The Beautiful Game?

David Conn is football's foremost investigative journalist. He was Sports News Reporter of the year in 2004 and is the author of *The Football Business* (Mainstream, 1997)

By the same author

The Football Business

David Conn

The Beautiful Game?
Searching for the Soul of Football

YELLOW JERSEY PRESS
LONDON

Published by Yellow Jersey Press 2005

2 4 6 8 10 9 7 5 3 1

First published in Great Britain in 2004 by
Yellow Jersey Press

Yellow Jersey Press
Random House, 20 Vauxhall Bridge Road,
London SW1V 2SA

Random House Australia (Pty) Limited
20 Alfred Street, Milsons Point, Sydney,
New South Wales 2061, Australia

Random House New Zealand Limited
18 Poland Road, Glenfield,
Auckland 10, New Zealand

Random House South Africa (Pty) Limited
Endulini, 5A Jubilee Road, Parktown 2193,
South Africa

The Random House Group Limited Reg. No. 954009
www.randomhouse.co.uk

A CIP catalogue record for this book
is available from the British Library

ISBN 0 224 064363

'Ossie's Dream' © Hodges/Peacock
Reproduced by permission of Snout Music Ltd

Papers used by Random House are natural, recyclable products made from
wood grown in sustainable forests. The manufacturing processes conform to
the environmental regulations of the country of origin

Typeset by Palimpsest Book Production Limited,
Polmont, Stirlingshire

Printed and bound in Great Britain by
Cox & Wyman Ltd, Reading, Berkshire

Contents

Illustrations
by Peter Robinson

Bootham Crescent, York
Hillsborough, Sheffield
The National Hockey Stadium, Milton Keynes
Surrey Street, Glossop
Sixfields Stadium, Northampton
Kingsmeadow Stadium, Kingston upon Thames
Wimbledon fans outside Selhurst Park
Valley Parade, Bradford
Old Trafford, Manchester
Arsenal victory parade
Stamford Bridge, Chelsea
Gigg Lane, Bury
Highbury, Islington
Ashburton Grove, Islington
The Football Association

Acknowledgements

A great many people readily provided research and information for this book, and several people in senior positions in football refused to be interviewed. The difference is always striking between the men running the game who are so difficult to reach and so often unaccountable, and the crowds who give of themselves to football and are always open and eager to help.

I would like to thank all the people quoted in the book for their contribution, particularly those who gave interviews in person, which took up considerable time. Particular thanks are owed to Graham Kelly, Graham Taylor, Steve Powell, Paul Matz, Alison Carmichael, Mike Winnett, Peter Hill-Wood, John Hemmingham, Alan Sykes, Joe Ashton, Chris Hobbs, John Hallmark of the Office of National Statistics, David Pendleton, John Dewhirst, Julian Rhodes, David Hindley, Albert Scardino, John Taylor, Andy Burnham, Gordon Sorfleet, Matthew Dunham, John Smith, Fred Mason, Paul Rawnsley, Steve Beck, Mike Shannon, Sophie McGill, David Allison, Colin Matthews and all connected with the supporters' trust at York City, Kris Stewart, Nicole Hammond, Kevin Rye and all involved with the story of AFC Wimbledon (the 'opposition', Charles Koppel and Peter Winkelman, were, to a journalist, always available and prepared to answer questions), John Bowler, the chairman of Crewe, who has always been exceptionally cogent and helpful since I first talked to him ten years ago, Hugh Hornby at the National Football Museum in Preston, Noel White, Sir

Geoffrey Dear, Dr Tim Kaye, Neil Watson, Neil Taylor, Joyce Powell, and Maggie Heavey and the staff and young people involved in the Positive Futures football scheme at Fairbridge in Salford. Particular thanks and appreciation to Adrian Priestley, Barry Jones, Peter Hammond, John Hamilton, David Atkinson and the former chairman Syd White for their help, hospitality and Herculean efforts at Glossop North End, and to Peter Heginbotham for dragging up the old files and painstakingly dealing with my enquiries.

A special tribute is owed to Phil and Hilda Hammond and all the families bereaved by the disaster at Hillsborough. Their strength and determination are an inspiration, even if the circumstances in which they have been forced to display them are so terrible.

The following people have for several years been an inspiration to me for their work and campaigning in football: Brian Lomax, Andy Walsh and Adam Brown. Dave Boyle and the staff at Supporters Direct deserve medals for their efforts, as do Malcolm Clarke, Ian Todd and all the stalwarts at the Football Supporters Federation.

The following fellow journalists were a great help with information or advice: Dan Gordon, Jonathan Foster, Brian McNally, Tom Bower, David Jones and Chris Lynham, Dave Stanford, Ivan Ash, Richard McIlroy, Kevin Mousley, Niall Couper and John Waples. My friend and colleague Chris Green was very helpful with advice, which unfortunately means I owe him a drink.

The press offices at the football authorities always manage to be professional and helpful with me, even when my questions might be called sensitive from their point of view, so thanks to Philip French and Dan Johnson at the Premier League and John Nagle and Ian Christon at the Football League. I am very grateful to David Barber in the FA's library for his help with historical detail, and to Alistair Bennett and Simon Taylor at the Football Foundation.

Profound thanks to Tristan Jones at Yellow Jersey for his care and patience editing this book and his unstinting support throughout. Thanks too to Peter Robinson for throwing himself so enthusiastically and expertly into the work of taking the pictures, to Matthew Broughton for the cover and Richard Collins for copy-editing. I am very grateful to Andy Farrington for taking so much care and trouble over the author picture. Sally Harrison was prompt and helpful as ever.

Bill Hamilton and Ben Mason of A.M. Heath were very supportive from the outset and many thanks to them for their help getting the book off the ground.

I will always be grateful to the following people who had faith in my work from the beginning: Frances Gibb, Matthew Kalman, all at Newsco Publications, Martin Regan, Andy Lyons, Mark Edmonds and in particular Peter Freedman. To those names I would now add Ian Bent and Angela Pertusini, and Michael Crick, for his very generous help and encouragement over several years.

I owe particular thanks and appreciation to Paul Newman, who, as the sports editor at the *Independent,* gave the original vote of confidence to commission my weekly column investigating football's cockeyed finances and, in his frantically busy working life, always found time to provide constant encouragement and support.

Thanks too to all my colleagues on the *Independent,* James Lawton, Glenn Moore, Phil Shaw, Tim Rich, Nick Harris, Steve Tongue, Jason Burt and Brian Viner: we help each other, which creates a real feeling of a team effort, even though we are spread across the country. I am also grateful every week to all the people working on the desk who, amidst their immense workload, have the not so enviable job of knocking sense and good looks into my columns: the deputy sports editor Nick Duxbury, Chris Maume, Jamie Corrigan, Stuart Robertson, Mark Burton, Andy Tong, Saul Brookfield, Simon Jones and many others. I am very grateful to Louise Hayman, Claire Stansfield and Imogen Haddon for their care and attention, and I would particularly like to thank

Vicky Yiasoumi and Nicole Wilmshurst for their endless patience and help.

Friends, through football and lots else: Andy Press, David 'DJ' Michael, Ric Demby and Sean Thorpe, thinking of you.

Finally, thanks are truly not enough for my wife Sarah and lovely girls Isobel and Emily, who, among all their wonders, have also somehow managed to put up for so long with me writing this book.

The Beautiful Game?

CHAPTER 1

The Marble Halls

L ondon, a brilliant Saturday, a few sunny weeks into the season.
I'm heading to Arsenal v Chelsea, a match the newspapers
have been chewing over endlessly all week; the aristocrats of the
Barclaycard Premiership against the team stocked from the
shameless wad of Roman Abramovich, a shy thirtysomething
who arrived at debt-soaked Chelsea in the summer of 2003 with
a fifth of the Russian oil industry to spend. The back pages, and
Sky TV, have been pumping it up: the battle of the managers,
Arsène Wenger v Claudio Ranieri; Hernan Crespo, signed for
£16.8m by Chelsea from Inter Milan, to round off the £111m
Abramovich spent in a summer of general recession. How, they
yammered, would Sol Campbell deal with Adrian Mutu, Edu
grapple with Makelele, Melchiot rein in Thierry Henry? This is a
local derby globalised, and surely decisive for the Premier League
Championship, because even this early in the season only three
clubs, these two and Manchester United, can possibly be imagined winning it.

Outside Finsbury Park tube drifts the sweet, autumn scent of
sweating kebab. Clumps of red- and white-shirted folk stand about
munching, drinking, chatting in the sunshine. Two women are
standing across the road in front of the Gaslight pub, drinks in
hands, their backs clad in new Arsenal shirts: SPANKY, says one,
GOONER BIRD, the other. I catch a look at their faces – they've
got to be forty at least.

The walk to the ground along St Thomas's Road is not the carnival of face-painted children and shiny, happy, multi-ethnic families which Sky would have you believe from their close-ups of fans at matches. Here is a procession of overwhelmingly white, mostly rough-shaven blokes, rumbling to their mates about what they did last night, what's up, how's business. There are a handful of children with their dads, not many teenagers at all. This is an expectant crowd, raw enough, its thinning hair flecked with grey.

Swagmen, selling Arsenal books, badges and videos, have set up in front yards, touting glumly for trade. The bloke in the garden of number 82 has a stall of colour photos of old Arsenal stars, signed and framed, for which he's asking big money. You wonder who he thinks is going to come along, after all these years, and give him £22 for Charlie Nicholas.

Those millions of us who breathed football in with the air of our childhoods, as I did in Manchester in the 1970s – playing non-stop in parks and playgrounds, catching glimpses of matches on TV before being taken, spellbound, to floodlit grounds in awesome crowds – we inhaled naturally some basic tenets of football knowledge. Notts County are the world's oldest League club – everybody knows that, although a great fuss always seemed to be made of Stoke City's age, too. Stanley Matthews – the wizard of the dribble; warming the nation's heart when he finally won an FA Cup winner's medal against Bolton in 1953, the year of the Queen's Coronation. Pele's real name, Bobby Moore's caps, the Twin Towers: articles of faith. Arsenal were in there too, with their marble halls.

I don't remember anybody ever explaining quite what the marble halls even were. They were a whispered hint of a club indescribably grand, the defining symbol of Arsenal's nobility, especially compared to the cocked-up scruffiness of the northern clubs, like the one I grew up supporting, Manchester City. Whenever Arsenal were mentioned, I always imagined vast, empty corridors, marble from floor to ceiling, the bust of the great manager Herbert Chapman standing massive at one end; maybe a lone, middle-aged gentleman in a suit, pacing along with echoing steps.

The odd fact might have come our way along with this vague lesson about Arsenal's distinction, something about their being the Bank of England club, football's version of posh. Their chairmen, going back generations, were the Hill-Woods, the only double-barrelled chaps in any football boardroom, several tiers of distinction above the likes of ours, Peter Swales, a sour bloke with a raked comb-over who made his money renting out tellies in Manchester in the 1960s. Hating Swales was an integral part of my footballing initiation, cursed into the Maine Road night. It was another thing nobody particularly explained, but they didn't have to. In some fundamental way, with his scheming and egotism, his *alone-ness*, he clearly seemed to betray us, the crowd, the clear, blue spirit of the club. As a kid, it was a fact of life: love the club, hate the chairman.

Of course I didn't know anything then about how football really worked; nor did I care. It was years later, after absorbing the game's history and being drawn inexorably, as a journalist, into its mechanics, that I saw how, while millions of people are transfixed by football itself, a few men are busy, networking and rising, working their way to running the clubs and Football Association committees which run the game. Before I set out to research this book, I had made a few connections: Swales, I knew, had been in business in Manchester with a man called Noel White – they ran a string of eponymous TV/hi-fi shops, White & Swales. They made a bit of money evidently, and took over their local club, non-league Altrincham, and were, I was told, instrumental in forming the semi-professional Northern Premier League. Swales, itchily ambitious, left after a while to mount his grimy *coup d'état* at City; White later found his way to becoming a director at Liverpool. Throughout, both of them worked their way into becoming Very Important People, sitting on fusty, influential committees and the ruling council of the FA, football's original and overall governing body.

In 1990, I knew, after a secret meeting of the self-appointed 'Big Five' First Division clubs: Manchester United, Arsenal, Liverpool, Tottenham and Everton – yes, Tottenham and Everton – Noel White was deputed to go along with David Dein, Arsenal's vice-chairman, to seek FA support for the big clubs' divisive and devastating plot to break away from the other three divisions of the Football League and form their own elite, the Premier League. Ever since the Football Association formed and established the rules of modern football in 1863, it had always regarded its role to be the protector of the sporting values of the game it gave to the world. For a long time the upper-class pillars of the FA were determined to keep the game amateur. They restricted money-making by players and directors, insisted on fair play and punished low behaviour which, as they saw it, dragged the core ethics of their sport into 'disrepute'. In 1888, twenty-five years after the FA was formed, twelve clubs established the Football League, the world's first ever. Although it was always professional, commercial and mercilessly competitive, the League, from its foundation, insisted that money be shared between its large and small clubs, a structure designed to keep all its member clubs reasonably strong, and maintain some rough equality between them on the field.

By 1990, the FA appeared to have long lost grip of its historic duty to guard football's soul, and shrivelled instead into a short-sighted clutch of bureaucrats, concerned mostly with perpetuating their own positions in the running of the game. So nervy had they become about the administrative rivalry with the League, the two bodies' squabbles about referees, club versus country, commercial rights and other turf wars, that the FA's chairman, Sir Bert Millichip, welcomed White and Dein as bearers of a solution. Fatefully, he and the FA supported the big clubs' breakaway, thus dealing a swingeing blow to the League. Following the 1990

World Cup in Italy, football in Britain was already recovering its image and popularity from its worst decade, the 1980s, which had seen crowds, penned behind cages and railings, fall to their lowest post-war, dozens of clubs come close to closing, and three major disasters, at Bradford, Heysel and Hillsborough, in which a total of 191 supporters were killed. The big clubs, having been careful to meet first with Greg Dyke, then an executive with ITV, who promised them a television windfall, knew that for all football's problems, the next deal in 1992 was going to be huge, given the emerging satellite competition from Sky TV. Enough money was coming in to make the game healthy all round, for all its professional clubs and – if the FA had only had some real vision – to rejuvenate football for a new era, a sport enriching the lives of the millions who play and watch it too. Instead, myopic and self-serving, the FA, historically wedded to amateurism, backed the breakaway of the already rich and let them keep the money to themselves.

Football boomed. It became suddenly acceptable after Italia '90, the top grounds all-seater, the media, awash with Gazza's tears, prepared to plug the game rather than scorn it. From 1992, huge money did indeed pour in – and the big clubs took it all. It took some years for most people, most fans, to realise what was happening; the new era was so refreshing after the caging, stigma and disasters of the eighties, that it seemed a new dawn: football was coming home. Yet even in the new Premier League, money was becoming the defining measure of sporting success. As Manchester United floated on the Stock Market and dispirited the nation with branding, merchandising, Champs Cola and other tat, while constructing some wonderful football teams, the other clubs mostly borrowed massively in failed attempts to keep up. An enormous financial gap opened up between the breakaway and the remaining three divisions of the Football League, but the system of three-up, three-down promotion and relegation was retained between them. For the clubs going down from the Premier League, relegation became an existence-threatening financial meltdown, rather than a gloomy part of growing up, as it had been for me when Swales' bedraggled City finally sank out of the First Division in 1983, Luton's manager David Pleat dancing hysterically across the Maine Road pitch in his Hush Puppies because his club had stayed up.

I wanted to understand what has happened to English football, why the Premier League champions will make £50m out of television alone in a single season and pay some of their top players £100,000 a week – £5m a year – yet since 1992 thirty-six of the Football League's clubs, exactly half of the League's seventy-two members, have been insolvent at one time or another. In our neighbourhoods, the million or so people who are reckoned to play the game, in teams and clubs registered to the same FA, still mostly scrap on the same municipal dumps on which I spent my youth, changing in cars or behind trees. While football and its players have never been more visible, more glamorous, while the grounds are packed again, crowds rising in number every year, actually going to a match is increasingly beyond the reach of poorer people, and particularly the young. I wanted to travel around the game and delve under its skin, to see the national sport and understand how it came to this.

Coming closer to Highbury, odd blokes, fifty-ish, are loitering in the middle of the road. 'Any spares? Any spares?' they're hustling, 'I'll buy any spares.' Canvas stalls are up in front gardens, selling programmes, scarves, sweets. Two blokes, about my age – knocking on forty, although it hurts to face up to it – come alongside with the first chant heard today: 'There's only one team in London! One team in London! There's only one team in London!' A lone woman, adrift in the stream of fans, is rattling a bucket, saying plaintively, 'Support St Thomas's Playgroup! Support the local children', without conspicuous success.

Arsenal, of course, had thrust themselves eagerly into the new age; it was what Dein had angled for. Dein has always claimed the credit for Arsenal's most important move – the appointment as their manager of the little-known-over-here Arsène Wenger, who recruited and burnished a series of sides to challenge United's corporate monopoly. United and Arsenal's rivalry itself points up how the concentration of money at the top, alien to English football, has crushed its unpredictability. Gone are the Derby County, Nottingham Forest, Aston Villa seasons, good sides of capable professionals melding together under inspired management to win memorable championships. Since 1992, only Blackburn, briefly finding the tax-free fortune of their owner Jack Walker sturdy enough to buy the title, have interrupted United's and Arsenal's duopoly. So dominant are the richer clubs now that winning the FA Cup as well – the near-impossible Double, we were told as kids – is no longer so tough. Previously in the twentieth century the Double was achieved only three times, by Tottenham in 1961, Arsenal in 1971 and Liverpool in 1986. Already since 1992 it has been claimed five times, three by United, in 1994, 1996 and 1999, and twice by Arsenal, in 1998 and 2002.

Now, since the summer of 2003, a third club has come to challenge them. It is not, however, a long-playing stalwart, wonderfully managed, spiriting a team of its own youngsters into the reckoning. Instead it's Chelsea, who were tottering financially under the defiantly unattractive Ken Bates, until he sold out to Abramovich, who introduced us to the shocking detail of Russia's post-Communist privatisations. We're not sure what end football serves for Abramovich, but here he is, a few droplets from his oil-riches fashioning for Chelsea an international shopping list of millionaire players.

The North Bank is suddenly in front. Revolutionary when it was built in 1993, one of the most stylish and generous of the new stands which bloomed after Hillsborough, it's looking a bit mucky. The old art deco East Stand, with its white frontage, cannon, and ARSENAL STADIUM in vast letters at neck-straining height, is still magnificent, although close up it's showing some wrinkles.

A peek into the main entrance as you pass and you can clearly see a very small bust of a man, peering impenetrably out.

The journalists' entrance is just on from there. A smiling press officer, Kate, hands me my pass, a nice touch, unusual. Then it's up some narrow steps, like backstage at the theatre, until you're into the warm, carpeted room where the press is nicely looked after and kept firmly in its place.

Up the stairs and out into the ground, the pitch is gleaming in the sunshine. Highbury is full, of course, and although a saggy-arsed mascot is imploring everyone to 'Watch the big screen', although Arsenal's multi-national side has O_2 on their shirts, and Chelsea's chests want us to Fly Emirates, the football spectacle is, as ever, timeless and seductive. The green grass, the classic proportions of the pitch, the dignified old stands, the new ones at each end, all packed. The thousands of faces, come to worship. The enduring vestments – red and white of Arsenal, blue of Chelsea – transport you effortlessly back in time, to generations who have come here before to see Chapman's team of the thirties, Cliff Bastin, Alex James, David Jack, or the fifties, football's golden age, when, here as elsewhere, people poured into the ground to devour football for its colour and drama as their lives settled back after war. History has seeped into this stately ground – and it strikes me how unsentimental fans have become about it.

Arsenal are leaving Highbury; they've been wanting to for years. Just a few years ago, such moves, like Sunderland's from Roker Park, Bolton's from their historic home at Burnden Park, had to be really sold to fans, assurances given that this was a new future, not a fracture with the past. Here, the fans don't need much convincing; they overwhelmingly back the move. The reason they're prepared to dump Highbury for the muck and speculation of Ashburton Grove, currently north London's garbage headquarters, is straightforward: money. United make more than them because they have a bigger ground; Chelsea are threatening because they have Abramovich. Money pays for players, the fans accept this, they want to win, so they all agree: we need a bigger stadium.

Five minutes after kick-off, Edu scores, a deflected free kick, and the crowd are up, all around me, roaring from their souls: '1-0, to the Arsenal, 1-0 to the Arsenal.' Football people are used to it, but it's worth remembering: this is unique in modern life, such an outpouring of noise, such passion, so openly and publicly expressed. Just four minutes later, Makelele, a steady midfield presence, newly signed from Real Madrid for a lot of roubles, strokes the ball to Crespo. Crespo is 25 yards out but Arsenal's defenders stand off him, leaving a pocket of space. He looks up, considers, then wallops the ball, to swirl, swerve, lob, dip. Thirty-eight thousand people are watching hushed, then they realise, a second after it's happened, that the ball is in the back of Arsenal's net and this guy Crespo really is phenomenal and the rump of Chelsea fans squashed into the corner of the Clock End abandon themselves to glee.

Minutes later, still chuffed, they're singing something, to the tune of 'Pretty Baby'. It takes a while to make it out, then it comes into focus: 'We're fucking loaded, na na na na na na, We're fucking loaded, na na na na na na, We're fucking loaded . . .' Then to the Arsenal fans: 'You're gonna groundshare with Tottenham, groundshare with Tottenham, you're gonna groundshare with Tottenham.'

Songs about money, and stadium size.

1-1, and the game settles down. Makelele and Geremi knock the ball about eye-pleasingly. Edu, for Arsenal, sits in midfield and prods about. Henry turns up on either wing, tricky. Pires, looking very much *le poseur* with his carefully tousled hair and white boots – the mark of players who fancy their skills rather too much, from Real Madrid to Bury – stuns a ball in the penalty area, expertly keeps his shot down. Cudicini clasps it, the last word in safety and security.

After a while, I can't help thinking: this is all a bit dainty. These are some of the world's best players, arrived here to earn the Premiership's unholy wages, their touch is admirable, their skills unarguable. It's certainly an enjoyable way to spend an afternoon. But for one of the biggest matches of the season, between two London rivals for the title, it's oddly passionless. There are just six English players out of the twenty-two on the pitch, no Scots, no Welsh, one Irishman – Damien Duff, for Chelsea. The English are midfield grafters or defenders: Sol Campbell and Ashley Cole for Arsenal, Wayne Bridge, Glen Johnson and Frank Lampard for Chelsea. The other Englishman is Ray Parlour, Arsenal's work-horse, a relic of the tradition, always more imagined by fans than real, that players felt a little like fans, had a sense of belonging to their club. He and Ashley Cole are the only players in either side playing for the club they joined as kids. I've seen a confidential document which goes round the battery of academies in the Premier League, giving the numbers of boys, from the fragile age of eight to eighteen, attached to each club. It shows that in 2002–3, the twenty clubs had 2,601 boys, supposedly being farmed for a home-reared future. There isn't much sign of fruits from that harvest at this showpiece.

Twenty minutes in, the crowd has gone quiet. I mean, silent. It's quite soporific, this, sitting in the sunshine after lunch and a couple of pints, watching the neat patterns of accomplished, mostly contact-free football. Since the Premier League launched and its clubs settled into their all-seater stadia, with their expensive tickets, foreign stars, merchandising and packaging, the view seems to have formed that the old, in-your-blood, working-class fans have been priced out and replaced by a wealthier, comfier audience; that football – the working man's theatre – has become middle-class entertainment. That idea was reinforced by Roy Keane's famous grumble about the taming of Old Trafford, that it was down to too many people sitting in executive boxes, munching prawn sandwiches with their little fingers exposed. This may be truer at Old Trafford, given United's huge 67,700 capacity, which allows plenty of room for new fans, football tourists and prodigious corporate scoffing. Look around Highbury, though, and despite Arsenal being the club of Nick Hornby's *Fever Pitch* and Melvyn Bragg, this is not largely a crowd of post-Italia '90 newcomers.

Some people have, without question, been forced out by the exorbitant cost of tickets – here they can pay well over £1,000 for an ordinary season ticket in a decent seat. But the excluded are a minority; most people who always went to the football still somehow seem to find the wherewithal to go. At Highbury, at intervals, there is no absence of passion; the blokes here get properly steamed up about the ref's decisions, tossing wanker signs to the linesman, to Jimmy Floyd Hasselbaink, to the stewards. No, the difference between fans before the grounds sat down and the prices went up doesn't seem to be predominantly class, but age. Look around, they're all thirty- or fortysomethings, at least. Crowds are rising across football, but there are very few teenagers in the grounds, as there were when I was sixteen in 1981 and paid £3 to stand on the Kippax at Maine Road, along with seemingly everybody else my age, teenagers and lads in their early twenties, cramming the terraces. Kids can't afford these prices now, not after the cut-price tickets – which, at Arsenal, are still £12 – stop, at all clubs, at sixteen. You can see the odd teenager here with his dad, but not groups of them, consumed, as we were, by the football – by supporting your club. My generation could afford it as a basic staple, and we didn't have such a choice of other, and – let's face it – cooler recreation. We were hooked.

Mostly, my generation, we and people older and slightly younger, still go, fill the grounds, continue to pay through the nose for the addiction. We've all grown older but we haven't generally noticed. At the ground we're still seeing the same faces, sitting next to the mate we've known for twenty-five years. He doesn't, and we don't, think of him as a grown man, forty years old with a job and a family and bad knees. He's still fourteen in our heads, reeking of fags at school, skiving off, coming alive at the football, slating the ref. It's no wonder, after half an hour or so of standing up, sitting down and shouting at the top of their voices, everybody needs a breather; we're not as young as we used to be.

With an hour gone, Parlour comes off, fondly applauded; Kanu comes on. Dennis Bergkamp replaces Wiltord. The crowd welcome Bergkamp with a low moan of appreciation, remembering past pleasures. These two, old-stagers for Arsenal by now – Bergkamp in his ninth season at Highbury, Kanu his sixth – change the game. Bergkamp, lovely skills and sharp elbows, crafts play beautifully, and Arsenal wake up. Joe Cole comes on for Chelsea – the outstanding English youngster of his generation, I saw him playing for the FA school at Lillieshall back in 1997 when he was fifteen; even then his skill, and, more particularly, his ease in expressing it, could make you weep. Now, having left his own club, West Ham, for some of the Abramovich booty, he looks lost. He should be at home, battling to lift West Ham back up, furthering his footballing education, not hanging around on the sidelines at Chelsea trying to blag a game with the superstars.

Late on, in this display of highly-paid technique, when the goal comes, it's a cock-up. Cudicini comes for a tame cross, the ball rolls underneath him and through his legs, bounces up, hits Henry on the knee and slithers into the goal. Chelsea's players troop back to take their places without saying a word to Cudicini – the reporters will remark on this on Monday, as a sign of the Chelsea mercenaries' threadbare team spirit. Highbury is on its feet all around us, triumphant, blokes punching the air, clutching each other, giving the Vs to the Chelsea fans in the corner. Finding their voice again, a song goes round at heart-shuddering volume:

> Hello, hello, we are the Arsenal boys;
> Hello, hello, we are the Arsenal boys.
> And if you are a Tottenham fan surrender or you'll die;
> We all follow the Arsenal.

A song from the Gooner, rather than the marble halls, tradition of supporting Arsenal, hailing from fighting days of yore, which these fans can well remember. Arsène Wenger, their talismanic modern manager, is on his feet by the touchline, fists clenched, defiant, looking, as ever, a little poorly. Arsenal coast in from here, Chelsea fizzle out, and the Arsenal fans leave chests out, job done, pundits corrected. The screens in the press box linger on Roman Abramovich, smiling wanly.

In the press room there is a bite to eat, then the managers come up eventually to give their ritual comments for tomorrow's and Monday's papers. Wenger, smart in his grey suit, is urbane, adept, even witty. He's very pleased, he says, he thought his team had more desire and organisation than Chelsea. He makes quite a funny joke about Arsenal's appalling disciplinary record under him: 'Please note we had no bookings today,' he says. 'You did,' someone pipes up, 'Parlour.' 'We'll appeal,' Wenger cracks, and everybody laughs. Then he's off.

The journalists – themselves mostly fortysomethings – want to know about pure footballing matters: the teams, whether Ranieri fears that Sven-Göran Eriksson has been lined up as Chelsea's manager, why Duff is playing in the centre and not on the wing, is Cudicini making too many mistakes. Ranieri, too, is impressive; his English is improved and he is engagingly open to the questions, even the pointedly personal. He acknowledges that despite all the money he has been given to acquire players, football is about men, whoever they are, combining as a team. He admits he doesn't have that yet.

'When Ashley Cole gets the ball, Wiltord knows what he is going to do, where to run. But when Mutu gets the ball, Crespo does not yet know where to be. This will take time.'

It is weird to hear him say that – why go round the world buying players if you complain of a lack of team understanding? But it seems, too, brave of him to admit it. At an appropriate pause, he smiles: 'OK?' Then he's gone too. It's heartening, watching two such considered, capable men, so in charge of their work, speaking forensically about their eclectic, cultured squads, managing the intricacies of modern Premier League behemoths. It makes me feel glad to be European, somehow.

I leave down the back stairs and whitewashed walls, out into the drifting rubbish and tide of self-satisfied Gooners. A little way along, outside the main entrance, a bloke with a mashed-up nose in a fluorescent steward's coat is standing halfway up the steps. You can peek behind him and see Chapman's bust, still peering out, oblivious. Inside, one or two elderly folk are hanging about in suits, saying their thank-yous for an afternoon's hospitality. I want a look at the marble halls and Chapman's bust. When I was ten or so, and used to be packed off in the summer holidays to stay with my auntie, who lived in Wembley, I was straight in for an Empire Stadium tour and the chance to lift a replica cup in the Royal Box. But, grown up and still living up North, I'll never, realistically, have time for an Arsenal stadium tour, just for an opportunity to see the mystical marble halls.

'Is there any chance,' I ask the steward-bouncer ever so politely, 'I could just go up and have a look inside?'

'No,' he says, looking not at me, but into the middle distance. 'Get off the steps, please.'

'I'm a journalist,' I say half-heartedly. It does not, it has to be said, do the trick. He seems, if anything, physically repulsed.

'It's just that I'd really like to see the marble halls; I'll only stand at the entrance, then I'll come back down again.'

'No,' he says, with just the beginning of a there's-an-easy-way-and-a-hard-way-to-do-this about him.

'Are they the marble halls?' I ask, pointing inside.

'Yeh, in there,' he says, without looking round. 'That's it.'

'Is the marble just on the floor?'

'Yes.'

'Are they massive, the halls?'

He's getting fed up with me. He's got work to do. It's been a match against Chelsea for Christ's sake. 'Look there,' he points 10 yards or so to the right of the door. 'Those are the dressing rooms. Look there,' he points, 10 yards to the left. 'That's the ticket office. From there to there. Those are the marble halls.'

'That's it?' I ask.

'That's it.'

He's keen to make himself clear: forget it, they're no big deal. The marble halls, they're just a bleedin' vestibule, at the end of the day.

I'm going straight home, from Euston. I wander back to the Arsenal tube station, famously renamed from Gillespie Road by Herbert Chapman, his greatest PR stunt. There's some problem; we're told to change at Finsbury Park and take the Victoria Line down. Only a straggle of football fans are left; the train is full of normal people coming home from shopping or days out. On the platform at Finsbury Park, a bloke next to me, bald guy with a major belly, has to be fifty, starts singing a song I haven't heard since school: 'Don't bend down, when so-and-so's around . . .' Kids used to sing it to taunt others about being gay, long before anybody had a clue what being gay meant. His mate is tall, very well built, grey-haired, at least forty-five, bulky in an amber, Stone Island woolly jumper, baseball cap, a couple of Arsenal badges on his chest.

'Let's go up to King's Cross for a ruck,' he's saying. 'Sheffield United'll be there.'

When I get on the train, I check the fixtures in the paper. Sheffield United are indeed in London, playing Millwall. Trains to Sheffield do leave from King's Cross.

The big guy starts talking about how he'd love to be at the Birmingham v Aston Villa derby tomorrow, how he went in the home end at St Andrews at an Arsenal match once and it was great. There's a younger lad with them, curly brown hair, with the remains of a lager in a plastic cup. He isn't drunk but he's acting it. They start up some Arsenal songs. They're really loud, but nobody cares. Then the big guy starts another song:

> Spurs are on their way to Belsen;
> Hitler's gonna gas 'em again;
> You can't stop 'em, the yids from Tottenham;
> The yids from White Hart Lane.

I can date that song instinctively. It goes back to the source of Man City fans' resentment of Tottenham – not hatred, more a grudge, splashed with envy, for the Spurs' side's style and flourish – their defeat of us in the mesmeric FA Cup Final replay at Wembley in 1981. Ricky Villa scored his winning goal at the other end from all the City fans so we couldn't see it properly, he just seemed to have the ball for a ridiculously long time. Its greatness as a Cup Final winning goal has been rubbed in every year since, in endless replays. We went back to Swales and strife and haven't made a Cup Final since. The following season, Spurs reached the Final again, against Queens Park Rangers, and they released an official team song featuring their Argentinian midfield orchestrator, Osvaldo Ardiles:

> Spurs are on their way to Wembley;
> Ossie's gonna do it again;
> You can't stop 'em, the boys from Tottenham;
> The boys from White Hart Lane . . .

So, this song, reworked by opposing fans tastefully along a Holocaust theme, dates precisely to 1982. These blokes have been singing it for over twenty years. I'm Jewish, but I have never felt genuinely threatened by the song; I've no doubt a very right-wing mind thought of it first, but it lost its menace for me on the Kippax when I looked at kids around me singing it and it was clear they didn't have a clue what the words meant – not even 'yids'.

But a young guy – he's twenty-five or so – with a grey Arsenal T-shirt on, his bag slung over his shoulder, standing in the corner of the tube by the doors, right next to the big bloke, thinks they're misguided.

'You shouldn't sing that song,' he says, earnestly.

'Why not?' the grey-haired guy challenges him.

'It's a very nasty song,' he says. He's talking as if he thinks they can't possibly understand what the words mean, that once he's told them what happened at places like Belsen, they'll realise and stop singing it.

'It's anti-Semitic, it's not good. It's just a bad song.'

'Why?' the bloke's turned round to face him front-on. 'What's it to you? Are you a Tottenham fan?'

'No,' he says.

'Are you Jewish?'

'No.'

By now, the fat guy and the youngster have stood up and begun to take a serious interest. 'Is he a yiddo?' the kid's asking. The big guy punches the boy full in the face, underneath his left eye. The boy's face is crimson, an egg sprouting on his cheekbone. Staggering, he maintains his dignity, does what people do when appealing to reason in the face of violence they can't defeat physically:

'What was the point of that?' he says, plaintively, shaking his head.

Then the big guy absolutely batters him, punches him with a left hook which sends him juddering, dazed, knowing he is in much deeper than he imagined when he first asked a middle-aged bloke on a crowded tube in London late on a Saturday afternoon not to sing a song at the top of his voice about Hitler gassing the Jews.

'Get off the fucking train,' the big guy says when it reaches Highbury & Islington – this has all happened in just one stop. 'Go on, fuck off.' He kicks the boy's arse and he meekly crumples off the train. Nobody, me included, has moved a muscle. The shoppers have mostly been oblivious, armed with that self-protecting

London skein of not wanting to know. 'Sorted,' grins the big bastard, arms outstretched in aren't-I-a-superstar pose. 'Fucking sorted.'

The younger one is beside himself, he's sort of writhing in his seat: 'Was he a yiddo?' he's shouting. 'Was he a fucking yiddo?'

The other, fat bloke, is grinning, he seems physically excited: 'I told you he was gonna get hit,' he's saying to the kid. 'Didn't I tell you he was gonna get hit?'

King's Cross is the next stop. They do get off. The big bloke strides away, warmed up now. The fat man trots after him. The young lad is left on the train next to me for a moment, unsure, then he shouts after the fat bloke: 'Dad! Dad! Are we off here?' Then he's gone too, with his plastic cup, the same amount of beer still in it.

I'm not telling this story because I want to give the impression that this sort of thing happens all the time, or because I set out to investigate 'hooliganism'. I don't and I didn't. It's just that I went to Highbury to see the ultimate in footballing sophistication which the multi-billion pound, multi-national English Barclaycard Premiership has to offer, and that's what happened on the way home.

CHAPTER 2

Lucky Arsenal

L ike all the proudest aristocrats, Arsenal, when you look into it, turn out to have built their status and fortune on long-ago, best-forgotten acts of piracy. The club's pristine Football League record was another building block in every child's football education: which club has been in the First Division, never relegated, since the First World War? Hands up: Arsenal! But while they taught us that Arsenal had never gone down, the solemn prefects of *Football Focus* never told us how Arsenal got themselves up in the first place.

The club's origin was earthy and commonplace enough. It was formed by a group of workers at the Royal Arsenal munitions factory in Woolwich in 1886. Like Manchester United, started as Newton Heath by men on the Lancashire and Yorkshire Railway in 1878, and thousands of clubs then and now, Arsenal's beginnings are a familiar story: a group of mates stuck working together, deciding to organise themselves, start a football team and play together, too. As sport, and other forms of modern organised leisure, flowered out of the grime and squalor of Britain's late nineteenth-century cities, workplaces, schools and churches were the main seedbeds for the new, eagerly formed football clubs.

By the time the men in the Royal Arsenal's Dial Square workshop were starting up their club, football was grinding into an industry itself, the clubs' natural ambition having already outstripped their early founders' impulse for a kickabout. The

Football Association, the group of public school and university men, had come together in 1863 to define and unify one set of rules of football, and so they became the game's first ever governing body. They were all players, and they were committed to their sport principally for people to play, for the exercise, team spirit, and, as they saw it, the moral and physical benefits of 'games' which had been inculcated in the public schools. The game was taken into the ragged industrial cities in the 1870s, in the knapsacks of upper- and middle-class educators and churchmen, with some more paternalistic employers soon also giving their support to works teams. However, the hordes of working men, famished for entertainment, devoured the new game with a more desperate hunger than the strolling gentlemen at their original London clubs. Football became a mass spectacle phenomenally quickly, the crowds drawn in their thousands to watch and roar on the new clubs – and very quickly the men backing the clubs saw they could charge the spectators to watch. Competition between the early clubs became intense, particularly in the North; the taking part never feeling as satisfying as winning, and it led inevitably to the commercialisation of the whole spirit of the game – paying money to tempt the better players; Darwen and Preston were the first to get caught. The FA remained vehemently opposed to what they saw as the corruption of their amateur ethos by men becoming paid mercenaries to play for clubs, but by 1885, faced, significantly, with the threat of a breakaway by the top clubs, the FA reluctantly caved in to the inevitable and ceded the idea of professional players.

Three years later, following an invitation from William McGregor, the shopkeeper-chairman of the Birmingham church team Aston Villa, twelve fully professional clubs, six from the north, six from the Midlands, agreed to take part in a competition of season-long, home and away fixtures, which would guarantee them a regular income and, they hoped, inspire interest from spectators and improve the standard of play. They called it, simply, the Football League, the first ever such league in the world. McGregor said from the beginning that there need be no clash between the FA, guardians of the values of a game they had established to play, not watch, and the League, a cartel of senior clubs, which was professional, money-driven, to its founding principle. For a while, the books tell us, relations were indeed quite harmonious, the FA responsible for the rules of the game, referees, the regulation of good practice by the clubs themselves, and running the FA Cup competition and the England international team. The League, affiliated to the FA, its clubs registered with the governing body alongside all amateur clubs, could get on with building a commercial business. From the start, League matches were a huge success, the raw competition and sense of occasion at the grounds filling a void in the lives of working men in the late Victorian industrial cities. What is startling, when you consider the game's origins as a sport, is how soon the competitive fortunes of these few clubs and players, the soap opera and silverware of the professional League, came to be what we all think of as football itself, separate somehow from the earnest strivings of millions of people out there playing it, week after week.

Royal Arsenal hardened into a serious side pretty quickly, winning the London Senior Cup in 1891, just five years after forming. That year, they became the first London club to pay their players – against appalled opposition from the London FA, who were true believers in the amateur faith. A lovely line unearthed from the local *Woolwich Gazette and Plumstead Times* in May that year captures the club's – and football's – genuine dilemmas of the time. By now called Woolwich Arsenal, the club's founders considered forming a limited company, as so many other new professional clubs were doing. As the early clubs' members found themselves responsible for a wage bill, then the formidable cost of building a ground, the idea of establishing a company was to protect the members from being personally liable for the club's expenses and debts. Forming a company, however, was also a launchpad for some clubs to sell shares to new investors, and build the club up financially. Woolwich Arsenal's local newspaper recorded that the members and players decided against forming a company because they wanted to avoid 'degenerating into a proprietary or capitalist club'. That particular resolution did not last long.

The Football League was expanding quickly, forming a Second Division within just four years, 1892, and a year later Arsenal were elected into it, becoming the League's first London club. They bought their own ground – the Manor Field, in Plumstead – and, faced with the same financial realities as the other member clubs, reluctantly voted to turn themselves from a club into a company. *The Official Illustrated History of Arsenal* written by Phil Soar and Martin Tyler, says the working-class founders were worried that the change was 'against the sporting ethos of the club and (rightly as it proved) endangering the control of the working men who had founded it'. Now any rich chancer could turn up, buy the shares, and become the club's owner. And, soon, one did.

Arsenal won promotion to the First Division in 1904, but, although gate income was shared between home and away clubs from the start of the League, Arsenal still struggled financially on lower home crowds at Woolwich than those garnered in new, purpose-built grounds by Chelsea, Fulham and Tottenham. The club was forced to sell its best players, but nevertheless by 1910 it was bust and up for sale. The man who came in to buy it, waving away the opposition of the hard-core fans, was the prototype football chairman: Henry Norris.

Norris was a property developer, the mayor of Fulham, and he already owned Fulham Football Club, for whom he had developed the always fondly appreciated Craven Cottage ground. Arsenal's own official history describes Norris variously as bullying, dictatorial, ruthless – 'a thin autocrat with a walrus moustache, he welcomed neither criticism nor advice, nonetheless he was influential and persuasive'. A blueprint for a chairman, some might say. The plans Norris developed for the two clubs he now owned, both struggling financially, will raise shivers of modern recognition. His first was the obvious heresy: merge the two clubs, gaining Fulham Arsenal's First Division status, but the fans were against it and the League turned him down. After that he launched his next, outrageous plot, to move Arsenal north, over the Thames, right across London, to a new site which would be more accessible and better positioned to suck in thousands more spectators. He landed on the playing fields and grounds of St John's College of the Divinity at Highbury, then secretly negotiated for years with the Church of England, which owned the site. When they finally did the deal, a twenty-one-year lease for a then huge £20,000 – Nottingham Forest were paying their council £30,000 a year rent in 2004 – the Archbishop of Canterbury himself put his signature next to that of Norris.

Floundering Woolwich Arsenal had been relegated back to the Second Division in 1913; the fans protesting back in Plumstead, that Norris was selling the club's roots and traditions down the river, had no chance. This was precisely the kind of dictatorship which the early members had felt would be anathema to their football club: Norris had all the shares, he owned the company, he made all the decisions. The fans had all the passion and loyalty, but no power. Arsenal were going north.

Norris carved the old church playing fields into a new temple for football, against well-organised local opposition, without even the scrutiny of a planning application. His move was wily, ruthless, commercially driven, bloody-minded, speculative; but it made Arsenal a modern football club. Known as The Arsenal, in 1913–14, their first season at Highbury, right by the tube, they drew in the Second Division's highest crowds, an average 23,000 people every match, and they finished third, behind Notts County and Bradford Park Avenue, who were both promoted.

Norris had spent £125,000, enormous for the time, buying and building the new ground, and Arsenal were still carrying £60,000 worth of debts. Few doubt that along with the ego boost, fame and defiant enjoyment he wrought from his ownership of the football club, Norris was motivated by making money for himself too, but it isn't clear how he thought he would do it. Along with the restrictions imposed by the Football Association on players making money – the maximum wage, which players loathed and formed their union to fight – the FA was also adamant that shareholders should not use the clubs' new company status to leak money out.

The FA wanted their great sport's necessary compromises with the mucky world of business to go only so far. If the history of English football has to some extent been a battle between those who saw themselves as upstanding gentlemen, and the rough lads, 'barbarians' – dirty players on the pitch, greedy schemers off it, drinkers and scrappers among the fans in the grounds – at this stage the FA, the governing body of gentlemen, insisted on its authority to make the rules.

In the FA's library, lovingly maintained now by the longserving David Barber behind reception in the new eight-storey offices in Soho Square, the old minute books don't explain the FA's thinking back when they had the confidence to rein in professional clubs and their chairmen. The first regulations imposed on the new football club-companies appear in 1892. The crusty old tome recording them simply notes that Preston North End, the first 'super club' – they won the Double in 1888–9, the League's first ever season – had applied to form a limited company. The FA's response comes across as dismissively high-handed: 'Agreed, but dividends must be limited to 5 per cent of the value of the shares.' So, the club could form a company, but the new shareholders, the likes of Henry Norris, could not pay themselves fat cheques at the end of a year through dividends.

By the end of the century, the FA had developed an armoury of rules to regulate the new professional club-companies, seeking to preserve the values of the game despite its unstoppable transformation into an industry. The clubs might be companies now, but the FA was determined to prevent businessmen exploiting them to make money. These were, the FA insisted, still sports clubs, not vehicles for keen-eyed speculators to cash in on an emerging leisure industry on the cusp of the twentieth century. The FA's 1899–1900 handbook, a slim brown hardcover in an orderly row of years of them on the library shelves, heralds the first appearance of a combination of rules which were to last a century. 'Formation of Companies' it announces at the top of page 31, and the governing body had no hesitancy about its purpose:

'1. *Dividends*. – No larger dividend to be declared than the maximum dividend allowed from time to time by the Football Association.'

The following three regulations restricted shareholders' benefits, including nailing them down to one season ticket per £10 of shares. The next was unambiguous:

'5. *Directors' Remuneration*. – No director shall be entitled to receive any remuneration in respect of his office as director.'

So, no getting money by paying yourself a whack out of the club, either with a salary or a dividend. The last restriction is still nominally in the FA's rulebooks today, although it is more observed in its avoidance. It says that if a club is wound up and its assets sold, then any money left after the debts are paid off does not go to the owners of the club's shares. Instead the surplus has to be paid to: 'Some other club or institute in the city or county . . . Or charitable or benevolent institution.' In other words, if a businessman, whether Henry Norris at loss-making, riverside Fulham in 1910 or any other, reckoned on making money by winding up the club and selling its ground, he couldn't keep the money. It would have to go to another sports club or charity. The FA was, quite cannily, removing the incentive for asset-stripping, institutionalising the idea that directors were custodians of their clubs, and their duty was to run a club for its and football's sake, not be in it to make money.

The FA sought to impose a similar restriction on the players themselves, succeeding in 1901 in imposing a maximum wage of £4 per week on all players. The high principle was that players would have the incentive removed from touting their talents to the highest bidder, that clubs would be more restrained in their relations with each other, and that competition would be more even. However, for all the revulsion many fans feel now at the enormous wages paid to top players, and the overpoweringly flash, brash lifestyles the money can buy, the maximum wage is not a distinguished feature of football's development. Lasting, amazingly, sixty-one years until the players' union, the Professional Footballers' Association, finally established that it was in fact illegal, the maximum wage held down generations of men who finished at thirty-five with very little put away, after playing for years in front of vast crowds. The clubs, too, found endless ways of getting round or under the rules and the ones caught bunging their players regularly trooped for punishment through the FA's pompous panels.

The following year, 1902, came the first of football's periodic disasters, when twenty-five people died after falling through the wooden terraces on the upper stands, watching the Scotland v England international. That the venue was Ibrox, Glasgow, one of the first great grounds, shows how far the professional game, with its strange, unsatisfactory structure, the ambitions of the clubs held back by the high ideals of the governing bodies, fell behind in being able to cater for the great numbers of people drawn to the matches.

How the early bosses evaded the restrictions on them, which they surely did, and earned returns for the vast sums that some, like Norris, threw at their new professional football ventures, is unclear, buried among the game's secrets. He certainly risked plenty; the First World War began within a year of Arsenal's move to Highbury, and – there is no tactful way to say this in the context of the slaughter in the trenches – the timing for the club and Norris was awful. Arsenal were consolidating – they completed more work on the ground, and finished fifth in the Second Division in the 1914–15 season, but the League was widely denounced for playing on at all, and after that play was suspended throughout the war.

The clubs earned next to nothing in the war, hosting the odd wartime friendly or army match, the grounds creaking unattended. But when, finally, the war ended, the country and its people were so eager to flock back and taste the thrill of normal life again that the League took the bold step of expanding. By 1921–2, just two seasons after the League restarted, it had four divisions, the larger clubs from regional leagues having been invited to form a Third Division (North) and (South) beneath the First and Second. Immediately, however, even in 1919, the League decided to enlarge its First and Second Divisions, from twenty to twenty-two clubs.

The choice of clubs to join the new, bigger First Division looked very straightforward. In 1915, the last season played, Chelsea and Tottenham finished as the bottom two clubs in the First Division. They, everybody assumed, would stay up, maintaining the same twenty, and would be joined by the two clubs which finished top and second in the Second Division – Derby and Preston, who would have been promoted anyway. Henry Norris, however, weighed down financially by his new ground and massive debts, had decided he had to get Arsenal into the First Division. He embarked on what Arsenal's official history describes as: 'The single most outrageous enterprise ever to be conceived in the history of English football. There is still no convincing explanation of how Norris achieved his object. Norris' aim, very simply, was to talk The Arsenal back into the First Division.'

How he did it, nobody knows. The authors of Arsenal's official history are comfortable enough with the idea that the club may have corruptly gained promotion, to openly wonder whether Norris offered backhanders to members of the League's Management Committee. In his official Football League centenary history, *League Football and the Men Who Made It*, Simon Inglis is also happy to ask whether the League's committee members took bribes, or Norris twisted hands through the Freemasons.

Whatever, there was no logical explanation. The League did not even attempt to explain why its members voted first to relegate Tottenham, then to elect Arsenal in their place, rather than Barnsley, who finished third in the Second Division in 1915, or Wolves, who finished fourth. What is known is that Norris tirelessly worked the Football League's back corridors and committee rooms, lobbying, probably bullying, promising, doing who knows what deals, wielding who knows what political influence, to earn the votes which produced the scandal of Arsenal's dodgy promotion:

'However one massages the facts,' Inglis wrote, 'the President, the Committee and the clubs had succumbed to a rich and powerful politician and property dealer . . . never has the League been so manipulated as it was in 1919.'

Barnsley fans would have to wait until 1997 before their club finally made it to their single, Room at the Top season in the top flight. Arsenal, as every child is told, have never been down since. Arsenal's golden age, which produced the marble halls, Herbert Chapman, five League Championships, the tube station named after the club and all the other trappings of this most respectable club, was built on that foundation. They have never, as the saying goes, looked back. However, although Norris appointed Chapman, the rotund, journeyman player who as a manager had seen Huddersfield to their remarkable three successive Championships from 1924 to 1926, Norris himself was not around to see Arsenal's glory days.

In 1927 an FA commission conducting a wide-ranging investigation into under-the-table payments to players and other financial irregularities managed to nail Norris and ban him from
football for life. His crimes look laughably small-time now, but
they did transgress the rule against director-owners making money
out of the clubs. Norris was found to have had Arsenal pay for
his chauffeur between 1921 and 1924, and in 1926 Arsenal had
bought his car for him. Norris sued the FA for libel, in the course
of which he and Chapman fell out, after Norris claimed they had
paid money under-the-table – cash on top of the suffocating
maximum wage – to bring the great players, including Charlie
Buchan, to Highbury. Chapman, who had been Leeds City's
manager when they were expelled from the League in 1919, having
been found to have paid players above the stipulated maximum
during the war, denied everything. Professional football, whatever we think of the past from our corporate, commercialised
present, was never pure, and the FA was always watchful.

The chairman who succeeded Norris at Arsenal, coming in to
work with Chapman, furnish Arsenal with their golden age and
make them over into a bastion of football respectability, was a
man with two surnames, Sir Samuel Hill Wood. For all the apparent nobility of his name, Sir Samuel's money was relatively new,
having been built up by his grandfather, John Wood, as a cotton
mill owner in Glossop, a small town near Manchester at the foot
of the peaty Peak District hills. Samuel, 'Young Sam', had inherited the business but, an Old Etonian, he was rather more interested in sport. He played cricket and football, and from 1898 he
took over the local football club, Glossop North End, and funded
them into the Football League.

Glossop stayed in the League for seventeen seasons, including
one, 1899–1900, in the First Division, making them the smallest
town ever to host a top-flight club in English football. In 1915,
the year Arsenal finished fifth, Glossop finished bottom of the
Second Division. In 1919, when Arsenal were leapfrogged up,

Glossop were voted out of the League. The adventure had cost Hill Wood big money, and, in 1921, with cotton entering a decline, he sold up and moved to London. There he found a new club: Arsenal. Within a couple of years, Norris had invited him on to the Highbury board, welcoming his money, class and contacts. When Norris was fingered by the FA and banned, Hill Wood was asked to take over as the chairman. He bought the shares and slid into the Highbury boardroom, from where he worked smoothly with Chapman, who was redefining the role of the football manager and, in doing so, Arsenal's image as a football club.

Chapman claimed football management as a professional responsibility, broad-ranging and far more sophisticated than the old compromised secretary-managers, who had scurried between the boardroom and the training ground bearing bad news for the players about contracts and selection. Chapman made himself the central figure in the football club. He was a tactician, motivator, selector and signer of the country's best players, and he was also a visionary, introducing state-of-the-art training methods and tirelessly promoting Arsenal's image. Chapman experimented with floodlit matches, invited the media to attend sessions with his team – there seem to be many more photographs of Arsenal than any other club in the 1930s. His greatest publicity coup was persuading London Underground to change the name of Gillespie Road tube station to Arsenal in November 1932, so putting the club literally, accessibly, on the map.

Under Chapman, Arsenal became the most drilled, formidable football team the country had ever seen. At the suggestion of Charlie Buchan, Chapman introduced and refined the 'WM formation', adding another defender, most prominently the red-haired Herbie Roberts, as a centre half between the fullbacks, thereby establishing Arsenal's trademark system of mean defending and ruthless counter-attacking. A club forever celebrated in the archives, around the country they were heartily loathed, like Liverpool in their seventies pomp and Manchester United now – dubbed 'Lucky

Arsenal' by opposing fans coming away from regular 1-0 home defeats to breakaway goals scored by Cliff Bastin or David Jack, with Alex James pulling the midfield strings. Arsenal were ready by 1930, when they won the FA Cup for the first time. They won League Championships in 1931 and 1933, and three more before the thirties were out, but Chapman was not there to see them; he died suddenly of pneumonia on 6 January 1934 having insisted on watching the reserves even though he was sick. In his time he had revolutionised English football, and, with Hill Wood steering unobtrusively, transformed Highbury from the cuckoo in Islington's nest to a seat of football nobility. At the time of Chapman's death, Arsenal already had its great West Stand, designed by the architect Claude Waterlow Ferrier, which opened in 1932. Four years later, in October 1936, came William Binnie's masterpiece, the East Stand, which awed football with its art deco finishes, grand Arsenal insignia and, yes, the marble halls. In a unique tribute to their great manager, the club had installed in the halls the famous bust of Chapman, created by the sculptor Jacob Epstein. In the 'people's game', watched by the working-class masses from uncovered terraces, this was incomparably classy.

Not that Arsenal were exactly the darlings of the wider public suffering the 1930s Depression, dole queues and hunger marches. Several clubs collapsed in stricken industrial areas: Thames in East London, Ashington in the North East coalfield, Aberdare in South Wales. Yet here were Arsenal, Hill Wood introducing Lords Lonsdale and Westmorland into the boardroom, swaggering at their monumental new home in front of 70,000 crowds, their players forever posing at tennis or golf days, the team sweeping away the silverware with clinical tactics orchestrated by Chapman.

Sir Samuel Hill Wood, apart from a ten-month break for Lord Lonsdale in 1936, remained the chairman throughout Arsenal's golden age, through the Second World War and up to 1949. Another gent, Sir Granville Smith, took over, then in 1961, Sir Samuel's son Denis, by then with a hyphen in the Hill-Wood, took the chair. His son, Peter, was to the manner born, becoming an Arsenal director in 1962, the chairman twenty years later. This monarchy-like hereditary succession is unique in the football boardroom. Now, with the club winning Premier League titles with a side of foreign superstars under their manager Arsène Wenger, and preparing to dig up Islington's garbage plant at Ashburton Grove to build a new £357m, 60,000-seat stadium, Peter Hill-Wood is still the Arsenal chairman.

He agreed to see me for an interview in his nice mews house in Chelsea, and we had a pleasant afternoon sitting round the kitchen table, discussing his family and Arsenal, his spaniel panting pleadingly for a walk. Peter wasn't what you'd expect, haughty and rarefied; he'd rung me back very quickly and said he'd be happy for me to come to his home. He answered the door in white chinos, trainers and a blue open-necked shirt. With his square glasses and crumpled brown hair, he seemed very grounded, matter-of-fact about his lot, not averse to a grumble or two about the cost of living nowadays.

'My grandfather had enough to live on, I think,' he said of Sir Samuel. 'And you could live well on very little in those days. I remember he had a cook and a maid for my grandmother, and probably a butler. You know, everything cost a few quid a week then. Nowadays,' he said, 'you couldn't dream of doing that.'

Sir Samuel never worked again after he came down from Glossop. 'What he did with himself all day I don't know,' Peter smiled. 'He had a perfectly good life, as far as I know. When I was a relatively small boy we used to go round there for lunch and I'd sort of sit in one room with the maid, and my father and my grandfather would have a drink or two in another room, then we'd go to lunch. He always seemed to be absolutely charming.

'He never thought of Arsenal as a financial asset in any way. The idea was to serve the club and try to do things the right way. For our family, when you've been involved in something for fifty years, you don't think of it as money.'

Like his forebears, Peter was sent to Eton. He served in the army, then moved into the City, where eventually he headed an investment department at Hambros merchant bank. He's retired now, with the odd directorship to keep him ticking over. He talked ever so plainly about his lifetime's involvement at the heart of one of the great football clubs. Arsenal was, he reflected of times past, 'run in a rather friendly, family way; it was a very small business', as if it was a sideline he had to pop in on every now and again to take care of.

I probed for a bit of passion, asked him about his first memories of going to Highbury, expecting to hear he was, as most football people can remember, overwhelmed by the spectacle, noise, the thrill of the crowd and the game. But it was all pretty laid back. He was taken to his first match in 1948, when he was twelve, which seems late for a boy whose family substantially owned the club and whose grandfather was the chairman. After that, his father took him maybe four times a year; he was away at school, after all. Once he was on the board, he said, he used to go to a lot of away matches, which he seems to have quite enjoyed:

'It was rather fun. You'd go up the night before, stay in Burnley or Bolton or wherever it was, have a nice dinner or maybe eat on the train going up. Then you'd have a walk around the town, go to the game the next day and come back the same night. Or if we went to Newcastle we'd come back on the sleeper. You know, I mean, it was all gentler; nobody was flying about all over the shop.'

His life in football was like a sepia British Rail advert, with weekend breaks in the provinces, before the arrival of modern inconveniences like the European Champions League.

'One was brought up to be Arsenal,' he said of the *noblesse oblige* which came with the privilege. 'You dedicated your efforts to continuing the traditions and taking decisions for the good of the club, not for any other reason. I know it sounds rather pompous, but actually that's probably how it works.'

It was never, for him either, he said, a route to making money. The Hill-Woods never took a salary – they would not have been allowed to by the FA's rules, still in force. Nor did they take money out in any other way. There was, though, a hint of pragmatism in his answer:

'I never looked upon Arsenal as basically a financial asset. I mean, one couldn't see where the big money was going to be.'

In 1983, somebody arrived on the Arsenal board who would see where the money was to be made. David Dein was very different, in class and upbringing, from the public school merchant banker running the club. For a man who has now been in football for over twenty years, negotiating Arsenal into the modern era, proving himself an expert at working the committees first of the Football League, then the FA, there is surprisingly little detail on record about Dein. I asked him for an interview and had an e-mail from his secretary to say Mr Dein was unable to help. A search of newspaper archives reveals not a lot; there is one long profile from the *Daily Mail*, which is a model for the embarrassing sycophancy which newspapers seem to reserve for exaggerating the talents and vision of businessmen coming into football.

According to that article – 'The rise and rise of David Dein' – he grew up in Golders Green, London, captivated from an early age by playing football and supporting Arsenal after his uncle took him to Highbury in the fifties. Dein was bestowed by the paper with the standard innate gifts ascribed to football's money-men: 'indefatigable energy and enterprise', he was 'mercurial', and – the inevitable – 'a visionary'. An anonymous friend was quoted saying Dein never discusses his humble origins, but he was said to have helped out in his father's tobacconist's shop as a child, then, later, on his mother's grocery stall on Shepherd's Bush market importing yams, avocadoes, mangos and other Caribbean fruit and vegetables to serve London's new West Indian community. Later, the Deins imported food from Nigeria and elsewhere to cater for the Africans in London. The *Mail* piece and others said he dropped out of a French and economics course at Leeds University because he was so excited by the idea of building the family's business – wanting to become a 'fledgling tycoon', as the *Mail* puts it – although his biography in the Football League's official centenary book, written when Dein was on the Management Committee, said he actually graduated from Leeds, before 'making an extremely successful career as a commodity broker, principally in sugar'.

In 1964, when David was twenty-one, he founded a business with his brother Arnold called, initially, London and Overseas Express Freight. It seems to have grown steadily if modestly enough; in 1972, for example, they made a profit of £512. He married well, an American, Barbara Einhorn, and bought a house in 1974 on the nouveau-exclusive Totteridge Lane in north London, home to such giants of stage and screen as Des O'Connor and Bruce Forsyth.

The huge leap in their company's financial fortunes came in 1982. The accounts show that the previous year they turned over £1.7m, making a decent profit, £113,587. For the times, Dein was paying himself well, a salary of £80,000. But the following year the company recorded a galloping £42m turnover, although for the first time a small part of it was qualified by the accountants, saying they could not be sure some money owed from Nigeria would come in. That warning would be repeated every year after that. Despite this enormous rise in business, the company still made a loss, £2.7m. Dein took nearly double out in salary: £148,200. The following year, 1983, the company nearly tripled its losses, to £6.3m, its short-term debts, including trade creditors, ballooned to £20m, but Dein doubled his own salary again, to £281,333.

And that matches very closely the price, £292,000, he paid the same year for 16 per cent of Arsenal, buying previously unissued shares, a ticket to the blue-chip boardroom for the wheeler-dealer from Shepherd's Bush market. Peter Hill-Wood had been looking for someone to come and invest, to move the club on a stage. He had been, he told me, very glad to welcome David Dein in. At the time, Hill-Wood had famously said he was bemused as to why Dein would do it.

'I think he's crazy. To all intents and purposes it's dead money.'

His comment stands like an epitaph, more poignant as the years go on. Not necessarily naïve at the time, his words can be said to mark the beginning of the end of a long phase of football history, in which the clubs shared money and directors at least claimed to subscribe to the FA's ethos that they serve the clubs, not themselves. The rules, and the purity of the idea that directors were custodians, had routinely been bent, few doubt, with a dodge or two, a rake-off of cash from a turnstile, a slice of a transfer fee. It was, however, stamped into the game's version of itself that, despite professionalism and the way the League had come through to dominate the football experience, clubs were just that: clubs. Hill-Wood's family had been involved in football for eighty-six years, and learned, by paying out, that chairmen, shareholders, did not make money. That, though, was all about to change.

CHAPTER 3

Property Values

Supporting football clubs hoards millions of people into a collective experience, yet each fan has his own personal journey. The 1980s go down as the bleakest decade in football's history, the game's watershed and the excuse for the 'whole new ball game' of the Premier League, which began in 1992. Yet my memories of the 1980s are, I have to say, not predominantly of decline and disaster; Manchester City opened the decade with trips to Wembley for the FA Cup Final and – although we lost – the magical midweek replay against Spurs. The fans who had grown up with City as a top club had their shattering realisation that football is a fragile dream when City were relegated in 1983, an event with which many glum fortysomethings are still struggling to come to terms. Then, yes, looking back, we watched the remaining scraps of a team in thinning crowds, from behind fences, with regular mayhem going off outside the grounds. To me, though, the poisonous fighting, fences, police horses and miserable grounds were just inconveniences, to be avoided or hurdled while following the football soap opera, in our case a parade of careworn managers, kids thrown in too early, and eventually the odd new signing we could afford, like Trevor Morley from Northampton, who came for £200,000, had us wondering when he took his first pass in the penalty area, then fell over.

City fans reacted to the cheerless arenas, the railings, trouble, police horse shit and haggard grounds not with earnest arguments but with silliness – the inflatable craze, which started with blow-up bananas dotting the Kippax, and reached its popping point at a midweek game at West Brom, when fans wandered into the away terrace, the Smethwick End, with whatever they had grabbed from their kids' toy boxes: inflatable alligators, hammers, dinosaurs. When one guy finally, after several tries, managed to land his blow-up dolphin in another fan's paddling pool, a huge cheer went up. The crowd started singing: 'Paddling pool, paddling pool, paddling pool', and on it went. City did their bit by losing 1-0, their goal scored after our centre half, Brian Gayle, the newly-signed rock of our promotion hopes, ducked under the ball.

The loyalty of supporters saw football through, and they were still there in their millions, the captive market at the end of the game's darkest decade, exploitable for Sky, which based its survival plans on winning the TV rights to English football exclusively. Seen from the perspective of today's era, the problems then were huge, even if most fans were too busy bloody-mindedly enjoying themselves to do anything about it. In the general malaise, most clubs below the successful few were having serious financial problems. A report on professional football's finances in 1981–2, cited in Inglis' *League Football and the Men Who Made It*, found that all but four-teen of the ninety-two Football League clubs were technically bust, and were losing, overall, £6m a year. Yet it is interesting that the League was still making plenty of money – why wouldn't it be when millions were still turning up and the game was still a TV staple? Match receipts in all four divisions were totted up to £35m, and the League received £5.9m from television and sponsorship – quaint figures in the age of Sky but still good money. It is a familiar picture to us now; the clubs made losses not because they had no money, or because they spent it all on their grounds, or on safety, facilities or policing – about whose cost they moaned relentlessly. No, it was the innate problem: the clubs and their chairmen were so obsessed with competing against each other for the football prizes that they spent money they didn't have, £22m that season, in over-the-top transfer fees and unaffordable players' wages. The major First Division clubs, with apparently sound grounds and crowds holding up, were mostly making money, while the lower division clubs were sagging trying to keep up. The response of the League's chairmen was split, wracked by division: between those who saw that the game required a united, collective response to its troubles, and the big clubs themselves, who increasingly wanted to break away and keep the money. Leadership, from the League's own central management and the FA, was desperately lacking, and the major clubs moved through to exploit that vacuum.

They made their first fundamental breach in the ramparts in 1983, the year David Dein bought into Arsenal. From its estab-lishment ninety-five years earlier, the Football League had main-tained the system of sharing a match's gate money between the home and away clubs, whoever they might be. William McGregor had originally proposed that gates should be shared equally, but at the first ever meeting of clubs, on 17 April 1888 at the Royal Hotel in Manchester – which, appropriately enough, appears to have been something of a squabble – McGregor was voted down.

The clubs agreed instead that the away side would be guaran-teed £15 per match, a decent fee for the time. Besides simply ensuring clubs a regular, weekly income to enable them to pay their way, the principle was established that some sharing was necessary to safeguard the competition. Otherwise the big city clubs, having more of a population to draw on, would make so much more money out of their crowds than the smaller town clubs, they would pay for more and better players, and therefore dominate on the field. That was not, the clubs decided at the start, the basis of a good, exciting league.

The guarantee was reduced to £12 the following season, and stuck there until the First World War. Then, to help clubs relying on odd wartime games for their survival, gate money from friendlies was shared more equally, 20 per cent paid to the away club. When the

League restarted in 1919, the clubs agreed to keep that split, and it was maintained at 20 per cent throughout football's phenomenal growth up to and after the Second World War. Gate-sharing, and, from 1965, equal distribution of television money, underpinned the rough evenness of English football on the field, where, apart from bursts of exceptional management – Chapman at Huddersfield then Arsenal, Stan Cullis at Wolves, Matt Busby at Manchester United, Shankly and Paisley at Liverpool – League Championships were usually close and could be won by several different clubs.

Gate-sharing was done away with at the League's Annual Meeting in the summer of 1983. For the first time the visiting club from then on was paid nothing. The change favoured and had been lobbied for by the bigger clubs, who had grown to resent sharing the takings from their larger grounds and crowds. The significance of that change has been too little understood; it is being felt ever more keenly as the years pass. Now, the club with the biggest stadium, Manchester United, with 67,700 people at Old Trafford paying credit-card-busting prices, is required to share none of the proceeds, and so makes more money to continually strengthen its team than all the other clubs. Although the money from television and sponsorship has exploded in recent times, stadium size is coming to define which clubs will be successful.

The FA had already, in 1981, relaxed its historic prohibition against directors being paid; they were now allowed a salary, as long as they worked full-time at their clubs. The idea was to introduce a more professional approach, while preserving the principle that clubs were not there to leak money out to nominal placemen on the boards. Martin Edwards, whose father, Louis, had bought up the bulk of Manchester United in the 1960s, and whose family meat business had been sold, almost immediately became one of football's first chief executives, well paid from the beginning.

The annual payments permitted to shareholders from dividends were also raised, from 5 to 15 per cent, which the FA were persuaded would encourage investment in the professional game.

At United, the Edwards family, advised by Roland Smith, a professor at Manchester University's Business School, had anyway in 1978 found a way to make big money out of dividends, despite the restriction. Called in to look at the prospects for the meat business, Smith tuned instead to the opportunity to make money out of United, seeing that the Edwardses could boost their dividends simply by increasing the number of their shares. The resulting mechanism was a 1:208 rights issue, by which a shareholder had the right to buy 208 shares for every one he held already. It was opposed by Matt Busby himself, United's own secretary Les Olive and some clear-sighted fans, but they were overridden. The Edwards family embarked on another round of share-buying from small and larger shareholders before the rights issue, which took their holding of United to 74 per cent. The number of shares they held was then multiplied by 209, and suddenly the annual 5 per cent dividend was a proper windfall out of United, to a family whose own business was in serious trouble. United declared a dividend worth £50,000 the very next year, following it with similar amounts for the next two. Then in 1981, when the FA increased the permissible maximum to 15 per cent, United immediately paid it – £151,284. The Edwards family became one of the first to live, very comfortably, off a football club.

There were other figures in a new, younger generation of commercial men arriving in the football boardrooms. Irving Scholar was a property dealer, now living in the tax-free haven of Monaco, who had manoeuvred himself a takeover of the club he supported, Tottenham. In 1983 he decided to float Spurs on the Stock Market, the first football club to do so. Scholar argued that a float would enable investors to put new money into Spurs, and it would also make him a fortune if it went well and the share price increased. Working on the intricacies of the deal, his lawyers came across the FA's longstanding restrictions against paid part-time directors, unlimited dividends and the distribution of any surplus if the club were wound up. If the FA had known its business back in 1892 when the clubs first formed limited liability companies, and developed the rules to balance what they saw as the dangers of commercialism, by 1983 the governing body seemed to have lost its way, and its eyesight. Scholar's lawyers decided the easiest, neatest way to deal with the restrictions was simply to dodge them. They could form a holding company, free of the rules which applied to clubs, make the football club itself, with its ground and players' contracts, a subsidiary, then float the holding company. They were duly allowed to do it, no problem, floated Tottenham Hotspur plc, with Tottenham Hotspur FC as the subsidiary, the rules, now meaningless, attaching to the club but not the company. That same device was adopted by every club which lined up to float afterwards, bypassing the FA's own rules, which were aimed at protecting their clubs from precisely this: financial speculation.

I asked Scholar if he recalled what the FA's response had been when he first proposed bypassing the rules in this way. He's a great talker, still an engaging enthusiast for the game, for all that his time at Spurs ended with a financial crisis in 1991, and his 1997 float and chairmanship of Nottingham Forest was, if anything, unhappier still. He told me he didn't remember what the FA said; in fact, he wasn't sure his advisers ever had a reply. It is pointless asking the FA – I already have. They can't remember. The proposal does not seem even to have come up for discussion at a meeting. The rules, ninety years old by then, could be evaded, and football clubs could become public companies, profit-making vehicles for investors, contrary to the governing body's own principles. Perhaps the old gents on the FA council thought, as the money men danced around them, that it all sounded very go-ahead. The rules stayed in the governing body's handbooks, but, from that moment, they lay flaccid.

David Dein was another of this new breed of younger, financially motivated men, casually written up as visionaries by a football press which did not have the time or inclination to pick more inquiringly at the game's fabric. There is a legitimate question to be asked about whether doing well in your own small business, which tends to require the hard-headed pursuit of self-interest, is a suitable qualification for running a football club, which serves its fans and community, let alone for occupying a senior position in the FA or leagues running the sport itself. Anyhow, investigating the careers of many of these people, it is clear that making money by ploughing on with a small company is tough, strewn with pitfalls and failure, and some of them have not been as successful as the superficial football write-ups would have us believe. Looking at how much many of these people have gone on to make out of football, they seem to have found it all rather easier.

Within months of buying into Arsenal, David Dein's own company was plunged into crisis, weighed down with debts of £11m it was never to shake off. Dein had come to know an Indian businessman, Rajendra Sethia, who ran a trading company called Esal Commodities and put a tremendous amount of business Dein's way, importing huge quantities of sugar and other foodstuffs. The association with Esal apparently accounts for the huge increase in Dein's company turnover in 1982. The two men are said to have enjoyed each other's company, playing tennis and flying around the world in Sethia's private jet. Once Dein had bought into Arsenal, Sethia was invited there, too. Somebody who knew them at the time told me he thought Dein originally bought the football shares much as Louis Edwards had – as a passport to the boardroom of the club he supported rather than because he thought then that there was money to be made.

In late 1983, Esal imploded, suddenly and dramatically. The company unravelled when several banks discovered that they had all lent money against the same, single cargo of sugar, bound for Nigeria in a ship, the *Sea King*, which was sitting in port at Dunkirk. Memories of Esal have been overtaken by larger City debacles later in the 1980s – Maxwell, BCCI, Lloyds – but at the time it was a major financial scandal. Esal, it turned out, was a house of cards, a pyramid constructed with massive borrowing to fund, it was alleged, Sethia's playboy lifestyle. The Metropolitan Police Fraud Squad launched a long investigation but Sethia fled to India, from where he has protested his innocence but has never returned. I talked to Richard Coleman of PriceWaterhouseCoopers, the accountant who acted as the liquidator of Esal after it went bust. He recalled that they had spent years, and been in court several times, trying to trace assets which Sethia had bought. Coleman's firm repossessed a private plane with gold fittings, racehorses, even an Indian tea plantation. But not much else.

'Most of the money had gone,' he said. 'It was spent. We worked a long time tracking it but in the end we only recovered 6p for every pound lost by the creditors.'

Dein was one of Esal's biggest creditors, his company owed millions. Dein himself ultimately wound up Esal on 7 November 1984; it had total debts of $350m, owed to an armada of banks, traders and other businesses. Dein apparently fought hard against this enormous setback; Arnold, his brother, left the company a month later, and since then David's wife Barbara has always been named in the records as the sole other director. In February 1985, Dein is reported to have made Sethia bankrupt. He made *The Guinness Book of Records* as Britain's most catastrophic bankrupt, with personal debts of £168m.

Dein still carried on trading through his company, now called London and Overseas (Sugar) Co., and made, by the looks of it, good money, paying himself handsomely: £269,000 in 1984, £138,000 in 1985, nearly £200,000 in 1986. But every year the same note was stubbornly made in the company accounts: debts exceeded assets by around the same: £10m–£11m.

Yet in football, Dein, Scholar and Edwards were written up as dynamic business whiz kids. They worked quite closely together throughout the 1980s, pursuing the interests of their own clubs. Dein, more than the others, also took eagerly to the business of winning friends and influencing people in football's politics, soon getting himself voted onto the League's ruling body, the Management Committee, then steadily working his way into senior positions in the committees at the FA's hidebound Lancaster Gate headquarters.

Television and sponsorship money was still distributed evenly throughout the League, as it had been from 1965, when the BBC paid £5,000 for a new Saturday evening highlights programme called *Match of the Day*. The League duly shared that out equally to the ninety-two clubs in the four divisions – not much more than £50 each. By the 1980s, for all football's growing problems, the game was still great, popular television, and the deals were getting bigger, although BBC and ITV had a mutual understanding to hold the price down. The big clubs, who were shown most, began to agitate to keep much more of the money.

The First Division clubs began to push openly in 1981–2, after Everton's chairman, Philip Carter, hosted a meeting of chairmen at Goodison Park. It was the beginning of the drive for a 'superleague', a threat by the First Division clubs to break away if the other seventy clubs did not cave in to their demands for more money. Martin Edwards, who would eventually make over £100m from his Manchester United shares, was centrally involved, and he made his famous comment at the time: 'The smaller clubs are bleeding the game dry. For the sake of the game, they should be put to sleep.'

When examining what has happened to football since then, it is worth keeping that remark in mind. It mustn't be forgotten, however, how bleak the backdrop was to the big clubs' plottings. Their crowds, at Old Trafford, Anfield, Highbury, even White Hart Lane and Goodison, were mostly holding up, but more widely, the League was in trouble. Hit by recession, mass unemployment and hooliganism at the crumbling, caged grounds, the number of people with the appetite to go through all this to watch a football match fell by 11 per cent in 1980–81. Crowds continued to decline by around a million a season, then in 1985 came disaster, first on 11 May at Bradford, where fifty-six people were killed in a fire, then just eighteen days later, in front of the world's cameras, at the European Cup Final between Liverpool and Juventus at Brussels' Heysel Stadium, where thirty-nine fans died when a wall collapsed after a rush by Liverpool fans. The following season, 1985–6, crowds fell to their lowest since the League expanded to four divisions back in 1922. It should be noted, however, that even after such horror, this total attendance figure was still 16.4m. England's professional clubs still called on the loyalty of a great many people, even at the game's lowest ebb, and in its most hostile landscape.

Financially, League football was in crisis, with many clubs on the brink of insolvency. The locked gates at Middlesbrough, who went into receivership, left perhaps the most lingering image, but many other clubs dangled. Charlton had to leave their home at the Valley and in 1984 came within minutes of going bust; Wolves, two sides of their ground disused, also came within minutes of liquidation. A debate evolved as to whether there were too many clubs in the League, whether ninety-two could be sustained. The League's president, one of the game's great and good, Jack Dunnett, the chairman and owner of Notts County and a Labour MP in Nottingham, actually agreed that they perhaps ought to let a few die:

'I believed in natural wastage,' he said, quoted in Inglis' *League Football*. 'If a community couldn't sustain its football club I didn't see why it should be propped up. We were quite prepared to see the League slimmed down to ninety or even seventy clubs.'

The policy changed, however, because every time a club was on the brink, with no saviour or solution apparent, somehow, with fans rallying round and local businessmen believing they could do better, clubs pulled through and survived. The League clubs have grown into a curious mixture – commercial organisations required to make money to compete, yet drawing on a deep well of support from fans who don't see them that way at all, but believe in them as spiritual homes, community institutions, havens of belonging. However self-destructive, malign or incompetent the people in charge of clubs have been, a core of supporters have always kept the faith and helped, over decades, to pull them out of a series of existence-threatening crises. In the 1980s, the League somehow clambered through with ninety-two clubs intact, each club saved at the last by campaigning, fundraising fans and some businessman appearing with a just-about-workable financial rescue package.

Not that the big clubs were at all impressed or committed to the preservation of all clubs; in fact, quite the opposite. In the summer of 1985, the big clubs renewed their demands for more money and power. The breakaway threat was genuine by then and the League came close to a split, averted only by the 'Heathrow Agreement', brokered over six hours by the PFA's chief executive Gordon Taylor at the airport's Post House Hotel on 18 December 1985. The compromise set the pattern for all that followed: the big clubs were given more money and voting power and so they agreed to stay in the League. The split of TV and sponsorship money now changed, from equal distribution throughout the League to 50 per cent to the First Division, 25 per cent to the Second, 25 per cent between them to the Third and Fourth. Perhaps that was fair; after all, television is interested overwhelmingly in showing the big clubs, and they argued they needed the money to compete in Europe against the major Spanish and Italian clubs. But the big clubs were not in a mood for debate; before the meeting, the chairmen of all twenty-two First Division clubs had agreed to walk out if their demands were not met.

'Vote yes or we break away' was Philip Carter's hard-faced presentation of the buffet of choices spread before the other chairmen.

David Dein joined the League's Management Committee the following year, when it was expanded as part of the cave-in, to give more places and influence to the First Division clubs. In 1988, the League did a four-year, £44m deal with Greg Dyke of ITV, in which the distribution of money was skewed towards the bigger clubs, whose matches were shown live almost exclusively. Still, though, the League clung together.

On 15 April 1989, the desperate decade finally reached its horrific conclusion with ninety-six Liverpool supporters, mostly young, crushed to death on the Leppings Lane Terrace at Hillsborough while watching the FA Cup semi-final between Liverpool and Nottingham Forest. The disaster was to be the end of football's slipshod, regularly fatal approach to safety. The Taylor Report, in January 1990, recommended that football grounds should become all-seater and safety be controlled by a strict system, legally binding, although he recommended the clubs should be given public money to help them pay for the rebuilding. He also called for football to overhaul the way it was run more generally, and he criticised the self-interest of club directors and poor governance by the FA and the League for having brought the national game, so close to the twenty-first century, into such disgrace and disaster. The game had to change – but the course of its future was still up for grabs.

In 1989, David Dein's company appears to have stopped trading completely. The turnover is given as '–'. Creditors were still owed £11m, and the company's debts exceeded its assets by the same amount. The auditors put a note on the accounts saying the company 'may be unable to continue trading without the continued financial support of its bankers, creditors and director'. The following year, 1990, Dein launched a legal action to try to get his money back. Sethia was bankrupt, Esal was in liquidation, so there was no prospect of any money coming from either of them. Instead, Dein sued the Punjab National Bank, which had worked so closely with Sethia that three of its managers were under investigation by the Fraud Squad. The liquidators had themselves sued the bank, but settled in the end for just $8.5m. Dein was unhappy with that, and issued his own action alleging that the bank had been complicit with Esal's frauds. The case, Dein's last chance to salvage anything from the collapse of his company, would take more than two years to be decided.

In the meantime, he made himself very busy pushing Arsenal's and the big clubs' interests in the stew of football politics which followed Hillsborough, in anticipation of the next TV deal, which was due for renewal in 1992. By now, satellite TV had been launched, introducing competition into the old cosy carve-up by the BBC and ITV, and the deal promised to flood the stricken game with new riches.

The Football League, not the FA, was the first to address the opportunities and challenges presented by this moment in the game's history, producing a document published on 18 October 1990. Called *One Game, One Team, One Voice: Managing Football's Future*, it still stands as a reasonably sound basis on which the game could have moved ahead in the new era. Its central message was the need for unity between the League and the FA. William McGregor's founding hope that the two bodies could dovetail rather than clash had not survived into the modern age. The League, which was, after all, only a collective of clubs, all of them hungry for money, had become frustrated with the FA for years over a number of areas. 'Club versus country' was one; the clubs all pledged loyalty to the England team, but always grumbled about the arrangements: the FA selects mostly the big clubs' players for England international matches, sells the TV rights and keeps the money, yet does not compensate the clubs, who pay the players' wages, then watch as they come back injured or jaded. There were always niggly matters such as referees and disciplinary issues, overseen by the FA with some self-importance, in which the clubs could lose valuable players to bans or suspensions imposed without obvious consistency by a panel of FA councillors who had never been involved in the professional game. The main area which really bugged the clubs, however, was, no surprises, money. The FA Cup is attractive to television principally because the big clubs play in it, yet the FA sold the TV rights, and, as with England matches, kept the money and decided how it was to be distributed. The League also believed the FA was presumptuous and arrogant, doing its commercial deals on the back of the big clubs and their players, but rarely troubling to consult or inform the League.

The League had dealt with these confrontations partly by seeking to influence the FA internally, by securing more places for its own representatives on the FA Council and the important FA committees. David Dein, along with the Chelsea chairman Ken Bates, Doug Ellis, Peter Swales and others, got himself voted in there quickly. The other FA councillors, chairman Bert Millichip and paid officers did not react to the problems with vision, by actively seeking to discuss and resolve them. They took the view that they had conceded some authority and now the League could be listened to inside Lancaster Gate, but they were not prepared to, as they saw it, further compromise the pre-eminence of the FA as the overall governing body.

One Game, One Team, One Voice proposed solving the turf wars by forming a single, joint board on which five delegates from the FA, five from the League, together with the chief executives of each body, would sit together, discuss the issues and produce a joint approach on the significant issues. Reading it now, you can see it was not a document which was motivated most centrally by concern for the health of football as a whole, from the grass roots up to the England team, for all of which the FA is responsible. It did touch on those areas and said the game could only be helped by close co-operation between the bodies. But the document dealt principally with the areas of commercial frustration; they suggested a joint approach to television and sponsors by the League and FA, which they argued would bring more money in, and said the touchy areas of club versus country, disciplinary issues, ground safety and a host of others would be resolved more effectively after joint discussion and with a unified approach.

The document will disabuse anybody of the notion that the big clubs' directors, the likes of Dein, Edwards, Scholar, were somehow visionary in seeing that big money was coming in from television. That was plain to everybody; the League noted that the BBC and ITV cartel had 'very successfully' kept the price paid by television down, and that this was going to change because of the emergence of satellite.

'With respect to television, football is about to enter an era of unprecedented opportunity,' it said.

All in the League saw that the game was poised to be transformed: 'There can be little doubt that the 1980s provided football with the most problematic decade in its history. There can also be little doubt that the 1990s will be the decade of most dramatic change.'

The question was how football would manage itself to take advantage of this change, and its new wealth and opportunities, and the League was clear that it would be best done if the two bodies were united. Bill Fox, the chairman of Blackburn Rovers and president of the League, signed off the document: 'We, the administrators of the game, are responsible for taking a positive step forward to work together.'

The League's commercial director, Trevor Philips, was dispatched on a roadshow around the country, to local County FA headquarters, to sell the good sense of the new thinking. Yet just a month later, the big clubs completely undermined this policy, which had been agreed by all League clubs. The League's self-proclaimed 'Big Five' – Manchester United, Arsenal, Liverpool, Everton and Tottenham – held their own private meeting, over dinner with Greg Dyke, then of London Weekend Television, to discuss their wish to break away from the League completely. They asked him if ITV would pay them big money for the rights, and Dyke, very aware of the threat from Sky, said he would love to. The clubs then deputed two men to go to the FA to ask the governing body to support the breakaway. The two were Noel White, by now a director of Liverpool, and David Dein.

White and Dein found the FA, led by Bert Millichip and Graham Kelly, gripped by insecurity in the face of *One Game, One Team, One Voice*. Millichip did not view the League's call for a joint board as a sensible starting point on which to base a more considered approach to the game. The new money coming in at the top could have been used, in a unified sport, to make football better run and more appealing not only to the ninety-two professional clubs but for all the other 43,000 clubs, amateur and semi-professional, for which the FA is responsible, the million or so people who play it regularly, as well as those who watch it and support clubs. The FA could have come together with the League and looked to create a true pyramid, a strong sport with a coherent purpose to which everybody adhered. Instead, the FA had become so obsessed with its own standing, the position and privileges of its ninety-two-member ruling council, that it saw the League's proposals only as a threat, a challenge to the FA's supremacy. When Dein and White approached with the idea of the breakaway, Millichip embraced it more warmly than they could have hoped, seeing the proposal as a way to fatally undermine the League.

That decision, to back the rich clubs to break away and keep all the money, was clearly contrary to the FA's principles, philosophy for its game and *raison d'être* since its foundation in 1863. The result of petty politics and vanity, it was also flawed in a very important way. Millichip was misreading the proponents of *One Game, One Team, One Voice*. He saw it as 'the League' seeking to power share with the FA, but the League is only a body of clubs. And the clubs who were most frustrated over such things as the England team, the distribution of money from the FA Cup, sponsorship and the rest were not the smaller clubs, which never provided players for internationals, but the big clubs. They, clearly, were behind the proposal for the joint board. But the FA misread it, seeing 'the League' as the enemy and, instead of dealing with the underlying concerns, supported the big clubs' breakaway as a way of defeating 'the League'. Crazy.

The FA gave its formal support to the breakaway in June 1991, in *The Blueprint for the Future of Football*, a one-hundred-page flimflam of ideas for the game, most of which the FA never implemented, wrapped around one bombshell: the establishment of the Premier League. The blueprint claimed that the rationale for this was pure football: it would be an elite league reduced to eighteen clubs, streamlining the matches played by the top players, which would benefit the England team. The real reason was to smash the League; the FA never prevailed on the Premier League to slim down to eighteen clubs, and Millichip never held them to it. Dein, White, Scholar, Edwards and Philip Carter of Everton were triumphant: the game was heading for a TV windfall, and yet somehow they had won the backing of the game's originally amateur governing body for a breakaway from the tradition of sharing money with the clubs in the other three divisions, or with the rest of football.

Crucially for the future, nothing in this breakaway, which was to mean that the new money came in but was swallowed up at the top of football, dealt with the big clubs' concerns at the heart of *One Game, One Team, One Voice*. They got to keep all the millions paid by Sky for Premier League matches, but club versus country, the separate TV deals done by the FA and the distribution of that money, referees, disciplinary and the other issues – none of that was resolved. Despite the cataclysm of the FA's backing for the breakaway and its savage effect on the League, those problems between the FA and the big clubs were to drift on into the new era.

David Dein proceeded to consolidate his hold on Arsenal's shares. As recorded in the 1990 accounts, Peter Hill-Wood still had 1,016 shares, the family silver, hallmarked when his grandfather took over in the 1920s. Dein had 1,461, with most of the rest held by the five other directors. By the following year, 1991, Hill-Wood had suddenly sold his shares, 960 of them, leaving him with just fifty-six, 1 per cent of Arsenal. Dein's holding was hugely up, to 42 per cent. The price Dein paid Hill-Wood has never been revealed, and when I talked to Hill-Wood around his kitchen table he wasn't about to tell me; but you only had to look at the regret in his eyes to see that, compared to modern fortunes, it wasn't much. In 1983 Hill-Wood had not seen the changing times and said Dein's investment was dead money; it looks as if he got it wrong again in 1990–91, when the game and his club was finally on the threshold of multi-millions.

'I shouldn't,' he said, looking over his glasses, his voice shaking slightly, 'have sold the shares to him when I did.'

I asked him if he regretted it.

'Well, I have done, but there's no point thinking about it because I haven't got them, so there.'

He was ever so brave about it. You could only imagine the nights he'd spent lying awake, beating himself up about selling the damn shares so cheaply. He was phlegmatic, though:

'Back then it was completely different. No one had envisaged Rupert Murdoch coming in and us getting a billion pounds for a three-year contract as we just have. You couldn't see where the big money was going to be.'

Dein, lobbying for the breakaway, must have known well enough – as, it has to be said, did most of the men involved in professional football.

'Well my situation is history,' Hill-Wood told me. 'There's no point taking any other view than to look forward and positively. You've got to be relatively relaxed.'

If Dein's rise in football had been slick so far, his next major plan hit concerted opposition, from the fans on Arsenal's North Bank terrace. All the clubs were raising money to finance the rebuilding of their grounds to comply with the Taylor Report. Manchester United floated in 1991 – forming a holding company, bypassing the FA's rules – raising £10m to finance the all-seating of their Stretford End. The float made Martin Edwards an immediate £6m in cash, the first in his epic series of share sales. United's flotation did, though, allow supporters who gave money to the club to have a shareholding and a stake in it. Arsenal, who wanted to raise up to £16.5m towards a rebuilt North Bank, one of the game's better-appointed terraces, were to allow no such thing. Fans arriving for the final game of the season, against United in May 1991, saw their solid, mostly British team presented with the League Championship, George Graham's second, and handed to all of them was a document showing how Arsenal intended to raise the money. Somewhat embarrassingly trying to entice fans with football language – Arsenal's 'goal' was to rebuild the North Bank, that type of thing – the document boiled down to asking the fans to pay £1,500, or £1,100, in debentures, what came to be known as bonds, for the following chief benefit: 'A Debenture will entitle the Bondholder to purchase a season ticket prior to each football season.'

It was hardly the deal of the century; fans were offered a way to spread payments over up to four years, at an annual interest rate of 10 per cent, bringing the total for a £1,100 bond to £1,536 – for the right to buy a season ticket. Following an outcry from fans, a revised scheme was announced, on 14 August the following year, which cited an instructive benefit: the bondholder would be able to buy a season ticket with inflation-only price rises for nine years. A table showed fans the saving this could make – a bondholder's season ticket might be up to £370 by 2002, while for fans without bonds season tickets might cost £630. In other words, the club was explicitly saying it was going to ratchet up the cost of tickets well beyond the rate of inflation and wanted fans to pay big money up front to avoid that. Arsenal have in fact steepled the prices to almost double what they threatened – to £1,220 in the North Bank. Those who bought bonds have 'saved' money, but who thought it would turn out anything like this expensive when fans were still paying a few quid a match to stand on the North Bank?

The clear threat behind the bond scheme was that fans would not get a season ticket at all if they didn't buy one. Many people initially scratched around for the wherewithal, but gradually resentment grew from fans who felt ripped off. IASA, the Independent Arsenal Supporters Association, was formed specifically to fight the bond scheme, which Mike Winnett, one of the leading opponents, dismissed as 'the Blind Scheme'.

'We opposed it,' he told me, 'because it was introduced without any consultation with fans, and because it effectively deprived many fans, who didn't have access to big money or credit, of the opportunity to sit on the North Bank. Those loyal fans were summarily evicted for the benefit of bigger spenders.'

At the time, he said he could see that the bond would be hugely profitable for the shareholders, of whom the largest was Dein:

'There was never any doubt that it would benefit shareholders, since their assets would significantly appreciate at no cost to themselves. But it killed the atmosphere, and many people I know were alienated and never came back.'

Opposition hardened to the bond scheme throughout 1991–2, culminating in a sit-down protest by thousands of fans after the last match ever in front of the North Bank terrace, a 5-1 win over Southampton.

'It was a peaceful protest,' Winnett remembered. 'We had had "stay-behinds" at a number of games before that. But on that final day, we were forcibly removed by stewards and police, some people were dragged off by their hair. It wasn't pretty.'

A petition with 8,000 signatures was handed in at the entrance to the East Stand. The fans had asked Dein to accept it personally but in the end a commissionaire took it from them. Arsenal did change some of the detail for the revised 1992 scheme, but the bonds remained; as so often, the supporters' protests were largely ignored. The club did not disclose exactly how many fans bought bonds; it was several thousand, although the club fell short of its target. So Arsenal financed the rebuilding largely using money from fans, who received no shares in the club, only the right to pay for a season ticket. Even dreaming up such a scheme testifies to the power of football over the loyalty of fans, and the club directors' preparedness to exploit that loyalty, however they dressed it up. In the close season, the North Bank was demolished and, famously, a mural put up as a veil over the building work, featuring smiley happy people, and not a single black face.

Almost immediately, Dein sold a chunk of his shares. In 1991 when the bond scheme was launched, although the fans were offered no shares for their investment the directors enjoyed a 'bonus issue' of shares for free; for every one they held, they were issued with seven more. Arsenal's 1991 accounts showed Hill-Wood with 448 shares – in reality fifty-six old ones – while Dein had 23,816 shares. The following year, by May 1992, Dein was shown to have sold 10,000 to Danny Fiszman, a new face on the Arsenal board, a man who made his apparently large pile of money in Hatton Garden, London's diamond centre. What Fiszman paid Dein is, again, private, but there is no reason to think Dein sold a large portion of one of England's most prestigious football clubs, on the brink of the satellite, moneyed, seated, breakaway era, for anything other than a decent profit. In September 1992, as planned and plotted for, the FA Carling Premiership was launched, 'live and exclusive' on Sky, the rights seized with unprecedentedly huge money, £305m over the next five years, none of it needing to be shared with the rest of football.

It has been said that Dein sold the shares to finance his expensive legal action against the Punjab National Bank, which was heading for the High Court in late October and early November 1992, with eye-watering hourly-rate QCs and law firms on each side. On 5 November, after a five-day hearing, Judge Lindsay came back with his decision. The case established some minor precedent in a small corner of insolvency law but the upshot was that the judge threw out Dein's case. He lost. London and Overseas, Dein's company, was finished.

In 1993, they filed their last accounts. The company doesn't appear to have traded. All Dein's other ventures, London and Overseas Finance, Petroleum, Commodities, appear to have since been dissolved. A long list of companies run by the Dein brothers back in the good days, Imaginative Printing, Jaycon Soft Drinks, Deins' Food Stores, Dein Bros (Food Importers) Ltd, have dropped off the companies register. London and Overseas' auditors noted that the company was 'dependent on the continued financial support of [its] creditors', and its debts exceeded its assets, still, nearly ten years on, by over £11m.

At Highbury, the North Bank was completed for the start of the 1993–4 season with some dignity and style, compared to the soulless units being thrown up in all-seater uniformity across the country. In 1995, with football cleaned up, its image made over, the media relentlessly hyping it, the money pouring in, Dein's shareholding dropped by nearly 5,000, taking his holding down to 17 per cent. Fiszman's increased by 4,500, giving this obscure but clearly very rich man 27 per cent of the club. Because, according to Arsenal's accounts, Dein and Fiszman had a joint interest in some of the shares, it is not clear whether this was a sale or not.

The following year, 1996, in June or early July, Dein did sell, another 3,000 shares to Fiszman. This time you can hazard an informed guess at the price; in October 1995 Arsenal moved onto a Stock Exchange market called OFEX, which allows shares to be more easily traded. The OFEX price at around this time was £1,350. It was a private deal, so the price was unknown, but if Fiszman paid him anything like the market price Dein would have made £4.05m. A nice profit, this, from 'dead money', for the tycoon whose own company had collapsed.

Dein then salvaged his own stock with the Arsenal fans, reinventing himself from somebody seen as a self-seeking opportunist by making one inspired appointment. George Graham had gone, following the episode when he was found to have accepted £425,000 from the agent Rune Hauge following his signing of the midfielder John Jensen from the Danish club Brondby. Bruce Rioch had come in as the manager, signed Dennis Bergkamp and David Platt, but was considered not of the stature Arsenal were looking for. Dein pushed for a manager of whom few but the most hooded world football anoraks can have heard, a Frenchman then managing Grampus Eight in the manufactured Japanese League: Arsène Wenger.

Peter Hill-Wood was at pains with me to stress that the whole board agreed to bring Wenger in, but conceded that Dein was 'very largely responsible' for the choice. Yet Dein's own account of it in a book, *The Glorious Game*, co-authored by Alex Fynn and Kevin Whitcher, makes the selection process for Wenger a little harder to admire. Wenger, Dein said, was managing Monaco when they first met at Highbury while Wenger was watching Arsenal. Dein, the book has it, 'generously took him to dinner', after which Wenger 'made an immediate impression on Dein' in a game of charades. They kept in touch because 'Dein had a yacht moored at Antibes along the coast from Monaco, and would often take in a game and dinner with the coach afterwards.'

Such is life for the men who made millions out of football in the 1990s. Wenger's first signing was not well known either, a tall midfield player burning up in AC Milan's reserves: Patrick Vieira. Wenger retained the English defence of Dixon, Bould, Adams, Winterburn and goalkeeper David Seaman, but overhauled the players' training, preparation, diet and the tactical approach to the game. He also made over Arsenal's image by freeing the players' spirits, encouraging skill and daring, and he signed foreign, mostly French, players to introduce the va-va-voom: Nicolas Anelka, signed for just £500,000 from Paris St-Germain in February 1997 and sold for £23m to Real Madrid in 1999, Emmanuel Petit, who also made Arsenal a huge profit when he was sold to Barcelona with Marc Overmars for £22m in 2000. Later, flush with success, Arsenal signed Sylvain Wiltord, Robert Pires and the uncontainable Thierry Henry.

If Wenger shook up English football management in similar ways to Chapman and his landmark professionalism some seventy years earlier, he also made Arsenal a great deal of money. TV payments in the English Premiership are linked to where a club finishes in the League and how many times they are shown live, so the successful clubs make more money. As the game was rebranded from filthy habit in the 1980s to legitimised state religion in the 1990s, the money swelled. In 1997, Sky, which had orbited from the brink of insolvency for Rupert Murdoch's empire to international domination on the strength of capturing English football, renewed their exclusive live deal with the Premier League, this time more than doubling the bonanza to the top clubs, to £670m over four years.

In 1997 Dein's company, London & Overseas Sugar, was finally dissolved. They had filed no accounts since December 1993 and so were struck off the company register. Dein's favourable write-up in the *Daily Mail* quoted an anonymous 'well placed source' saying Dein is 'an honourable man' and settled with all his creditors. There is no way of knowing if this is true without Dein's cooperation, and he has never talked publicly about his troubles. The company was dissolved rather than being wound up by creditors seeking payment, so they may indeed have been paid. Given Dein's fortunes at Arsenal, he did have the wherewithal to do so.

In December 1999 Dein sold to Fiszman again, another chunk of his Arsenal shares: 2,840 of them. All the changes in football, the fortunes made by the clubs and Arsenal's success, had swollen the value of the club to £2,500 per share. If Fiszman paid anything like this going rate, the sale made Dein another £7.1m. Dein had also enjoyed being paid handsomely for some years as a director, Arsenal apparently having become his full-time job since the collapse of his businesses. Arsenal did not identify directors' earnings by their names until 2001, instead just giving a figure for the highest paid director. Through the 1990s, two were usually on over £100,000 a year. In 1999, the highest paid director's salary was engorged to £500,000, which halved the following year, to £250,000, after a new managing director, Keith Edelman, joined the club on £409,385. The £250,000 earner from 2000 turned out to be Dein. In 2001 he was paid £275,000, the following year he was back on £250,000, and in 2003 he was paid £255,000.

Ken Friar, who had been at the club since he was sixteen, for over forty years, was the managing director before Edelman arrived, so he was responsible for running the club day to day.

Dein's job was to be responsible for the football side; Hill-Wood told me Dein was forever on the phone to players' agents. He confirmed that in recent years the Arsenal board became concerned about Darren Dein, David's son, working as a legal adviser with Jerome Anderson, an agent who has for years represented several Arsenal players.

'How healthy that is, is a matter of personal preference,' he said. 'I think it's better if you're a little more distant.'

The board, he said, had been sufficiently concerned to ask for assurances from Dein that the deals Arsenal did with players were not made cosy by his son working in some capacity for the agent.

'We paid Jerome Anderson money for deals that he did for us and one needs to know they are at arms' length. We received assurances from David Dein that they were and we accepted that.'

Keen to say the right thing, and, it seemed to me, rather trying to persuade himself, he said: 'I'm delighted David Dein has done well. I'm delighted that he came; he pushed us to build the North Bank and South Bank and a lot of his suggestions have been innovative and very helpful.'

Mike Winnett joined in a discussion on an Arsenal message-board, where fans were praising Dein for his vision and achievements. He said:

'I criticised Dein over the Blind Scheme and my opinion is that he acts in his own self-interest, but that includes making Arsenal successful and profitable. I've always argued that he must be quite a shrewd businessman, firstly to buy into Arsenal so cheaply, then to persuade a bunch of complete strangers in the North Bank to finance rebuilding the stadium while not diluting his shareholding at all, thus making him a very rich man. I also have to admire the fact that he has remained solvent despite his own business collapsing into penury. In fact, I feel he is the kind of guy who, if he fell into a latrine, would not only come out smelling of roses, but would talk you into buying the turds too.'

One of the bitterest anomalies of the modern era for the

supporters who stayed with the game through its glum, fenced days, is that far from using the billion-pound TV bonanza to keep the cost of going to games steady, the clubs inflated ticket prices up on top. Arsenal were relatively restrained for a few years, but later their approach to pricing became as extravagant as a Thierry Henry pirouette. In 1989–90, the season after Hillsborough, the average price of a ticket at Highbury was £6.71. By 2003–4, fans who could plan and call and book early enough for the few matchday tickets available had to fork out up to £48 in the North Bank upper tier, down to £31 on the fringe of the East and West Stands. Bottom price, for adults – under-sixteens can get in half-price in the Family Stand – is £26, at the edge of the North Bank.

Steve Powell, an old IASA veteran and now a leading figure in the national Football Supporters Federation, has graduated from standing on the North Bank to a seat quite central in the East Stand. He pays £1,650 for his season ticket.

'I know many people who can't afford it any more,' he sighed. 'My neighbours are both postal workers; they can't afford to go. A friend works in Tesco; he can't afford it. Arsenal are pricing people out, and they're pricing out the next generation. I just look around me; everybody is in their forties and fifties.'

At Highbury, my eyes didn't lie. The Arsenal fans *are* ageing. Dein himself has said the fanbase is being gentrified, the atmosphere tamer than it was. The helpful people in the club's press office told me they do not document the age of their season ticket holders, and referred me to the Premier League's National Fan Surveys, which are compiled from questionnaires returned by nearly 30,000 Premier League club supporters. The surveys showed that season ticket holders are getting steadily richer; in 2003, 37 per cent of season ticket holders across the clubs were earning over £30,000 a year, the London clubs having the most, Sunderland the least white-collar fans, still surprisingly high at 32 per cent.

The results on age were so striking it is remarkable that the Premier League doesn't publicly acknowledge they are storing up a problem for the future. In 2003, just 7 per cent of season ticket holders were aged 16–24. That looks about right from what you see at matches, but it's startling to see it in print. Nearly half of season ticket holders were 25–44 – my generation. Another 24 per cent were 45–54. The Premiership's 2001 survey noted supporters were 'generally getting older'. The average age in 2003 was forty-four for a season ticket holder, thirty-nine for non-season ticket holding fans. Sad for people my age to reflect on but I'm afraid that's us. If you were twenty-two in 1979, when Alan Sunderland stretched a leg out to win Arsenal the FA Cup, a minute after Sammy McIlroy had dragged Man United from 2-0 down to 2-2 – jumping round the room if you were a City fan – you fall into the 46–55 category. If you were eleven in 1976, as I was when City last won a trophy, beating Newcastle 2-1 in the League Cup Final with an overhead kick by Dennis Tueart, the wondrous picture of which decorated 10,000 bedrooms, you are now solidly in the 35–44 range. It hurts, but it's true.

Teenagers today aren't getting in and they can't afford it. In the Football League that's even truer; their own research showed their clubs' fans on average older than the Premiership's. This is perhaps surprising, because ticket prices are cheaper, but that's relative. At Bury, for example, still surviving in the Third Division, adult tickets in the side stands are £14; the home fans still pay £12 to sit in the archly named Cemetery End. Perhaps the ageing supporters of League clubs are testament to a more basic truth: to be a diehard fan of Bury, Notts County or York City now you have to have grown up supporting them when it was cheap – the average price at Bury in 1989–90 was £2.84 – and a great local experience, better than anything else on offer round about. The clubs wove themselves into local lads' sense of belonging, and showed them a good time, or at least one worth putting up with. Now, there is Champions League football on telly and cooler stuff for teenagers to do, but anyway for those hanging about bored, the football is too expensive. They have never been drenched in the obsession of following a club, and when their old men get too upset about life at the football ground, the kids mostly tell them to get a life. The worrying upshot for the professional clubs is that they have always relied on the irrationally stubborn loyalty of fans, prepared to keep coming despite all the ignominy, expense and disappointment heaped upon them, but now the clubs are pricing out the next generation.

Steve Powell is forty-seven; he's been going since he was introduced to Arsenal and Highbury in 1967, aged eleven.

'I was fifteen when Arsenal did the Double in 1971 and saw the whole magical season. I paid 10 shillings (50p) for a Wembley ticket for the Cup Final against Liverpool, which was twice the price of entry to the North Bank. All my mates went and the Arsenal end was full of teenagers and kids. The 1998 and 2002 Doubles were special for me too, but the cheapest ticket at the Millennium Stadium is now £40, and the most expensive £80. The support is getting older, and nobody is doing anything about this exclusion of the poor and the next generation of fans.'

Dein's write-ups hail him as a visionary, mainly for buying into football at the 'right' time, helping to engineer changes to football's structure in his favour, and the single appointment of Wenger. At Manchester United, Martin Edwards was so widely loathed by the fans for his separateness from them, and the dry fortunes he made, that few will even grudgingly credit him with their Premier League domination. United, however, can be seen as a model of long-term development, the cantilevered rebuilding of Old Trafford having been planned back in the 1960s and followed through. United saw where the 1990s changes were heading, however resented by many football people, and had the vision to expand Old Trafford, quietly and regularly slapping extra tiers on the stands, without borrowing to pay for them or implementing as brazen a scheme as the Arsenal bond. While United plc's clinical marketing men have rolled out a plan for global 'brand' awareness, with tours of the Far East and commercial tie-ups with the New York Yankees, they did not forget to look after their home too, expanding the capacity of Old Trafford steadily to 67,700, in a ground girdled with 180 corporate entertaining boxes, all full, and with a ten-year waiting list.

The result of the squeezing of money at the top is that English professional football became dominated by a couple of clubs more than ever before. Arsenal finished third in Wenger's first season, 1996–7, and after that, whenever they didn't win the Premiership, they finished second to United. With no gate sharing, huge salaries paid to top players and the TV rewards going to the already successful, the rich clubs drew away from the others, many of which, like Leeds, borrowed unsustainably to keep up. Arsenal, too, despite their success on the field, have struggled frantically not to fall behind United.

In 2002, the year of Wenger's second Double, arguably their greatest-ever triumph, Arsenal made £90m – huge money, nearly seven times the £13.7m they made in 1991–2, the last year before the Premier League breakaway. Yet they lost £23m.

United finished second but made 60 per cent more: £146m, with a tidy profit of £25m. On matchdays, United took in £56.3m, more than twice Arsenal's income from the overcharged crowd at a sold-out ground half the size. The Arsenal World of Sport shop at Finsbury Park tube cannot compete with United's fuck-you megastore, which makes millions for United when there isn't even a match on. In 2002–3, 200,000 people paid for the Old Trafford stadium tour and to go to the museum; 100,000 went to non-matchday dinners and conferences at Old Trafford.

I went there on a windy Monday, two o'clock-ish, and lo, it was true: groups of South Africans, Scandinavians, middle-aged, middle-class Chinese, were strolling away from the forecourt clutching megastore shopping bags, passing the bronze figure of a hapless Matt Busby, bodies leaning into the Salford gale, Lowry figures for the globalised age.

For all Wenger's managerial miracles, United's relentless earning power is taking them out of Arsenal's and Liverpool's reach. Such are the economics of the Premier League. Money buys players, buys success. And while they can all compete for the TV cake, without any gate-sharing, the club with the biggest stadium makes more every fortnight, and can pull away financially. Partly this is planning, partly an accident of location; Old Trafford is sited in acres of car parks which cut down on planning problems when they were whacking their extensions on. Arsenal spent £36m on seating and rebuilding Highbury, yet they began to realise in the mid-1990s, after they had done the work, that they needed more paying customers. Highbury, the grandest of English grounds, looked suddenly old and stifling.

Their campaign to escape has not been glorious. They blundered into it first in 1997, simply announcing they wanted to expand Highbury to 48,000 by rebuilding the West Stand and Clock End. This, the club said peremptorily, would make it necessary to demolish twenty-five neighbouring houses. They even put in a planning application. It seems that, fretting over the football imperative to make more money to keep up with their competitors, Arsenal's directors hadn't given quite enough thought to what the neighbours might think. Not surprisingly, in hindsight, there was an outcry.

'We had just formed the Highbury Community Association,' recalls Alison Carmichael, who became a tireless campaigner against Arsenal's expansion plans. 'There were vulnerable and old people living there, and they turned to us and said: "What can we do?" We had to fight it. We realised this football club was a business, and we learned it was mostly owned by a very few people, including David Dein and Danny Fiszman, who of course stood to make millions themselves. They showed with that first plan how much they cared about the people living around the club.'

For all the brutality and presumptuousness of the proposal, there were still earnest national debates about the pros and cons and whether Arsenal should be allowed to do it. Eventually, the club abandoned the idea; they decided 48,000 would not be big enough anyway, and considered leaving Highbury altogether. In January 1998, after trickles of rumour, Arsenal confirmed publicly they were considering bidding for Wembley Stadium. At the time, the FA was considering buying Wembley with a £120m Lottery grant, to turn it into a new national stadium, and Dein was a senior councillor and committee man at the FA. His strange position was not lost on Ken Bates, later the chairman of the Wembley project, a longstanding enemy of Dein's, who wrote to all Premier League chairmen in 2003 arguing that in this and many other episodes Dein had a conflict of interest which he always resolved by pushing for his own and the big clubs' interests, to the detriment of all the others. Dein circulated a letter replying to Bates, saying the claims were inaccurate.

At the end of March 1998, Arsenal officially withdrew its bid, without much explanation, and in July the FA bought Wembley, the start of a saga which would fracture and nearly sink the governing body financially. Arsenal's search was constrained by the lack of ripe sites in London, unlike the former industrial cities which are spattered with derelict land. Eventually they fell back on their own neighbourhood, having been talked into it by an estate agent, Anthony Spencer, who had been up in a helicopter, mapped out the area, then proposed Islington Council's own huge, grey, rubbish processing plant, and the surrounding Ashburton Grove industrial estate, as a potential new stadium site. The waste station, a concrete eyesore with endless bin wagons queueing to enter its maw, would have to go, and the eighty-three businesses on the industrial estate moved too. Arsenal would have to find huge money to pay for a new stadium, but could make a profit by developing the surrounding land and Highbury itself, for flats, which would go for millions in desirable Islington.

Arsenal submitted a planning application for a brand new 60,000-seater stadium in November 2000. What followed in their discussions with Islington Council was a lesson in planning realities.

'We always made it clear,' Keith Edelman told me, 'we only wanted a stadium.'

Islington emerged after seven months' discussions having wrested from Arsenal a great deal more. The club agreed to build a new, cleaner, modern waste plant, across Holloway Road near the tube station, on Lough Road, two developments of 'affordable' flats for poorer people – also on Lough Road, right by the new waste station; to pay for improvements to the tube station and roads, to build four new health centres in the area and replace a children's playground with a new play area. The campaign to win over the local population made huge play of Arsenal's commitment to the area – 'Let Arsenal Support Islington', went the slogan. They kept rather quiet about the fact they had been considering moving to Brent just a year or two before. In Islington, however, more people were unhappy with the new scheme than the old. Sixteen local organisations, including the Highbury Community Association, residents' groups, trades unions and businesses, united as the Islington Stadium Communities Alliance, ISCA, to oppose the plans. Alison Carmichael, who moved on to that campaign, summed it up:

'We live here. The vast majority of Arsenal fans, 95 per cent according to the club itself, don't. It may look like Arsenal are doing great things for the area, but in its detail, the plan is awful. We blame the council; the football club just wants to expand to make more money, we can see that, and the council has grabbed a few extras which it has never managed to complete itself. This is not true regeneration, but a botch job.'

After the planning application went in, in June 2001, 75 per cent of those who responded were against the scheme: 2,133 residents objected, while 712 wrote in support.

Finance was another problem. Arsenal never publicised the overall figures for this awesome inner city development; Anthony Spencer told me the overall cost was between £700m and £1bn, quite a difference. Still stuck in their stadium half the size of

United's, but competing well on the field, Arsenal looked for money where they could. Along with Wenger's transfer fee windfalls for Anelka, Petit and Overmars, the club's other coup came in 1999, from Granada, who paid £47m for 5 per cent of Arsenal, plus a stake in AFC Broadband, Arsenal's poke at the dotcom bubble, and a role as the club's exclusive commercial services and media rights agent. Granada were also tied in to paying another £30m for a further 4.99 per cent of the club once the arrangements for the new stadium were finalised. Granada's interest in football media rights has cooled since, and, together with Carlton, they managed to drop all seventy-two Football League clubs £185m short when they pulled out of ITV Digital, but Arsenal have made it clear they have a signed contract and will enforce it.

In summer 2003 Arsenal organised another bond scheme. Times change. Now there were many relatively rich, middle-aged blokes on the season ticket waiting list and the club wanted to raise £15m by selling 3,000 debentures at £5,000 each. All the bonds did was provide a jump of the season ticket queue, allowing, again, 'the right to purchase a season ticket', at Highbury, then at Ashburton Grove. There was no inflation-only price freeze, just annual interest on the bonds of 2.75 per cent and some 'win dividends', for example £60 off the following season's ticket if Arsenal won the Premiership. With the North Bank lads long subdued or priced out, there were no protests this time. The club has never announced how many bonds were sold but they raised several million pounds.

The amount the club has borrowed is now known; the cost of the stadium alone was to be £357m, and after several false starts, which led to a year's delay, in March 2003 Arsenal finally secured loans from a group of banks led by the Royal Bank of Scotland: £260m repayable over fourteen years. Around Arsenal, they say that Dein was cooler on the scheme than other directors, and Hill-Wood seemed to acknowledge that:

'We've got various resolutions saying we're unanimous to

proceed; so whether he's not as totally overjoyed with it as the rest of us I don't know. He certainly agreed to everything we've done but it's a big project and people are right to be nervous.'

Steve Powell formed a new AISA to campaign for the move, principally because he believes the 60,000-seater stadium will open up support for the club to the poor, the young, the local. The majority of Arsenal fans do support it, because they are sold on the financial arguments. Arsenal are saying 10,000 of the extra 22,000 seats will go to local Islington residents, but there is no commitment that they will be affordable to ordinary, threadbare wallets. While United pound on, and Chelsea draw on Abramovich's slice of Russia, Arsenal will be repaying their massive loans and interest, so there is not much incentive for price-cutting.

The opposition locally rallied around one particular aspect of the stadium scheme which seemed so unjust it was difficult to believe it was legal. Islington Council decided that the project was so beneficial to the area that it should have the right of Compulsory Purchase Orders, CPOs, to force out the businesses occupying the Ashburton Grove industrial estate. The mathematics are simple: Arsenal must try to relocate the businesses but if they cannot reach agreement the council has the right to evict them, paying the value of the property calculated at industrial prices. The council will then pass the land to Arsenal, who will sell it at residential prices, far more – perhaps twenty times more – profitable in Islington. At Ashburton Grove, no old or vulnerable residents are facing eviction, but while many businesses gladly took Arsenal's money and moved out of their run-down area, several have put up a fight.

For the full flavour of this clash of worlds, you have to go down there. It isn't the Islington of Georgian gentility, Tony Blair country, meals at the Granita restaurant where deals are done to determine the future running of the country. Down on Queensland Road, the lorries build up early, laden with rubbish, lopped off branches, litter. The waste station is a horror, a faceless concrete block, all around it a belching queue of lorries, and the nagging, fetid smell of decomposition.

The Alliance Spring Company is directly opposite. They were there a long time before the rubbish; in fact they started in 1913, the year Henry Norris moved Arsenal to Highbury, and they moved onto Ashburton Grove in 1967. Theirs is not a business plated with glamour, but it's long-established; they manufacture springs for food machinery. The company employs seven people and is run by Raymond Pinn, aged sixty-two, a tall, working man with greying hair and thick glasses, who has been here since he left school at sixteen. He, like other companies here, was scathing about Arsenal's treatment:

'It's going to put us out of business,' he said, looking across at the rubbish procession without really seeing it. 'To buy a similar sized factory and equip it would cost £1m; they, through Anthony Spencer, have offered £540,000. Why should we move? Why is the local council putting CPOs on us and eighty-two other companies, to give one – Arsenal – the right to make more money? Just because it's a football club. It's bullying.'

Spencer told me they hadn't bullied anyone, but when I talked to Edelman he stressed there was a financial formula beyond which the club did not need to go. They could rely on the CPOs and the businesses would be forced out. All the legal avenues went in favour of the club: the council were always certain to grant planning permission, and although the development, the biggest in London, looked sure to be 'called in', assessed, by the Government and a public inquiry held, instead the Office of the Deputy Prime Minister, John Prescott, declined. ISCA took the council's planning permission to the High Court, a difficult case to win, and lost. Two residents, Edward Bedford and Elizabeth Clare, went to the European Court of Human Rights, arguing that their right to enjoy their home would be infringed by the invasion of 60,000 people every two weeks to an area which will struggle to cope. They are, at the time of writing, waiting to hear back from Strasbourg.

As part of the CPO process, an independent inquiry is held by a Government Planning Inspector, specifically to advise on whether the CPOs, which will deprive people of their homes or businesses, are based on the 'compelling public interest' the law requires. The businesses, and ISCA, presented their objections to the Inspector, Rupert Grantham, at his inquiry, held over five weeks starting in January 2003 at a freezing Islington Town Hall. He delivered his report to Prescott's office in summer 2003 but it was not made public until the following December. His verdict vindicated every argument ISCA had made against the development. Grantham acknowledged that the stadium itself would be 'world class . . . appropriate to London's role as a world city', and said the stadium's 'positive impact' would be a boost to the area, along with the transport improvements.

But for fans, and the media, entranced by football, seeing the move in terms of what it will do for Arsenal and the balance of power in the English Premiership, the report comes as a physical jolt. Regeneration in our lumbering old cities is a difficult business, not something football can lightly presume its own expansion provides. Grantham said the scheme is 'opportunistic'; the council grabbing some extras from Arsenal rather than applying 'a properly planned approach'. This is not regeneration but 'simply a redevelopment scheme' which favours Arsenal's 'private interests' rather than 'benefits to the community', which were, he said, 'disappointingly low'. His language was painstaking, legal, but you get the sense he was shocked it had so sailed through the political process.

The stadium project, he said, would seriously disrupt the area on matchdays yet would be unlikely to deliver more jobs compared to the numbers moving into the area, and would lose green space. It was also socially divisive, because the affordable homes would be on Lough Road next to the already poorest people, so ghettoising the poor across Holloway Road, leaving the wealthier in the apartments by the stadium. The most unappealing aspect of the whole project, he decided, was the one trumpeted most by the council: the new waste station, which Arsenal are building for £60m, more in itself than it cost Sunderland to build their 48,000-seater Stadium of Light on the sight of the disused Wearmouth Colliery. The waste station, he said, was state-of-the-art, but the council should have developed a new, modern facility at Ashburton Grove, which is not bordered by houses. Instead, the residents, many of them deprived, living on the Ringcross council estate, and the new people stuffed into the affordable flats on Lough Road, will be hosting the 1,000 garbage lorries a day, on their doorsteps.

'I can understand,' Grantham said, 'how the residents of the Ringcross Estate feel stigmatised and further marginalised by the introduction of a large waste handling facility into their neighbourhood.'

Angela Clare, who lives in Adams Place, by the Ringcross Estate, told me she and her neighbours were watching the new waste station go up with horror:

'It's in our faces and it's a massive blight. Only now are we realising it's coming and will be here to stay. What message does it send to the children of this area that the rubbish for the whole area is going to be dumped on them? And all because everybody is expected to bow down to the football club – it's the new religion.'

She gave powerful evidence at the inquiry. She was asked by the council's barrister to accept the new brighter world the club was bringing to the area. Surely, she was challenged, she will like to drink coffee in the café Arsenal is building in the tower blocks on Lough Road.

'No,' she said, 'we can't afford £1.50 for a coffee – that is not the sort of "regeneration" me and my neighbours need. We need decent homes that don't have leaking roofs or windows, grass for our kids to play on and clubs to keep our kids off the street – we don't need fancy, overpriced coffee bars.'

Grantham concluded emphatically there was no 'compelling public interest' for the businesses to be forced out of Queensland Road to make way for Arsenal's stadium, offices and four tower blocks of pricey flats. Prescott's office ignored his detailed report and granted them anyway. Ray Pinn and the other businesses were forced to appeal that decision.

Grantham, objective, addressed Arsenal's pressing, frantic need for a new larger stadium and he wasn't convinced. This, too, is sobering for football followers. He observed that Arsenal were pretty successful already at Highbury and were not in any danger of crumpling if permission were not granted. He did not reflect on the wider conditions in football which have produced Arsenal's push to leave the marble halls and spread themselves across Islington. He didn't note that Arsenal need the money from 60,000 people because they compete in a sport which, under pressure from clubs like them and their shareholder-directors, scrapped gate sharing, then sanctioned the breakaway from a more even distribution of the new TV riches, and now places ever more money in the hands of the already rich. Money, to a great extent, determines footballing success, and the clubs, rather than preserve a League system which balances income to encourage competition, have undone the founding structures so that every club is a business seeking to increase its own wealth. A more responsible approach might reconsider the structure itself, to make it more equal, and ask where will it all end: even as Arsenal were announcing delightedly they had their bank loans, United were floating the idea of expanding Old Trafford to 75,000. Will Ashburton Grove look too small, sometime soon? However, while the overwhelming majority of people involved in football believe the Premier League has too much of the game's money, there is no prospect of the breakaway process being undone, because the men with the money run the game.

A more considered inquiry could look also at the question of stadium sharing, in London, Liverpool, Nottingham and elsewhere, to see if breaking that English football taboo might help solve the local problems of clubs which have outgrown their historic but cramped inner-city neighbourhoods. The idea of Arsenal and Tottenham occupying Wembley has never been genuinely thought through. Football has no general approach to these dilemmas; its clubs, competing with each other, batter on. Arsenal thrash around for a new stadium, the local council believes it has grabbed a good deal and the poorest people of the area get a waste station outside their front doors.

For Danny Fiszman, the Ashburton Grove scheme will determine whether he personally will eventually make money from his steady purchase of shares from David Dein. For Dein, the vice-chairman of Arsenal and of the FA, his initial £292,000 share purchase in 1983, plus what he paid for the Hill-Wood shares, has, since the breakaway for which he lobbied, turned out not to be dead money at all. His take from the declared sales to Fiszman can reasonably be estimated at £11.15m, on top of any profit from his first sale. The value of his current stake, 9,072 shares, is worth, at the time of writing, £13m. He's made more than £24m already. And counting.

CHAPTER 4

Hillsborough

Thinking about how football changed, the rebirth of its image and explosion in popularity after Italia '90, the rebuilding of the grounds, the Premier League breakaway, cash windfalls and subsequent financial collapses of the Football League clubs, you return, every time, to Hillsborough. The disaster, so recent, so long ago, ended a century of the game muddling through in ramshackle grounds which risked the lives of supporters. Taylor reported and the Government made it law that the top two division clubs' grounds had to be all-seater and gave clubs £2m each in public money to help them build. Taylor accepted supporters' objections at the time, that the all-seater requirement could lead to clubs charging higher prices, but said this needn't necessarily be so, and he referred for a guide to the then price for a seat at Ibrox which was £6. The clubs took the public money then promptly ignored what he said about cost, and increased their ticket prices sevenfold or more. Still, crowds swarmed back to the game, the top clubs made fortunes, then blew most of the money paying players salaries large enough to keep tower blocks of accountants in work.

You come back to Hillsborough not only because it was football's historic watershed but because in so many ways the game never learned its lessons. The clubs simply clattered on with their rows, plots and demands for more money. Safety improved only because the Government made it law. The League and FA remained at odds; there was no purposeful leadership of the game. When you have met some of the families of the ninety-six people who died, in colour, on the BBC, on a Saturday afternoon on the edge of the 1990s, the disaster, the appalling depth of its tragedy, stays with you; the families' unanswered questions nag, they don't fade. For the families, there has been no forgetting. Their lives are changed forever, emptier, full of pain and outrage. In football, it is difficult to see any lasting, heartfelt recognition of the lives its failures blighted. With Hillsborough, as for all the times when real life intrudes shockingly on the football dream, the game has its standard response: a minute's silence. Stand, think, be sorry, dip your head – but just for a minute. Then the whistle blows, and let's get on with the game.

Fifteen years may have passed, but in large parts the game is still in denial about what really happened at Hillsborough, how much Sheffield Wednesday itself and football more generally was at fault, how culpable the FA was for its lack of decent governance. I listened, open-mouthed, as a Sheffield Wednesday supporter, an intelligent, decent guy who I won't name because he is only one of too many owls at Hillsborough who think the same, chatted away about the disaster, trotting out the old, tired falsehoods. The Liverpool supporters were to blame because they arrived late and without tickets, thousands of them had been drinking. I'm always struck by the po-facedness of this from football fans; as if drinking before a match, then cutting it fine to get in for kick-off, are capital crimes, rather than the standard pre-match ritual for millions. He went on with his account, my blood running cold:

'The fans all rushed into the back of the Leppings Lane terrace, and crushed all the people in the front. It was sad, really, but they killed theirselves.'

Then he came out with a Sheffield Wednesday lament which was new to me: 'We feel we've suffered because of it.'

Come again?

'Our club's been tarred with it – it's called the Hillsborough Disaster; a lot of Wednesday fans think it should be called the

Liverpool Disaster. Our club didn't get semi-finals for a long time, so we lost money. If there aren't enough away fans to fill the whole of the Leppings Lane when we play a match, they leave that lower area, where the disaster happened, empty, which looks really bad on telly. Wednesday fans feel bitter that the Liverpool fans caused it, we didn't do anything wrong, but we've lost out.'

You can get too close to a subject when you know about it; you can think everybody knows the truth too. I was shocked that this whining and astonishingly false account is not only still doing the rounds but embedded in Wednesday supporters' sense of themselves and their club. I told him: no, these allegations were considered by Lord Justice Taylor in his report and comprehensively rejected. Yes, some Liverpool fans arrived late after having a drink before they went to the ground, but even a law lord saw that this was no crime, but normal life. If you read the report, Taylor deals with it directly: 'The fifteenth of April was the sort of fine spring day which tempted fans to sit or stand about in the sun with a drink. If you had a ticket it would seem more pleasant and sensible to relax in that way than to enter the ground early and stand on the terrace for an extra hour.'

'Pre-match entertainment in the ground,' he noted, 'had been advertised but did not take place.' So that was par for the course.

Taylor found that when the fans did get to the ground, not at the last minute, but even at 2.30, they couldn't get in. The arrangements to segregate the Liverpool and Forest fans meant that only twenty-three turnstiles at the Leppings Lane end were designated to cope with the 24,256 Liverpool fans who were to fill that stand and the whole West Stand. The 10,100 supporters with tickets for the Leppings Lane terraces were to be serviced by just seven turnstiles.

'Both the police and the club should have realised that the Leppings Lane turnstiles and the waiting area outside them would be under strain to admit all the Liverpool supporters in time,' his report said.

The crowd built up outside and fans grew frustrated because the arrangements were a shambles, a crush was developing and they were worried they weren't going to get in. As for drink, Taylor addressed it:

'I am satisfied that the great majority were not drunk nor even the worse for drink.'

There were, he said, some 'youngsters influenced by drink and bravado pushing impatiently at the rear of the crowd [outside the turnstiles] thereby exacerbating the crush. But the more convincing witnesses . . . were in my view right in describing this element as a minority.

'In my view, some police officers, seeking to rationalise their loss of control, overestimated the drunken element in the crowd.'

Not much doubt there, yet the police's story, notoriously splashed by the *Sun* immediately after the disaster, has been a stain difficult to remove. That so many fans still believe it is a legacy partly of how poorly the Taylor Report itself was reported. People are not only ignorant about Taylor's findings, they mostly don't even know he produced two reports. One dealt in detail with the causes of the disaster itself and who was to blame – the Interim Report, produced in impressively quick time, by August 1989. The one the fans do know about and think of as the Taylor Report was the next one, the Final Report, which in January 1990 came down on the side of all-seater stadia.

As is better known now because of the families' unending campaign and the 1997 TV docu-drama by the screenwriter Jimmy McGovern, the police officer in charge on the day, Chief Superintendent David Duckenfield, in charge of his first match, said immediately afterwards that the Liverpool fans had forced open an exit gate, C, and poured through it. In fact, Taylor found, he had ordered the gate to be opened because he could not cope with the crush outside Leppings Lane. The fans did not rush in, but as they walked through the gate there were no police or stewards to direct them to the terracing at the sides of the stand, where there was lots of room. Instead, they were faced immediately with a wide tunnel, and a sign above it, which led them naturally into it.

It took them down a steep slope, into the centre of the Leppings Lane stand. Throughout the 1980s, with the emphasis on containing hooliganism, the Leppings Lane terraces had gradually been subdivided by railings, into five separate pens. The central pens, 3 and 4, were the most popular with fans because they were right behind the goal. Neither the club nor the police had any way of accurately counting in the numbers of fans in the separate pens, but when the central pens looked full, they would direct fans away from them. They had done that at the previous year's semi-final: closed off the tunnel when the central pens were full and diverted the fans to the sides. Duckenfield told Taylor it 'did not cross his mind' to do that when the central pens were full. That, Taylor reported, was 'a blunder of the first magnitude', the primary cause of the disaster.

The fans who came in did not push from the back and crush those crammed in front. Another myth, that one. Besides being nasty human cages, the Leppings Lane pens were unsafe. There were fences around the front of the terrace to keep fans from invading the pitch, and when the crushing started the gates at the front were not wide enough to allow people to escape. In pen 3, a crush barrier, number 144, had been removed in 1986, leaving nothing to break a clear fall through to the front. Another barrier had had a gap inserted in it in 1985. Many of those who came through gate C arrived at the back and were propelled to the front. A police witness, Inspector Bullas, told Taylor the movement down the terracing was like 'a river of people ... going directly towards the pitch'. The front barrier, number 124a, was corroded, and under the pressure of the excessive number of fans allowed in, it collapsed after Peter Beardsley hit the bar at 3.04. 'That collapse caused a number of deaths,' Taylor found. Of those who died at the front, Taylor found 'at least sixteen and probably twenty-one' came through gate C after 2.52. Of the 730 injured, he found about 30 per cent probably did so.

Nearly half of the dead, 38, were under 20; 39 more were aged 20–29 – 80 per cent, then, were under 30. The coroner had ordered blood samples of the dead to be taken and tested for alcohol – which outraged the families – but in any case they found that none of the dead girls had drunk anything, 51 of the males had 'negligible' traces of alcohol, 15 had over 80 milligrams per cent in their blood and six had over 120 milligrams. His dismissal of the idea that drunk fans played a major part in the disaster was therefore based on solid scientific evidence. He was clear that the chief factor was police failure to handle the crowd:

'The immediate cause of the gross overcrowding and hence the disaster was the failure, when gate C was opened, to cut off access to the central pens which were already overfull.'

He could hardly have been clearer, and the failure subsequently to prosecute or even discipline any of the police officers responsible has been the main basis of the bereaved families' ceaseless quest for justice.

Of Duckenfield's statement that the Liverpool fans had forced the gate open, when in fact he had ordered it to be opened, Taylor said:

'The likeliest explanation is that he simply could not face the enormity of the decision to open the gates and all that flowed therefrom. That would explain what he said . . . He froze.'

Standing talking to the Wednesday fan, I told him some of this. 'Well,' he smiled, 'maybe I should read the Taylor Report.'

It would, I told him, be a good idea. Wednesday fans prepared to enrol for that education will find plenty in there about how far their own club was at fault, and the ground, apparently one of England's most prestigious, was unsafe. Taylor said that 'in general' the club had 'adopted a responsible and conscientious approach to its responsibilities', and used a skilled consultant engineer, Dr Eastwood, to advise on the ground. 'Nevertheless,' he found, unambiguously, 'there are a number of respects in which failure by the club contributed to this disaster.'

At the time, the Government required major sports grounds, including Hillsborough, to be licensed with an official safety certificate by the local authority, in this case Sheffield City Council. The safety of a ground was assessed according to the detailed standards set out in the 'Green Guide', the Home Office Guide to Safety at Sports Grounds, a system introduced after sixty-six people were killed in a crush at the Rangers v Celtic derby at Ibrox on 2 January 1971.

Sheffield Wednesday had no valid, up-to-date safety certificate for the ground at all. The one it was first issued, in December 1979, had never been updated, despite all the changes to the ground, including the carve-up of Leppings Lane into pens in 1981 and 1985, the removal of barrier 144 and the enlargement of the Kop, Wednesday-ites' home end, in 1986.

The legal responsibility to issue a safety certificate lay with Sheffield City Council and Taylor described their failure to revise or amend the certificate as 'a serious breach of duty', and 'woefully inadequate'. Nevertheless, he said the club itself was the owner of the ground and responsible to all paying visitors – fans paid £6 to stand, £12 to sit that day – to ensure the ground was safe.

At the time, Sheffield Wednesday's secretary was Graham Mackrell. He described himself to the Taylor inquiry as, in effect, the club's chief executive. His duties meant he was officially the club's safety officer. Taylor noted that in April 1987 Mackrell had raised the question of amending the safety certificate, particularly in relation to the enlargement of the Kop, with Dr Eastwood's firm, 'but nothing resulted'. The safety certificate sat unchanged and redundant in the offices of the council while matches went on, and the FA continued to award Wednesday the privilege of hosting semi-finals at Hillsborough.

In several specific areas, directly relevant to how people died, Taylor itemised that Wednesday were in breach of the Green Guide.

- in pen 3, 'four out of five' of the gaps between the crush barriers were 'well in excess' of the prescribed maximums, which meant fans had nothing to stop them falling forward;
- 'in pen 4, nine out of ten [did] not conform';
- 'some 40 per cent of [the fans] in pens 3 and 4 were more than 12 metres from an exit', contrary to the aim of paragraph 96 of the Green Guide;
- 'four out of five of the crush barriers in pen 3 and six out of nine in pen 4 were below the height prescribed. The point is not academic since, in the event, many fans were bent painfully over barriers under great pressure'.

Although the Leppings Lane terraces had been divided into five pens, Taylor found the club was still using the old, overall figure for the whole terrace of 10,100, which the police had said was too high back in 1981. 'Yet despite that, and the sub-division into pens, the figure remained'.

There was no way of counting numbers into the individual pens of the Leppings Lane terraces. The club, Taylor said, notionally used the figures of 1,200 for pen 3 and 1,000 for pen 4. These, he said, were too high. 'When all relevant factors regarding the configuration and the Green Guide are taken into account, the maximum capacity for pen 3 should have been 822 and for pen 4, 871.'

The tunnel down which all the fans went into the overcrowded pens, after being allowed through the opened gate C, was much steeper, 1 in 6, than the prescribed Green Guide maximum: 1 in 10.

Taylor spelt out a litany of the club's failures, in a sad list taking up the whole of page 52.

'The Leppings Lane End was unsatisfactory and ill-suited to admit the numbers invited';

'The club . . . ought to have alerted the police to the risks of the turnstiles being swamped';

'The club had a duty to its visitors and the club's officials ought to have alerted the police to the grossly uneven distribution of fans [between the middle and outer pens] on the terraces';

'The removal of barrier 144 was the responsibility of the club although it clearly acted on the advice of Dr Eastwood . . . which in this instance was misguided';

'Poor signposting . . . tended to produce . . . over-filling of pens 3 and 4';

'Poor signposting outside the turnstiles and the unhelpful format of the tickets also led to confusion, aggravating the build-up in the turnstile area'.

'The breaches of the Green Guide,' Taylor said, 'were matters which the club should have appreciated and remedied.' The gates at the front of the pens – against which the victims were crushed – were 0.82m and 0.79m wide, significantly narrower than the 1.1m specified in the Green Guide. However, Taylor said even that was inadequate – and aimed more at giving the police access to quell trouble than allowing a swift evacuation of the terraces for the safety of supporters. 'Certain it was, that once the crush occurred on 15 April, [the gates] were wholly inadequate for rescue purposes.'

Yet the club and most of its fans seem never to have been prepared to acknowledge any of this. Wednesday went to the Taylor Inquiry determined to defend itself completely. Mackrell, safety officer at a ground with no valid safety certificate, found to be in breach of the Government's safety guidelines in ways which Taylor found contributed directly to the disaster, never resigned. Nobody else connected with the club ever resigned, nor did the club ever officially say they were sorry.

Phil Hammond is the chairman of the Hillsborough Family Support Group. He lost his son Philip, who was fourteen then, crushed to death at his first-ever away match, on the Leppings Lane terrace watching the Liverpool he loved. When I called to talk to Phil, he and his wife Hilda had just been to their son's grave, because it had been Philip's birthday. He would have been twenty-eight.

'We had fourteen years with him,' Phil said, his voice a familiar mix of human warmth and suppressed outrage. 'And now we've had fourteen years without him. It's a landmark for us and our family, but it doesn't get any easier.'

For the families of those who died, their shock and grief has been compounded by seeing nobody take responsibility for the disaster. Football moved on, took the money and did its best to forget, but the families were sent on a black journey through legal processes. If there was a flaw to find in our system, they suffered it. Another police force, the West Midlands, was appointed on behalf of the Director of Public Prosecutions and the coroner to investigate what happened, including the failures by their fellow force, South Yorkshire Police. The DPP announced there were to be no prosecutions. Bereaved families were not entitled to legal aid for representation at an inquest, and there they listened outraged as the coroner summed up and the jury returned a verdict of accidental death. The families appealed the summing up to the High Court, but lost. When they look back at it all, they still cannot accept that not a single person took responsibility and resigned. Disciplinary action was recommended against Duckenfield, and his second-in-command, Superintendent Bernard Murray, but both retired before they had to face them.

That search for official justice has dominated the families' efforts since, rather than the failures by the club, and the FA which selected the ground on such thin criteria, and Phil Hammond, a Liverpool fan and season ticket holder himself, told me they are still quite raw about that:

'We never had anything from football; from the club, or the FA. Why didn't the FA ask, as a matter of routine, to see the safety certificate, or check that there was one? They didn't; they asked nothing, they didn't care about safety. They just wanted the money.'

When the families, and the injured, sued for compensation, the club paid up, sharing the cost with South Yorkshire Police and Sheffield City Council. The terms of that agreement and the percentages in which they split the liability have never been revealed.

'They got off very lightly,' said Phil Hammond. 'Not one person, at the FA, Sheffield Wednesday, the council, the police, lost one day's pay as a result of ninety-six people dying at Hillsborough. Nobody from the club even talked to us properly, never mind showing genuine human sympathy or remorse.'

Delve further into the history of the club and the game and Sheffield Wednesday's failures, the safety breaches which contributed to the disaster itself, and their conduct afterwards, seem even worse. That it should all happen in Sheffield makes the disaster yet more emblematic of football's general failure of its supporters. Sheffield was one of the birthplaces of the modern game, long a source of pride in the city. A match is recorded between a Sheffield team and one from neighbouring Norton way back in 1793. In 1857, two worthy middle-class Sheffield chaps, Nathaniel Creswick and William Prest, wanting to play a sport and keep the generous new Bramall Lane cricket field busy in the winter, formed Sheffield FC. It is, as keen young football-following schoolboys ought to know, the oldest football club in the world, and still going.

Sheffield played to rules drawn from different public schools, Harrow and Winchester, in which football had developed while the old rough folk games were mostly being snuffed out by the mass move of workers to the industrial cities in the early and mid-nineteenth century. The FA, the university men and ex-public schoolboys who came together in London originally to unify all the separate codes, didn't reply to a letter from the new Sheffield FA asking to join, so the two played on by separate rules. Sheffield's lasted until 1877 before they unified, and they claimed the credit for the introduction of crossbars, corners and other refinements.

On 4 September 1867, the Wednesday Cricket Club formed a football section, which battled quickly to become one of Sheffield's strongest clubs. By 1870, two brothers who were to become significant in football joined the Wednesday as players: Charles and William Clegg. The early history of the club was written in 1926 in a wonderful book, one of the earliest comprehensive club histories, *The Romance of the Wednesday, 1867–1926*. Written by Richard Sparling and reprinted in 1997, it is one of the few decent things for sale in Wednesday's dismal club shop. Sparling picked out a telling detail about the Cleggs, following William Clegg's first match, a 3-0 win against Attercliffe Christ Church:

'Up to that term, each winning team had a gallon of beer allowed, the defeated team having to be content with half the quantity. Then it was decided that the practice of allowing refreshments to players after a match be discontinued.'

When the Cleggs arrived, the beer stopped flowing. They were both solicitors, Methodists and active in the temperance movement, and they became central influences on Wednesday for decades. An interesting historical twist, given the 1989 Hillsborough disaster and the discernible air of resentment around Sheffield Wednesday at the families' continuing campaign, is that the Cleggs' father, William, became a solicitor and subsequently Sheffield's mayor, after teaching himself legal skills battling for compensation for families devastated by another disaster, the Sheffield flood of 1864. In this strangely little-known but terrible episode, 250 people died and thousands of homes were ruined when a dam on a reservoir up on the hills serving Sheffield burst and flooded vast areas of the ramshackle city, including the Hillsborough district itself. William Clegg senior is said to have worked tirelessly to secure some recompense for families from the water company, against whom negligence, a crack in the dam wall, was established by the long, traumatic inquest. Fired up, Clegg rented two small rooms in London, leaving his wife and children in Sheffield, to work at a law firm and study morning and night, until, at forty-two, he qualified as a solicitor. Both his sons, educated in Sheffield, followed their father into the law – and into a militantly temperance approach to the demon drink.

According to a forthcoming book called *Football's Christian Heritage* by Peter Lupson, Charles Clegg, who became the chairman of the FA for a prodigious forty-eight years from 1889 until he died in 1937, saw football and Christian values as intertwined. 'Clegg believed that in addition to promoting health and fitness, football should be a great moral force in people's lives. He constantly fought against anything which could bring the game into disrepute.'

Clegg was for the purity of the sport, teamwork, fairplay. He fought alcohol, gambling, violence and foul language implacably – and not always successfully. He opposed professionalism and transfer fees for players until he was forced, like the FA generally, to accept them because they were happening anyway. He believed it was anathema for a man to be paid to play the sport, far less to be paid for being a director of a club. He insisted on rigorously above-board dealings at Wednesday, with whom he remained associated, becoming an original shareholder when the club formed a company in 1899, and chairman in 1915.

'We are the guardians of the game,' Charles Clegg used to proclaim of the FA.

His motto, quoted by Sparling and all the reference books, could, in our smirking times, be the catchphrase for a spoof of a Victorian pillar of northern society: 'Nobody gets lost on a straight road.'

Wednesday became a major club as football grew in popularity, and they were elected straight into the First Division when it expanded from twelve to sixteen clubs in 1892; they twice won the League two years running, in 1903 and 1904, then in 1929 and 1930. They won the FA Cup in 1896, 1907 and 1935. In the old team photographs hanging around Wednesday's current, dreary reception, the Cleggs are there at the edges in the later line-ups, buttoned up in waistcoats, leaning on their sticks. They say that when Charles died in 1937 Wednesday took years to recover stability. Indeed, they were relegated that year and stayed in the Second Division until 1950. They yo-yoed, then won promotion to the First in 1959, where they stayed for eleven years, their best season being 1961 when they finished runners-up to Double-winning Spurs. In August that year they established a genuine landmark: the opening of the North Stand, a sleek marriage of scale and design, the first cantilevered stand at a British football ground. You can only imagine how Charles Clegg would have reacted to the match-fixing scandal involving three Wednesday players, David Layne and the England internationals Tony Kay and Peter Swan, who were found to have made sure Wednesday lost 2-0 to Ipswich in December 1962, and made £100 by betting on the result. They had got lost on an unstraight road, presumably.

Hillsborough had become recognised as one of England's finest grounds, selected to host matches in the 1966 World Cup, for which, with Government money, the club built the Leppings Lane stand. In 1970 they were relegated, then in 1975 went down again, spending five years, until 1980, in the old Third Division.

They were eventually dragged up by another chairman, cast from different material from Clegg: Bert McGee. The chairman of a firm of toolmakers, Presto, who had as a boy stood in the rain on the famous open, sloping Kop, McGee was an autocrat, the archetypal 'old-style chairman', smelted in Sheffield's engineering and hard business traditions. When he took over as the chairman in 1975 with the club relegated to the Third Division, it was laden with nearly £400,000 of debt, massive then. McGee attacked the club's finances with bottom-line, earn-more-than-you-spend common sense, and he also instituted a share issue which raised vital cash to shore up Wednesday.

Arsenal in 1992 and 2003 may have minted the ingenious method of raising millions from fans without opening up a single share; McGee kept his club tight, while widening the Wednesday ownership a little. After the share issue raised £129,000, buying Wednesday leeway from the bank, no individual owned more than a minimal stake in the club, an important principle of McGee's who, according to his write-up in Inglis' *League Football*, believed, 'Football clubs shouldn't be used as ego trips or possessions by individuals.' He was said to be 'much opposed to the exploitation of football clubs by wealthy outsiders'.

In 1984, with Howard Wilkinson as their manager and players like Mel Sterland, Mike Lyons and Imre Varadi forming their backbone, Wednesday fulfilled McGee's promise and returned to the First Division. Daniel Gordon, now a writer and TV producer, covered this momentous season in his book, *A Quarter of Wednesday*, a labour of love meticulously recording Wednesday's history from 1970 to 1995. That promotion season, he recalls 8,000 fans staying on for twenty minutes after the end of a midweek 2-0 defeat by Middlesbrough at Ayresome Park chanting, 'We Love You Wednesday'. Sterland scored a penalty to beat Crystal Palace at Hillsborough and win promotion, and the midfielder Gary Megson paid homage to 'tremendous' fans, who had 'never waned' throughout the Third Division humiliations. At Ninian Park after the final match against Cardiff, Gordon was on the pitch with thousands of others: 'Songs were sung, players' names were chanted, the turf was kissed. As one banner put it: "The Hibernation is Over: The Owls are Back."'

Within two years, McGee had made a mark he had longed for, putting a roof on the Kop, levelling out the slope by adding more terracing to it. In the bruised years of hooliganism, fences and falling crowds, Hillsborough was still regarded as one of the country's best grounds, regularly hosting semi-finals. Taylor noted in his report that there had been a serious crush at the Leppings Lane end at the 1981 semi-final between Ossie Ardiles' Spurs and Wolves, after a large number of fans arrived late. There were, Taylor noted, 'broken arms, legs and ribs, and thirty-eight people were treated in hospital or by the St John Ambulance Brigade'.

That did not, though, make any headlines. In 1986, Dr Eastwood was telling Sheffield City Council that Hillsborough was 'probably the safest ground in the country'. McGee, said to be considering retirement by then after fourteen long years, was still the chairman in 1989 when the realities of his ground were laid bare by the disaster.

All the documents submitted to the Taylor Inquiry – from the police, council, club, the Football Supporters Association and thousands of witnesses, together with transcripts of the evidence of the 174 people who appeared before the inquiry during its thirty-one days – now fill some of the 100 miles of shelves at the National Archive in Kew. It is a quiet, eerily efficient operation, the files guaranteed to be delivered for reading within half an hour of a click on the online catalogue. I went down there one Friday in the summer; the seats were crowded with people hunched intently over old papers, their bags and pens left, as required, in the lockers downstairs, taking notes in pencil only. Most people go there to look up their family history. The Hillsborough files can make you cry – and angry, too.

The business of selecting Hillsborough as a venue was a revelation to me. It was so routine that Graham Kelly, who had recently taken over as the FA's chief executive, did not even write the letter. It was sent on 24 February 1989 by an S. R. Clark, Competitions Secretary, to Graham Mackrell, saying simply:

'As is customary this time of the season, I am writing to enquire whether your club would be interested in staging an FA Challenge Cup Semi-Final Tie on Saturday 15 April 1989.'

There is little in his letter relating to fans' safety. First off, he talks about money, running Mackrell through the details: the club would keep 10 per cent of the gate receipts, 'clarifying' they could have 50 per cent of the money from executive boxes. Clark wanted details of 'spectator segregation', and whether 'safety fencing is provided round the pitch'. The letter made it clear that Wednesday were not entitled to reserve any part of the ground for itself: the whole stadium had to be given over to Liverpool and Nottingham Forest fans – 'with the exception of Directors Box, which will be controlled by this Office'. Millichip, the FA chairman, and invited dignitaries were reserving the choicest seats, 350 near the Directors' Box 'for use of FA Council members and guests'.

Evidently, the FA was satisfied that Mackrell, and Hillsborough, proved they could do the necessary. The next letter from the FA in the Kew files is dated 17 April 1989, two days after the disaster. This time it was from Graham Kelly, to all member clubs:

> Dear Sirs,
>
> **Re: Ground Safety**
>
> Following the tragic events at Sheffield Wednesday FC last Saturday, you are instructed to undertake, in conjunction with your local licensing authority, an immediate review of ground safety . . .

Just a little too late.

The files at Kew also contain Sheffield Wednesday's own submission to Taylor, a transcript of Mackrell giving evidence and details of the safety work carried out on the stadium. A body called the Football Trust administered a fund of public money, redirected from the pools companies, to give grants to clubs for improvement and safety work. Between 1978 and 1988, the Trust's statement said, Sheffield Wednesday received grants of £431,180 for twenty-one different schemes on the ground. They had also received a grant for McGee's work on the Kop, £595,099.

Knowing now Taylor's verdict on the club's safety record, Wednesday's submission, 105 pages of it, seems extraordinarily belligerent. It isn't so much the case they made; that was clear. They laid responsibility for monitoring and managing the crowd with the police and maintained that the sole cause of the disaster was Duckenfield's blunder in not redirecting supporters away from the tunnel after he ordered the gate to be opened. The safety certificate, and all the issues relating to the changes to the pens, barriers and fences, were, the club argued, the council's responsibility. That was no great surprise; they had a very arguable point. It was the council's job to license the ground and the club argued that they complied as they were asked. They also relied on the expertise of Dr Eastwood. However, the striking aspect of the submission was its tone. The club comes across as indignant, dismissing outright, not merely denying, the suggestions, based on evidence, that Hillsborough had been unsafe and the club bore some responsibility for it.

They paused at the beginning of their 105-page submission to devote three lines to a human response: 'The club and its officers have been deeply affected by what has happened. The sympathy which they have for those who have suffered and who are suffering is sincere.'

It then states that 'such criticisms as have been material and justified have been accepted with candour and humility'. It isn't clear which criticisms they are referring to. The rest of the document seems to be a rejection, point by point, of just about every criticism made of the club. It has to be remembered that, at the time, they feared not just a damning verdict by Taylor, and civil claims by the families and the injured, but possibly criminal prosecutions for manslaughter if they were accused of being reckless about the safety of the visitors to their ground. So, tough as it is, the club had the right to assert that it had behaved lawfully and carefully. They just came across so insensitive and unrepentant. Criticisms of the club and ground – some later upheld by Taylor, some not – were, according to the club, 'misconceived', or 'manifestly absurd'; they agreed it was 'clearly regrettable in the extreme that the Safety Certificate was allowed to become seriously out of date', but Mr Mackrell had acted 'sensibly' in checking there were no amendments to it and it would be 'unfair and unreasonable' to have expected Mackrell to pursue the council further. Why exactly they don't say. Of the removal of barrier 144, 'the club should not be criticised'; of the fact that there was no system for stopping the pens from overcrowding, or ensuring even distribution of fans across the Leppings Lane pens, that criticism was 'misconceived'.

Giving his evidence for the club, Mackrell was taken on a somewhat uncomfortable ride by the barristers, particularly Andrew

Collins, counsel for the inquiry itself. Mackrell gave his background first; he had started in football club management at Bournemouth in 1974, moved on to Luton in 1981, then joined Wednesday in November 1986. Among his duties, he confirmed he was, officially, the club's safety officer.

Questioned about the safety certificate, he said it was 'obvious' that work had been carried out on the ground since the certificate had been issued and he had 'assumed' the certificate was out of date. He had made one phone call, a few months after he arrived at the club, to Dr Eastwood's firm. They had said the council was supposed to be making amendments, and Mackrell had not followed it up after that. On the crucial defect of the ground, that no individual capacities were established for the Leppings Lane pens, Mackrell answered at first that it didn't matter because there was movement between them. He was then questioned by Taylor himself: 'Is it not worth having a figure for each pen, as a guideline, if nothing else?' He said: 'Possibly, sir, yes.'

Soon after, Mackrell admitted that because the club did not employ stewards to direct fans at the Leppings Lane end it was 'inevitable' the central pens would become overcrowded. He was pointed to a specific part of the safety certificate, out of date as it was, which required the club to be able to record the numbers of people admitted to different parts of the ground. There was, it turned out, no way of doing that for the North West and West Stands, and Mackrell agreed with Collins it 'would appear' the club was always in breach of that part of the safety certificate, every match. Then he accepted there was 'a failure of communication' which meant that the club doctor, Dr Purcell, believed he was there solely for the team, and not, as required by the safety certificate, as a club doctor, ready to give first aid to fans. Then Mackrell agreed the club was in breach of the safety certificate in not maintaining signs over all exits at the ground.

Mackrell was taken rigorously through some detail about the match tickets. The map of the ground printed on the back of tickets was actually wrong, he admitted. He said one of his staff would have done the drawing, but he took responsibility for it. The tickets showed Liverpool fans that they were apparently to go onto the Leppings Lane terrace through entrance B. When they came through the turnstiles or gate C, they were met with a large B above the fateful tunnel. The back of the ticket, which was inaccurate, encouraged fans, Collins argued, to go down the tunnel, because it showed that part of the ground as a B. The ticketing, he said: 'is not only not good, it is worse than useless, and as it has turned out thoroughly dangerous . . . because it encouraged people . . . everyone, to go down that central tunnel?'

'I take your point,' Mackrell replied. 'I hear what you say sir, yes.'

The club's submission later took issue with that point, saying no witnesses had claimed that that had been a problem. However, Taylor concluded in his report: 'The unhelpful format of the tickets . . . also led to confusion.' Mackrell did not resign, despite having been the safety officer for a ground in serial breach of the Green Guide and whose safety certificate was invalid because it was ten years out of date. At the end of Mackrell's evidence, Taylor asked a question which clearly pointed to his thinking about football's skewed priorities.

Since the disaster, just a few weeks earlier, with the families still enduring the first throes of grief, Taylor wanted to know whether Sheffield Wednesday had spent any money on players. Yes, Mackrell replied, he would estimate the club had spent £800,000 that summer.

Taylor produced his Final Report – the second one, the one fans know about because he called for all-seater stadia, again impressively quickly, on 18 January 1990. In it he said: 'Transfer fees have reached a level which many regard as grotesque and certainly out of all proportion to the amounts spent on ground improvement.' Taylor did not hold back in his criticism of what he had found out, by a 'wider and deeper inquiry', about the way in which football was run. He found that safety standards at many other grounds were as wretched as at Hillsborough, and described the facilities for ordinary fans as 'depressing . . . below the standard necessary to give spectators dignity . . . in stark contrast to the different world, only yards away, in the boardroom'. No surprise there, then. Fans, he saw, were never consulted about anything. Beyond the legally imposed new basic safety standards at grounds, Taylor called for a 'new ethos for football', a better way to run the national game, 'more consultation with supporters and more positive leadership'. It required, he said, 'the fullest reassessment of policy', to create a sport fit for the stubborn love and reverence which millions still had for it. As he noted, since the low point of 1985–6, crowds were even at the time of the disaster rising again – after all, at football's darkest hour, 53,000 people had woken up aquiver with excitement at the prospect of going to an FA Cup semi-final.

Many fans still resent Taylor's decision to recommend all-seater grounds, blame it for the price rises, lament the loss of atmosphere, the more brotherly, shoulder-rubbing way to support their club, and long for a return of standing in the top two divisions, believing the terracing did not have to go to ensure the grounds were safe. Terracing itself was not a cause of the disaster – the causes were neglect, police mismanagement and the fences around the front. Read Taylor's report and you can see he was persuaded of the argument for seats mostly to address concerns about hooliganism, which the authorities had pressed very strongly, rather than the fans' right to watch their football safely. Having said that fans needed to be consulted more, he went against the submission of the supporters organisations, who called for safe standing. Even now, whenever the discussion pops up again, the Government will never countenance a return to terracing more because they fear it might herald a return of serious hooliganism, with bad lads massing together more easily in particular areas, than because they truly believe terracing is inherently unsafe – it clearly isn't, because it has been retained in the lower two divisions. The police have always said that seats, combined with CCTV, have done the most to prevent hooliganism because individuals can be more easily identified and arrested. The big clubs, although they resented the expense of converting to seats, and lobbied for the grants to help them, did mostly feel that raising the cost of tickets would price out many of the hooligans. The evidence for this is shaky, as we know; they have priced out the young, and some of the poor, but many of the fighters are still there, with grey in their hair, enough money to pay for a ticket, ready for a ruck, for old times' sake.

'As for the clubs,' Taylor said in his report, 'in some instances it is legitimate to wonder whether the directors are genuinely interested in the welfare of their grass-roots supporters. Boardroom struggles for power, wheeler-dealing in the buying and selling of shares, and indeed of whole clubs, sometimes suggest that those involved are more interested in the personal financial benefits or social status of being a director than of directing the club in the interests of its supporter customers.'

At Wednesday, Bert McGee was soon gone. Joe Ashton, then the Labour MP for the Sheffield constituency of Bassetlaw, who joined the Wednesday board himself shortly afterwards, told me McGee was shattered after the disaster, mostly by the stigma. He had very shortly afterwards asked the FA for money to compensate the club for its own losses, but Graham Kelly had turned him down. McGee's replacement as Sheffield Wednesday's chairman in March 1990 was a man who had first become a director only a few months before, in October 1989, a man about whom Wednesday fans knew not much: Dave Richards.

Richards was an engineer, like McGee and many in the managerial backbone of what is still a mucky, industrial city. A steelworker's son, he had completed his apprenticeship in the early 1960s, then in 1970 joined a firm, Three Star Engineering, which had been formed a year earlier by three Rotherham-based directors. On 11 September 1973, Richards, then not quite thirty, was himself made a director. He has always been very reluctant, despite his prominent positions in football, to talk in detail about his background; he told the *Sheffield Star* at the time that he was a Wednesday fan who had been taken to Hillsborough by his dad, watched the club's fifties legends Derek Dooley and Albert Quixall, and had 'enjoyed the banter on the Kop'. Richards was involved in South Africa before the end of apartheid, although the detail of this is scant. He refused my request to interview him for this book, and the only record I could find about his South African activities was quoted in the South African newspaper, the *Weekly Mail*, in September 1993 when Wednesday went to the country to play three friendlies. Richards, the piece said, was keen to turn 'longstanding business and family ties' with the country into a closer link with Wednesday. He was quoted as saying: 'I've had close ties with South Africa for many years. I had a business there and travelled there for the past twenty years, and my family lives there.'

Some say the contact with McGee was through McGee's wife, Phoebe, who is South African, but others dismiss that, saying he was a local businessman McGee grew to know and brought on board. Anyway, Richards stayed throughout as a director of Three Star, which expanded, made profits of £471,639 in 1990, apparently paying Richards the decent salary of £60,000. Although he said he was a lifelong Wednesday fan, his credentials for becoming the club's chairman were never crystal clear. In June 1991 he gave an interview to the *Sheffield Telegraph*, talking about his relationship with the manager, Ron Atkinson:

'When I became chairman, I told Ron that what I know about football you could write on the back of your hand, but I believed in employing the best.'

This was the man taking over at Sheffield Wednesday less than a year after the worst disaster of the many which blighted English football from its beginnings. Dave Richards inherited in the Sheffield boardroom the tradition of Charles Clegg, the pioneer of football and sobriety, who believed it was anathema ever to take a penny from the game, the weathered old gent who always claimed high moral values for Sheffield Wednesday, the FA and the game of football itself.

Richards was coming into a club and a game which had gone rather astray from the ramrod avenue insisted upon by Clegg. Even after ninety-six blameless young people needlessly died, Sheffield Wednesday seems never really to have acknowledged and accepted its own part in football's bleakest failure. Under Richards' leadership, for ten years they never even put a memorial up to the disaster, despite being continually pressed to do so by the families and supporter groups. Soon Mackrell was talking publicly about the club's desire to 'move on'. They did so armed with those original lies about the disaster, comprehensively unpicked by Taylor, lingering in Sheffield, protecting the club and many of its fans from interrogating Wednesday's own part in the tragedy. Wednesday carried on into the world with which the men who run clubs are more naturally comfortable: the football soap opera, results, promotion and relegation, managers, points, cup ties, the game's involving, magical bubble. Plus, the money was coming. Football had no time for 'the fullest reassessment of policy for the game', as Taylor had urged, with matches to play, a TV deal to be done and breakaway talk in the corridors. The game dips its head every year, gives a minute's silence for the Hillsborough victims, stands solemn, its mind mostly empty. Then, as in 1989 when the semi-final and final were played despite the tragedy, the ref blows his whistle, real life can be forgotten and football moves on.

CHAPTER 5

Cashing In

It would have been interesting to have had a third Taylor Report, some years later, setting out what the good judge thought of football's response to his call for the fullest reassessment of policy and a new ethos for the game. While Trevor Philips, the League's commercial director, was taking his unity roadshow round the country to seriously unimpressed audiences at County Football Associations, David Dein and Noel White were nipping into Lancaster Gate and schmoozing the FA to support their break-away. A myth has grown up around the carve-up, that, had the FA not backed the big clubs, they would have broken away anyway. That is not true. The FA is indeed constantly worried that its authority is based only on the voluntary membership of clubs, and since the dawn of the big clubs' wealth and power has compromised with them for fear that they would break with the FA. That diplomatic balance lay behind the amateur FA's land-mark decision back in 1885 to allow professionalism, and further concessions had been chipped away ever since.

However, the big clubs were in no position to break free of the FA in the modern era; they had too much to lose – the infra-structure of referees, officials, registration of players, the ground-work the FA provides to facilitate organised football at all levels. And the clubs would have fallen foul of the European governing body, Uefa, which would have probably seen them excluded from continental competitions, once the English clubs' ban following

Heysel was over. At the time, in 1990, the big clubs needed the FA's support, which was why they went looking for it; Irving Scholar confirmed that to me. The FA, tremblingly insecure, was wretched in giving its blessing so easily, wresting nothing from the big clubs in return.

Millichip, seeing the breakaway as the FA's victory in the parochial rivalry with the League, worked with Graham Kelly and the FA's technical director, the never knowingly charismatic Charles Hughes, to produce their response, *The Blueprint for the Future of Football*, supporting an elite division of eighteen clubs, separate from the Football League, which would keep all the new money to themselves – a move, the FA claimed, which would help the England team.

Yet England had a year earlier, under the old, sharing, four-division structure, reached the semi-final of the World Cup in Italy, their best performance since they won it in 1966. The backbone of the inspired team had come through the 'pyramid' of the English system, many players having learned their football in the lower divisions or non-leagues, like Chris Waddle (Tow Law Town in the Northern League), Peter Beardsley (Carlisle United), Paul Parker (Fulham), Stuart Pearce (Wealdstone), Mark Wright (Oxford United) and David Platt (Crewe). The drama and glamour of the tournament, Gazza's tears, Lineker's finishing, Lynam's twinkling and Pavarotti's singing, ushered a swarm of interest back to football, before the Premier League or Sky launched two years later and began to claim the credit. The fact that England have not come close to that level of achievement since *The Blueprint* has not caused anybody to question or review its wisdom; everybody in football knows its true aim was petty politics, not the England team.

Club chairmen in the lower divisions and officials at the League itself howled against the breakaway, warning that if the top clubs were released to keep all the new money it would mean a deep financial crisis for the other seventy-two League clubs. It is surprising, looking back, how few other senior football figures spoke out against the 'superleague' at the time. Gordon Taylor, the chief executive of the PFA, who had spent much of the 1980s on rescue plans for hard-hit clubs, or brokering agreements to hold the League together, was appalled by the FA's treachery:

'The FA is trying to diminish the Football League and with it most of the professional clubs in this country. Its blueprint is a way for the leading clubs to seize virtually all the money, leaving the remaining clubs to wither and, for some, die.'

Graham Taylor, the England manager, was notably another, deliciously causing embarrassment for his employers, the FA, at the very launch of *The Blueprint*. Of the idea that the breakaway would benefit the England team, Taylor told the assembled press: 'People think there must be a lot of my thinking in this Premier League. There is none, and I'm not totally convinced this is for the betterment of the England team. I think a lot of this is based on greed.'

That view, that the FA had not been motivated by what was best for the England team, but were simply giving the big clubs what they wanted, was depressingly reinforced after a meeting in early 1991, notorious among FA staff, between Millichip and the First Division clubs. Ken Bates, the Chelsea chairman, was opposed to reducing the top division to eighteen clubs; Chelsea were then a yo-yo struggler and Bates argued that a smaller Premier League would exclude middle-ranking clubs like his. He always railed against Dein for promoting Arsenal in a breakaway of the super-rich, but here Bates was arguing for Chelsea's own membership of the elite. Millichip, rather than insisting that eighteen clubs was the very rationale for *The Blueprint*, its purpose to create a slimmed-down season and fresher, better-prepared players for internationals, shrugged:

'Well, how many clubs you have is up to you.'

That abdication of leadership gave the clubs notice that they had a free hand, that the governing body wasn't up to doing much governing at all. The clubs were required to give three years' notice of any intention to quit the Football League, but they wanted out immediately, in time to do their own TV deal for the 1992–3 season. The League went to court to seek to enforce the notice period but it lost. Instead, the bodies agreed to retain promotion and relegation, and the FA itself, not even the Premier League clubs, agreed to compensate the League for what it was losing in TV money by losing its First Division clubs. The figure was valued on the basis of the deal at the time, not the new millions about to come in, so the rump of the clubs in the other three divisions were thrown a paltry figure of around £3m. The ethics of the FA supporting a move by the nation's biggest clubs which, whatever its other implications, was contrary to their agreed membership of their own League, were never considered in the realpolitik.

So, somehow, they'd pulled it off. Dein and White and the 'Big Five' had managed to get the governing body for the whole of football to back their breakaway from sharing the upcoming TV bonanza with the other Football League clubs, let alone being required to distribute some of the riches down the pyramid, to strengthen the sport at large. The FA had even dressed it up as being good for the game. So, in August 1992, the FA Carling Premiership – the new name for the twenty-two First Division clubs – kicked off, backed by football's governing body and a brewer of weak lager. 'A Whole New Ball Game', Sky called it, but the truth was that Rupert Murdoch was throwing everything, a five-year, £305m bid with the BBC, to salvage his ailing News International empire on the generations-old, in-the-blood loyalties of English football fans. They were still there, solid, after all the game's traumas and disasters, the only group of people in Britain, Sky had finally worked out, addicted enough to their TV fix to be prepared to pay for a satellite dish. Betrayed and battered and warning of trouble ahead, the League renamed its divisions, promoting the Second to First, Third to Second, Fourth to Third, and played doughtily on.

It is striking to reflect that not a single old First Division club refused to join the breakaway. Not one held out on principle for the unity of the League. Perhaps more surprisingly, neither did any object out of self-interest. A tremendous financial gap was opening up between the Football League and the Premier League, which was taking the new Sky millions free of the old requirement to share it 50:25:25 with the other League clubs. However, they were retaining the old three-up, three-down system of promotion and relegation between the Leagues. Not one club seems to have thought about the possibility that they might be relegated, and the financial problems they would have when they fell out of the Premier League. United, Arsenal, Liverpool, Everton, Tottenham, the self-anointed, presumed to think only about Europe and trophies, but you have to wonder what delusions of grandeur had descended on several of the Premiership's other original clubs: Coventry, Crystal Palace, Ipswich, Man City, Norwich, Queens Park Rangers, Sheffield United. Did their histories tell them they'd never go down, that they were rightfully part of an elite? Wimbledon, in the Southern League as recently as 1977, who the year before left their Plough Lane home to become tenants of Crystal Palace: did they really consider they belonged in a Premier League, and stuff the seventy 'little clubs'? As for Oldham: what can you say?

Sheffield Wednesday, with Richards as their chairman, were in it as eagerly as all the others. The reality, somebody senior at the club at the time told me, was that nobody wanted to miss it. 'You're there to do the best for your club. Here were the biggest clubs in the country breaking away and huge money was coming in. How could we turn it down? We didn't think about relegation; we thought: we're really going places now.'

Within the Premier League, from the beginning, the new TV and sponsorship money was split in three ways. Half of it was shared equally between all twenty-two clubs. A quarter was reserved to pay out in hefty match fees to clubs selected by Sky for live coverage. The other quarter was paid in increasing slices according to where a club finished at the end of the season. So Manchester United, who ended their search for a first Championship title since 1967, received a great deal more at the end of the first Premiership season than Nottingham Forest, Middlesbrough and Crystal Palace, who were relegated. That financial structure was intended to ensure that there was a base of equality, that no club was totally, hopelessly, out of its depth, but success would earn more money. The effect was that the already rich were to get richer.

In retrospect, compared to the Premier League's moneymaking and global reach now, those were innocent times: Sharp, makers of ghetto blasters, microwaves and tellies, were on United's Umbro shirts, rather than Vodafone and Nike, who paid the astonishing £303m in 2000 for the right to make United's shirts for thirteen years. Steve Bruce was the captain, Clayton Blackmore picked up a medal, Alex Ferguson wasn't a knight or a significant racehorse owner; one of his major buys was Dion Dublin. The team was British or Irish except for Peter Schmeichel, Andrei Kanchelskis and Eric Cantona, who seemed dazzlingly exotic, playing to all our caricatures of what Frenchness entails. The Stretford End was rebuilt, making Old Trafford's capacity 45,000. With what their annual report unblushingly called the 'improved arrangements' for television income in the Premier League, and the 'additional revenues from winning the Championship', United's total income was up a quarter, but this still added up to a mere £25m. How quaint. If you look carefully at the *Rothmans Football Yearbook* that year, you'll find a seventeen-year-old called David Beckham, born in Leytonstone, listed in the clutch of trainees.

The Premiership's early years, with the shame of Hillsborough still fresh in the memory, were hailed as an unqualified rebirth for football. New stands were going up, huge money pouring in, Sky's coverage, for those who bought the dish or assembled in pubs, glorified and hyped up the game. The Sky millions, ticket price increases and new commercial operations afforded the top clubs enough money to attract foreign stars we'd seen previously only on telly in World Cups. Jürgen Klinsmann dived in, and the arrival of the Brazilian Juninho, at Middlesbrough's new Riverside Stadium in October 1995, said it all about the game's reinvention, a dash of glamour in one of England's smoggiest corners.

The foreign players, and the overseas managers like Wenger who mostly arrived shortly after that, helped to overhaul the quality and style of play. United, when they first returned to European competition in 1993, were embarrassed by the likes of Turkish side Galatasaray, and learned painfully that they needed to keep and pass the ball, not hurtle around. For fans, all of these elements combined with the media opening up to the game and football came out of the closet. It was no longer a seedy impulse satisfied furtively in dark urban spaces at the weekends, but flamboyant, triumphant. Football was no longer untouchable, but thrilling showbiz; *FourFourTwo* launched, *SHOOT!* for grownups, Radio 5 was turned over almost wholly to football, and suddenly the nation's lust for football was unashamed. The fact that there had been no real reform of the game's clubs or institutions since the horrors of a few years earlier, that the Premiership was a breakaway opening up huge financial division, that problems of a different kind were being stored up, were never mentioned, except under the breath or in fanzines. Perhaps it was a question of timing: when you have emerged from hell to a brandnew home, it seems bad manners to complain about the fixtures and fittings.

The reaction in the boardrooms of the top clubs was that they had finally arrived into an environment in which there was big money to be made. It had all the ingredients of a boom 'industry', for those who wanted to think of the sport in that way. Gerry Boon, an accountant at Deloitte & Touche, pronounced himself a 'missionary' for football's new, commercial age and the personal profits the chairmen of clubs could make, although his own annual analysis of football finance, given massive coverage, showed the clubs mostly spending the bonanza on vastly increased players' wages. In 1993–4, Boon's report noted the English professional game was making massive money compared to pre-Sky days, but the clubs were still, as in the 1980s, inclined to spend it all on paying more for players they thought would make the difference. The evidence showed that money determined playing success, because the better players were only attracted with more money. United, which made the most money, won the Championship again. The three clubs with the lowest wage bills, Sheffield United, Oldham and Swindon Town, were all relegated. Fourteen Premier League clubs did make a profit, mostly a small one, while the other eight made a loss, and in the Football League half the clubs made a small profit, which was due almost entirely to being able to sell their better players to the Premier League clubs. Overall, professional football's bonanza was worth £387m, but the ninety-two clubs made a total profit of just £12,000: 0.003 per cent. This seemed to shock the accountants, so much they mentioned it in their report three times with exclamation marks. They concluded that controlling the wage bill was 'long-term, football's greatest challenge', and described the lack of profits being made on the new money 'a salutary statistic for potential investors'. The clubs did not generally accept the challenge of not spending all their money on wages, but this did not have a salutary effect on people coming into the game looking to make money.

By 1997, Manchester United had won the Premier League four times, coming second in 1995 to the blip; the single time Blackburn Rovers won it when Jack Walker's Jersey-based fortune was briefly enough to pay for a title-winning team. Alan Shearer, Chris Sutton, Graeme Le Saux and the rest took the money at Ewood Park, before the bigger clubs' earning power relegated those £10,000 per week wages downtable. The Premiership did reduce to 20 clubs, Old Trafford was by now rebranded as the

'Theatre of Dreams'™, the home-developed young players, Beckham included, had slipped into the spine of Ferguson's side, United's merchandising developed yet more lines of tat for sale, and Manchester United plc's turnover reached £87.9m, more than four times its level six years earlier. The dividend declared earned Martin Edwards £393,059, on top of his salary package of £536,000, which included a £220,000 bonus.

The Premier League's storming popularity led to Sky more than doubling its money to renew the deal in 1997: £670m over four years. The Football League rejected a late offer from the Premiership to sell their TV rights together, a lost chance of limited reunification – although the League's officials said they hadn't been given enough time – which infuriated several Football League club chairmen. The League managed to do a respectable deal of its own with Sky, £125m over five years, but the gap between the two Leagues was yawning. United earned £12.5m from television that year, half as much as all the Football League clubs put together.

By now the moneymen circling around football – accountants, bankers, investment analysts, the people, frighteningly enough, responsible for managing ordinary people's pension funds – were convinced there was a gold rush, that football, repackaged, recovered, was the passport to multi-millions. They began to advise the clubs that more fortunes shone in the near future via charging fans to pay-to-view on television and for internet coverage. The men in charge of most clubs did not need too much convincing to cash in, and between 1996 and 1997 a flood of clubs floated on the Stock Market, making fortunes for the chairmen or other major shareholders, who had bought into the clubs much more cheaply a decade or two earlier.

Ken Bates had bought Chelsea for £1 in 1982, and in 1996 he floated the club onto the Stock Exchange for smaller companies, the Alternative Investment Market. At the time, more than 66 per cent of the shares were held by a company called Rysaffe Limited, based on the eighteenth floor of a tower block in Hong

Kong, on behalf of owners whose identities were never revealed. Shortly afterwards the shares were transferred to another company, Swan Management, in the Channel Islands tax haven of Guernsey. In the twenty-one years he lasted before he sold a rebuilt Chelsea, laden with huge debt, to Abramovich for £17m, Bates never said who the shares belonged to, except to deny that they were his.

Leeds United were bought for £16.5m in August 1996 by Caspian, a loss-making media company chaired by Chris Akers, who said: 'We intend that Leeds should form the corner stone of our strategy to create one of Europe's leading sports, leisure and media groups, underpinned by a unique multi-sport and leisure facility in Leeds available for the local community.' Not much of that ever came to pass, but the outgoing shareholders, Leslie Silver, Peter Gilman and Bill Fotherby, made £5m each when they sold.

In December 1996, Sunderland, which had made a loss in each of the previous three years, floated on the Stock Exchange aiming to raise over £10m by selling new shares at £5.85 each. One of the stated aims of the flotation was to 'widen public, and in particular, supporter share ownership' in the club. Brian McNally, a journalist who covers football in the North East with a weathered eye, wrote in the *Sunday Mirror* that hard-up Sunderland fans, living in a Wearside lashed by recession and the closure of the shipyards and pits, should not buy the shares at that price. He was banned from Sunderland's matches ever after, writing his match reports after sneaking into the ground and sitting in the stand. The shares, at the time of writing this book, are worth 60p each. Many fans, wanting to play a part in the club's new future at its landmark new stadium, lost fortunes.

Across the way at Newcastle, John Hall had bought into the club steadily between 1989 and 1992 for around £3m, promising to make it the centre for a reborn North East, a rallying point for the 'Geordie nation' and other such talk. He floated Newcastle on the Stock Market in April 1997, when the City was at the peak of its overexcitement with this new entertainment industry called football. Hall's shares were valued at £102m, a gain of £99m. In May 1997, Aston Villa floated, its shares valued at £11 each, the club at £126m. Its prospectus, the glossy document which goes out to encourage investors to buy shares in the expectation of making a profit, boasted in similar vein to the other clubs' about: 'High quality revenue streams and tightly controlled cost base', the 'significant levels of income the club receives under the BSkyB contract as a member of the Premier League'. The directors, it said, were: 'confident that the club can continue to grow profitably through its strategy of building sound commercial revenue streams to supplement match day income'. Doug Ellis sold a portion of the shares he'd bought fifteen years earlier for £500,000, pocketing £4m, and still held on to 33.4 per cent of the club, worth £42m at those peak prices. He has had a handsome salary every year since, and over £200,000 most years in dividends, a record of relentless moneymaking. At the time of writing, Villa's shares are valued at £2.83, and that is significantly boosted because of the constant speculation that somebody, somewhere, will finally buy Ellis out.

Arsenal never floated, but the price of their shares quoted on the OFEX market rose in this period of City flirtation with football, and David Dein cashed in some of his, selling in chunks to Danny Fiszman. Some of the unlikeliest clubs fancied themselves as Stock Market-listed companies: Queens Park Rangers, Bolton Wanderers, Millwall, Sheffield United.

And what did the FA do, as its football clubs floated off to make money? A version of all three restrictions imposed back in the 1890s to protect clubs' sporting character when their founders formed limited companies were still on the FA's handbooks, at Rule 34. Dividends were restricted to 15 per cent of the face value of shares. Directors could be paid but had to work full-time and be approved by the FA and the League. If a club were wound up, the shareholders could not sell the assets and pocket the profit; any surplus still had to go to another sports club or charity.

All the floating clubs followed the lead set by Irving Scholar when he floated Tottenham back in 1983. They formed holding companies and made the football club a subsidiary, announcing explicitly in their prospectuses that the governing body's long-standing rules no longer applied to them. From Aston Villa's prospectus, referring to Rule 34:

'These regulations apply only to member club companies such as Aston Villa FC Limited. Aston Villa PLC is not subject to these regulations.'

From Newcastle's: 'These rules apply to the Club but not to the Company.'

They all did it. The whole purpose of the regulations was to prevent people exploiting football clubs to make money when they formed limited companies, and here they were going further, floating to become public companies, which makes it very much easier for the shareholders to make money. The directors were bypassing the rules with holding companies, yet the FA had nothing to say. It did not insist that its own rules must apply to its top clubs, nor did it provide any leadership in this period, counselling about whether flotations were advisable, or in any other way give guidance about the clubs' management of the financial boom. Southampton Football Club floated by 'reversing' into Secure Homes, a company which built flats for old people. They also made it clear that the FA's Rule 34 restrictions no longer applied to the club. One of the Saints directors, who made an instant paper profit of £721,000, was Keith Wiseman. At the time, he was the chairman of the FA.

Irving Scholar's chairmanship of Spurs had ended in 1991 when their shares were suspended by the Stock Exchange, and he eventually sold to Alan Sugar, who bought close to half of Tottenham altogether, for £8m. Sugar's company, Amstrad, was making the satellite dishes for Rupert Murdoch's failing BSkyB, and Sugar's vote as the Spurs chairman was crucial in swinging the Premier League's original 1992 vote to Sky, with the required two-thirds majority, 14-8. Scholar popped up again as part of a consortium which took over and floated Nottingham Forest on AIM in October 1997. It was the last football club flotation and not the most dignified. The prospectus represented Forest's 1979 and 1980 European Cup wins, arguably the most extraordinary achievements ever by any English football club, on the cover, in the form of coins. Apart from Phil Soar, a businessman and Forest historian, Scholar's partners in the consortium were London-based businessmen looking to make money: Nigel Wray, a property developer and owner of Saracens Rugby Union Club, Wray's associate Nick Leslau and another property developer, Julian Markham. The merchant bank Singer & Friedlander, which had been the most notably enthusiastic financial institution for football speculation, launching a Football Fund fronted by the Liverpool legend turned TV pundit Alan Hansen, supported the Forest deal financially.

It did not turn out well. Forest were promoted in 1998 but relegated disastrously the following season, which is remembered most for the sulk by the Dutch striker Pierre Van Hooijdonk, who flounced off refusing to play for the club. With Forest crippled by debt, the old directors fell out with the consortium, and after what Wray described as 'a pretty miserable experience', in April 1999 he resigned as the chairman. A Forest fan and rich corporate financier, Nigel Doughty, then called the bluff of the holding company device. He agreed to put £6m into Forest, but insisted he would not put it into the plc; he wanted it to go directly into the football club, the subsidiary. Scholar, and his associate, Julian Markham, sued him, arguing that the arrangement, which would dilute the plc's ownership of the club, should not be allowed. They lost, but the judgement is most notable as a football landmark for the comments of the judge, Mr Justice Hart, who seemed to confirm what fans felt about so many of the people coming into the football club boardrooms during this gold rush:

'The board were seen as a collection of out-of-town investors who had invested for narrow financial motives . . . Mr Scholar was known to be a passionate supporter of Tottenham Hotspur. Mr Markham was also a Spurs fan. Neither Mr Wray nor Mr Leslau were natural fans of the game of football. None had local Nottingham connections . . .'

Leicester City floated on 24 October 1997, with Hansen again involved, paid £15,000, given 10,000 shares worth £1.10 each, and 100,000 share options, for advising a company, Soccer Investments, on the merits of buying the club. People involved in the deal told me he thrilled some of the young City professionals by turning up at meetings, a breath of real football among the roster of suits. The directors were, the prospectus said, 'confident that the club could continue to grow'. One line below that and other feverish enthusiasm for Leicester's prospects drew investors' attention to 'the risk factors set out in Part 9'. This was to be found in rather smaller print, towards the back. It talked about a few problems in the football 'market'; especially holding on to players, particularly after the Bosman ruling in December 1995, which meant clubs were no longer paid transfer fees if a player moved once his contract was over. The document even explained that players could get injured, which 'may impair the player's future performance'. It also pointed out that Leicester, an up-and-down club throughout their Football League history since joining in 1894, were relying financially on continued fat Premiership TV and sponsorship deals:

'The Premier League is very competitive. Three of the 20 clubs in the Premier League will be relegated at the end of the season. Relegation may have a significant negative impact upon sources of the club's income.'

Dave Richards and the Sheffield Wednesday directors watched the money come in and the City institutions taking an interest for the first time in the people's game, and they thought hard about floating. In 1990, for all the money spent by Ron Atkinson on players immediately after the disaster, Wednesday, now with

Carlton Palmer, Nigel Worthington, David Hirst, John Sheridan and other good players, had been relegated on the final day of the season, losing 3-0 to Forest.

Wednesday came straight back up the following season, but, more memorably for their fans, they actually won something: the League Cup, then sponsored by Rumbelows, Wednesday's first trophy since 1935. Even better, they beat Manchester United, 1-0, Sheridan scoring the goal. For all but ancient Wednesday-ites, it was the greatest day in their supporting lives. 'Sheffield Wednesday,' Paul Thompson wrote in the *Sheffield Star*, 'laughed all the way to Wembley and left weeping tears of joy.' It was, he said, 'a wonderful emotional triumph'.

Then, on the day of the civic reception at Sheffield Town Hall to celebrate the win, the news leaked that Ron Atkinson was leaving for Aston Villa, closer to his home in the Midlands. Dave Richards desperately wanted him to stay and Atkinson later said Richards offered him a package which would have made him the highest paid manager in English football history. After three hours of discussion, Atkinson reconsidered, and Richards went on local radio, announcing: 'I am delighted to tell you that Ron Atkinson is staying.'

A week later, Atkinson changed his mind and he was gone.

He was followed by Trevor Francis, whom Atkinson had brought in as a player, still marauding to wonderful effect, aged thirty-seven. Wednesday brought the Leppings Lane, which had stood vacant since the disaster, back into use, laying seats on the terrace at a cost of £800,000. They were given a grant of £488,000, public money from the Football Trust, towards the work. Graham Mackrell said in the programme for the match against Millwall on 30 January 1991: 'The empty terrace has been a constant reminder of the tragedy and although it will never be forgotten, we do need to press on. That is not a callous remark. It is a truthful one.'

Under Francis, in 1991–2 Wednesday took to their regained

First Division status in exciting style, finishing third – qualifying for Europe – convincingly claiming their founder membership of the Premier League breakaway. Mark Bright and Chris Waddle arrived, and Wednesday reached Wembley twice in 1993, losing to Arsenal in both the FA Cup and League Cup finals. They finished seventh twice, then thirteenth, but the fans never greatly warmed to Francis and he left in May 1995. David Pleat came for a time, then in 1997, when Wednesday finished seventh again, Atkinson came back for another year.

In March 1997, Dave Richards produced a document for shareholders setting out Sheffield Wednesday's proposals for their march to success in the new commercial age.

'Your Board,' it began, 'believes that it is necessary to raise further finance to maintain the progress of the club and to enable it to take advantage of opportunities which are available. The Directors have considered various options including the flotation of the club on the London Stock Exchange or the Alternative Investment Market.'

He said they should aim for a full listing on the London Stock Exchange, but: 'It is likely to be more beneficial to achieve this in two or three years time.'

The reason for delaying, he said, was that 'key full-time executives' would have to be appointed, and also that Wednesday had not done too well financially the previous year. They'd been knocked out of the cups, sacked the manager and entire first team backroom staff, turning over £10m on which they made a £2.5m loss. The wage bill had risen, as at all clubs, as players and their agents simply argued for a share of a much more lucrative pot. Wednesday's debts, at August 1996, were given as £16m.

'After careful consideration,' Richards said, the directors had decided instead to raise money, which would enable Wednesday to reduce their overdraft, buy more players and also improve facilities at the training ground and at Hillsborough itself, 'including additional catering and leisure facilities'. Boosted by this investment, Wednesday would float in a couple of years. The proposed deal was with the venture capital part of a merchant bank, Charterhouse Development Capital. Charterhouse agreed to pay £8.5m for a 20 per cent stake in Wednesday, but underwrote the whole deal and, because too few fans and shareholders took up shares, Charterhouse ended up paying £16m for 37 per cent. Compared to Villa, floating at around the same time valued at £126m, Wednesday seemed to the bank pretty cut-price.

'The idea was terribly simple,' a Charterhouse spokesman told me. 'Invest relatively cheaply, get Sheffield Wednesday among the top six clubs, fill the big ground, then two years later float at a massive profit.'

A Charterhouse director, Geoff Arbuthnott, was to become a Wednesday director. In an interview in the *Financial Times*, he was described as having 'no particular affinity for the sport'. He told the paper that Wednesday were 'good value', 'securely placed in the lucrative Premier League'. Wednesday, he said, had huge potential: 'Whether the new management team can unlock that potential is the bet we're taking.'

Keener-eyed Wednesday fans reading the document, mulling over whether it was a good deal – £16m seemed decent money, but they didn't see why so much of Wednesday was being sold so cheaply – were suddenly struck by a table on page 112.

'Actually,' Dan Gordon recalls, 'I couldn't believe it when I saw it.'

The page showed that in the months leading up to the Charterhouse deal, which increased the value of Sheffield Wednesday shares, all the directors, except Joe Ashton, the MP, had bought shares. They had made an immediate profit, quite a lot of money. The document listed how much each of them had bought the shares for, and showed that the shares were being valued at a great deal more now the Charterhouse money was coming in. Some of the directors bought them knowing the deal, or at least some deal, was in the offing. Richards' letter made clear that the board had spent months considering and negotiating the best way to bring new money into Wednesday. Arbuthnott had told the *Financial Times* that he had been discussing the deal with Richards 'late last year'. Graham Mackrell told me the Charterhouse deal had been under discussion for six months by the time the document was published in March 1997.

All the directors had bought shares within that time except one, Geoff Hulley, who made £28,000 profit on eleven shares he had bought just over six months before, on 5 September the previous year. Richards had bought six shares the previous October, then one on 11 December 1996. As late as 27 January 1997, just a couple of months before his letter went out setting out every worked-out detail of the Charterhouse deal, he bought four more shares, at £6,250 each. They were worth £18,360 each when the deal was done. The Wednesday chairman's total profit from the shares he bought while he was negotiating the deal which increased their value: £137, 960.

Other directors had sold in late January – the shares used to come up to the board for sale, from people wanting to sell up or the families of shareholders who had died. Howard Culley, a partner in the respected Sheffield law firm Irwin Mitchell, bought a share as late as Valentine's Day, 14 February 1997, not six weeks before Richards' letter was printed. Keith Addy, a director who, the document said, was a builder, with 'particular responsibility for ground alterations and improvements', had been on the board at the time of the disaster. The table showed that he had bought shares in July, August and December 1996, then he bought six shares on 27 January, which made him an immediate profit of £63,010. Bob Grierson, an accountant, whose main responsibility, the document said, was 'the financial management of the club', had bought two shares the previous April for £5,500, and one on 27 January, for £6,250 – it was now worth £18,360.

To say there was uproar would overstate it. They had not done anything illegal. 'Insider dealing' – making money by dealing in shares with inside knowledge that their value is going to increase – is not a criminal offence where companies are not listed on the Stock Exchange. That principle was established in old legal cases where directors had cashed in on shares in private companies, knowing they were about to do deals which would make them a nice profit. One director, Graham Thorpe, who bought a single share in November 1996, told me he had not then been aware a deal was in the offing, and recalled that when the club appointed professional advisers for the Charterhouse deal, the directors were then not allowed to buy or sell shares. The directors had committed no offence. However, the appearance of gold-rush profiteering left a bitter taste.

Joe Ashton told me he knew what was going on: 'The shares came up in front of the board when people wanted to sell. I knew they were buying them up. But there was no way I was getting involved with it.'

David Coupe, a shareholder, organised a small shareholders' association and began to campaign against the board. I went to see him in his shop selling mobile phones in the flat South Yorkshire village of Dinnington. He's a big bloke, with shades, bling, boxes full of mobile phones for sale and a rich store of language when he gets going on what has happened to his beloved Wednesday:

'I've put it straight to them, all these directors,' he said, leaning back. 'The way you operated was totally unethical. They just said what they've always said, that it wasn't illegal.'

'I thought it was outrageous,' said Dan Gordon. 'The directors, including Richards, the chairman, had been buying shares cheaply, knowing they were going to be worth more when the deal was done. I think it was a betrayal of Wednesday as a family club, and it definitely alienated people.'

The directors, including Richards, always maintained they did nothing wrong, paid the going rate at the time, and acted in the best interests of the club. Geoff Hulley told me that when he bought the shares, he had no idea they were going to increase in value, because Richards, Grierson and Culley were the directors working on the financial proposals. 'Even if I had, I wouldn't have worried. There was nothing sinister in it. They were all for the welfare of Sheffield Wednesday.'

The directors might have been forgiven more had the team done better. Wednesday had already backed Francis to bring in some exotic talent; Benito Carbone, the perky striker, signed from Inter Milan in October 1996 for £3m, nearly half of it borrowed from the Co-Op Bank and repayable on demand. Then the Charterhouse money came in and they signed Paolo Di Canio, the former Juventus player, from Celtic in August 1997, also for £3m. Danny Wilson replaced Ron Atkinson as the manager in summer 1998, then on 26 September 1998 came the famous incident, one of those equilibrium-upsetting events which can happen any time in football, and which some feel set Wednesday into decline. Di Canio, playing to the archetype of the Italian wind-up footballer, pushed referee Paul Alcock, who staggered backwards like a stunned weeble. Di Canio was banned for eleven matches for laying hands on a ref, but he was unhappy, felt Wednesday hadn't backed him sufficiently and in January 1999 he left for £1.75m, a loss of £1.25m, to unfurl his skills at West Ham.

By now, the Premier League bounty was seriously inflating wages. Chris Sutton's £10,000 a week at Blackburn had shocked football, but now the tabloids were acclimatising their readers to figures of £20,000 and £25,000. The lurid stories of misbehaviour, champagne-soaked gang bangs and sexual 'roastings' had not yet made the headlines, the TV soap *Footballers' Wives*, camping up a world of obscene wealth, had not yet begun. But the top players were earning over £1m per year and their houses, cars and other prizes were in the tabloids, a world beyond the imaginings of most supporters. The Premier League renewed its exclusive sale of live televised matches to Sky from 2001–4, in a package worth overall £1.6bn. Roy Keane set the benchmark for players shortly before the deal was concluded in 2000 when he successfully argued at United for a contract reported to be paying him £52,000 per week. When the TV deals went up, the agents arrived to argue that their players were the clubs' product, who made them all the money, and they should be commensurately rewarded. The clubs have never discovered a way to defeat that argument, however much they hate paying the money, and the agents in particular. Reviewing the game's finances for 1998–9, Deloitte & Touche found that players' wages had increased by 18 per cent in a year, while clubs' overall turnover had increased only 10 per cent – in other words, clubs were spending more of their money on players' wages. The ninety-two clubs, in this time of greatest ever plenty, were only breaking even; and the gap was growing between the Football League and the Premier League, which had 85 per cent of professional football's assets.

At Hillsborough, as at all clubs, Sheffield Wednesday spent to try to keep up. In August 1998 they signed Wim Jonk, the Dutch international, from PSV Eindhoven for £2.5m. The following close season, on 10 July 1999, Wednesday signed the Belgian striker Gilles De Bilde from PSV for £3m and, to partner him, Gerald Sibon from Ajax, for £2m. Those players were said to be being paid the going rate for coveted foreign strikers of the time, up to £1m a year, and were given four-year contracts. Simon Donnelly and Phil O'Donnell both signed from Celtic, on free transfers, said to be on similar sized modern pay packets.

After Di Canio left, Carbone waited till his contract was up, then left in October 1999 for Aston Villa for a nominal fee, a loss to Wednesday of £3m. Phil O'Donnell was injured throughout his time at Wednesday and in four seasons played only twenty games. De Bilde and Sibon played, but not to the effect envisaged by the headlines when they were signed. In the 1999–2000 season, Danny Wilson's Wednesday shuffled into a lamentable losing spiral. They didn't win for ten games. They lost 4-0 at

Man United, then on 19 September went to Newcastle and lost 8-0. They were already bottom of the Premier League in August, and they stayed bottom until 22 January, when they moved up to nineteenth.

In January 2000 four local MPs, Ashton, Clive Betts, formerly the leader of Sheffield City Council at the time of the disaster, Bill Michie and David Blunkett, went to see Charterhouse to discuss Wednesday's imminent plummet, wanting to know why the club, having received £16m, now had debts of £16m, and asked the bank to use its influence to intervene with the board. The MPs were savaged within football when it emerged they had also, Ashton says as an afterthought, told Arbuthnott they thought the club wouldn't survive in the Premier League with Wilson as the manager. Football people rallied round Wilson, saying it was a disgrace that the MPs had 'tried to get him the sack'. The board insisted Wilson was staying, then, on 21 March, after a 1-0 defeat away at Watford, they sacked him. At the end of the season, Wednesday went down, having won just eight games. They had deep debts from the spending spree, were saddled with fat players' contracts, which, because of the security long fought for by the PFA, could not be reduced. Football clubs cannot make footballers redundant, although they sack their backroom, administrative staff in droves when times are tough. Sheffield Wednesday were about to discover for themselves the financial realities of relegation, in which the breakaway gap between the Premier League and Football League First Division means that clubs suffer a huge loss of income, but have to pay costs which they can't reduce.

Before the slide, in June 1999, Graham Mackrell had left to become the chief executive at West Ham. Alan Sykes, formerly the secretary at Huddersfield Town, his home town club, took his place. Just six months later, Mackrell resigned from his job at West Ham. His club had fielded a player, Emmanuel Omoyimni, in the last eight minutes of extra-time in a League Cup quarter-final against Aston Villa. A call from a member of the public to the

Football League pointed out Omoyimni was ineligible, cup-tied, because he had previously played for Gillingham in the competition. West Ham won the game, but were ordered to replay it. Mackrell himself hadn't been responsible for checking the eligibility of all players but it fell within his department's responsibility. He immediately announced he was leaving: 'I felt the only honourable thing to do was to resign.'

For this minor administrative oversight, for a trifling footballing error, Graham Mackrell resigned, immediately.

Dave Richards was soon to leave too, rather than stay with Wednesday on their journey to the First Division. Richards had become the acting chairman of the Premier League, then, in February 2000, with Wednesday stuck at the bottom, he resigned as Wednesday's chairman to take up the Premiership job on a paid, three-year contract. When Wednesday were relegated, Dave Richards, who had been their chairman for the ten previous years, was elsewhere, presenting the Premier League Championship trophy to Manchester United. The Premier League told me he worked between one and two days a week, and the accounts for his first full year as chairman show he was paid £176,667.

Dan Gordon still struggles to comprehend Richards' promotion to heading the Premier League as a whole: 'We simply could not believe that with Richards having been Wednesday's chairman when the Charterhouse deal was done, appointed the managers, and signed the players' contracts which got us into so much debt and trouble, that he bailed out and was appointed chairman of the Premier League. I cannot see what his credentials are for being in such a senior position. And anyway, I thought football was about digging in and battling, not jumping ship.'

Joe Ashton continued the ocean-going theme: 'It's like the captain of the *Titanic* being appointed First Lord of the Admiralty.'

CHAPTER 6

The Romance of the Wednesday

Sheffield Wednesday sank. After three seasons of miserable defeats in the First Division, their expensive signings injured or not performing, in 2002–3 Wednesday were relegated to the Second Division – the Third, in pre-1992 language. Talk to Wednesday fans about the club's slide, weighed down with debt, and the detail which really irks them is that, throughout this time, the chairman who got them into it, Dave Richards, far from staying and taking responsibility for dragging the club back up, glided away to become football's most senior administrator, the very well paid chairman of the Premier League, chairman of the Football Foundation, which succeeded the Football Trust as the game's grant-giving body, and a central influence on the main board of the FA itself, the body which runs football.

If his qualifications for these senior roles are unclear, given his football record at Wednesday, his business career does not reassure. Richards had run his company, Three Star Engineering, steadily since first becoming a director back in 1973, making decent profits doing general engineering work for the steel, mining and defence industries. Three Star were taken over by a larger company, Bimec, in 1991, but it didn't work out; Bimec soon went into receivership and Richards bought Three Star back through his own company, Globalfare. He seems to have paid himself a good but not excessive salary, around £60,000 a year, when the company was doing well. In November 1994 he launched Three

Star into a new future, moving to a large, handsome factory in a modern industrial estate on President Way, a little distance from the oily fingernails and Victorian workshops in the centre of Sheffield.

Three Star did well at first, but in 1999, the year Sheffield Wednesday were heading downwards, Richards' company was staggering into trouble. In the year to 30 June 1999, Richards declared a £158,312 profit and said of a new waste treatment division: 'Long term prospects are considered excellent.' However, by then, they were losing work to cheaper suppliers overseas, and, in the whole of 1999, Three Star won no major contracts for work at all. At the same time, costs increased because of the new, more expensive rent at the factory and investment needed in equipment. In January 2000, Richards laid off workers, although not too many because he believed business would turn round. Personally, he was working his way up in football, networking prodigiously, and a month later he won the backing of the other Premiership clubs' chairmen, led by his ally Ken Bates, to take on the job as chairman of the Premier League itself, £176,667 a year for his one or two days a week in London. In June, sighing that it had been 'a very difficult' year for Three Star, Richards declared the company's first ever loss, £353,081, and the following month laid off more workers.

In June 2001, Richards sold off the waste treatment division, which was described, straight-faced, as 'a drain' on the company. Three Star owed the Co-Op Bank £1.5m, was struggling to pay its PAYE tax bill, creditors were beginning to sue for unpaid bills and Three Star's credit was stopped with several key suppliers. On 6 July 2001, Richards called in the insolvency practitioners. His company was put into administrative receivership, the accountants appointed to get what they could for the bank. Nobody was interested in buying the company, so it was closed down and all 120 staff were laid off. Three Star owed £213,000 in tax and VAT, the bank lost big money, unsecured smaller creditors and trade suppliers, owed £959,000 in total, got nothing. Richards' holding company, Globalfare, also went into administrative receivership. It owned the worthless shares in Three Star, together with 237,600 5p shares in Sheffield Wednesday, the ones which were intended to make Richards a fortune when the club eventually floated. The receivers are not thought to have had much luck getting rid of those.

I went to Sheffield to talk to people about the state of the football club and had a drive up to President Way to see the Three Star site. You wind through Sheffield's inky heart, then out onto a dual carriageway, and off after a mile or so into the industrial estate. There is a sweep of large modern factories; this is heavy, technical territory, acres of factory, yards of pallets, forklifts, the odd bloke walking about in overalls, companies with names like Bestobell Valves. In the middle is a high, wide, purpose-built unit, with a blue slanting roof and corrugated face: the Wood Group Rotary Electrical Company. Bruised into the front and back, you can just make out the name of the previous occupant: Three Star Engineering. I popped into reception; there were no frills, just a small hatch behind which a woman broke off from some typing to tell me that, yes, this used to be the Three Star factory. There was an aerial photograph, taken when Three Star had newly moved in. They must have been pretty pleased with it at the time.

Hillsborough itself was a trip back to the past, compared to the new stadia and all-seater makeovers which have changed the face of football since the disaster. From the outside, the Leppings Lane end still looks formidably grim, a gloomy concrete grey, squashed into the corner of Leppings Lane itself, an ordinary terraced street made infamous by the disaster. The memorial the club finally put up in 1999, shortly before Richards left for the Premier League, is across the river from the main stand's entrance. It seemed to me a pretty passionless, token effort for so catastrophic an event, tucked away on the pavement, a low brick wall carving a little quiet for it from the traffic whistling down Catchbar Lane.

Walk across the river to the main entrance and you pass through high doors with a large club badge, picture of an Owl, est. 1867, and then you're into reception. Hitting you in the eye are huge colour pictures of Wednesday's 1991 Rumbelows Cup Final victory. The scale of this celebration really only drives home how long ago it was, John Sheridan scoring the winning goal, the two Manchester United players stretching but failing to block him were Brian McClair and Neil Webb. United have done a bit since then; Wednesday, the club's very entrance tells you, haven't.

Inside, the reception, blue, wooden and a bit tatty, makes the sort of corporate impact you might have expected if you'd turned up for a job interview at a regional headquarters of C&A, sometime in the seventies. There are some more pictures of Wembley '91, which gives the impression not that the club is enduringly thrilled with its triumph but that they haven't had the money or the get-up-and-go to redecorate. There are some sepia photographs of bygone days: Wednesday's 1928–9 League Championship winning team, a collection of pale, hard-looking players with, resolute among them, the waistcoated, unsmiling figures of both Sirs, Charles and William Clegg, formidably crusty. You half-expect Miss Havisham to pop her head round the corner and try to sell you a Lottery ticket.

Alan Sykes, the club's chief executive, sent instructions for me to come up in the lift to see him, as arranged. He arrived at Hillsborough from Huddersfield in the summer of 1999, to replace Mackrell. He had originally trained, he told me, as an accountant, but he had spent twenty years in general management in the timber industry. Imagine a man who spent much of his working life in senior positions in timber companies and you would picture a man not unlike Alan Sykes: tall, lean, upright. He looked the kind of man who would be comfortable with the notion that you never get lost on a straight road, even if he wouldn't necessarily see the point of saying it.

He had a hardwood handshake, then we sat in his office, which was as plain as could be, partitioned off from the open-plan secretarial space, which would struggle to be described as a nerve centre. Sykes, I have always been told, was well respected by the officials in the Football League, who found him, among many blusterers, to talk sense, based on experience. He proceeded, painstakingly and convincingly, to talk me through the factual circumstances which have led Sheffield Wednesday to find themselves so deeply in the shit.

He joined when Wednesday were still in the Premiership: 'I thought when I came that I would spend the rest of my career in the Premier League.' He didn't say that as if he felt sorry for himself; it was a simple fact. Wednesday had finished twelfth the previous season with Danny Wilson as the manager, they had spent much of the Charterhouse money on new, highly rated players and expected to do well. Then they had their dreadful start to the 1999–2000 season, one point from the first eight matches: 'I think everybody realised two months into the season that there was a very real prospect of us being relegated.'

They went down with Wimbledon and Watford, to the shrunken lands of the Football League, with players to pay on Premiership wages. Sykes said the finances down there weren't a shock; he knew what was in store: 'I'd spent six and a half years at Huddersfield working in the First and Second Division, so I knew how much of a gap there was in the money we would get from television, and how much money you lose in other ways, like sponsorship and smaller crowds. What was a surprise was the number of highly paid players who didn't perform.'

He didn't want to talk about how much they were on but once he was flowing he said, 'Twelve, thirteen, fourteen, fifteen thousand pounds a week.' Footballers' contracts have to be honoured in full whatever the financial circumstances of the club, and, although Des Walker and Wim Jonk had only one year to go, of the other top-earning players the left back Andy Hinchcliffe had two years left, and De Bilde, Sibon, Donnelly and O'Donnell all had three years left out of four-year contracts.

Sykes clearly agreed with what I had been told by Wednesday fans; Walker was tremendous: 'He gave us everything, and credit to him.' But in the First Division the other players were no advert for the new era of galactic wages. Jonk, the Dutch international and former Inter Milan striker, went off injured at half-time in the second game of the season, at home to Huddersfield, and never played for Wednesday again. O'Donnell and Donnelly were both injured, Andy Hinchcliffe struggling. De Bilde tried a bit, but the fans felt Sibon – and this is putting it politely – was doing rather too little on the field for the money he was collecting. The other players, paid a good deal less, failed to gel as a team; they all played neurotically in front of an exasperated crowd with high expectations. Wednesday did not fulfil the role of big club yo-yo-ing back up; they finished seventeenth.

'Meanwhile,' I asked Alan Sykes, 'you're having to write cheques or pay direct debits of £15,000 a week to these guys?'

He looked me in the eye: 'And there's nothing you can do about it.'

He addressed the question raised by many people about the motivation of modern players, who are paid enough out of one contract to live in luxury for the rest of their lives, earning more in a year than most supporters can make in a lifetime's hard work:

'There are players earning £50–100,000 a week in the Premier League now,' he said. 'It sounds obscene, but there are players who give absolutely everything they've got: Roy Keane, Sol Campbell, Henry, many others who are really top players. Equally, there are some below that top level whose earnings put them in a comfort zone, and they don't try hard enough for their team. With the players we had at our disposal we should have been in the top half of the table. We shouldn't have been fighting a relegation battle, but from the start, we were.'

'And the money was leaking out of the club?'

'Absolutely haemorrhaging out. Our debts climbed gradually. The contracts were a millstone round our necks but we had to deal with them. Then we ended up in a relegation battle, so that is a pretty potent combination of problems.'

This was it: the financial consequences, for relegated clubs, of the gap which opened up when the Premier League broke away. The separate leagues retained promotion and relegation, and players' contracts are fixed, a security which the PFA, having fought the likes of Charles Clegg early in the last century simply for the right to exist, are not going to give up limply now. So clubs go down with wage bills they have amassed in the Premier League to pay the kind of players they hope will enable them to compete up there. When they are relegated, they receive 'parachute payments' from the Premier League – half of the previous season's television money – to cushion the drop, but very often this cannot fill the gap between the huge reduction in income down in the Football League First Division and what they are still committed to pay out in wages.

I asked Sykes about the measure which is often presented as the obvious way to deal with this. As clubs' income drops on relegation, many argue that the clubs should negotiate with players to take a reduction in their earnings if the club goes down. Some in the Premier League sneer at clubs – their own – which have been relegated without such 'drop clauses' in contracts, deriding them as irresponsible, implying the clubs deserve the trouble they get into. Yet several people involved at clubs have told me that it isn't that easy, that top players simply will not accept such clauses and so will not come to the club, which then cannot compete in the Premier League as it and its fans want to. Alan Sykes took me through this, again in plainly persuasive detail:

'Take De Bilde and Sibon – they might not be the best examples because they didn't do it for Sheffield Wednesday ultimately. But they were the players we were trying to attract at the time to help the team do well in the Premier League. One was coming from PSV Eindhoven, the other from Ajax. You have to pay them better money than they are on if you want to attract them to your club. You're trying to sell players the attractions of coming to Sheffield Wednesday. If you go into the negotiations saying: here's what you get in the Premiership, but if we go down, your wages will have to come down by 25, 35 per cent, that could put them on less than they are on at their present club, so they have no incentive to come. You're also not presenting much ambition, talking about relegation when you're trying to attract the players, and attempting to insist drop clauses are written into their contracts. Most players at the top level won't move on that basis, because they don't have to, they just won't accept it. It's different if you are signing players from the First Division, giving them a step up, but top players don't have to accept those terms and they won't.'

The income gap between the two leagues therefore means that clubs which are relegated face serious financial problems, and there is no easy mechanism the clubs can employ to deal with it. And clubs on the decline, with a mix of overpaid underperformers on long contracts, a few youngsters and British scrappers signed on the cheap, do not have a tendency to be happy places of work. Wednesday didn't bounce back from the First Division, they fell through it, under a series of managers – Paul Jewell, Peter Shreeves, Terry Yorath – none of whom could turn it round. The frustration of the supporters, who believed their club was bigger than this, deepened the bad mood.

All the while the debts climbed, up to £16m, then nudging £20m. In 2001, paying out millions in wages but earning Football League incomes, Wednesday made a £9m loss. The pattern of football's finances in the modern, soaraway, breakaway age, was now establishing itself. Apart from the top clubs – Manchester United plc going global, Martin Edwards agreeing a £625m sale to BSkyB in 1999 which the fans fiercely opposed and the Government eventually blocked – most other clubs were sagging.

The huge money pouring into football had produced hyper-inflation of wages, so the money was leaking through clubs to their players and agents, a process described memorably by the perennially grumpy Alan Sugar, as 'like drinking prune juice while eating figs'. Football clubs' management of their money was not markedly better than in the 1980s – why would it be, with so many of the same people involved and the same lack of leadership? But the scale of the wages paid and the lifestyles the money furnished for the players were more frighteningly excessive. In 1999–2000, while top-level wages climbed to tally with Roy Keane's standard of £52,000 a week, English professional football clubs overall lost £145m, £35m in the Premier League, £110m in the Football League. The City's speculators, seeing that the 'industry' did not have control of its costs, quickly lost interest in the game as a 'sector'. The share prices of all the clubs fell, even United's. Some of the large shareholders who had bought into clubs before the boom did sell and make money. Sugar himself, who described his time at Tottenham as 'a sad failure' because of the money he'd had to pour out to players and their agents, saying he hadn't enjoyed much of it, sold to an investment company, Enic, in December 2000, for £22m. That was £14m more than he paid for his shares when he bought the club from Scholar in 1991 – and he still held on to a 13 per cent stake.

In a series of sales, Martin Edwards made more than £100m from the United shares he and his father had accumulated for around £1m in the fifties, sixties and seventies. Sir John Hall sold just 9.8 per cent of his Newcastle shares for £16m to ntl, a cable company buying extravagantly into football clubs in an ultimately failed effort to establish itself as a rival to Sky. The gold rush, however, did not deliver the expected bullion to those who had poured in in the mid-1990s because the clubs were leaking money. With the Premier League structured to pay more to the successful clubs, Manchester United, carrying no debt, now with a 67,700-seat stadium and burgeoning commercial operations, could pay top whack to their players and still make a major profit every year. That left all the others extending themselves to pay wages for players who could compete with United, an inflationary tendency in football which extended right down the leagues. Clubs overreached themselves to live with United, Premiership clubs below the top few were spending more than they had desperately trying to avoid relegation, the relegated clubs were in serious trouble, the top clubs in the First Division were usually gambling to get up to the big money in the Premiership, and so on. Arsenal had their windfalls from transfers and Granada, and earned well because of the success brought by Wenger's inspirational management, but still made losses, hiked ticket prices and face the expense and effort of Ashburton Grove if they are to remain at the top. Leeds, a plc headed by the chairman Peter Ridsdale, seemed a new model club of bright young starlets under the unctuous charm of the manager David O'Leary. The reality – besides the tarnish which came with the players Jonathan Woodgate and Lee Bowyer being charged with grievous bodily harm after the beating-up of an Asian student, Sarfraz Najeib, Woodgate convicted of affray, Bowyer acquitted – was that it was all a mirage. Leeds had tried the short cut to reach the big money success in the Premier League and European Champions League would bring by borrowing hugely to buy the players to take them there. On 26 September 2001, Leeds borrowed £60m from a group of financial institutions, secured on future ticket income for twenty-five years at 7.695 per cent interest – £4.6m a year. They even sold and leased back some of their top players to a strange footballers' hire purchase operation, Registered European Football Finance (REFF). All to get money in up front to fuel their march on glory. They had reached the European Champions League semi-final in 2001 – Ridsdale was paid £645,000 that year – but when they missed out on qualifying for the competition for the following season, their income fell, their debts became unpayable, they had to sell Rio Ferdinand, Woodgate and others, and Ridsdale was up blinking in the media's lights, coining ruefully the classic phrase for the wasted boom years: 'We lived the dream.'

On coming to power in 1997, the new Labour Government had set up a Football Task Force to look into football's problems, chaired, oddly enough, by a former Conservative minister, David Mellor, who had a phone-in football show, 606, on Radio 5 in which he took fan's complaints reasonably seriously. Rather than legislate to reform football, the Government's idea was that the Task Force would bring relevant parties together: the FA, Premier League, Football League, PFA, football supporters' groups, League Managers Association, referees, academics and others with something to contribute. Out of that, it was hoped, agreement would come on what to do about a number of serious concerns darkening football's revival: high ticket prices, merchandising rip-offs, the paucity of disabled access in grounds, the persistence of racism, players' poor behaviour and image, and also how to balance the interests of supporters and shareholders where clubs had floated as plcs. It was, in hindsight, a fascinating period for the Task Force process to happen; they sat arguing in tortuous, bitterly fought meetings, the football bodies mostly unwilling to contemplate any reform urged upon them by the majority, from July 1997 to December 1999. It was a pocket of time, shortly after the boom but just before the clubs began to collapse. The financial management of clubs was, therefore, not dealt with in any depth, because it was not a central issue, although the supporters' groups and a majority on the Task Force did argue that the Premier League breakaway had sliced off far too much of football's money and that more redistribution had to be restored. The FA and leagues opposed that – even the Football League. The League is in an awkward position; the hurt of the breakaway still seethes underneath, but they need the cooperation of the Premier League clubs to play in the League Cup, which is the League's main attraction for television. So, even on the question of whether the breakaway should be reversed and more money shared with the Football

League, the League is forced to stay silent for fear of antagonising the Premier League clubs.

The Task Force came to sensible agreements on increasing disabled access and outlawing racism in grounds. The Task Force's administrator, Andy Burnham, also pulled off a shrewd, opportunist coup, securing from the Premier League an agreement that 5 per cent of the next TV deal would indeed be redistributed, not to the Football League clubs but directly to improve grass-roots football facilities for the mass of people who play the game, mainly in public parks, which had been neglected through the boom and stood dilapidated, half without changing facilities. Burnham was able to get the Premier League to agree because at the time they were facing a court challenge from the Office of Fair Trading to the clubs' right to operate as a cartel to sell their TV rights exclusively to Sky. The OFT argued that collective selling pushed up the price to the consumer and limited the number of matches which could be seen. The Premier League countered that it had to be allowed to sell matches collectively, because that ensured some equality between its clubs – if the clubs sold their rights individually, Manchester United, Arsenal and the big clubs would make fortunes, while the smaller Premier League clubs would struggle for a deal at all, and there would be no competition in the League. It was a deeply strange moment, the rich, breakaway league arguing for its legal right to operate as a collective so that it could share money among its members. In order for the Premier League to persuade the court it was in the public interest for the clubs to operate collectively, Burnham persuaded them, in the teeth of bitter opposition at first, that their case would be more convincing if they were sharing some of their vast wealth with the wider, amateur game, army of players who were consigned to the municipal mudbaths. The pledge was finally agreed after many wrangles and given in the report *Investing in the Community* in January 1999, which also called for professional players to devote a set three hours a week to community work. The new grass-roots funding led to the formation of the Football Foundation, which receives the 5 per cent from the Premier League, which is £20m a season from 2001 to 2004, matched by the FA and – with some struggle – by the Government from various Lottery pots: £60m, the first contribution ever put back by the professional game into the grass roots. The Premier League, which has Dave Richards as the Foundation's chairman, boasts relentlessly of its good works, but Burnham, now the Labour MP for Leigh, is clear that self-interest was at the heart of it:

'Some of the people involved were genuinely ready to put something back into the community and contribute to the wider welfare of football. But there is no question that had it not been for the threat to the Premier League from the OFT court case, there would have been no 5 per cent, and no Football Foundation.'

The Premiership has since resisted all arguments that it should redistribute more of its windfalls down to the wider game.

The Task Force's other achievement was the establishment of a Government-backed body, Supporters Direct. Again, the Government seemed to have a real problem actually coming up with the modest funding for the organisation it enjoyed crowing about at press conferences. Supporters Direct's role was to encourage supporters to form trusts, democratic bodies which had been pioneered at Northampton Town by a fan, Brian Lomax. Supporters paid into a fund which could be used to contribute to the club's coffers and buy shares and, if the clubs agreed to the deal, elect a director onto the board. Lomax himself had been an elected director of the Cobblers for seven years. This idea, which drew on his philosophy that football clubs should not be companies, bought and sold by businessmen, but mutual bodies of supporters running their clubs as sporting, community institutions, struck a chord with fans disenchanted by the commercialisation in the game, or whose clubs had lurched into crises. By the spring of 2004, in just three years, supporters' trusts had been formed at more than eighty professional and semi-professional clubs in

England, around half had a shareholding in their club, more than thirty with a director on the board. Along with the moneymaking, the mismanagement, the rip-offs which attended the new era, there was a fightback, and a body of more enlightened thinking was built up by many football people who believed the game ought to see and run itself very differently.

On the thorny clutch of what became known as 'the commercial issues' – ticket prices, merchandising, plcs – there was, however, no agreement. A majority of the Task Force, marshalled by Dr Adam Brown, the Manchester Metropolitan University academic and Manchester United fan, called for much firmer regulation by the FA and leagues. Research had been done by Leicester University which showed, rather unsurprisingly, that poorer people, lifelong fans, had been excluded from going to see their clubs live by the ticket price rises. It was, however, difficult to compile figures because by definition these were people who had melted away. The researchers conducted interviews with fans, many of whom spoke of a sense of betrayal, that they had stood there, loyal, throughout the years of decay, and now they were being excluded from the good times. The overwhelming majority on the Task Force called for a 'Football Audit Commission' which would develop rules to steer football in the direction of more equality, better management of clubs, more responsiveness to supporters and the grass roots. The FA and leagues rejected that idea and trashed it in leaks to the press, issuing their own, minority report, which rejected the notion of firm regulation, arguing instead for an 'Independent Football Commission', funded by the football bodies themselves, which would report annually on their running of the game and make recommendations. The Government, reluctant to legislate or, seemingly, to upset the football authorities, backed the minority, insisting on the implementation of none of the majority report.

On plcs, the majority report had drawn attention to the way in which the FA had allowed clubs to float free of its Rule 34, and argued that while those old rules could now fairly be said to be out of date, the FA needed urgently to create a new body of rules to help manage the fury of the commercial feeding frenzy while protecting the clubs and the character of the sport:

'In effect, what is needed is a modernised Rule 34,' the report said. 'This will allow clubs to take advantage of the opportunities of the Stock Market while remaining football clubs in their nature and purpose.'

The FA's lawyer and company secretary, Nic Coward, had sat through the Task Force process in which Rule 34 was discussed and concern aired about its avoidance. Not once did Coward mention, as I discovered in 2000, that he had in the summer of 1998 organised the removal by the relevant FA committee of the first two aspects of Rule 34, the restriction on dividends and on directors working part-time. Coward had originally been brought into the FA from the law firm Freshfields, to undertake a thorough review of the rules, and this was the result: a weakening, not a strengthening, of football's only financial regulations of clubs, at a time when the governing body was being urged to get a grip on the game's runaway finances. The FA did, however, keep the third restriction of Rule 34, the one which prevented owners winding up clubs and keeping the proceeds. When I found out about the removal of the first two rules I questioned Coward on it. He said:

'As the rules weren't working, there was no point keeping them.'

For all the arguments about the need for the FA to step in rather than flop out of governing its sport, there were no more flotations of clubs anyway. The City's interest in football burned away as they saw the clubs spend their money on players' wages in the chase for footballing success. The financial analysts turned their brilliant minds to the next exciting industry which was sure to make them a fortune – dotcoms. Singer & Friedlander, which had loved the publicity in the boomtime, putting up their executive Tony Fraher to lecture the media about the 'discipline' which 'the market' would inevitably inspire in football clubs, quietly closed the Football Fund. When you call the bank to ask them about it, nobody phones you back.

Slowly, football people, not just supporters, saw the results and said that the plc structure, besides being contrary to the game's ethos by providing a vehicle for profiteering, didn't work for football clubs. Stock Market companies are required to make profits every year and pay much of them out in dividends to shareholders. Football clubs, some of the game's executives began tentatively to realise as they woke up to the reality, were there to win matches, play sport, serve supporters and plough any profits back into the club. Yet still the governing bodies had nothing to say. The majority of the Task Force had called for the FA to set up a strong 'Financial Compliance Unit'. Coward's department instead watered it down to a 'Financial Advisory Unit'. The Premier League supported no meaningful changes at all as its clubs ran up huge debts, all the while cosying up to the Government to boast about the magnificent, selfless contribution they were making through the Football Foundation, murmuring that no actual reform was necessary.

When the Premiership did its 2001–4 TV deal, negotiated the year before at the height of the media rights and dotcom bubble, they reaped £1.6bn from Sky and a roster of other broadcasters paying for highlights and other packages. Sol Campbell immediately set the new standard wage for top players. His move from Tottenham, an agonising and drawn-out saga as he renegotiated the contract due to end in 2001, led ultimately to his move to Arsenal, loathed fiercely by Spurs fans, where he has always been reported to be on £100,000 per week – £5m per year. The very highest paid players in the English game are now assumed to be on that kind of money.

The Football League had a result in the TV market too: a £315m, three-year agreement with Carlton and Granada's new ITV Digital channel, which bought up the rights to matches in the

League's three divisions in a campaign to establish itself with pay-TV subscribers. They advertised the launch with a cloth monkey, which turned out to be very much more popular than the channel itself. Stories did the rounds that only 1,000 people had watched some lower division games, leading to jokes that it would have been cheaper to fly all the viewers there first class than buy the TV rights. By March 2002, the rumours that Carlton and Granada were losing so much money that they were thinking of closing the channel turned out to be true. ITV Digital went into administration and was closed down at the end of April. Carlton and Granada, two media giants who later merged to form a single mighty ITV channel, had said in their bid to the League that they would stand behind ITV Digital and guarantee the payments to the League. The League did not, after agreeing the deal, move to a 'long form contract', incorporating that guarantee and all the commercial details, which seems surprising but was common practice in the broadcasting industry at the time.

When Carlton and Granada closed the channel, it still owed the League clubs £185m for the two years left on the deal. The League had suffered similar internal demands for a greater share of the money from its own senior clubs as those which had led to the Premier League breakaway, and the lower division clubs had agreed, for the sake of unity, to distribute most of the money to the First Division clubs, £2m each per season, while the Second Division clubs were paid around £200,000 and Third Division clubs £150,000. The League had to sue Carlton and Granada to try to enforce the guarantee, but they lost because it was not specifically contained in the final signed contract. No shame seemed to attach to Carlton or Granada, whose chairman, Charles Allen, was knighted just a few months later for being the chairman of the Commonwealth Games in Manchester. We live in a strange country.

The League's chief executive, David Burns, moved quickly to do a replacement deal with Sky, £96m over four years, very much less than ITV Digital's level of folly, but still generous-looking with no other broadcasters left to compete. The larger clubs, however, Wolves, Millwall, Crystal Palace, Watford and others, were furious, and there were claims that Burns had not consulted fully enough with the League's board before doing the deal, which was not true. After a stormy meeting in London where some First Division club chairmen tore into him, Burns resigned.

ITV Digital's collapse did not cause the Football League clubs to make losses, run up debts and end up in financial trouble; they were doing that very naturally already. However, Carlton and Granada's withdrawal did cause all clubs serious difficulties, reducing the First Division clubs' expected incomes, on the basis of which players had been signed, from £2m a year from television to £700,000 a year. Its other major impact, which has been underestimated by those who believe the clubs brought the problems on themselves, is that it caused the transfer market within the Football League almost completely to collapse. Premier League clubs had already begun to buy foreign players rather than prospects from the Football League, so removing a very important historic element of lower division clubs' finances. Shortly after that came the first major financial collapse in the post-1992 era: Bradford City, which sank into administration having been relegated from the Premier League the previous season, committed to a wage bill the club simply could not pay in the First Division. At the end of the 2001–2 season, Leicester City and Ipswich Town were relegated, and both fell insolvent very quickly and went into administration. Leicester had been regarded as one of the Premier League's better-run clubs, but they soon earned notoriety by securing an agreement from the Inland Revenue to take a tenth, rising to a fifth when Leicester were promoted, of an outstanding tax bill of £6m. Ipswich, whose chairman David Sheepshanks had prided himself on being a 'new-style' chairman, talking at length on television of his steady, prudent, five-year plan for the club, imploded with debts of £45m. He said:

'We must take responsibility for our own problems and the creditors we cannot pay, but still, at the root of all this is the gap between the two Leagues which means that relegation, which ought to be a shock to the system, turns into a financial disaster.'

Five years earlier, football had published its commercial pretensions in glossy prospectuses, boasting of the money to be made for investors in clubs floating on the Stock Market. Now, clubs were churning out legal documents of a rather different kind, reports by accountants on the hopeless insolvency of some of the most senior clubs, containing pages of tightly typed lists of scores of creditors owed money they would never see again. Even when clubs are insolvent, the FA, leagues and PFA insist that all the players are paid in full, while ordinary employees can be sacked and other creditors left unpaid. This, the football establishment argues, provides some competitive discipline, preventing clubs from taking on players they know they cannot afford, then simply laying them off when the money gets tight. However, it did not prevent the tumble of clubs into insolvency; it made it a great deal harder for them to clamber out, still saddled with the crazy wage bills, and its morality didn't look good at all, paying millionaire players while sacking receptionists and the assistant kit washer. The administration procedure was that, apart from 'football creditors' – players and other clubs owed money – a settlement could be made with other creditors, banks, the Inland Revenue and smaller suppliers, to be paid less money, in order to allow the club to carry on and pay them something. If football clubs are completely wound up owing tens of millions and, often, with a mortgage on the ground, the creditors would get nothing, so they are usually forced to agree to Company Voluntary Arrangements (CVAs), settling, usually, for 10p in the pound. The administrator calculates how much is required to pay off the debts as agreed and puts the club up for sale, hoping to find a buyer prepared to stump up that amount of money. If it happens, the footballers get paid in full, the smaller creditors take a hit, and the club, owned by a new hopeful, rumbles on.

At Sheffield Wednesday, Charterhouse realised very quickly after the club was relegated that they'd chucked their money away and were never going to get anything for their 37 per cent. They sold out eventually to the directors Keith Addy and Geoff Hulley, and principally to a new director and, from June 2003, the club's chairman, Dave Allen, the owner of Napoleon's Casino in Sheffield and the Owlerton dog track. His first love is pigeon racing – don't laugh, there's big money in gambling on that.

Charterhouse never said how much of a loss they made; a spokesman at the bank simply summarised for me: 'It all went horribly wrong.' People around the club say reliably the figure paid was £2m, a loss to Charterhouse of £15m. In venture capital, you win some, you lose some. Elektra, also a venture capital firm, did a similar deal in 1997 with Derby, paying £10m for 25 per cent of the club, in the expectation of a fat profit when the club feasted on the Premiership plenty and floated a couple of years later. Elektra were similarly disappointed. Derby were relegated in 2002 owing many millions to the Co-Op Bank, run up on overspending on players to try to stay up in the Premier League. Eventually the bank appointed receivers, who sold the club to a three-man consortium, John Sleightholme, Jeremy Keith and Steve Harding, financed with a £15m loan from the anonymous ABC Corporation, based in Panama. That faceless offshore entity, whose owner is unknown, now has a mortgage on Pride Park, which had been one of the brightest new homes of football's 1990s recovery.

In 2002–3, Sheffield Wednesday's Premier League-sized contracts were fizzling out, but they were still struggling under the weight of debt. One of their own, their former goalkeeper Chris Turner, was brought in from Hartlepool as the manager, but he could only fiddle while the fans were put out of their misery and the club was finally relegated to the Second Division. The overdraft had swollen to £22m. When ITV Digital collapsed,

Dave Allen put in, according to Sykes, around £2m in loans. This, together with loans from other directors (none of whom had made the money they hoped for from the Charterhouse deal or a float), kept Sheffield Wednesday just short of the insolvency precipice. Sykes said the directors had done it because they were determined not to take the club into administration but instead work through the financial morass if possible.

'It would have been very easy to allow the club to go into admin-istration, and keep their money back to buy it back out again, having cut its debts like so many other clubs did,' Sykes told me. 'But the board here chose to try to keep the club afloat, for which I think they need to be applauded.'

He went on sternly to criticise the procession of clubs going into administration, leaving a stream of people unpaid:

'People tend to focus on the bank or the Inland Revenue who lose money and think there are no real victims. But what's often missed are the local businesses, where the loss of money is very painful indeed, perhaps makes the difference between staying in business and going bust. At this club we were not prepared to shaft our suppliers. It might sound corny, but the board believe it's the honourable thing to do. There is a responsibility to do the best we can.'

He seemed very genuine. The heart of the club's predicament, he told me, is the gap between the leagues. The Premier League broke away to keep all the money, but still three clubs go down, so relegation is financially shattering. It's the startlingly obvious consequence of the breakaway.

'The problem is not that there isn't enough money in the game. If you add up all the money that comes into the Premier League, the FA and the Football League, it's absolutely massive. The problem is that it is not equally or fairly distributed, that far too big a percentage of that money goes into the Premier League and the gap between the Premier League and the First Division is such that it's just a disaster zone when clubs get relegated.'

We talked about the clubs which had collapsed into serious financial trouble since they had come down from the Premier League: Bradford, Ipswich, Leicester, Barnsley, Wimbledon, QPR, all in administration. Derby in receivership. Sheffield Wednesday, Nottingham Forest – losing £100,000 a week as they wasted Nigel Doughty's investment too – Watford, who had to sell their ground and lease it back to raise £4m cash; Coventry, with debts of £60m.

'The list goes on,' Sykes said, mournfully.

Of the idea that football generally had to see sense, and realise this financial structure could not work, that money had to be shared out more evenly, he was not at all optimistic: 'You cannot see where the pressure is going to come from. The FA have got a part to play and should make the argument, but the Premier League are not easily or willingly going to surrender their money. There's no incentive for them to share. The Football League can't exert any pressure; they were defeated back in 1992.'

I said that the men running the Premier League and its clubs must be pretty thick-skinned, to see other clubs going bust as soon as they drop, leaving millions of pounds unpaid to creditors, large and small.

'I just don't think it concerns them,' he said. 'I just don't think they can relate to it at all.'

Hanging in the air over all of this, to me at least, was Dave Richards. He was the chairman here, the man who signed all the contracts which did the damage, then left just before relegation. As the club faced the drop, he had been cementing his influence and securing his payday at the heart of football. While his club was left in a financial hole, put there by football's unequal structure, Richards was walking into meetings representing the Premier League, batting away any suggestion that it should share more of its money. Indeed, he appears to have been looking, on instructions from the men who put him in that position, to extend the Premier League's power over the game and its wealth. It is difficult to understand the qualities he brings to the Premier League chairman's job, because the appointment was made privately, the job was never advertised, and the Premier League has never announced his qualities. They tend to talk vaguely about his heart being in the right place and, regarding his chairmanship of the Football Foundation, that he is committed to the game's grass-roots. People in football tell you the Premier League clubs are a series of rivalrous, if not warring, factions; nineteen clubs envious and wary of Manchester United, Bates, when he was there, lining up against Dein, the smaller clubs angling timidly for their interests. Richards, they say, is inoffensive and emollient to most. He garnered votes there and at the FA by talking to all and sundry and he's always on his phone, always around, knows everybody in football now. When you need something, Richards is often the man to ask. Whether he can deliver you don't know, but he'll often try. In London, he's Mr Football, the fixer, the man to know, the man with the ear of Government, someone you want on your side, somebody even, as the chairman of the Football Foundation, on whom the good causes now depend. It is, however, strange that he can square chairing the Premier League with the demise of his own club. It's not as if he doesn't know what financial problems are like.

Since Three Star Engineering went bust he has tried a couple of other businesses, without notable success. In February 2001, Richards set up a company, Call Excel, to operate as a telephone call centre, but in November, just nine months later, its accounts said, 'Due to mounting losses, it ceased to trade.' He appears to have moved his address to New Romney, in Kent, where he is a director of the local bowls club, giving his occupation as 'retired'. In 2002, for his second full season as part-time chairman of the Premier League, he was paid £140,000.

In Sheffield, they're mostly not too keen on the disparity between their club's fortunes, and Richards' own: 'Richards took this club to the brink,' said David Coupe, chair of the Sheffield Wednesday Shareholders Association. 'Rather than stand and fight,

he bailed out and left for his cushy job in London. I don't understand his qualifications to be Premier League chairman; how
come he's the man they want on all these boards, running the
game?'

Alan Sykes had said beforehand he wouldn't talk about Richards
and he stuck to his word. He also said he couldn't talk about the
disaster, because it was before his time. He said he received occasional requests from the bereaved families to come to Hillsborough
on the anniversary, if they are not going to the memorial service
in Liverpool. 'It's obviously very difficult and we try to be as helpful
as we can,' he said.

A teak cabinet of a handshake, a slow walk to the lift, a manful
goodbye. Within a few months, Sykes was gone, too, one of those
sudden departures after which nobody says anything illuminat-
ing. Sykes was simply quoted in the *Sheffield Star* wishing the
Wednesday fans, 'the success they so richly deserve'.

They stayed loyal in the Second Division, 20,000 of them
turning up to see awful, halting displays by a cobbled-together
side. When Allen, Addy and Hulley bought the Charterhouse
shares they gifted 9.4 per cent to the Owls Trust, a democratic,
1,000-strong body of fans, formed with the help of Supporters
Direct. The Trust had a small office at the ground, tucked away
in the ticket office, and a couple of part-time employees; the chief
executive was John Hemmingham, who found fame of a sort as
the trumpeter in the band of Wednesday fans, and went on to
play, so to speak, for England.

He's been a Wednesday fan all his life and has a twinkly good
humour about how crap they've become. He told me the fans had
been enjoying the season in the Second Division at first because they
felt like a big club, taking 3,500 fans away to clubs like Peterborough
and winning a few games: 'When you've spent four years in the
bottom three, losing every week, it's been pretty miserable.'

In the Second Division, Wednesday duly started losing again.
The Trust was fundraising, but the debts, £22m, were way beyond

help. The Trust asked the members what they should do with the money and they'd said overwhelmingly that, rather than buy up a few worthless shares to take their stake creepingly up to nowhere significant, they'd prefer to spend it on something which would make a real difference to the club. As the facilities on the Kop are so poor, they'd decided to spend it there: putting in a new concrete floor at an upper level behind the stand, and equipping it with decent toilets, including one for women – which will be an innovation – and a kiosk selling decent food.

To install those basic requirements, the club had an estimate for the building work of £160,000. They had applied for a grant of half of it, £80,000, from the Football Foundation, so the Trust was going halves with the club on the rest, £40,000 each. The money from the kiosk would go to the club, but the Trust would have a half say in how it is run; for instance, they could decide that hot pork sandwiches, not awful burgers, would be served up there. When I saw Hemmingham, the Trust had scrabbled together £22,000 from regular events and were looking forward to a black tie do coming up, at £100 a head, to raise most of the rest of it.

I went to see Wednesday play Plymouth on a chilly winter night with Dan Gordon, the film-maker who wrote *A Quarter of Wednesday*, the twenty-five-year modern history of the club. He told me he'd sat in the same seat in the main stand for twenty-four years, since he'd first been brought along as a boy by his dad, their common support for the football club binding them together.

During the match I found it difficult to stop looking at the Leppings Lane end; knowing what happened, what the families have been through since, how much is still unresolved. It is surreal to see the ground given over wholly to football's soap opera, the disaster forgotten here. Still, absorbed in their football mire, the Wednesday fans seem a friendly bunch, except for the replica Burberry brigade of young thugs, gesturing away at the Plymouth fans, 2,000 of them, who have travelled midweek to sit in the upper level of the Leppings Lane end. The lower tier, where the ninety-six died, is empty.

Plymouth, well-drilled under their manager Paul Sturrock, playing nice, flowing football, danced round Wednesday and were 1-0 up at half-time. A few people behind us shouted some futile observations about the defence, had the odd go at Chris Turner, which didn't go down well. A guy, about fifty-five, sitting in front of Dan Gordon, leaned back in his seat with an hour gone, arms folded, shook his head and sighed: 'It's what you call shite, isn't it?'

Wednesday had a late rally and scored, but Plymouth, on their way up, strolled away with the match, then wandered over afterwards, fists up, to salute their fans, who made tremendous noise. We drifted out, everybody with his own take on how and where it all went wrong. You don't want to mention Richards' name at Sheffield Wednesday. Outside, John Hemmingham smiled wistfully:

'You get used to losing,' he said. 'It was nice to win the odd match but I recognise this old sinking feeling.'

We went round to the back of the Kop. He wanted to show me where the new floor is going, and why the toilets and kiosk were so badly needed. The Kop is a huge stand. You can see, once Hillsborough is empty, why it was considered one of the country's best; it has an old-style grandeur, scale and integrity. Going on appearances, not on the safety certificate, you can understand why the FA was continually superficially impressed. When, with Richards as the chairman, Wednesday put the seats in the Kop, which he has claimed as one of his proudest achievements, they simply reconfigured the terracing and fixed seats to them, rather than knocking the stand down and rebuilding, as other clubs did. It was a bit of a poor job, leaving the old banking there, still with tree stumps in the ground, leaving no room at the back for new facilities for 11,200 fans, the capacity of the Kop. There is a single hatch serving refreshments. Just one.

'You can't get any food,' Hemmingham grimaced.

Then we went to see the toilet which serves the crowd. It really was a step back in time: an old, small, brick square, weakly lit, a drain at the bottom, which, Hemmingham assured me, runneth over on match days. Rivers of piss; if you miss them, come to Hillsborough before the fans raise the money themselves to build some twentieth-century toilets, or Ken Bates arrives with his booty from selling out to Abramovich and takes over the club for one last ego trip. That smell, the deep, acrid stench of generations, etched into the walls, a dark, dank humiliation for the paying people who need to take a leak while watching their debt-ridden club get hammered again. It's all here, the legacy of the man who is now the chairman of the Premier League, a main board director of the FA, the chairman of the Football Foundation, football's most senior administrator, seeped into this dripping Sheffield pisser, the modern day Romance of the Wednesday.

CHAPTER 7

Six Weeks of Madness

Sunday morning, 11 May 2003, Bradford city centre. Wondrous, intricate stone architecture, monuments to the Victorian pomp of Bradford's wool industry, jostling with concrete hulks from more recent, make-do-and-mend decades. A small huddle, perhaps fifty souls, is gathered in the gusty main square, the odd girl wearing a claret and amber scarf, one or two men in replica shirts. At eleven o'clock there is silence. The Town Hall clock chimes out – tinnily it might be said – a just-recognisable version of 'Abide With Me'. When it's over, it clangs out 'You'll Never Walk Alone'. Everybody is solemn, thoughtful. One or two of the women cry, hug each other. There are some prayers. On the fringes of the group are some footballers: David Wetherall, Bradford City's current captain, and the recognisable ginger hair of the club's former star, Stuart McCall. The prayers over, people walk slowly over to a small memorial and lay flowers. Then everybody is invited into the Town Hall for tea.

Largely unnoticed by the nation, they have been performing this annual service for eighteen years. The fire at Bradford City's Valley Parade ground in May 1985 is somehow football's less-remembered disaster, although it was truly horrific: fifty-six people died when the wooden main stand caught fire during the final game, against Lincoln City, of the 1984–5 season. Bradford were the Third Division champions; before the game they were presented with the trophy, and the manager, Trevor Cherry, was named the division's Manager of the Year. The Deputy Lord Mayor of Bradford was there with civic dignitaries from Bradford's twin towns in Germany and Belgium, 11,000 people were in a bumper crowd, celebrating a sparkling side, including the young McCall, which had won promotion for Bradford in tremendous style. Just two years earlier, in 1983, the club had gone bust, was in receivership and, like so many other Football League clubs in the 1980s, narrowly avoided going into liquidation and folding completely.

Reading the official report into the disaster, by Mr Justice Oliver Popplewell, makes you think it should be seared into the consciousness of every football person in the land. If at Hillsborough, four years later, police mismanagement exposed Sheffield Wednesday's and the game's ramshackle approach to the safety of supporters, the Bradford fire can be said to have high-lighted football's dysfunctional priorities even more starkly. The cause of the disaster was not in dispute, and as Popplewell itemised it the fire unfolded with horrible inevitability. There were, no surprises here, breaches of the Green Guide. Bradford was not a senior ground designated by law to require a safety certificate, but Popplewell said that the Green Guide had strong persuasive force as a set of standards and should have been followed. At Valley Parade the main stand was wooden and had hardly been changed since it was built in 1908. Because of the natural slope of the hill on which Valley Parade stands, there was a void beneath the stand's wooden floor and the ground. Such a void was explic-itly stated in the Green Guide, at paragraph 8.11, to be a fire risk, because litter could catch fire from a chucked fag end above. Every stand, the guide also said, should have sufficient exits to allow for 'orderly evacuation' in 2.5 minutes if the stand was a fire risk.

At Bradford there were gaps between the floorboards of the stand and litter had indeed built up in the void. After the fire, the senior police officer picking over the charred site found litter which had been there for years, including a copy of the *Bradford*

Telegraph and Argus from Monday 4 November 1968 and an empty packet of peanuts costing six old pennies – decimalisation was introduced in 1971, fourteen years before the fire. Popplewell concluded that the fire started 'due to the accidental lighting of debris below the floorboards'.

The fire engulfed the stand within five minutes. Evacuation took substantially longer than 2.5 minutes, and, even then, many people escaping behind the stand were trapped, because several exits to the street were boarded up or padlocked. Some managed to force doors open and get out. Others did not. More than half of the fifty-six people who died were over seventy or under twenty; all were Bradford City supporters except for two, Bill Stacey and Jim West, who were Lincoln fans. At Lincoln's Sincil Bank ground, a stand, the Stacey West, is named after them.

'Had the Green Guide been complied with,' the Popplewell Report said, 'this tragedy would not have occurred.'

But the neglect of the ground's safety, exposed by the disaster, was worse even than that. The potential fire risk, of litter under the floorboards of the old, homely wooden stand, was not just a breach of the Green Guide but had actually been specifically drawn to the club's attention in writing, by the Health & Safety Executive, twice, in 1981, and by the county council in 1984, just a year before the fire. Both wrote officially to the club asking it to remedy the fire risk and stressing that evacuation had to be achievable within 2.5 minutes. Neither body received a reply from the club. Bradford had, however, arranged to meet the county council to talk about future safety requirements, because promotion to the Second Division would mean that the ground was to become designated and require a safety certificate. The meeting was scheduled for the Wednesday after the disaster. It was a bitter coincidence that the club had made an application for a grant, and work was going to start to replace the main stand's timber flooring with concrete – the Monday after the match.

Popplewell described the ragged circumstances Bradford City

were in at the time: 'The financial position of the club was not substantially different from a number of others who lurk in the depths of the Third and Fourth Division. The gates of these clubs are insufficient generally to provide adequate financial stability. Thus, directors and chairmen, often local businessmen themselves, devote a substantial amount of their own money in order to keep their football clubs afloat. Football at this level is run on a shoestring.'

Bradford had limped along desperately trying to maintain their Football League status for years, and had finally gone into receivership in 1983 after they failed to pay £10,000 for Trevor Cherry whom they signed as a player from Leeds, their overbearing West Yorkshire rivals. Leeds grew fed up with waiting for the money and issued a winding-up petition. Bradford owed £400,000 in total and looked a suitable case to go out of business and the League. Popplewell recorded that the policy of the League at the time, following its president, Notts County chairman Jack Dunnett's notion of 'natural wastage', was that the League should reduce from ninety-two clubs to eighty. Bradford's new chairman, Stafford Heginbotham, a local businessman, long-term Bradford fan and former director, saved the club by putting together financial proposals with just hours to spare, and he had to work hard to persuade the League to let Bradford continue. Football's insolvency rules were slightly different then; indeed, they were tightened up to include paying 'football creditors' in full after the series of club insolvencies in the 1980s. At the time, Bradford were still made to pay more than ordinary companies would have to when they go bust: they had to meet their debts to the Football League in full, and to the bank, and pay 60 per cent of what the creditors were owed. They were also making a continuing loss on their operations of £100,000 a season. In this struggle, the main effort of the club was to find the money to get a team out, and safety, or any work on the ground, suffered as a result: 'A very low priority was given to additional expenditure,' Popplewell said.

The letters from the Health & Safety Executive and county council failed to reach Heginbotham by a series of mishaps; the second one, from the county council, was opened by the receiver, passed on to the club secretary, who took it into a board meeting stapled underneath another letter. The vice-chairman, Jack Tordoff, did, however, see the letter. It could hardly have been clearer, saying, as point 1 (b): 'The timber construction [of the main stand] is a fire hazard and in particular there is a build-up of combustible materials in the voids beneath the seats. A carelessly discarded cigarette could give rise to a fire risk.'

Tordoff misunderstood and thought the letter referred to rubbish on the surface of the stand, not underneath, and asked for the area above to be swept. Heginbotham told Popplewell that even if he had seen the letter he still would not have done anything about it because he regarded it as applicable to more senior clubs, designated to require a safety certificate. It would also, he said, have necessitated almost dismantling the stand, a major job: 'the cost would have been considerable'.

This was not only extraordinary evidence to give to an inquiry after fifty-six people had died following a fire caused by that identified fire hazard, but the club's financial straits have to be put rather more seriously into context. Popplewell took Heginbotham at his word, that lower division football was run on a shoestring and was a struggle. He didn't question whether it had to be this way. In fact, Bradford's accounts for 1984–5, a successful, winning season from a bright young side, show that gate receipts, season tickets and the share of the League's TV and other sponsorship deals added up to a pretty good income of £621,000 – £1.21m in today's terms. Then, as now, professional football clubs drew on great loyalty from fans, who paid good money for their support. Bradford made a small loss that season, £13,600 (£26,250 today). But that was not because they spent money on their ground or other equipment – only £4,000 (£7,800 today) was spent in the year. No, nearly 70 per cent of the club's income, £419,000 (£817,050 in today's terms) was spent on wages. Popplewell was gentler on the club than he might have been, saying it was not his aim to apportion blame for the disaster, although he did say that financial difficulties were no excuse for the disaster, because 'the public are entitled to expect that sports grounds will be reasonably safe'. He might, however, have pointed out in very plain terms that here was a club turning over £621,000 a year, whose chairman was still, even after people had died, saying he would not have sanctioned expenditure to remove the fire hazard which killed them, but who had spent £419,000 on paying players to form a team which would win promotion. Bradford's was a mostly young side, featuring McCall, John Hendrie and Peter Jackson, which would not be regarded as extravagant, but clearly these successful players had to be relatively well paid to stay at Bradford. The money, in other words, was there to make the ground safe but the club chose not to spend it in that way, but on the players' wages, to chase the football dream. They would, no doubt, argue that all clubs were spending at that level, so they had to as well if they wanted to compete or stay in that division. And no doubt this was true, that all the clubs were bleating about financial difficulties, not because they had no money but because they were spending too much of it in players' wages while ignoring the most fundamental housekeeping. Professional football's priorities.

Heginbotham – regarded by fans as a genuine enthusiast for the club and decent man who went to all the victims' funerals – made a statement to the inquiry in which he said he accepted responsibility: 'I am prepared to say that there are a number of things we all wish had been done or had been thought of prior to this terrible tragedy.' But he never specified which ones.

Popplewell concluded his report by paying tribute to the 'enormous heroism' shown by many Bradford people, from all walks of life, who played their part in saving lives. All the emergency services, particularly the fire brigade, were praised for their response. There had also been ten members of St John Ambulance at the match, expecting, no doubt, to deal with the odd sprained ankle or funny turn, but they ended up administering first aid in an inferno. St John is a voluntary, charitable service which has been attending to the sick and injured at major events for decades, and football clubs make a donation to meet the cost of equipment and expenses. Popplewell said they 'undoubtedly did an enormously valuable service attending to those injured . . . there can be no doubt that, but for their help, the casualty rate would have been higher'. St John Ambulance did not give oral evidence but sent in a written submission to the inquiry. They complained that adequate first aid equipment was rarely provided by the clubs, and also: 'There was a feeling that the members did not receive proper recognition at football matches, nor was appropriate recompense paid to the St John Ambulance.'

Perhaps the Bradford fire has never received the attention it deserved because this was a lower division club and the TV coverage was mercifully limited. Heysel came just eighteen days later, live on television across Europe featuring two of the Continent's biggest clubs. It is amazing to think how little was done immediately after Bradford to make the grounds safe and ensure they complied with the Green Guide, and that football was allowed to bungle on into Hillsborough four years later. Perhaps it is not as well remembered nationally because, unlike Hillsborough, there was no real dispute over the cause, no bitter fallout from the families, no continuing campaign for the culpable people to take responsibility. The victims were killed at their home ground because of the deficiencies of the club they supported, and it is a phenomenon of the passionate loyalty inspired by football clubs that many of the families appear to have regarded the fire as a tragic accident and reacted emotionally not by criticising the club for its neglect but by rallying round it.

'The supporters really came together after the disaster,' Dave Pendleton, a lifelong supporter who organised the club's centenary exhibition in 2003, told me. 'City are a small club really, and most people, if they hadn't lost a loved one themselves, knew somebody who had.' One of Pendleton's young neighbours, a boy with learning disabilities, died in the fire – his parents had bought him a ticket for the main stand as a treat.

'The relationship between the club and the fans became indivisible,' he said. 'It became one community, a group of people who had been through the worst imaginable horror, but wanted to support the club even more as something positive, an affirmation of life carrying on.'

Stuart McCall's father was badly burned in the fire, and McCall was greatly moved, as were all the players. He visited his father daily on his hospital ward and one day took the Third Division championship trophy in:

'I was amazed that the sight of this piece of silverware could lift so many people who had gone through so much,' McCall wrote in his autobiography, *The Real McCall*. 'They had all suffered and yet, apart from the strength of their families, what kept them going was their love for Bradford City. The thought of seeing us play in the Second Division gave them that extra target for recovery. There were powerful emotions at the time, quite astounding. Football then should have been the furthest thing from their minds, yet it was such a big part of them.'

More than a football club, in this deeply affected way, Bradford soldiered on. They played their home games at Leeds, Huddersfield and eventually Odsal Stadium in Bradford before Valley Parade was rebuilt and reopened on 14 December 1986 – by Oliver Popplewell himself. A couple of games in, Trevor Cherry was sacked, an experience which put him off management for good. Bradford spent most of 1987–8 in the top three of the Second Division, and McCall wrote that a couple of shrewd late signings would have seen them promoted to the First Division, a glorious revival. But the club, now led by Tordoff after Heginbotham had a heart attack following a club tour in Magaluf in June 1987, did not sign players, and Bradford ended up losing in the play-offs to Middlesbrough. The team was broken up, McCall getting his major, £875,000, move to Everton, Hendrie leaving for Newcastle. Two years later they were back in the Third Division, without much gleam of footballing promise.

Tordoff, who built up the JCT 600 car dealership, which still sponsors the club, eventually sold Bradford to another local businessman, Dave Simpson, but under him the club floundered and began to run up large debts again. In January 1994, Simpson did a deal with Geoffrey Richmond, the chairman and owner of Scarborough Football Club. Richmond was a Leeds boy who had left school in the late sixties and started off selling children's encyclopaedias door-to-door. He proved himself good at making money and, via car bulbs, then printing and producing bumper and window stickers, in 1983 he bought the Ronson lighter business, which had gone into administrative receivership, for £200,000, running it from an industrial estate in North Shields, Tyne and Wear. He fancied getting involved in football, and in 1987 he bought a fairly local club, Scarborough, who had won the Conference, becoming the first club to be automatically promoted to the Football League, but were – wait for it – in financial trouble. Richmond did well with Scarborough. He told me they kept it 'tight', he didn't spend big money, they sold players every year to balance the books, for example Craig Short, who went to Notts County for £100,000 in the summer of 1989. That season they had reached the Fourth Division play-offs, losing to Orient. Richmond had brought them some respectability, loved the involvement, and although Scarborough fans never warmed to him because they regarded him as an outsider, he passed the club on solvent, in the Football League, and with money in the bank.

In January 1994, Richmond sold Ronson for £10m to Hoskyns Brewery, a £7m gain on his initial investment and the money he'd put into building it up. With Bradford City, closer to his Leeds home, falling into serious trouble under Simpson, Richmond offered to take over. The Football League's rules, introduced after

Robert Maxwell's ownership of Derby and Oxford in the eighties, forbade one person from owning substantial stakes in two clubs. So Richmond did him a swap: he gave Simpson Scarborough and Simpson gave Richmond Bradford. It was Yorkshire businessmen's version of swapping football stickers in the playground.

Richmond arrived at Valley Parade to find the club, then in the Second Division (Third in pre-breakaway terms), £2.3m in debt, facing twenty-seven writs from disgruntled creditors and threats of winding-up petitions. He put in £2.3m as a loan, saying that when the club was in a position to repay him, it would. Then he applied all his skills as a grafter and a salesman to drag Bradford up. He told the fans – there were, on average 6,500 at each home match – they would be in the Premier League within five years. A big guy in an open-necked shirt who drove a convertible Bentley Azure but liked his fags and had come up the hard way, Richmond is a truly gifted talker and the fans, finding him accessible and seeing great progress, took to him. In 1996, two years after he arrived, Bradford, managed by Chris Kamara, won the Second Division play-offs, beating Notts County 2-0 at Wembley, a game to which the club took 30,000 supporters. By the following year, Richmond had turned the club round commercially: gates were up, they were making a profit and he had paid himself his loans back.

Such was football fever in the City of London that the scruffy bantams of Bradford even considered floating. Richmond eventually found one of Bradford's most successful businessmen, David Rhodes, a Leeds University electronics professor whose company, Filtronics, makes telecommunications equipment, and his son, Julian, both of them Bradford fans, to invest. They bought 49 per cent of the club's shares for £3m in 1997. Richmond and his son, David, kept hold of 49 per cent.

Richmond's ambition swelled: 'I said to the professor: look, this First Division is hardly the greatest league in the world. With a bit of investment, we could get promotion. We decided to take out a loan, he put up the security, I put up a guarantee. We borrowed £5m from Singer & Friedlander and went to the manager Paul Jewell, and said: "Right, you've got £5m to spend." He was completely astonished. The best signing he made with that money was Lee Mills, from Port Vale for £1m, who scored bag-fulls that season.'

They then borrowed money to begin a grand redevelopment of Valley Parade, first a £2.5m all-seating of the Kop, then a £6.5m mortgage for a new main stand, a monster, which dominates the landscape up on its hill in Manningham. Jewell, a Bradford player since 1988, had made a winning first signing: Stuart McCall. Bradford finished thirteenth in 1997–8, mounted a genuine challenge the following season and surprised everybody by maintaining it, with Jewell a shrewd tactician, McCall the midfield general and Richmond the chainsmoking showman in the boardroom with the big vision and the common touch. On Sunday 9 May 1999, they went to Molineux and beat Wolves 3-2, joyfully clutching their place as the most romantic, improbable new members of the moneyed Premier League since Barnsley, who had popped up for their one year of life at the top in 1997–8.

Their attitude, Richmond said, was to enjoy the ride, probably expect to be relegated and not bust the bank to stay up. The only major signing was the centre half David Wetherall, £1.4m from Leeds. They were everybody's second favourite team, strapped together on the cheap but with some clever senior pros: McCall, Peter Beagrie, Wetherall, Dean Windass. Bradford scrapped around the relegation zone all season until, at home to Liverpool on the last day of the season, Wetherall headed them in front after thirteen minutes and they clung on, eye-poppingly, to sneak into seventeenth place and survive.

The joy about the place was, as they say, unconfined. It was the summer of 2000. Bradford were in the Premier League for the second successive season. The fans were disbelieving, Richmond a hero. He was honoured for his achievements, having transformed the club completely, in all its activities, bringing one positive beacon to a city wracked with poverty and deprivation, which would suffer awful riots the following year. In July 2000, Richmond was given an honorary degree, a doctor of letters, by the University of Bradford. The citation, a speech which must have been almost unbearably embarrassing to have to sit through, held back no droplet of praise, blessing Richmond, among other things, as 'a breath of fresh air', 'unique among chairmen', saying he had achieved 'an astonishing turnaround'. Which, to be fair, was true. In an extremely idle moment, you can still click on to the website at www.bradford.ac.uk/admin/recruitment/annrept/2001/honours2.htm and see Geoffrey Richmond looking rosy, happy and utterly incongruous, wrapped and topped in a gown and mortar board. Perhaps, for a guy who left school after one year of the sixth form, it was this sort of acclaim which went to his head.

He says not. He told me he simply got carried away, thinking that, just as they had gambled a little on promotion and succeeded, if they pushed the boat out, they could establish the club in the Premier League. 'We saw the bright lights. Looking back, staying up was the worst thing which could have happened to the club. Had we gone down, I'd still be a hero in Bradford; they'd have put up a statue to me.' He had built his football clubs by keeping the finances tight and marketing flamboyantly, but in July 2000 he lost it. Jewell left abruptly, a departure never fully explained, replaced by his former assistant Chris Hutchings. Bradford were suddenly spenders: David Hopkin, the Scottish midfielder, was signed from Leeds for £2.5m, a club record; Ashley Ward, whose goals had helped Barnsley up in 1997, arrived from Blackburn, bought for £1.5m. Dan Petrescu, thirty-two by then, was an exotic sort for Valley Parade, £1m from Chelsea, but not as glamorous as Benito Carbone, who arrived in Bradford in early August. He was a free agent, having spent a year at Aston Villa, but although Bradford paid no fee for him Richmond gave him a four-year contract and agreed to pay proper, in-with-the-big-boys, Premiership wages: £40,000 per week.

It does an injustice to the misery of what has happened since to say that the high spending didn't work. As Julian Rhodes told me: 'If only we had carried on what we were doing, made Valley Parade a difficult place for away teams to come, scrapped for points away, we might have survived. Certainly, going down would not have been so catastrophic. Instead, we suddenly acted like we were Man United.'

Stocked with players used to more rarefied football existences than West Yorkshire relegation battles, as early as November 2000 Bradford were obviously going down. Terrified of staggering into the barren fields of the Football League with Premiership-sized commitments on players' wages, Richmond hired Jim Jefferies from Hearts as the manager with a hatchet to wield. They managed to shuffle Petrescu off to Southampton in January 2001 and Hopkin to Crystal Palace at a £1m loss in March. By then they'd had it; they won just five games all season and finished bottom of the Premier League with twenty-six points.

Geoffrey Richmond did not immediately endear himself to his new colleagues among the seventy-two clubs in the Football League. He started a row almost as soon as he arrived, joining with a couple of other clubs to threaten legal action against the League, which had, authorised by the clubs, distributed £300,000 to each club in advance when the ITV Digital deal was signed the season before. Bradford didn't get it, because they had been in the Premier League at the time. The League, led by David Burns, their irrepressibly enthusiastic chief executive who had arrived from running cruises and timeshares for the pile-it-high holiday company Airtours, saw them off. Richmond backed down: 'I wasn't making myself very popular,' he told me.

Richmond won no more friends when, in November 2001, he was revealed as one of the chief plotters, along with Bryan Richardson, the Coventry chairman, angling to form the so-called 'Phoenix League', a desperate breakaway plan by the bigger or more self-deluding First Division clubs to form a second division of the Premier League. Dave Richards, now, of course, the Premier League chairman and the man to contact if you wanted a deal discussing, had, it was confirmed, a couple of conversations with the plotters. The story destabilised the League and ruptured the First Division's relations with the other two divisions, and never had a chance of coming off. The problem with a First Division breakaway is that it requires the Premier League to invite the First Division clubs to join them; since breaking away from the old Second Division in 1992, however, the top clubs have shown no sign of wanting to reverse the process.

In May 2002, Bradford having finished fifteenth in the First Division, Richmond became the representative for another idea to boost the First Division clubs' earning power – inviting Rangers and Celtic to join the League. That one didn't run either. Then, after the collapse of ITV Digital, there was a strange episode – a presentation to all the clubs by an insolvency accountant, David Buchler, at a meeting in the Tara Hotel in Kensington on 3 May. Buchler's proposal was for a temporary suspension of the requirement in the League's insolvency policy that all 'football creditors', most substantially the players with their wages, had to be paid in full. The clubs, Buchler proposed, could then do a 'mass administration': make all their players redundant, agree not to poach from each other then rehire the players at significantly reduced terms.

Some clubs, overspent and in the mire, did think this might be something to grasp at. Others, the majority, whose chairmen had prided themselves on having run their clubs responsibly, on being able to handle the ITV Digital blow somehow, dismissed it as a bizarre, ugly interlude, and asked to get on with the meeting. Alan Sykes apparently stood up immediately and tore into it, saying it was utterly dishonourable even to suggest that the Football League clubs should agree collectively to shaft everybody. Geoffrey Richmond was conspicuously keen on the idea: 'Certainly,' he told me, 'it had my very strong support.'

It did not take long for the other clubs to understand why. Just thirteen days later Richmond was forced into the indignity of putting Bradford into administration. It was a major collapse; Bradford, the club everybody had loved, owed £36m, had a wage bill they couldn't afford on First Division income and were massively, appallingly insolvent. They had hoped Carbone would move to Middlesbrough but he had come back from a loan period leaving Bradford still liable for his wages. David Buchler's firm, Kroll, were appointed administrators.

They decided to take on the League's insolvency policy, which many accountants were arguing was illegal because it ranks footballers and clubs above the Inland Revenue and other creditors, contrary to the spirit of insolvency law. Seven administrative staff and the thirty-two employees in the shops Richmond had opened in Dewsbury and Wakefield were sacked immediately and they had no comeback. But Kroll also tried to terminate the contracts of nineteen players, including Wetherall, McCall, Carbone and Ward – the whole first team.

There was an outcry from the PFA, stung by this challenge to its members' hard-won security. However, the League held firm to its policy, as it did throughout the subsequent collapse of many clubs. The League believes that clubs which overstretch themselves have to suffer the consequences, otherwise, to take the logic to its extreme, Rotherham could sign Zidane, Ronaldo and Beckham, win everything but not pay the players, then just lay the team off and continue. David Burns wrote to all clubs, saying Bradford would be kicked out of the League if they did not pay their players and other football creditors in full.

It was all a humiliation for Geoffrey Richmond, the worst experience of his thirty years in business, as he told the clubs at a meeting on 7 June, giving what one witness described to me as a 'tear-jerker' of a twenty-minute speech. Most lasting of Richmond's soul-baring *bon mots* was that the summer of 2000, when the expensive players were signed, was his 'six weeks of madness'.

Bradford's administrators' report, published by Kroll in July

2002, set out the gory consequences. Carbone was in there, sure enough, on £40,000 per week, and therefore owed, for the contract due to run until June 2004, £3.5m. The club had also bought him a house in Leeds with seven bedrooms and five en suite bathrooms.

There was something about the five en suite bathrooms which got me, seemed to sum up the schlock of football's waste of its windfall. Whenever I thought of areas of football – the grass roots, schools, community programmes – which could really do with some money, I used to think of Beni Carbone with his £40,000 a week and five bathrooms en suite. Ashley Ward was owed £1,276,000, Wetherall £734,000, and so on and so on.

The march to glory had been done on tick. Everything was rented: the floodlights, furniture, kitchen fittings, CCTV, the shop tills, everything. To raise cash, some players had been sold to and leased back from REFF, the same Guernsey-based company with whom Leeds had done similar hire purchase deals. At Leeds, when the dream died and Trevor Birch, an insolvency practitioner, moved from Chelsea as the chief executive to try to sort out the mess, REFF were owed £22m. At Bradford they were owed £7.3m. Richmond argues with justification that the club's plight was greatly worsened by the collapse of the transfer market, meaning they could not offload the players, and that the income gap between the two leagues makes relegation disastrous, but he also admits it was madness for a club like Bradford to take on so gross a wage bill. The club's £5m 'parachute payment' was mortgaged to a finance company, GE Capital. The ground, symbol of Richmond's ambition, was mortgaged to another, Lombard, owed £6.5m. Bradford also had a £4.6m overdraft with HSBC Bank and owed the Inland Revenue £919,000. There was a long list of other smaller creditors.

The document contained some uncomfortable revelations for Richmond. In 1999 and 2000, the Premier League years, Bradford City had paid Bradford City Holdings, which owned the football club, large amounts of money described as 'management fees'. The holding company had then paid these out in dividends to the shareholders, the Richmond and Rhodes families, personally. In total, between April 1999 and 25 August 2000, they had been paid £8.125m, plus VAT, in dividends. In both years, the payments pushed the club from making a small profit into losses close to £3m. The largest payment, £3,750,000, had been made just after the six weeks of madness, when the club was borrowing prodigiously. In October 2001, after Bradford had been relegated and with its financial position perilous, Geoffrey Richmond had also been paid a consultancy fee of £250,000. The administrators concluded that the dividends were 'reasonable' because Bradford had been in the Premier League at the time, and the fee was justified because Richmond had never previously taken a salary. He says himself: 'We'd taken significant risks guaranteeing debts and making investments, and I worked there full-time. When we were promoted to the Premier League, then when we survived, that was mine and the professor's reward.'

Dave Pendleton was, along with many other fans, taken aback: 'I'm realistic enough to realise that shareholders can be entitled to a reward for money invested. But to learn that money had been taken out on that scale at that time felt to us absolutely disgraceful.'

The administrator's report lists the ordinary creditors: players' agents, the local newsagent, the Leeds infirmary, credit card companies, Kirklees Metropolitan Council, which was owed £27,616; signwriters, food suppliers, Trimilin UK, a physiotherapy equipment supplier, owed £40,463; Leeds Metropolitan University, Holme Valley Fire Protection, £625.73 unpaid . . . on and on, thirty-four pages of a football club's bare necessities, £1,421,613.68 in total. One of these bad debts leaps out, encapsulating the financial mismanagement of the game. Just above the £9 owed to Sheikh's News: St John Ambulance, owed £5,475.50. Richmond, in over his head in leases and wages and mortgages, had left St John Ambulance, at Bradford of all clubs, unpaid for the season. It was a shock, but it became routine. At every football club which collapsed into administration, St John Ambulance were found on the list of creditors. Bradford's was the highest until Wimbledon went into administration in May 2003, owing the charity £8,000. Darlington collapsed just before Christmas 2003. Their chairman, George Reynolds, had built the club – average gates around 3,000 – a brand new 27,000-seat stadium for £20m, naming it after himself, the George Reynolds Arena, as part of his vain, doomed promise to take that club, perennial lower division strugglers, into the Premier League within five years. They ended up in administration, battling to survive in the Third Division. Among the club's vast debts was a new record, £9,040, owed to St John Ambulance. Altogether, the charity was left around £35,000 out of pocket by bust football clubs, and mostly had to settle for 10p in the pound.

At Bradford, much of the club's borrowings, £13.7m, had been guaranteed personally by Geoffrey Richmond and David Rhodes. This meant that if Bradford City went bust, or couldn't find the money to pay its creditors, these banks and companies could call on Richmond and Rhodes personally, jointly, to pay up. The Rhodes family's wealth was mostly tied up in the share price of their company, Filtronics; when it is high, they are multi-millionaires, but at the time City analysts were undergoing a 'correction' to their fevered overvaluation of dotcom and telecom companies and the Filtronics price was so low that the family were facing possible bankruptcy.

'We got together,' Julian Rhodes told me, 'and we said we wanted to save the club, because we're Bradford people and fans, and we would fight for the club until we were down to our last penny. But people could also look at our situation and say fairly that we were in so deep, in terms of our personal guarantees, that we had to keep the club going; or we could have gone bust.'

The threat of ruin seeped as far as the Rhodes family home, which Mrs Rhodes agreed to put up as security for a loan from the PFA. Of the dividend payments, Rhodes said: 'Yes, we took them, and we were glad to have them; we had put big money in and that was some reward. But we fully expected that if the club needed money again, we'd have to put it back in.'

And that was where they fell out with Richmond. Administration freezes a company's debts while the accountants look for a solution, but the administrator needs cash to keep the company going while he works on it. David Rhodes knew he would have to put money in, and assumed Richmond would too; they were already talking about a combined deal to bring the club out of administration. But Richmond told him: 'I am unable to.' David Rhodes put in £400,000 cash, money down the drain. Richmond wanted to carry on, proposing deals first where he would have a half share, then a third, of the club, without actually putting any money in himself: 'They would have my expertise,' he said. The Rhodes family eventually told him they didn't want him to be part of it if, having had so much out, he was not prepared to put any money back in to saving the club. Instead they did a deal with Gordon Gibb, the owner of the Flamingoland zoo and theme park in Malton, North Yorkshire, who had decided this was a good time to 'invest' in a football club. He paid £1.875m to HSBC, taking over Richmond's shares. Richmond walked away. His personal guarantees were indemnified, in effect taken over, by the Rhodes family. He had worked hard for eight years at Valley Parade, but he'd had £4.31m out of it in dividends and the consultancy fee, an average of nearly £540,000 a year. He argues that he had 'fourteen very successful years in football and just six weeks where it all went wrong'. True enough, but Bradford fans, rather than forever begrudging that rash of extravagance, resent Richmond more for leaving them in trouble, putting not a penny back in.

Julian Rhodes and Gibb put together a CVA settlement, agreeing to pay 'football creditors' – the players, mostly – in full: £8.8m. The tax and VAT were to be paid in full too, a requirement at the time, because they were 'preferential creditors' – over £1m. The 'unsecured creditors', suppliers, leasing companies, St John Ambulance, but also including the £7.4m outstanding to REFF, were to be paid 17.5 pence for every £1 owed. The creditors agreed to this, but that all added up to £3.26m to be paid in instalments by August 2005.

Bradford's new manager, Nicky Law, brought in because he had kept Chesterfield up through administration during a crisis there, had no budget to speak of. Several players left, but, as contracts have to be honoured in full, they were still being paid. Ashley Ward went to Sheffield United in August 2003, but Bradford still had to pay him, in batches, the full £880,000 left under this contract with them. Carbone had gone to Como, in Italy, a pleasant enough bolthole, with a settlement on his Bradford wad. The Leeds house was sold, with all its bedrooms and all its bathrooms, but there was a mortgage on the house so it realised no cash.

Gibb paid off part of Lombard's mortgage by having his family pension fund buy Valley Parade for £2.5m, then lease it back to the club for twenty-five years. The Rhodeses, though, were forced to keep putting money in. In 2003–4 the crowds dropped. The Premiership dream had died. There was no immense appetite in Bradford to watch Nicky Law's loan signings and kids chasing around to avoid relegation. In November 2003 he left and Bradford invested their survival hopes on old-stager Bryan Robson's desire to revive his own managerial career. The slump led Julian Rhodes, who was working full-time at the club, to call in John Dewhirst, an accountant who runs his own firm, Vincere, and also a lifelong fan. He found the club was still in a wretched state; it needed £2m more just to make it to the end of the season and they couldn't afford to keep paying the CVA payments on top of that.

'The company,' he wrote, 'is likely to become insolvent without a further injection of funds.'

The Filtronics shares were up again and the Rhodeses were prepared to throw in more money: £3m if the team survived, £5m if they sank to the Second Division, but they wanted to cut the old debts further before they did. Julian Rhodes tried to renegotiate the settlements with REFF and Lombard, and he wanted Gibb to sign his shares over to the Rhodeses, as they were having to put more millions in. Gibb, however, was so upset he resigned as the club's chairman in January 2004, and even went on the pitch before the home match against Crewe, telling fans he felt let down by the Rhodes family. David Rhodes issued a terse statement dismissing that and setting out the millions they had sunk into the club to keep it going. Julian Rhodes came painfully close to a new agreement with the creditors but the club missed a deadline and, at the end of February, Bradford were forced to go back into administration. Rhodes, through all this, remained engagingly chipper, although he had his moments of considering putting a stop to it all, which would have meant the club having to fold. He never wanted to do that, out of duty, but through all the financial juggling, you could sense the football dream still beating in his heart: 'You never know. One season in the Premiership, and we're in the big money, £25m. It's still possible.'

In mid-April, after a 3-2 home defeat to the bottom club, Wimbledon, who were already relegated, Bradford went down to the Second Division.

Meanwhile, Geoffrey Richmond's reason for being 'unable' to pay up when Bradford went bust had become publicly clear in a court case in May 2003, which he lost. The judgement runs to thirty-seven pages but can be summed up simply: he was sued by the Inland Revenue for £2.3m tax, unpaid from his original sale of Ronson back in 1994. Richmond had tried to 'roll over' the tax into another venture, but the judge rejected that scheme, saying the money was not going into a genuine new business but one devised solely to avoid paying the tax. He ruled that Richmond and another director had been 'in breach of their duties' and had 'failed to satisfy the court that they had acted . . . honestly and reasonably'. So he was hit with the bill for £2.3m, plus interest on the nine years it had been overdue.

Richmond, the hustler, dealmaker, was in trouble. Soon the number plate, GR1, which had decorated his Bentley Azure, was advertised for sale in the newspaper. None of these developments appear to have found their way onto the University of Bradford's website. However, neither could they keep the good man down. In late February 2004, the very week that Bradford went back into administration, Richmond admitted, after denying it for months, that he was indeed 'advising' the consortium considering taking over Leeds United, and his son David was involved as a possible investor. Leeds had collapsed by then, and were in a series of 'standstill' agreements with their major creditors, the bondholders and REFF, owed £82m combined, as the chief executive, Trevor Birch, sought a solution. Various consortia came to look at the mess, which included £24m of other debts and the huge wage bill on contracts signed by Peter Ridsdale in his time, and none would touch it. But at the end of March, Richmond's consortium, including his son and a couple of minor Leeds property developers, fronted by a local insolvency accountant, Gerald Krasner, decided they could see a way through. They cobbled together £5m, two of them remortgaging their own houses, then borrowed a further £15m via the former Watford owner and property developer Jack Petchey. The bondholders and REFF accepted that £15m as the best they would get.

Richmond, battling to rehabilitate his reputation at this huge football club in the glare of the world's media, could not own shares because of his liabilities to the Inland Revenue, nor, it seemed, could he be paid a salary. David Richmond – who, proportionately, had been paid £1.3m of the dividends at Bradford – swiftly became a full-time director at Elland Road. Soon, the consortium elaborated on their plan: they were going to raise money by selling Elland Road and renting it back, which would bring them a lump sum of, Richmond hoped, over £15m, enough to pay back Petchey. Then they announced a scheme to reap cash today by selling twenty-year season tickets to 2,000 supporters for effectively the cost of ten years, hoping to raise around £8m up front. These schemes do not have a happy history at desperate clubs; Richmond himself had sold 1,000 twenty-five-year season tickets at Bradford a couple of years before the club went into administration. When it went bust, the club did not even have to honour them in its CVA – the fans were mere unsecured creditors – but Julian Rhodes decided they had to, so for the next twenty-two years a hard core of Bradford's most loyal fans will be coming to matches without providing the club with income, the money they originally paid lost when the club went into administration. At Huddersfield Town, four-year season tickets were sold to fans, but after the club went into administration they were not honoured in full. Apart from that risk to the fans, here again is a form of gambling on the future, getting money in from years ahead to deal with today's debts, borrowing from here, borrowing from there, selling the ground, leasing it back, finding cash now, all for the pot of gold just over the hill. Richmond, smoking fiercely in his Elland Road office, told me: 'In business terms, this is an extraordinary deal, because if all goes well, the consortium will have bought a massive Premiership club for just £5m. They fully hope to get a significant return.' Many before them have come into football with similar hopes.

With Leeds shaken roughly from their dream, and the fans in ferment over the new owners' plans and Geoffrey Richmond's involvement, in mid-April the club abruptly released a statement saying Richmond had left 'for personal and health reasons'. It took just a few days for the extent of his difficulties to be clarified: on Monday 26 April at Leeds County Court, Richmond was made bankrupt. He had been chased by the Inland Revenue for payment of the £2.3m bill, to which, with interest, another £1m had been added. For a man who had so thrived on the action and the glory, it was a spectacular, public fall. A couple of weeks later, Leeds fell too, to the First Division.

At Bradford, feelings about Richmond were mixed, at least until he became involved with Leeds, the enemy. To the fans, this was the ultimate insult when Bradford were so deeply back in trouble. But some will always be grateful to him for the glimpse of the high life, beating Newcastle, Arsenal and Liverpool at Valley Parade, if only for one decent season, even at such huge cost. Dave Pendleton, organising the well-attended 2003 Centenary Exhibition at Bradford's Industrial Museum, reflected that it was quite appropriate that the club should be fighting for its life in that landmark year. He did feel Richmond had plenty to answer for: 'Geoffrey had talent and ambition and he did a lot for the club, but people here have been through a great deal personally and emotionally for Bradford City. Richmond, in overreaching himself, damaged the club, and so people felt he was violating something very personal and precious to them.'

Pendleton, researching the club's past, had found they had faced similar crises three times before, in the 1930s, the 1960s and then in 1983. The search for money was at the heart of the club from its beginnings; it was a rugby league club originally and only switched to football in 1903 because that code was going to be more popular, attract more supporters and so be more lucrative. An excellent book on this history, by the academic A. J. Arnold, is entitled *A Game That Would Pay*. For those who think football has become a cynically commercial business only in recent years, it is enlightening to learn that Bradford were invited to join the Football League's Second Division immediately, before they even had a team to kick a football, because the League wanted a club in West Yorkshire to establish football in rugby league territory.

Throughout their history, as in 2000, they made money from their fans, but, particularly after the players' maximum wage was abolished, in the sixties, in 1983 and under Geoffrey Richmond, they fell into trouble because they spent too much of it on players rather than look after the basic finances of the club. That is it: professional football's disease. The consequence in 1985 was horrific: fifty-six people dead. Since Hillsborough, the Government has forced the clubs by law to keep their grounds safe, so now, partly encouraged by football's very structure, which offers huge money to reward the sporting glories at the top, when clubs gamble recklessly the fallout is financial wreckage, unpaid bills and a needlessly shaky future. It's madness.

CHAPTER 8

The Oldest Professional Club
in the World

Notts County: hmm, what do we know about them? Well, they were founder members of the Football League in 1888, but in all the time since have won only one trophy, the FA Cup, and that was over 100 years ago. Oh – and the Anglo-Italian Cup, that famous midweek bad idea, in 1995. There is that nugget of their story, the Italian connection, made through Nottingham and Turin's links in the lace industry, which led in the 1900s to a Turin football club ditching their pink strip and taking on Notts' black and white stripes. But that story only puts into stark relief the gulf in achievement since between Notts County and their Italian cousins, who were called Juventus. So what else? OK, yes, there is that little known fact, which I can now exclusively reveal in these pages: Notts County are the oldest professional football club in the world. Bet you didn't know that.

Notts County's venerable age may be learned in the reception class of football's school of history, but it is, when you think about it, some record to hold. Official Notts historians have the date the club formed as a meeting at the city's George Hotel in 1864, although some have put it two years earlier. Nottingham, like Sheffield, was an early cradle for the great new sport and representative sides from the two cities played each other at the dawn of organised football. Notts' thunderously average playing record is somehow fitting; that the world's oldest club should be a tale of dogged survival, rather than unalloyed triumph, which decorates only the fewest clubs – now needing outsized megastores or bandit capitalists for owners to have a chance. At Notts County, 140 years has seen many thousands of games, crowds of players, generations of supporters taken along and enraptured for life; effort, sweat, hopes, plenty of disappointments, and barely a trophy in sight. The history even records that Notts were lucky to be invited to be one of the League's twelve founder members in the first place, having in 1888 just had an awful season in which, according to *Athletic News*, they only just avoided 'an ignominious collapse'. Seeped into Meadow Lane's walls, therefore, is experience, knowledge of how they have made it this far. It is now a modern, neat, all-seater stadium, too grand really for the 4,500 faithful who congregate there regularly, but it has seen a thing or two about how the old game works.

Keener followers of football's post-Premiership implosion, the bust it fashioned from the years of boom, will know Notts County claimed another record more recently, an appropriate one given their place in the order of things: they now have the distinction of having been in administration longer than any other football club, ever. Eighteen months, from June 2002 to December 2003. Their saga had many familiar elements; an ambitious new owner, naïve about the limits of the club's potential, buys the club from an old-style local businessman-chairman who'd sold players to balance the books in his day, bunged loans in when necessary and now wanted his money back. The club overreached itself, signed players it could not afford; money the new owner hoped would come never arrived and they became insolvent and went into administration. There was then no shortage of people examining the bones to see if they were worth picking over. There was, however, one unusually intriguing aspect to the story.

The setting was appropriately cockeyed: Notts' West Stand – it faces east. The local council owned the Meadow Lane ground and the club rented it for a token annual payment. When Notts collapsed into trouble, the administrator asked if the council could revise the lease, to allow land around the ground to be developed, thereby making the club more tempting to a businessman to buy, because there would be a profit to be made from the property. Looking into that, the council, which wanted to help, discovered that all was not straightforward.

The West Stand, it turned out, was 'owned' by the old chairman, the heating and plumbing merchant, gruff-talking, hard-dealing Derek Pavis. The arrangement was cute: Pavis paid 'a peppercorn' to rent from the club the rooms inside the stand, and the executive boxes looking out on the pitch. He then rented the exec boxes back to the club for £90,000, and the rooms to a social and a sports club, for £45,000, £135,000 in total. Yes, you read that correctly; he rented the exec boxes from the club for nothing, then rented them back to the club for £90,000. What an ingenious way for a chairman to make money out of his football club while not taking a salary or a dividend. It turned out, on making a few inquiries, that this arrangement had not belonged to Pavis for very long; in fact he had bought the leases relatively recently from the former owner, a man whose name rings a bell: that old president of the League in the 1980s, who believed clubs had to balance their books or suffer 'natural wastage', Jack Dunnett. He had sorted the little twist out, shortly before he sold to Pavis in June 1987.

Dunnett was a figure I remember vaguely from my youth, one of football's great, good and grey: Bert Millichip, Ted Croker and Jack Dunnett, that sort of man. The breed you'd find pulling the balls out of the bag at the draw for later rounds of the FA Cup, or quoted in a crisis. And here he was, in the privacy of his own club, arranging to be handed a stand, then renting it back to the club to rake in, proportionately for the time, over £100,000 every year, after he left. The old-style chairmen, eh: you always wondered how it worked. They were never allowed to make money from

their clubs, and they always presented themselves as the custodians, taking nothing from the club, only serving it, but the fans,
on terraces whose squalor differed so starkly from the shagpile
in the boardrooms, always suspected the chairmen were doing all
right out of it. At Manchester City when I was a kid there was
always that suspicion and resentment in the air that Peter Swales
was helping himself to a few extras, although he may not have
been and I have never troubled myself to find out for sure. At
Notts County, here we had it, not just any old chairman but the
president of the League, his hand solemnly on the tiller, handing
out proclamations throughout the 1980s crisis, working himself
a funny mirror at Notts County, an arrangement that would see
the club continuing to pay him large amounts of money long
after he'd handed it on. 'If a community couldn't sustain its
football club,' Dunnett had been quoted in the League's official
history, 'I didn't see why it should be propped up.'

Described in various other accounts as 'manic', 'saturnine' and
'of demonic energy', Dunnett was involved in property development and had been the chairman of Brentford in the 1960s, where
he had fans protesting and defeating his idea to merge with Queens
Park Rangers. He went to Nottingham, where he became a powerful figure in the local, ruling, Labour Party, and was elected an
MP for Nottingham constituencies from 1964 to 1983. He took
over Notts County in 1968. The old club was at the time – prepare
to be not very astounded – seriously on its uppers.

Dunnett worked frantically with the club's gnarled, iconic
manager Jimmy Sirrel to drag Notts up from the old Fourth
Division. From 1981 to 1984 they even made it up to the First. He
had a go at developing Meadow Lane, but with the same pessimism
for football's future as that which brought a supermarket onto
one end of Bolton's Burnden Park and the block of flats jutting
into Southend's Roots Hall. Notts County's West Stand was built
in 1978, costing £800,000. It had no seats, just the executive boxes
and, inside, to make some cash, a sports facility and a social club,

the Meadow Club. Facing the pitch was just a blank brick wall, topped by the exec boxes.

The stand's facilities were first leased by the club to Dunnett's company, Park Street Securities, nine years later, in May 1987. Just two weeks after that, Dunnett sold the club, then back in the Third Division, to Pavis, for an undisclosed amount. Pavis told me the arrangement was not part of the deal, as it might look, a way to pay Dunnett for selling him the club. 'The leases were in place when I took over the club,' he said. He continued, he told me, to pay Park Street Securities the hefty rent, every quarter, for the club to use the exec boxes.

Pavis was a local businessman who had made a lot of money in plumbing, latterly in bathrooms and kitchens. He had previously been a director of Nottingham Forest. As the chairman, with Neil Warnock as the manager, they assembled a side including centre half Craig Short and striker Tommy Johnson which made it back to the old First Division for a season in 1991–2, only just missing out on being part of the Premier League breakaway. With £2m available from the Football Trust to First Division clubs for ground redevelopment post-Hillsborough, Pavis figured he should do up Meadow Lane before Notts inevitably dropped again and less grant was available, so, financed by the £2m and the sales of Short and Johnson for £3.5m and £1.5m respectively, he had three sides of the ground rebuilt, including seats installed in the West Stand, in just seventeen weeks in the summer of 1992, a remarkable achievement.

He ran the club as many old-style directors still do, lending money to cover shortfalls, then paying himself back when the club sold a player. Notts County went down in 1992, hovered in the Football League's First and Second Divisions for a couple of years, then went down to the Third in 1997, before coming back again as champions. Dunnett retired from Parliament in 1983, but continued to be involved in property and other businesses, including a major development of an old mental hospital in Nottingham.

He retired as a director of Park Street Securities in 1993 and was not named recently as a shareholder. He'd run into plenty of trouble and in October 1994 the ex-Football League and Labour Party grandee was made bankrupt – he is, at the time of writing, still bankrupt, aged eighty-one. Every year, Park Street Securities received the equivalent of £90,000 from Notts County, for the right to use the club's own executive boxes.

Park Street at some point mortgaged their West Stand lease to Barclays Bank; then, in 1998, receivers were appointed. So eventually Pavis bought the arrangement from the receiver in 1999, for, he said, around £500,000. From then, Notts County, the Meadow Club and the sports club paid rent to Pavis' company, DCP Holdings. As did the club itself, to use the boxes, a nice earner. Shortly afterwards, Pavis decided he wanted to sell the club and retire. His loan account was up to £2m, he was seventy. He told me he had many offers but eventually agreed to sell to an interesting and persuasive incomer, Albert Scardino.

Scardino was a curious figure to become so deeply immersed in the taps and washers of Nottingham football affairs. A native of Savannah, Georgia, Scardino arrived in this country in 1993 with his wife Marjorie, a major media figure who had been appointed chief executive of *The Economist* group, then become chief executive of Pearson, the conglomerate which owns the *Financial Times*. Back home in the seventies, while Marjorie earned the regular salary as a lawyer, the couple had co-founded a weekly local newspaper, the *Georgia Gazette*. It was tiny, with a circulation of just 2,600, but Albert crusaded against local corruption scandals and won a Pulitzer Prize for this investigative journalism. However, the newspaper never made money and eventually the Scardinos sold it; later it closed down. Albert then worked for the *New York Times* and as press secretary for David Dinkins, New York's mayor, before coming to London.

He was not a natural to be doing deals with the likes of Derek Pavis, but perhaps he was unfortunate, arriving in Britain at just the wrong time, when football clubs were being hyped by boys in suits as hot investments, sure vehicles to television millions. Even Notts County.

He looked first at Forest and was part of a consortium, supported by Mercury Asset Management, a venture capital firm which became seriously interested in a £20m bid for Forest in 1996. But at a late stage Mercury withdrew, leaving Scardino short, and Forest were taken over by Irving Scholar and Nigel Wray's ill-fated consortium. Scardino rated a mention in Scholar and Markham's subsequent court case against Forest, being described by the judge as: 'A North American who is enthusiastic about the merits of UK football clubs as investments, having regard in partic-ular for their potential role in the development of local television channels.'

Oh dear. Scardino, an engaging, gentle, rather dreamy guy, told me then that he believed English clubs could benefit from links with local television as happens in the States, and that, while it was difficult to make money directly from football clubs, it was possible to do so from 'ancillary activities' like these: 'US sports clubs have close links with local TV. It has been slow to take off here but it will come eventually, and local sports clubs will benefit from continued increases in media rights values.'

This thinking – doomed because in England only the very top clubs wallow in big money from television – led Scardino to go shopping for a football club. He looked at Stoke, both Sheffield clubs and Wolves, before he entered discussions with Derek Pavis. The judge in the Forest case had said of Scardino, when he tried to make another bid for Forest, that he was 'perfectly well-intentioned', but his ability to raise the money in time was 'highly suspect' and 'his ability to raise it at all was open to serious doubt'.

Scardino and Pavis talked, then agreed a deal. Pavis would sell Scardino his 90 per cent shareholding for £300,000, and Scardino would raise money to enable the club to repay Pavis his £2m loans, in three instalments, on 15 November 2000, 2001 and 2002.

Not publicised at the time was the fact that this still left the West Stand arrangement providing Pavis with around £90,000 a year rent from the club; he offered this lease to Scardino separately, for another handsome cheque, but Scardino did not agree to buy it from him.

Scardino had some positive discussions with Nottingham's city and county councils, who have a very good record of supporting their local football clubs, designating a councillor, John Taylor, to work with them. Scardino emerged confident that they had agreed to provide £3.4m in loan guarantees to the club, which would enable Notts in turn to borrow to pay Pavis back. The city council in 1994 had provided £4.3m in guarantees to Forest, so Scardino did have reason to believe it would happen. However, he had no formal contract with the council. He raised a loan to enable Notts to pay Pavis' first instalment of around £560,000, but then the council guarantees didn't come. Scardino looked for funding else-where, but never quite managed to secure it. He missed the second instalment due in November 2001 and Pavis was incandescent, fuming, roaring that the deal had been breached and Scardino had not delivered.

By this time, however, Peter Storrie had arrived as the chief exec-utive from West Ham, where he had been replaced by Graham Mackrell. In the expectation of cash arriving from the loans Albert Scardino was going to get backed by the council guarantees, Notts had begun to pay big money to attract players, like Darren Caskey, believed to be on around £130,000 a year all in, for a push for promotion to the First Division. The plan was to garner regular crowds of 8,000 to help fund it, but under the manager Jocky Scott they finished eighth in 2000–2001, four points off the play-offs. Expected to challenge again the following season, as the war raged between Scardino and Pavis and the money shrivelled as the loans never came in, Notts tumbled instead into relegation territory. Gary Brazil replaced Scott, then Billy Dearden came in, and they just avoided going down to the Third, finishing nineteenth.

Of the war between Scardino and Pavis, Storrie told me: 'You couldn't get two more different people. Albert is so mild-mannered, you couldn't meet a gentler bloke, but one day I heard him absolutely tearing into Pavis. I can't imagine what had pushed him so far.'

What each man says about the other in private is not printable. It would be a fair summary to say that Pavis, the Nottingham plumbing merchant and decades-long habitué of the football boardroom, and Scardino, the urbane, media-savvy Democrat, did not like each other very much. In January 2002, with Notts unable to pay the wages because the loans had never arrived, the PFA loaned the club £100,000 to cover the payroll and a transfer embargo was imposed. Notts were late paying the Inland Revenue and several other creditors issued writs. ITV Digital's collapse came in April, bringing a full stop to the idea that lower division clubs were lucrative TV vehicles.

Storrie went on what the club described as 'secondment' with his old West Ham manager Harry Redknapp at Portsmouth, then left permanently. This rancorous chapter of Notts' history finally ended on 6 June 2002, when the councils came back with their final answer: circumstances had changed, ITV Digital had made everybody more wary, they could not provide the loan guarantees. Scardino felt betrayed, although he accepts he never had a signed commitment from the councils. Notts were left with a wage bill they simply could not pay, and unable to borrow money without guarantees. The world's oldest professional football club was insolvent. Scardino, as the chairman, was forced to put it into administration.

I asked him at the time whether he regretted doing the deal with Pavis without having the finance absolutely in place. He said: 'I haven't really thought about it. It seemed too good an opportunity to get into Notts County and I thought we had several layers of safety net if we didn't get the loan guarantees. In hindsight it may have been a misjudgement.'

Nor was it cheap. Pavis was still owed around £1m in loans, but Scardino himself had raised £1.8m to allow the club partly to pay Pavis and keep going. He lost all that. The club's total debts were around £6m; NatWest, secured on the ground, were owed around £700,000, outstanding tax was nearly £400,000, VAT £105,000, while the total unsecured creditors, besides Pavis', Scardino's and the other directors' loans, were £1.5m, the usual sorry list.

The administrator was Paul Finnity. He would end up spending eighteen months on the job, sitting in his season ticket seat at Derby County, listening for Notts' result on his earphone. He waited a long while for Scardino to find another backer, but finally, in December 2002 it became clear that it was not going to happen.

Finnity approached the council to reorganise the Meadow Lane lease, which prohibited use of the ground and the seven acres around it for anything other than football. That old-fashioned arrangement used to protect clubs from property speculators, but now the only way to save the club was to offer the land for development, as long, the council insisted, as the club was guaranteed a 10,000-seat stadium there or somewhere else nearby. The council did want to help both its clubs, who were in trouble – Forest had appointed David Platt as the manager and spent Nigel Doughty's money on a push for promotion to the Premiership, which failed and led to them losing £100,000 *a week*.

It was when the council was looking at how to rework the Meadow Lane lease that it came across the curious money-leaking arrangement with Pavis on the West Stand.

'People were very surprised,' John Taylor told me. 'We never found out exactly why Jack Dunnett arranged it that way. We insisted that the ownership should be cleaned up, the stand fully owned by the club, before we signed the new lease. We believed that was the fit and proper way to go forward.'

The council duly redesigned the lease, to allow development of the land around Meadow Lane, as long as the club was guaranteed a home. Long term, Nottingham City Council would like the two clubs to move in together to a purpose-built super-stadium, leaving both their Trent-side grounds to be developed, but that's another story for now. Finnity, armed with the new offer of a lease, looked then for a deal from somebody interested in the club as a property deal: he was asking around £4m for the club and the long lease on the land. That included buying out the West Stand arrangement, now owned by Pavis. His price, asked of the administrator, was around £500,000, what he paid for it in 1999.

The people most interested were Raj Bhatia, from Essex, in partnership with a well-known businessman in Scotland, Frank Strang, the owner of Prestwick Airport. They were former RAF colleagues; Bhatia, it turned out, was finding the finance and was more interested than Strang, who was paying for professional advice on the deal. It wasn't quick.

In April 2003, the Football League noted gloomily that in the midst of the financial meltdown after ITV Digital, among the clubs insolvent or wobbling on the edge, Notts County had been in administration all season. This, other clubs could argue, gave Notts an advantage, because the club's old debts were frozen, while other clubs were paying theirs off. The League decided it had to deliver an ultimatum: if Notts were not out of administration by the end of the season, 27 May, they would be expelled from the League. The symbolism was not lost on anybody: the loss of the world's oldest League club would have been an awful reflection of the state of the game in the twenty-first century.

Finnity continued to talk with Bhatia and Strang and the deadline was missed. The sudden arrival of Geoffrey Richmond in the summer of 2003, giving long interviews about the plans for the club, talking about himself as the chief executive, did not greatly clarify Notts' future. Suddenly, without much of an explanation, Richmond was gone, not to appear in the public eye again until he arrived at Leeds.

The League was caught between not wanting to see its authority flouted and its extreme reluctance to kick out a member club, particularly Notts County. Finnity was given a couple of extensions, as he said the deal was very close. Finally, the League agreed to extend it through the summer, leaving the week of the start of the 2003–4 season, Monday 4 August, as the final, final, final deadline. On the Friday before, true to form, the deal collapsed. Bhatia maintains, still, that it was unfair because he had the money and could have done the deal. Finnity disputed that, saying he wanted a certain, concluded deal for the Monday, and he was not confident that Bhatia could deliver.

Instead, Finnity went to the League with a request for another extension. They agreed, giving him another three months, making Tuesday 9 December Notts' final, final, final, really absolutely and completely final deadline, and this time everybody knew the League would have to enforce it if they weren't utterly to lose credibility. It was, Sir Brian Mawhinney, the League's new, somewhat unlikely chairman, went out of his way to say: 'The last opportunity.'

This time the fans and local businessmen reacted. A supporters' trust had formed, and after the Strang–Bhatia deal collapsed, when it was clear the club really was staring at the end of its history, the trust began to play a more active role. They grew to 1,200 members out of a home crowd averaging 4,500, and set a target to raise £250,000, which they believed would be substantial enough to make them part of the solution and gain a seat on the board. At the home match with Luton in September they unveiled the new accessory required for fans of lower division football: the collection bucket. The chairman, David Hindley, a lecturer at Nottingham Trent University, saw a heartwarming reaction of loyalty and commitment. 'Hucknail Magpie', a 6 feet 4 inch skinhead, raised £220 in sponsorship by going to work at his factory wearing bra, knickers and suspenders. Hindley met a Southampton supporter who travelled up to Nottingham to hand over the holiday money she had saved up: 'She said it was more important to save the club than for her to go on holiday.'

David Johnson, Forest's striker, made a name for himself by dropping £500 in a bucket at the Luton match. County's own Darren Caskey threw away his chances in the supporters' player of the year vote by chucking in a coin which turned out to be foreign. His agent, Eric Hall, asked for a donation, said: 'I don't think so. This club owes me enough money as it is.'

The abiding image of football's extremes of inequality came on Wednesday evening 9 September 2003, when England's multi-millionaire players came to Manchester United plc's packed 'Theatre of Dreams' to play their Euro 2004 qualifier against Liechtenstein. Outside the ground were five Notts County fans, rattling buckets, like *Big Issue* sellers at the doors of the Ritz. Helped locally by the Independent Manchester United Supporters Association, which argues for better distribution of money in football, they raised, from the near 65,000 crowd, £600, on average less than one penny from each person there. It was a long trudge back to Nottingham.

The coffers, though, were slowly filling. Pavis, who was a major creditor and wanted £500,000 for his leases, tried to rally a consortium but it did not solidify. He rang the local newspaper then and did an interview in which it was reported that tears were rolling down his cheeks as he called for somebody to save the club. Not included in the piece was that, throughout the eighteen months the club had been insolvent and in administration, Pavis was being paid £7,500 every month, £90,000 a year, by the club, to rent from him the West Stand executive boxes and the Pavilion Lodge Hotel, which houses the young players. Pavis was also down to be paid £45,000 from the Meadow Club and Sport Nottingham, which rented the rooms in the stand, making the total £135,000, although it was a little less because the Meadow Club was empty during that year.

Pavis was unapologetic, when I talked to him, saying of the West Stand lease arrangement:

'I made an investment [when he bought the lease from the receivers] and I expected a return on it.'

The piece in the newspaper worked. A group calling themselves the 'Blenheim Consortium', including former Notts directors Peter Joyce and John Mountney, and the former Leicester City director Roy Parker, had formed, but most importantly a supporter came forward, a Meadow Lane season ticket holder who turned out to be a dotcom entrepreneur who had made money from a banking website. He wanted to remain anonymous but agreed to pay £3m for the new, cleaned-up lease from the council – which paid off Pavis – then rent Meadow Lane back to the club for a peppercorn, complete with its executive boxes, with which the club was reunited. The Supporters Trust triumphantly met its fundraising target of £250,000, and earned a seat on the board, the first ever Notts County director who would actually be elected by a large body of fans. The council approved, John Taylor saying: 'That has to be the future for clubs like these: community clubs working with their supporters.'

Pavis was, as he acknowledged himself, 'kicked upstairs' to become life president of the club, with sundry privileges. 'I'm delighted the club survived,' he said. Of the supporters electing a director he said: 'They used to ask for a supporter on the board, and I used to say: "Don't you think I'm a supporter? I've invested millions in this club."

'It's foreign to me,' he shrugged. 'But good luck to them.'

David Hindley, who, like all fans forced to fight for their club's existence, found it ate up his life, said it had to mark a new era: 'The club has to be run professionally and also transparently, so the supporters know exactly what arrangements there are, and what deals are being done. It is our club, we are the people proud of its long history, who fought for it to survive and prosper.

'The club's community programme is excellent here; the staff go out to difficult areas of Nottingham and reach out to alienated young people with football, a very powerful attraction. We are going to dedicate ourselves to building up that community presence, and have a football club we can be proud of.'

I went down to London to have a chat with Albert Scardino, who had recently been given an executive editor's job at the *Guardian*. He lives in Knightsbridge, near Harrods, and he mentioned a nice Viennese-style coffee shop where we could meet and talk. It was an early autumn evening. We ordered tea for two and talked it through. The twists, the nearlies, the money he lost, the trouble with Pavis. He had, he said, liked the club very much and became personally attached to it and the fans. Paul Finnity had told me the same thing, that it was a nice family club and the longer he was there the more drawn in he became. The fans always said that the one thing you had as a Notts County fan was the fact that it was the oldest League club in the world; no glory, no trophies, just that, and in the end that was what they had fought for.

Scardino told me he had tried everything to make it work and he explained why he had become involved: 'I had come to this country and was out of newspapers, which I had been in for a long time, and I couldn't see at that time when I would get back in. The football club offered a great opportunity for me to be involved in an English community, in a way no American could have. I'd still like to help the club; I haven't walked away, but obviously the idea of me taking over has gone.

'I learned the difficult way that that economic model of football does not work. Maybe, in my enthusiasm, I allowed myself to be blind to various aspects of the business deal. The council reacted positively to our discussions and perhaps I talked too early in public about getting the guarantees. These things were my own stupidity,' he said over his tea. 'It was nobody's fault but mine.'

The staff were sweeping up around us; they were closing, it was seven o'clock. I told him it was surprising that a guy could still smile, reflect so calmly on his experience, still be positive, when he'd lost so much money and gone through such ordure. He shrugged, smiled and we shook hands. I thought, weaving back to the tube through the early evening crowds, of all the people involved in football's overblown crack-up, this is the first and only time that anybody I've met has looked intently at their part in it and said, genuinely: I got it wrong.

And so, the world's oldest League club limps away from its latest crisis. Perhaps after all they've been through, Notts County will know themselves more thoroughly now, understand their limitations, the junior club of a small city, and realise their job is firstly to ensure they survive, extend their record-breaking history, run themselves properly, openly, with genuine people in charge who care about the club. Be committed to living within their means, and grow not by gambling with money they haven't got, but by weaving more fans into the club, and reaching out to the community. Aim for success realistically, not sink into the red to chase it, all the while, maybe, campaigning for a fairer share of money through football. Perhaps all this trauma was for a reason, showing those in charge a better way, and all the lessons will be learned. Or, on the other hand, maybe they won't.

CHAPTER 9

The Cemetery End

I was at home one Friday evening, work done, playing with our baby, the telly chuntering in the background, when a weary-looking guy with curly grey hair came on, trembling a little, to say Bury Football Club were in trouble. The caption named him as Fred Mason, one of Bury's acting chairmen, and he was pleading with people to come to Gigg Lane for the following day's home match, saying that without more support locally the club would not survive. 'It really is desperate,' he said, his words made all the more insistently believable by his being a long way from a TV natural.

I went to school in Bury, and, like most football fans from the north side of Manchester, have a soft spot for the club. I didn't go to Gigg Lane too often; once, when City weren't playing, I saw the celebrated Wrexham side of the seventies, Mickey Thomas, Dixie McNeil, Dai Davies, beat Bury 3-2 – we watched the game, as I remember it, from wooden seats in the main stand. Later, on rare Saturdays if our school team played in the afternoon rather than the morning, I went down there with a couple of other lads after playing our game. It was half-time and already dark; the gates were open and we just walked in and watched the second half from the terraces. I remember standing up down the bottom of the side terrace opposite the main stand one time when Preston's striker – I can never remember his name – ran the ball out of play and muttered 'Shit!' right in front of us. 'Yeah,' said an old bloke next to us, not missing a beat. 'It were.'

Bury never did a great deal on the field; they were in the Third Division until 1980, when they were relegated to the Fourth; in 1981–2 their nippy striker Craig Madden was scoring tons of goals, thirty-five in the League, but he never went on anywhere much, unlike the goalkeeper, Neville Southall, who became Everton's scruffy genius in their mid-eighties heyday. Bury never did much in the giant-killing stakes either. They'd draw one of the big clubs, everybody would get really excited, then Bury would get truly hammered. In September 1980 they drew Nottingham Forest in the League Cup, and the few Bury fans at school – most boys even then supported Man City or United, with a sprinkling of Bolton fans – believed that football's mythology demanded a humbling for Forest, who had just won the European Cup twice. Cloughie brought his side to Gigg Lane and they won 7-0. The following season, Bury drew the West Ham of Trevor Brooking and Alan Devonshire, who delivered some fundamental truths about football's Darwinian hierarchy, underlining the lesson 10-0.

There was, though, something venerable about Bury, and invitingly cosy about the ground. Gigg Lane itself is perched above the main Manchester Road, so I passed it every day; from the top deck of a bus you could see the blue stand and square floodlights, nestling behind the trees. That was before I knew any of the history, that Bury were one of the game's early stalwarts, elected to the Football League Second Division right back in 1894, then spending nearly twenty years in the First Division playing the Woolwich Arsenals and Manchester Uniteds, twice winning the FA Cup, in 1900 and 1903, when they beat Derby County 6-0, still the most thumping victory ever in a Cup Final. I knew that in the sixties Colin Bell, City's greatest ever player and the sky-blue icon of my childhood, had come from Bury, so the place was precious anyway. Gigg Lane's main claim to fame back then was the natural lushness of its turf, said to be among the loveliest in the League, when City's was still a claypit. All of it made you think well of Bury and want the best for them.

In recent years I'd had a vague eye out for them, and they'd suddenly been doing really well, playing above themselves. They won successive promotions in 1996 and 1997 and made it up to the First Division, where they came to Maine Road and beat City 1-0, one of the more depressing afternoons even in a City fan's routinely morose existence. Peter Swales had been finally chased out of Maine Road in 1994 by a mass, bitter reaction from fans following his sacking of our then manager Peter Reid. Swales was replaced by the saviour from our dreams, none other than Francis Lee, the blond, cherubic, tubby centre forward from City's great, Championship-winning days when we were kids. Grown–up life turned out to be more complicated; Franny was a businessman who was looking to float City and make money, and under his chairmanship City fell apart. Swales, said to be a broken man, died in the spring of 1996, and with painful timing, a minute's silence was held for him before the final match of the season, against Liverpool, when City were looking at relegation. Who can say what was in 30,000 people's minds as they bowed their heads – the minute's silence 'meticulously observed', as the papers would have it – then the whistle blew, City played ninety minutes of extreme farce, and went down. The defeat against Bury came on Valentine's Day, 1998; our manager, Frank Clark, struggled to say anything at all afterwards and on the way home, one of the directors, David Makin, the co-owner of the retail chain J-D Sports, actually called Greater Manchester Radio's fans' phone-in, almost in tears, saying he'd be dedicating himself from then on to 'Getting the chairman [Francis Lee] out'. Within weeks, Franny was gone. That saved him from having to make good on a promise rashly given in public that he would jump off his new, expensive, all-seater Kippax if City went down to the Second Division – the third flight – for the first time in the club's history. City did, at the end of the season, but Franny didn't. In 1998–9, Bury were playing in a division above City. But after those heady two years, Bury's experience was down, down – and a touch bizarre.

It turned out that Bury had been able to splash the cash and pay the wages, for the manager Stan Ternent's solid side: Dean Kiely in goal, the huge centre half Paul Butler, tidy striker David Johnson, because they had been bankrolled by a man who, when he first appeared, must have seemed the divine answer to any fan's prayer for a football fairy godfather. Hugh Eaves was originally from Bury and had apparently gone on to make fortunes in the City. In 1992, when the club had fallen on hard times, a perennial state for Bury, with ten players on part-time contracts, Eaves contacted the chairman, Terry Robinson, and said he'd like to back the club. For Bury, flailing in the modern era to survive at all on falling gates, the town's football fans forever drifting off to season tickets at the big Manchester clubs, the local kids wandering about in United shirts, this must have seemed like deliverance. Eaves bought 89 per cent of the club's shares and, although Bury still paid the bills by selling players every year – Johnson, to Ipswich for £1m in 1997, Butler, to Sunderland for £1m the following year, Kiely, to Charlton for £1m the year after – Eaves' support bankrolled wages of an average £70,000 a year for each player, huge money for a club of Bury's size, meaning they could afford players who could compete in the First Division.

Robinson was a practised player of football politics, on the FA Council for a while, and he hustled for all available grants, completely redeveloping Gigg Lane into a 12,000 all-seater stadium, SHAKERS emblazoned in white across the blue seats, a pattern sadly visible even on most matchdays.

Then, in April 1999, the wheels suddenly fell off the Hugh Eaves gravy train. It was written up as one of the financial scandals of the year and Eaves confessed to it. In the City, a world remote to Bury fans, Eaves had, it seemed, an unpaid, administrative role for a large fund of money belonging to himself and thirty-one others, including his former partners in the stockbroking firm Philips & Drew. They had cashed in in 1985, selling their firm to a Swiss investment conglomerate, UBS, for £50m. Eaves had taken on the apparently mundane job of sending out an annual dividend and interest payments and sorting out the details if partners wanted to sell.

In April 1999 he had gone to see a solicitor, David Speker, of the firm Kingsley Napley, well known for acting for people in it up to their white collars. Speker had framed a letter from Eaves to all his former partners in wretchedly hand-wringing tones. Eaves, a sober man not, from all accounts, overblessed with personality, a 3D definition of the word unassuming, had succumbed to the temptation of all men working with massive amounts of money, dipped into it himself and gone on a fantastically uncharacteristic spending spree. He'd spent a large part of his former partners' nest eggs on, it was said, buying Nannau Hall, a three-storey manor house in north Wales, property around Hampstead, where he lived quietly with his wife, and buying Bury Football Club, his first true love. For a fling, he'd bought Swinton Rugby League Club too, who had moved in to share Gigg Lane. Eaves' letter, drafted by Speker, was a detailed written confession to his partners when the game was up. It was a sad story: Eaves was suicidal, than said to have gone on the run and to have been variously last spotted in Hong Kong or Thailand – although, talk to some people at Gigg Lane and they say he's sneaked in to the odd match since.

The former partners instructed their lawyers and Eaves' assets worldwide, which included 89 per cent of Bury, were frozen by the court. The *Sunday Times*, though, didn't think there would be much point bothering to repossess the club; they wrote of the scandal: 'The most valuable assets owned by Eaves are his Hampstead properties, but their value is way short of the £8m he plundered. His stake in Bury is said by football experts to be worthless – the club is just one of many struggling to survive in the lower reaches of the game.'

Bit harsh, that. Bury had gone back down to the Second Division in 1999, but only on goals scored; they hadn't been doing too badly before this unfortunate bit of news from bloody London about the true source of the sugar daddy's cash. The old club was really shaken to its bones now. Theirs is a salutary tale about benefactors, the idea and longstanding practice at most English clubs, from Chelsea to Chesterfield, of running at a loss every season and relying on one rich backer to pick up the shortfall and keep the show on the field. Fans are told that such people 'put money in' to clubs, which is true, but in almost every case, once they have bought the club's shares and gained control, they fund it not with donations but loans. If anything happens to the benefactor, the loans are outstanding and the club is deep in debt. At Gigg Lane, even a man as apparently made as Hugh Eaves, the house in Hampstead, pinstriped job in the City, a Bury fan from birth – the ideal, manna-from-heaven, model of a saviour – accepting the worship of Bury fans when they won their promotions, had put it all in in loans. Albeit interest free, his account was up to £750,000, and he also appeared to have guaranteed personally a large loan from Lloyds TSB, which was mortgaged on Gigg Lane. Or, at least, the bank only lent the money because it was secure in the knowledge that Eaves was backing Bury.

So when Eaves ended up red-fingered, shame-faced and on the run, Bury were facing collapse. Terry Robinson was the full-time chairman and chief executive, working closely with commercial director Neville Neville, so good they named him twice. Neville, the father of the two United players, Phil and Gary, had from 1994 made use of the Old Trafford link, earning a few bob for Bury, £2,500 a time, by having United's reserves play their matches at Gigg Lane. His wife, the boys' mum, Jill, also worked in the office at Bury for years.

Robinson and Neville put a brave face on and tried to pull the club through. Robinson argued manfully that it was not so much the 'well-documented problems of our major shareholder' which had scuppered them as relegation, which had cost £500,000 in television income and a fall in gates to around 4,000. The wage bill had reached £2.4m, and relegation had landed the club with a near-£2m shortfall and no backer to scoop it up.

Redundancy blew through Gigg Lane; eighteen people were laid off or not replaced, including nine players whose contracts were not renewed, three youth development officers and administrative staff. Then, in December 1999, as a cost-cutter, manager Neil Warnock and assistant Kevin Blackwell left and were replaced as co-player-managers by the senior pros Andy Preece and Steve Redmond. Bury had to take what they could for players now; top scorer Ian Lawson was sold to Stockport for just £150,000. Neville talked bullishly about the club having always scrapped to survive, pre-Eaves, and being able to 'cut their cloth' accordingly:

'We've been down this road before,' he said, but that was only partly true, it had never been this bad. With Eaves' backing gone, the banks were pressing for repayment. The wage bill for the remaining highly-paid players simply could not be met out of ordinary income and the club was in financial crisis.

In early 2000, Robinson wrote an open letter, calling for support from the people of Bury, but it was spiky, too, laced with put-downs of fans who'd voiced their cynicism and criticism of the way the club had been run: 'Our main task is to maintain the club on an even keel until its long-term future is clarified,' he concluded. 'Painful decisions must be taken . . . We have a responsibility to keep football going in Bury, and we're determined to fulfil that.'

The next I knew was when Fred Mason came on the telly, his voice quivering, saying the club was staring like never before at the possibility of folding. I went up there to see what was up. I hadn't been back to Bury for a long time, but it seemed just the same: pinched, miserable town. The combination of mills and Methodism never did much for anybody's élan. There, though, was Gigg Lane, still snug in the woods; a haven, as comforting as a bag of chips.

Terry Robinson had gone, left. After twenty years at Gigg Lane he'd shortly afterwards taken a job as Sheffield United's 'football executive'. Neville had left sometime before, to do his own thing. Fred Mason and another director, John Smith were the only two left, sat holding the club at the gates of ruin. I found John in the chairman's office, a dour, decent man in his fifties, baseball cap pulled right down over his reddish face, clutching a mobile phone and a packet of fags. He told me he ran a local haulage company and had always been Bury; he'd felt when he made a few quid that he had a duty to put money into supporting the club because the town, for its pride, needed a club in the League. He didn't exactly pour forth. There was nothing much on the desk, except a letter he skimmed over to me. It was on plain paper from somebody in Anglesey, asking whether Fred and John were still interested in a loan facility for Bury which had apparently been discussed previously with somebody else at the club. John dismissed it mournfully, said it seemed much too expensive, just another problem, and they hadn't known anything about it. He told me they were facing very shortly a court action from a company with a mortgage on Gigg Lane, suing to repossess the ground.

Terry Robinson had been frantically trying to broker a deal to sell Bury to a company called Mansport Developments, then he'd left, Robinson had said, to allow it to go through. But the *Manchester Evening News* had, a few days after Robinson left, revealed that Mansport's sole director, Paul Barrett, and David Jones, who had become Bury's company secretary to facilitate the Mansport takeover and at whose offices Mansport was registered, were convicted fraudsters. They had been sentenced to eighteen months – reduced to twelve on appeal – and eight months in prison respectively in 1997 after being convicted of obtaining services by deception. Several of Barrett's companies had also been put into liquidation and were under investigation by the Department of Trade and Industry. Jones turned out to be a former bankrupt who in 1998 was disqualified from acting as a company director for twelve years following irregularities in his running of another company, Burling Bond (1986) Limited. The revelations had given Fred and John Smith what could legitimately be described as serious concerns. The deal to sell Bury to Mansport collapsed. That left them with no escape route and a court action in four weeks' time, which could see them lose Gigg Lane.

'We're in a very serious situation,' Smith told me, staring down at the desk. 'At the moment we can't see a way out.'

I looked around the room in which Robinson had spent twenty years, harrying to keep Bury going. It was pretty bare, like a waiting room in a minicab firm late at night. There was a tatty chair, the chairman's cheap desk, by the wall a stand-up ashtray powdered with ash. It was mind-blowing to contemplate how many fags might have been smoked in there over the years.

Fred Mason arrived. The telly hadn't done him justice: he is a nice man with laughing eyes. Not that he was having much fun at the moment. He let me see some of the paperwork for the legal trouble they were in. We had a chat, then we shook hands and I wished them luck. On the way out I spoke to the press officer, Gordon Sorfleet, who was sticking some match details up on the official website, soldiering on, having a fag and a coffee in a plastic cup. Oh yeah, he said, the club was in big trouble but they didn't know too many details. There were only eight staff left because everybody else had been laid off. Outside in the corridor players were wandering around, carrying their boots, training over. There was still a friendly, if harassed, air about the place. The commercial manager, Peter Young, told me all this doom and gloom was no good, because he still had to sell sponsorships and bring money in.

I drove back past the old Bury Convent School, out to the M66, and home, to have a look at the documents. It turned out to be pretty horrible. Seriously worrying. When Bury lost their backer and Eaves' assets were frozen, the court repossession documents said, 'Lloyds TSB [which had the mortgage on Gigg Lane] had been extremely nervous of their position'. Evidently Robinson hadn't been able to find any other bank willing to lend to Bury and take on the loan instead, so on 12 May 2000 he'd turned in desperation to a £1m loan, paying 15 per cent interest a year, from a scheme run by a firm of solicitors called Richard Prentis & Co. Prentis had advertised to the general public to pay into a fund, which, he had promised, would go into investments guaranteeing 15 per cent interest a year. The £1m had paid off Lloyds TSB, and the investment scheme now had the mortgage on Gigg Lane instead. The loan was described in the documents as 'a true lending of last resort'.

Just a couple of weeks afterwards, Prentis' firm had been closed down by the Law Society, which ruled that he could not legally operate such 'collective investment schemes'; later he was struck off their roll of solicitors. Nevertheless, the £1m loaned to Bury had come from fifty-three different people and they did still have to be repaid, with interest.

With no backer, ebbing gates and a punishing wage bill, Bury hadn't managed to pay anything, not a penny of interest, let alone chip away at the capital, and on 29 May 2001 new lawyers acting on behalf of the investors had sued to reclaim the money and repossess the ground. They had delayed after Robinson told them negotiations were under way for the Mansport takeover, but had written twice in June 2001, then called on 23 and 27 July and 1 and 2 August but received no information in response. So, on 6 August 2001 they had served the repossession papers.

Bury had put a defence in, in which Robinson said that, although the interest was indeed originally 15 per cent, he had agreed, in a conversation with somebody acting for Prentis, that the interest would drop to 'a conventional rate of interest' after the first year. The court hearing coming up was because the scheme's lawyers had applied for that defence to be struck out because, they claimed in the application, it was 'inconceivable,' 'unbelievable' and 'plainly untrue'.

After Robinson left, Fred and John, who'd always been part-time directors because they had their businesses to run, stepped in to find the lawyers for the Prentis investors applying to repossess Gigg Lane, plus repayment of £1.35m, plus costs.

Interest was running at £984.59 every day. Of all the football clubs falling into crisis, Bury seemed to me the most genuinely critical. It was hard to see a way out. For me, it was like visiting a great-uncle you always remembered fondly but hadn't seen for a long time, and finding him in the grip of loansharks, chain-smoking, with his flat about to be repossessed.

Fred and John sighed, flapped and panicked, then went to see some sympathetic lawyers and accountants. Just three days before the court action, which would surely have closed the club down, Bury went into administration. That froze all the debts, including the mortgage scheme and the lawyers for the former Philips & Drew partners demanding Eaves' £750,000 – and, it turned out, lots else besides, the Inland Revenue and others waiting for debts amounting in total to £4.8m. Bury, however, were so skint that they had enough money to carry on in business, to pay their players and skeleton staff, for only two weeks. After that, the club would definitely have to close because an administrator cannot run up losses himself. Matthew Dunham, the administrator from the accountancy firm Robson Rhodes, made it very clear that the club needed £370,000 to make it to the end of the season, or Bury would be wound up and that would really be that.

Bury people, the ones who cared, reacted by digging very deep indeed. Neville Neville came back, unpaid, doing what he's good at: fundraising. He cracked on with sportsmen's dinners and celebrity auctions, tapping up his contacts, then he had an idea with mass appeal: sponsor a seat. Gigg Lane had 12,000 of them, new and shiny, but the ground itself was facing the bulldozer. So Bury offered, for a £10 contribution to the cause of staying alive, that donors would get their names on seats. Gordon Sorfleet, press officer turned first lieutenant of the rescue operation, leapt into the job, pounding out the message on the official website:

SOS: Save Our Shakers: two weeks to keep the club afloat. The reaction astounded him.

There was real solidarity out there. The official websites of thirty-seven other Football League clubs ran the threat to Bury as their main story. Bury's own website – never, in truth, at risk of crashing when, say, Andy Preece's post-match reflections went up – started to receive forty thousand hits a day. Sorfleet was flooded with e-mails from people wanting to sponsor seats: 'They came in from everywhere,' he told me, bubbling with it. 'Obviously there were a lot of local people, but we had donations from all over the country. It was emotional at times; there were people asking for a seat to be named in memory of a loved one.'

Players gave money too. Chris Lucketti, backbone of Bury's defence in the promotion years, who'd gone to Huddersfield in June 1999 for £750,000, came in, dropped his credit card in reception and said: 'Take a load of seats off that.' They nibbled £500 out of him. Henning Berg turned up with £3,000 from a whip-round of Blackburn players; Man City players raised £2,000. Cynical comments about how much those donations really amount to in terms of top players' wages, or reflections that such a level of loose change in players' pockets, while whole clubs go bust, illustrates the game's waste of its boom years, are not welcome here – this is supposed to be the heartwarming bit.

'The one which stands out in my memory,' Sorfleet recalled, 'was a really small boy, he might have been only four or five. He turned up with coppers Sellotaped to a card. He said it was all he'd got, but we could have it. It was 37p. We put his name on a seat: Ben Alcott.

'Donations came in from everywhere. We had someone from the Congo – I mean who on earth, in Congo, cares about Bury Football Club, and why? We had a couple from Russia, Australia, a lot from Canada, quite a few from the US, all round Europe of course, a couple from Kenya, Namibia. There were a couple of

Bury fans in Mombasa – this is true – and they were taking collections there, in buckets, for Bury. It was unbelievable.'

They raised £100,000 in a week. Neville formed a richer man's appeal fund, the Save Our Shakers trust, while ordinary fans held a public meeting in the Town Hall advised by Supporters Direct, and agreed to form a trust to raise money in return, they hoped, for shares and a seat on the board. Every match, Bury fans held bucket collections, raising around £2,000 a time. At a Tuesday night local derby against Oldham, 8,000 turned up, twice the crowd Bury would normally have expected. The home match against Notts County was designated a Fans United day, and supporters came from all over the country. Sorfleet talked to fans from Ipswich, Charlton, Kidderminster, Arsenal, Tottenham, and one man who had travelled from Plymouth. 'They all said they couldn't bear to see any club fold, and that there but for the grace of God went theirs.' Club owners see football in terms of self-interest, their club's and too often their own too, but the fans don't; they see a collection of great names, who were there a long time ago and which they hope will be there for a long time to come, each sustaining the other, from the base to the top.

Bury didn't surprise anybody on this big day, losing 4-0. The sad display prompted John Smith to lose his temper with the players, saying here was the public rallying round to pay their wages, yet they played like they didn't care.

Bury raised the money. When the seats scheme closed, with much of the ground sponsored, they had raised £225,000, some people having paid over £10 for theirs, and this money went to Dunham to keep the club going in administration – money lost but securing the club's future. Neville was raising cash and also talking to Bury's richest and likeliest backer, Ron Wood, owner of the massive local greetings card factory, who'd flown Alex Ferguson about in his private jet during Fergie's testimonial year – that sort of bloke. Wood ended up buying the ground for £495,000 – the investment scheme receiving a reduced pay-off.

Neville also found a small group of wealthy men to pay into his own fund, accumulating enough money eventually to give to Dunham to pay off creditors and own the majority of the club.

The supporters' trust were still gathering members and cash to try to be part of the future and I went up to their official launch meeting, held at 7.30 on a Sunday evening at the leisure centre. Another place I hadn't been to for years, I always remember decent times there; a load of kids from school all arranged to go swimming there one half-term and afterwards we'd all gone to the chippy next door and had wonderful fish and chips, mouth-burningly hot.

Driving in, though, looking more carefully around, Bury looked different. I'd walked everywhere in my schooldays, so maybe the ring road, soullessly skirting the town, was there already. Retail parks are encamped at intervals around it; a huge Halfords, TK Maxx, a vast Wickes. I don't remember one superstore in Bury in my day; now the multi-nationals have got the place surrounded. I pulled into the leisure centre car park; a bunch of fans were sheltering from the drizzle under the entrance. The chippy was closed down, empty, as were several other shops. There were 'fun' pubs and peeling billboards, an empty, hollowed-out feel to the town.

When Bury won the FA Cup, more than a century ago, it was still a town with its own separate character and its football club was a formidable battler drawing good local crowds. Now, Bury is paddling for any sense of identity at all, trying not to be washed into Greater Manchester's suburban sprawl. The sight of United's reserves, trotting about at Gigg Lane in their Adidas Predators throughout the crisis, although a little earner for Bury, also reinforced a sense of town and club overwhelmed by the big city, now just half an hour away down the main road. The hundred or so people huddled in the drizzle outside the leisure centre were of a certain age, mostly mid-forties and older. A few of them told me there was little else left which was really Bury except the football club, and that was why they still went and why they were going to fight to keep the club going.

We waited outside. The leisure centre was all dark inside. Eventually, an embarassed manager came out to say there had been a power cut, wiping out just that area of Bury. Wouldn't you know it: pissed on and pissed on again. Everybody trooped away, the launch postponed. I had a drink in a fun pub, which was a lot of fun, then went home.

Forever Bury, the trust, did launch successfully. They fundraised vigorously, organised duck races, bucket collections, social evenings, bought shares and earned a seat on the board. Neville's rich man's trust raised the rest, enabling Dunham to organise a CVA and take Bury out of administration. The unsecured creditors added up to £1.1m, and they all got 10p in the pound. Most of it was the £750,000 owed to Eaves' former partners but it also included the usual public bodies – £23,505 owed to Greater Manchester Police, nearly £3,000 owed to the local council, and suppliers, including £44,567 owed to a local building company, the water, electric, gas. The unpaid bill to St John Ambulance was £983.72.

The fans have some respect for Neville for putting his back into saving the club. Few, though, have much time for Terry Robinson. For all his work over the years, many resented that, while the club racked up losses and the Eaves backing collapsed, Robinson was still paid around £50,000 a year. When I called him about Bury's plight, he refused to discuss it:

'I'm employed at another club,' he'd said.

He didn't endear himself when he came back for Bury's goalkeeper, Paddy Kenny, whom many believe to be a £1m keeper in the same endearing, throw-yourself-about mould as Neville Southall. Robinson offered Fred and John £42,000 to sell him to Sheffield United and they were forced to accept it. Bradford Park Avenue, Kenny's former club, which got almost nothing for a sell-on clause they'd hoped might build them a new ground, complained to the FA but got nowhere. There was nothing under the table in the deal; Robinson really had offered only that, but it was a cold, stark way to do business.

I went up to Gigg Lane to see how they were getting on, one midweek match, when Bury played York. They were back on a more even keel, back to the perpetual struggle in the Third – bottom – Division. The Bury supporters had vowed that their club must never fall into so perilous a state again, that survival was the most important priority. John Smith had found it quite difficult to work with them; they were the opposite to the prejudiced assumption that fans would throw money away to buy fantasy players.

'They're very cautious people,' he told me, puzzled, still saying you had to have a little gamble at promotion, show some ambition.

Bury refuse to sanction living beyond their means any more. Gradually the bigger earners, those on £1,300 and £1,700 a week, reached the end of their contracts and were replaced by players on one month- or three-month stints. Not one player is now on more than £350 per week, and some of them came from big clubs. Their most promising young player, the striker David Nugent, lives at home with his mum and dad and on his new contract would probably struggle to move out.

The crowd that midweek evening was 2,282, which included 447 from York. People talk sniffily about lower division football being doomed but it is actually on the increase, crowds rising steadily every season since 1986. Football's general boom and hype has led to more people re-exploring their local clubs, although Bury compete with giants and it is a great deal harder than most. Still, nearly 3,000 people is more than will attend any other kind of event in Bury on a nippy Tuesday night. The major worry I could see is that there is a middle-aged spread to the crowd, not many teenagers seeing the point or being able to afford £12 to watch Bury stubbornly keep their heritage alive.

There is some history between the two sets of fans; a York girl broke her leg in a scuffle a few years before and police on horse-back were railroading a tiny group of York fans all the way down Manchester Road. Inside that evening Bury played some lovely stuff, on the deck in midfield between Paul O'Shaughnessy, a Bury lad, Gareth Seddon and the former City player little Terry Dunfield, who passed the ball daintily and found space devas-tatingly. Harpal Singh, the great hope to be the first Asian foot-baller to make it when he was coming through at Leeds, was on loan at Gigg Lane. He was fast and quite tricky, but you felt he hadn't done enough in the game yet to warrant wearing white boots, and he got a fearful clouting from the York fullbacks. Bury danced around all night and won 3-0. When they scored, the crowd was up and the roars were heartfelt; you could feel the stored-up passion, the depth of it, warming fans in Bury's home stand, whose name is a warning for the resting place of all lower divi-sion clubs, if they're not careful: the Cemetery End.

Gordon Sorfleet told me a bit about himself. He was brought up in Bury and first taken to Gigg Lane in 1968. He'd joined the navy as a caterer after school, was based for twenty years in Plymouth but never missed a match when he was on shore. For years he ran an unofficial Bury fans' website from the ship. His wife suffered from severe arthritis and in July 2000, after what he felt was rough treatment from the navy, he quit, just two years off his pension. Neville had offered him a job and he jumped at the chance, his salary dropping from £28,000 a year in the navy to £12,000 at Gigg Lane.

At the end of the crisis-hit season, Sorfleet had had a surprise phone call. It was Uefa. No, it wasn't an old mate winding him up. It was indeed Uefa. They had read about his part in the campaign to save Bury and had decided to award him European Supporter of the Year. They wanted to fly him out to the pres-entation evening in Monaco.

'It was,' he laughed at first, 'the first trophy Bury had won in a hundred years.' Then he said: 'It was a bit embarrassing, that they should single me out. Every supporter who made any contribution did their bit to save Bury.'

Uefa flew Gordon and his wife to Nice. He was sitting next to a mountain of a man, and somebody behind him looked vaguely familiar too, then he realised they were John Charles and Gérard Houllier. When the plane landed a woman was waiting, holding up a Uefa hospitality board with three names on it: 'Charles. Houllier. Sorfleet.' They were ushered onto a helicopter bound for Monte Carlo.

The Sorfleets' hotel room was as big as their house. At the do in the evening, Uefa showed a short film they'd made about the history of Bury and the battle to save the club. They'd recorded part of it at a pre-season friendly against non-league Chorley. When they showed David Nugent scoring a goal, everybody roared; Sorfleet looked around and saw Roberto Carlos on his feet, applauding.

'They gave me my award and Bobby Robson congratulated me. I sat down, someone slapped me on the back and said: "Well done, *mon ami*." I turned round and it was Zinedine Zidane. It was all too much, absolutely incredible.'

Sorfleet told me that Bury, now with fans on the board, are determined never to fall into the mire again, that they have to pay their way, work hard to attract more fans locally, and not be on the lookout for some rich backer, a chimera which got them so deeply into trouble. Bringing in the next generation is the biggest challenge, if only they had the time to do something about it. The Sorfleet family was itself rocked to its foundations when Gordon's teenage son spent his birthday money on a brand-new Manchester United shirt. 'The kids take the mickey out of me. They tell me to get a life. But I love this club. There's nothing else in Bury but the football club and the old East Lancs railway, which enthusiasts are maintaining. We're still here, we're still fighting and we're still needed.'

The crowd drifted off and Gigg Lane emptied. Only Simon Egan, who does the match reports for the official website now, was still there, tapping into a laptop, his young daughter Charlotte, waiting beside him, looking indulgent and long-suffering. I wandered down the steps. With everybody gone you could see the names on the back of all the empty seats: Stephen Holbrook, Sallyanne Eadie, I. Barlow: good Bury names. There were Derek and Iris Bowden, Charlton Athletic; Tarkan and Tarik Algin, Tottenham Hotspur. Row after row, back and back, serried rows of names, fixed with care to the back of seats. It's an eerie sight, makes you shiver. Looked at simply, it's blank, like a telephone directory, a list of the good people who would not let a football club die, a rollcall of solidarity, the football 'family'. Walking away, I kept wondering what else it reminded me of, then I realised: it was like a memorial, these ranks of unknown people, on blank mounts, sticking up from the ground. There was something of First World War graves about it, names from a lost world who didn't go down without a fight. With all the money washing through football there is no reason why clubs like Bury, still serving their towns, should be so starved of money, have to work so nerve-shreddingly just to stay alive, and the worldwide response to Bury's cause, and the sentimental gesture from the European governing body, showed a huge part of the footballing public believes this too. It's no way to run a sport, in a boom.

CHAPTER 10

Together We Make a Home

B ootham Crescent, York, 28 December 2002. A clear, crisp
winter's afternoon for the plum Christmas derby between
York City and Hull City, who are now the Third Division's big
noises, following the unheard-of 22,000 crowd which rolled up
for their first match – against Hartlepool, of all glamour games
– at the new Kingston Communications Stadium, built by Hull's
local council and given to the club. York, to most visitors, is a
sedate day trip, a gaze at the Minster, a wide-eyed shop in the
mummified medieval city, but the compact, atmospheric football
ground is outside the Roman walls, squashed into the real York:
a cold, northern, working place, striped with long streets of stone
terraces, punctuated by the occasional chippy.

I sneak into a parking space at the end of one of these streets.
A woman, frown on her brow, blue and red scarf round her neck,
is striding up the road so I ask her the best way. She points up a
narrow alley, its grey cobbles decorated with glass and desiccat-
ing dog turds.

'Up here,' she frowns, trotting on. 'It's not the nicest way, but
the quickest.'

We have a chat as we walk. It's not too good here at the moment,
is it, I ask her.

'It's terrible,' she shakes her head, eyes down, maintaining her
pace. 'I'm meeting my whole family here; my dad, my sons. We're
lifelong fans. It's an absolute disgrace what is being done to this club.'

The alleyway comes out right at the corner of Bootham Crescent, York's home for seventy-one years, crammed among the houses. Outside the main entrance is the standard twenty-first-century welcome to the national game: fans rattling buckets. There are a dizzying number: Save York City, York City Supporters Trust, Friends of Bootham Crescent. Like most collectors for charities having a decent day, they're quite cheery. A middle-aged bloke appealing for money for the local hospital looks bemused, as the people pass him by having chucked their spare coins at the football causes. Overhead is an arched sign: Welcome to York City Soccer Club, the club logo stuck to a black and white chequered flag. It looks ridiculous.

Inside, the ground is low, intimate and full of more than 7,000 people; the Hull fans, crowding cockily into a whole end, the home fans milling behind the opposite goal, in the David Longhurst Stand, built with fans' contributions in honour of the York player who died on the pitch during the home game against Lincoln in September 1990.

There is that post-Christmas feel to the crowd, everybody well fed and pleased to be out; mixed, here, with simmering outrage. The York team, in red with black and white flag bits on their sleeves, run out to a mix of passionate, anxious roars. A stadium announcer on the touchline, red face, blue blazer, fawn slacks, urges: 'Be loud, be proud, from the first whistle to the last! This is our club!'

York's players, a young side dotted with some bearing considerable reputations, like the goalkeeper Alan Fettis and elegant captain Lee Nogan, tear into the Tigers, who seem a collection of triers not equipped for the job of transforming Hull into appropriate achievers for England's seventh biggest city – or whatever the claim is these days for Hull's rightfully monumental status. With half an hour gone, York's right fullback Darren Edmondson cuts in from the touchline to the corner of Hull's box, switches the ball to his left foot, then curls it towards goal. It floats a wonderfully long time in the air, Hull's keeper diving vainly for it, then there is a split moment of silence as the net swells, suddenly everyone is up, jumping up and down, roaring, punching the air, Bootham Crescent shaking with defiance in its suburb. A chant breaks out in the Longhurst End:

'You'll never kill York City. You'll never kill York City. You'll never kill York City . . .'

At half-time two players from the 1970s, Chris Topping and Chris Jones, rangy and careworn, step out on the pitch. They take the microphone, make an appeal for money and support. Topping turns to the Longhurst Stand: 'We can survive,' he says, to applause. 'Some wonderful people have been associated with this club: players, managers and directors. Let's not let everything fall down because of one man.'

And everybody roars.

The one man who has been able to unite everybody here in such open, public protest was not the chairman who recently made a big noise for a few self-serving months but one who had 'served' the club for twenty-four years. During that time, although he was never popular with fans, he was a highly esteemed chap at the Football League. Douglas Craig, OBE, JP, BSC, FICE, FI, MUN E, FCI ARB, M CONS E, as his entry in the *Rothmans Football Yearbook* has him, was regarded as a respectable, upright, cerebral sort among the used-Bentley brigade elsewhere in the League clubs' boardrooms. How he managed to pitch York supporters into this depth of anger is a story of three carefully planned years, but the upshot is easy to summarise. In January 2002, Craig announced that he wanted £4.5m for the club and the ground, or else he was kicking the club out and would withdraw it from the Football League. He was selling Bootham Crescent, and he and three other directors, not the club itself, would take the money. Hence the rattling buckets outside the ground, the supporters' social club thick with intrigue, the weary-looking former players expressing their contempt on the pitch.

Way back in 1978 Douglas Craig had been invited onto York City's board precisely because he appeared to be a solid citizen, as measured by a deeply conservative approach to what constitutes a pillar of society. A Scot, he was, until his retirement, an engineer, who latterly sat as an authority on arbitrations, deciding commercial disputes. He had been something significant in the Church and a former Tory local councillor, very stiff, very firm. The football club's chairman then was Michael Sinclair, a businessman who made his money via a china and gift shop at the top of Stonegate, the York street most achingly preserved to attract shoals of Amex-wielding Americans and the wedding lists of North Yorkshire's plentiful bourgeoisie.

In 1990, Sinclair was at the World Cup in Italy when he was involved in a serious car crash, which caused him to re-assess his life, renounce his worldly strivings and retrain as a priest. Now he ministers to the old and bereaved in seven villages around York. Craig had been his steady ally on the board as they kept York City going through the constant financial struggles of lower-division life, so, in 1992, Sinclair sold him his shares and handed him the chairmanship. According to the tradition for football club directors, which had always been followed at York City, Sinclair had never looked to make money out of the club; he regarded being the chairman as a privilege and form of public service, even if it mostly involved battling to balance the books and there were rarely any thanks from the fans.

Sinclair never took a salary and he is known to have passed Craig his 123,000 shares, a majority, for no more than a nominal £1 each, not charged a market rate for the club, whose ground squats on potentially prime residential land in a city where planning is always a headache. Craig, difficult to approach, maintainer of the fierce, provincially snooty division between terrace and boardroom, was never a fans' favourite. Grudgingly, they supposed they could respect his prudent watching of the pennies, augmented by a profitable youth policy which yielded the likes of Jonathan

Greening, sold to Manchester United, Richard Cresswell to Preston. It was not exactly a recipe for unchained happiness.

Never one of the game's giants, York have survived on a hard core of local support since they were first elected into the old Third Division (North) in 1929. The club's most illustrious period was a brief two seasons in the old Second Division, 1974–6, where they battled with the likes of Manchester United and Aston Villa, before going down scrapping. Barry Swallow, the captain during that period, was named City's 'man of the millennium' in 1999, and, the owner of a moderate hotel in York, he became a director of the club. In May that year York were relegated to the Third Division (bottom, in real terms) after six seasons in the Second. The fans became properly disillusioned; the club under Craig was cold and unfriendly, making national headlines only for their chairman's refusal, alone among ninety-two clubs, to formally adopt the anti-racism campaign Kick it Out's ten-point code of conduct. And the football was crap. Craig came in for stick in the ground and on the web. Retired and at home with a wife who was known to be ill, Craig was obviously reading the stuff and evidently not as thick skinned as he liked to appear. There was also some unpleasantness in the campaign to get Craig out, a few fans talking rather more abusively about him. At times like that it does seem important to remember the old saying that it's only a game, and nobody in the wider body of York fans seeks to excuse any of the malicious stuff. But they say it was the work of a tiny number of people, while the vast majority were truly exasperated with Craig and wanted him to leave for somebody with a more generous attitude to the role of a modern football club. Most thought he was a mean old bloke who'd had his day. But they never dreamt he was liable to do what he got up to next.

When Craig sent a letter out to all York City shareholders on 14 July 1999, few fans or shareholders smelt what was happening. To the untutored, the dry, legalistic language suggested Craig was tidying up some niggling details, which he told them was for the long-term good of the club. The letter said Craig wanted to transfer Bootham Crescent to a new holding company. The club wouldn't own its ground any more; it would be transferred to the new holding company. The letter, for form, asked share-holders to approve the transfer, but Craig made it clear that he and the three other directors, Colin Webb, John Quickfall and Barry Swallow, owned 94 per cent of the shares and would be approving it anyway.

The fans had never heard of the FA rule, which Craig explained, explicitly, that he wanted to avoid by transferring the ground to a holding company: 'It is currently a requirement for member-ship of the Football Association . . . that in the event of a liqui-dation or a cessation of its footballing activities any club is required to pay any surplus funds to the Football Association Benevolent Fund or other charitable or benevolent institution.'

If you haven't seen that before, you would not necessarily work out why it is important. Craig went on to put his interpretation on the effect of the rule: 'Your directors are concerned that in certain circumstances these provisions could adversely affect the ability of [York City] to continue playing football at Bootham Crescent.'

So, according to him, the FA's Rule 34, still on the rulebook, framed all those years ago to protect football clubs and their grounds, was actually endangering the long-term survival of the club at Bootham Crescent. The York fans didn't know – as indeed the Football Task Force members campaigning for firmer regu-lation of the sport by the FA didn't know either – that this long-standing rule had been consciously retained by the governing body only recently, after Nic Coward's thorough review of the rules which had resulted in the removal of the other historic restric-tions. It is impossible to read the rule in the way Craig presented it. Try as you can, it doesn't work. Its purpose is to ensure clubs are more secure in their homes. To get technical, it only applies when a club is wound up, so it cannot have anything to do with affecting a club's future ability to play at its ground. The club is folding; the rule applies to what happens to the assets and its point is to take the proceeds away from the owners and redistribute them through football or local sport. It removes the financial incentive to asset-strip a club and therefore protects clubs' ability to remain at their grounds. I had never before seen it so specifically set out: that the purpose of forming a holding company and transferring the ground to it was to avoid this rule. When the clubs floated they just bypassed all the rules to be more appealing to Stock Market investors. This was concentrated archly on removing the restriction against winding up a club, flogging the ground and keeping the money.

Many York fans believe, looking back, that the letter was the first move in a carefully considered plan to do exactly that. Some of them later recalled a strange performance Craig produced in December 1999, in a Q & A session organised to address fans' concerns by the unofficial internet newsletter 'There's only one Arthur Bottom', titled after the York striker of the 1950s who was blessed with that as his name. Charm and diplomacy were not Craig's tools of choice for dealing with disgruntled fans and the abuse he had been getting.

'The unpalatable truth,' he said, 'is that if the foul-mouthed few and the media-obsessed people, who also appear to have nothing else to do except play with the new toy called the internet, were to absent themselves from Bootham Crescent, the atmosphere at home games would be infinitely fresher and more pleasant.'

Then came the lines York fans would remember when the hammer fell:

'In the absence of any buyer [for his shares, for which he wanted 'a market price'], I am more than happy to carry on, but I should point out that I do have an alternative. It is one, however, at which I am sure all the decent loyal supporters of the club would be horrified should I contemplate taking it. The alternative, put bluntly, is that I should use my shareholding to start a campaign to close the club down.'

Paul Rawnsley, thirty-one years old, a lifelong York fan and an accountant in the sports business department at Deloitte & Touche, has looked at how the club's finances changed after the holding company was formed. Previously, Craig had run York relatively prudently, its wage bill not so different from other lower division clubs, the books balanced by selling young players. From 1999, however, even though the club had been relegated and lost income, players' wages began to balloon, peaking at £2.2m in 2000–1. It made headlines in the Deloitte & Touche report because, in 2001–2, York's wages alone were over 50 per cent in excess – 151 per cent – of the club's total income. Hopeless. The average even in the Third Division, a snakepit of strugglers, was 86 per cent. 'As a result of the directors' actions,' Rawnsley said, 'York's financial position was one of the worst in the history of British football.' Craig, whose saving grace had been prudence, was now driving York City insolvent.

Bootham Crescent was transferred to the holding company in June 2000. The price BCH, a separate company, paid for it was £165,890, which puzzles many people, considering what they asked for it just eighteen months later. On 9 January 2002, Craig put out his statement, dry as dust. He had given notice to resign York City from the Football League at the end of the season – point 1. The club was available for sale, but it would have to: 'Vacate the ground and premises at Bootham Crescent by 30 June 2002 and relocate to another stadium.'

The owners of Bootham Crescent Holdings – him and his three associates – would contribute £1m to helping York do up the suggested new home, the bleak, out-of-town Huntington Stadium, where the York City Knights rugby league club plays. If, however, a buyer wanted Bootham Crescent too, the price would be £4.5m.

The point-by-point, icy legalities of the statement fooled

nobody. Craig was kicking the club out, happy to withdraw it from the Football League, and selling Bootham Crescent for £4.5m, of which the directors were prepared to give only £1m to the club. So different from the camel-hair coat, chancer-chairmen viewed with suspicion elsewhere, Craig had emerged as every football supporter's worst nightmare: the enemy within, kicking out the club, selling the ground, keeping the money. The result was uproar.

York's *Evening Press*, which was to be outstanding in its coverage, saw through Craig's plan clinically. In a leader the day of the announcement, the newspaper wrote:

> York City fans have been betrayed. Bootham Crescent is to be closed and demolished at the end of the season, barring a miracle. Those responsible for its destruction are not face-less outsiders, but the very people entrusted with the moral guardianship of this historic club: its directors ... What moti-vated this unseemly scramble to dump the club? The four major shareholders who between them paid under £200,000 for their 94 per cent holding and who stand to share a £3.5m pay out, are not saying ... The directors call themselves City fans. Today they sold the real fans down the river.

When I saw Craig's original letter to shareholders and the way he had presented Rule 34, I called him to ask about it. Bootham Crescent Holdings was grandly registered as a plc, but its official address, the HQ for Craig's corporation, was his house. I found a number from directory inquiries and rang him up. It was the first time I had ever spoken to him and he was immediately rude. I told him I was a journalist looking into the York situation, and he said: 'Well, you can't have anything very interesting to do.'

Good start. I was ready to challenge the intepretation of the FA's rule he had given his letter, but when I brought it up he volunteered a completely different explanation: 'It is not accept-able in the modern era that if a club closes, its proceeds go to the

FA or charity. The shareholders should have the right to the proceeds as with any business.'

So he plainly contradicted his letter to shareholders. He did not say it had anything to do with protecting the club's tenure of Bootham Crescent. It was indeed the opposite: the FA's rules were standing in the way of him making money by closing down the club and selling its ground, and that was why he had formed a holding company, to bypass them.

What Craig perhaps underestimated, as he viewed all fans through the prism of those who had slagged him off loudest, was the reaction he would provoke. York is a strange city, unreal, with its painfully sanctified centre and summer invasion by tourists on whistle-stop tours of Heritage UK. In this disorienting environment, the locals cling hard to the stuff of real life. York was, until recently, a centre for manufacturing locomotives, a city dominated for years by the Quaker sweetie factories of Terrys and Rowntrees, swarms of workers cycling out of factory gates in a tidal wave of overalls. They have, they tell you proudly, 365 pubs, one for every day of the year. To Yorkies, or at least 3,000 or so diehards, the football club is a rallying point for local belonging, reality. And they discovered very quickly they were not going to let a man like Douglas Craig kill it. They also questioned from the beginning the right of these four major shareholders to determine its future, pointing out the work the fans had done over the years, unpaid, literally to build Bootham Crescent itself.

Four days after Craig's announcement, Barry Nicoll, a lifelong fan, wrote to 'There's only one Arthur Bottom':

Dear Douglas,

When you finally get your hands on your £4.5million I would be very grateful if you would forward me a cheque for £15,467.57 in payment for my father's efforts on the following:

a) work on the popular stand (paid for by the supporters)
b) work on the transfer booths (both ends of the popular stand)
c) work on the first programme shop, including its relocation from York station platform in 1968
d) labour supplied to unload several thousand large blocks for the construction of the Grosvenor Road end external wall.

You will probably note that more sweat and effort was put in by my father and dozens like him for no payment than you have ever offered this great football club. You will always be remembered, along with the faceless three, as betraying the good people of York.

PS: When the cheque arrives, I will donate it back to the club I love. In memory of Victor Alexander Nicoll, died 1990, aged 71.

The fans had put their backs into the original move to Bootham Crescent, from the club's old ground in Fulfordgate, way back in 1932. When David Longhurst tragically dropped dead during the match in 1990, fans' contributions paid for the roof built in his memory. Now, they weren't having this from Craig. They used the 'new toys' of the internet and e-mail to organise impressively and quickly. Protests and marches were spectacularly well attended. York fans became the next group to form a trust, helped by Supporters Direct, which they launched within weeks, on 1 February at a public meeting with a revivalist air attended by 1,000 people, their fundraising soon boosted by a gig by local band Shed 7.

The trust gathered members with inspirational force, and also found, as fans were doing at clubs across the country, that they could draw on talent and experience in all areas. It was nonsense, the hidebound doctrine that the fans know nothing and football clubs have to be run by one dictatorial oddball. Paul Rawnsley was joined on the board of the trust by Michael Shannon, a fifty-seven-year-old solicitor in one of York's most prominent law firms whose previous campaign had been to have Yorkshire Terrier bitter stocked in the social club. Sophie McGill, a capable PR spokeswoman who had briefly worked for the club under Craig, and Mike Brown, a marketing techie, also became influential in the new trust. And indefatigable from the start was a huge man in every sense, Steve Beck.

Beck was unusual for a York City obsessive – he lived in Milton Keynes. He had grown up in York as a teenager and Bootham Crescent was at the centre of these, his happiest, years. The club was his link to his own sense of himself and he still followed them home and away, driving up from Milton Keynes at 8 a.m. for home matches, his wife Carol spending her weekends doing the same:

'I'd never have seen him otherwise,' she shrugs.

In the crisis after Craig's announcement, Beck worked all hours, trying to talk to Craig, raising money, organising the trust, the work eating up his time: 'People say I must be mad driving a 360-mile round trip to go to one meeting,' he said at the time, 'but there is no way I am going to allow Mr Craig to kill our club.'

York fans embarked on a journey of discovery, from simple support of their club to the organisation of football in this country, and then into how lacking the governance of the game is, the vaccum of leadership. They thought at first it was simple; the FA would step in. Craig had bypassed the governing body's rule and was intending to do with the club and ground just what the rule is there to prevent. Michael Shannon wrote to Adam Crozier, then the FA's chief executive, setting out the details of what Craig had done, asking for clarification about whether Rule 34 could indeed operate as Craig had claimed it, to adversely affect clubs' ability to stay at their grounds. It would seem odd for the FA to have such a rule, if that was its effect. Shannon asked why the FA had retained the rule – presumably the FA 'thought it a valuable protection'? – and why the FA allowed clubs to form holding companies to get round the rule: 'What view does the FA take with regard to the blatant evasion of its rules by member clubs?'

When Shannon had a reply three weeks later, it was from Nic Coward. It was hardly a masterpiece, even of dither. Coward didn't answer the questions about what the rule was intended to protect, how it worked or the FA's view of the formation of holding companies. He did say clubs had raised 'concerns' about the rule in the past:

'One of the issues raised with the FA has been that a risk that a prospective investor in a club may look at is the insolvency risk – clubs have in the past claimed that the existence of [Rule 34] is a disincentive to investment.'

Spending too long with that sentence can seriously mess with your mind.

'However,' Coward concluded, 'the rule persists.' That was it. As limp as that. From the FA's head of legal matters and regulation. No reason given, no information, no explanation, never mind any sense that the FA might actually do anything to address so blatant an evasion of the rule they had, after long deliberation, decided to keep just a couple of years earlier. Not even an expression of concern, or sympathy. No best wishes either. The York fans were not the first to be shocked at the hole where football's governing body should be. Richard Snowball, the trust's chairman, a semi-retired businessman, summed it up: 'The FA are the governing body, but seem to have no powers, no beef, no teeth.'

Another fan, Colin Matthews, organised a petition, calling for an investigation into the proposed 'asset-stripping' of the club and calling on the FA to put 'the interests of football clubs, their supporters and communities ahead of the financial interests of individual owners and directors'. It was signed by 6,000 people, including fans of more than 200 different clubs. Signatories e-mailed their names from Australia, New Zealand, the Middle East and the Virgin Islands. On Saturday 23 February, around eighty people walked from Hanover Square to FA headquarters in Soho Square to deliver it, the York fans joined by supporters of Ipswich, Bradford, Middlesbrough, Lincoln City and others.

Many other fans wrote separately to the FA, asking the governing body to step in. All they received were standard acknowledgements. Some weeks later, a line went up on the FA's website: it said Craig had 'broken no rules'.

Well, thanks a lot. York fans knew then that if they wanted a football club they were on their own. Another group formed, specifically to fight Craig's plan to turn the ground over to bulldozers, the Friends of Bootham Crescent, led by David Allison, who called Craig's actions 'shameless profiteering...unchallenged by the so-called governing bodies of the game'.

The supporters' trust considered bidding for the club, which was heading for insolvency and available for £1, but they hadn't a chance of affording the ground too. Others came, looked and went away. Then the only genuinely interested candidate rode into town with a baseball cap and a bootful of patter: John Batchelor. A good talker, Batchelor began by selling toilet paper door-to-door, then graduated to making some money in hygiene products. Latterly, he had reinvented himself through entering a team in the British Touring Car Championships – not everybody's idea of fun, but an event televised on ITV, so attracting a bit of money and sponsorship. He hot-rodded into York to talk to Craig. When he came close to an agreement, he told the supporters' trust that he was going to buy not only the club but the ground too. He also promised, later putting it in writing, that he would give the trust 25.1 per cent of the shares and invite two supporters onto the board. His big idea to make the club work financially and balance the books was to combine York City with his car team, which sounded laughable, but when you listened to him he could have you believing it. York's profile would be raised on television, encourage sponsors, all the rest of it. To fans who were desperate he seemed to have money they didn't; he was the only show in town and he was making the kind of promises they needed to hear, so the trust agreed to support his bid.

Batchelor took over on 15 March 2002. He was never, after that, backward at putting himself forward. Carlton and Granada made it clear that ITV Digital was collapsing just days later and Batchelor was right there straightaway on Radio 5, talking about the problems for lower division club chairmen. He never, however, came through with his promise to hand the fans shares and give them seats on the board. In early April he did announce a major sponsorship deal with the housebuilder Persimmon, whose head office is based in York. Then, in June, Batchelor unveiled York City's brave new 'rebranding'. Renamed York City Soccer Club – that apparently being of more appeal to sponsors – the logo and even players' strip were intertwined with the car racing team by incorporating the black and white chequered flag. And plenty else even more embarrassing than that.

Craig never budged, never relented on his plan, listened to no plea. He maintained he had every right to sell the ground for his personal profit and maintained BCH was being 'very generous' to the club. He told me he had bought Sinclair's shares originally for 'a market price' – I was told very reliably it was for under £123,000 – and was entitled to demand a market price, £4.5m, for Bootham Crescent.

Members of the trust went to see him, to negotiate, to reason. They said it was weird; at times he would drift from acrid, deathly discussions about rent, ground values, debts and all the other miseries, the vice in which he had the club, to suddenly musing wistfully about the team, lapsing, dewy-eyed, into talking about the talents of some up-and-coming kid in one of the youth sides. Yet he never gave an inch on his strategy of scything the club to make a killing himself. It was clear to the trust members that he was doing it because he had grown so embittered by the abuse he had taken from fans:

'This,' he'd say, 'is payback time.'

They argued that only a minority of fans had ever abused him, and that the majority would never condone such behaviour, but he wouldn't have it. One trust member argued that whether or not what Craig had done was illegal it was certainly immoral. His answer was: 'Don't give me that morality crap.'

In August 2002, Persimmon – motto 'Together we make a Home' – submitted a planning application to demolish Bootham Crescent and build ninety-two houses on the site. A record number of oppositions were lodged to it. Two months later the supporters discovered that Persimmon had already paid a deposit, buying 10 per cent of the shares in the holding company from Craig, Swallow, Webb, Quickfall and their wives, to whom 454 shares had been transferred, apparently a tax-saving device. If, as York property experts reckoned, £3.5m, not £4.5m, was in fact the price Persimmon would pay, the directors were already sharing a tenth of it, £350,000. Two-thirds of it, around £220,000, was Craig's, because he owned 64 per cent of the shares. Craig told me: 'It is just as if you had sold your house, or shares in Marks & Spencer.'

In November, Batchelor's ideas and credibility finally ran out of gas, as did the club's money. He had never bought the ground, only the club, for £1. The club could not now pay the players or staff, but Batchelor wasn't there to tell them because, he said, he was away on business. Steve Beck, who was always around still trying to dig York a future, had to tell them himself. The players agreed to defer receiving any wages for six weeks; some of the office staff were in tears. Beck said it was one of the hardest things he'd ever had to do. The trust declared Batchelor's position 'untenable'.

There was another bizarre episode on 26 November, at half-time in a midweek match against Swansea, when a protest by the Friends of Bootham Crescent was upstaged by Batchelor, arriving on the pitch with a microphone. He was, he said, to cheers from the crowd, going to hand 100 per cent ownership of the club to the trust. Then, the following day, when the trust prepared to sort out the details, it became apparent that Batchelor had retracted and was demanding continuing ownership and a role in the club. Beck then lost any remaining belief in Batchelor.

On 17 December, Batchelor had to face the fact that the club was insolvent and he finally put it into administration. The administrator, David Willis, said there was only enough money coming in to last thirty-five days, because upcoming home games against Scunthorpe, Lincoln and Hull were reasonable money-spinners. After that, without substantial additional cash, the club would close. So out came the buckets.

The trust began negotiating to buy the club, realising they should no longer rely on any incomers making promises. In doing so, the details of Batchelor's original deal were unravelled. It had been a three-way agreement, with Persimmon in at the start, agreeing to buy the ground from Craig. Batchelor had taken the club for £1, then he and Craig agreed that the club's twenty-five-year lease on Bootham Crescent be reduced to a single year. And here was another bit which hurt: Persimmon had agreed to pay £400,000 in sponsorship. It was clearly a sweetener from the York-based company to the football club, but Persimmon's rules don't allow local, only national, sponsorship. The company's managing director, Ian Hessay, had agreed the money should sponsor the 'York Sporting Club', which didn't actually exist, but which he took to mean joint sponsorship of the football club and Batchelor's touring car team, which would stick Persimmon's name on.

However, the contract was made out with Batchelor personally and did not even mention the football club. It talked only about sponsoring the car team, in 2002, 2003 and 2004. The trust found that Batchelor had put very little of this money into York City. He had, at first, put in a quarter, £100,000, as a loan to the club, but even this he had steadily withdrawn, marking down thousands for expenses, entertainment at Brands Hatch, tickets for Silverstone and other motor racing events, until eventually only £30,000–40,000, according to Batchelor himself, was left. The rest, £300,000, he kept. A couple of months after he was paid the money, Batchelor, it turned out, had bought a house for nearly £250,000 in Wilmslow, one of Manchester's posher satellite suburbs. He'd been renting before that. Six months later, he was looking to make a profit by selling it and buying another house for less, across the road.

Steve Beck told me at the time: 'We supported John at the beginning on the basis of promises he never honoured. Then it turned out that there had been good money from Persimmon, but he had put so little of it into the club, just feathered his own nest, while the club was going bust. He'd presented himself as the saviour, and we felt betrayed.'

Even on this Batchelor was unblinking. He told me the sponsorship of his car team was good publicity for Persimmon. Then he said it was his money: 'Look: I'm a businessman. That means I have to make a profit from what I do. And that includes football.'

I found that a fascinating insight to the modern attitude to making money: you still emerge with a fortune, even if the company you were running has gone bust, because you are 'a businessman'.

On the way to the Hull match in December 2002, with the club in administration and the fans still in ferment, I picked up an old man who was thumbing a lift. He had a wispy beard, weathered knapsack and cagoule. He was visiting his sister and couldn't be bothered waiting for the bus. I told him I was going to the football and he asked me about it. 'York's a nice club,' I said, 'but they've had one chairman sell the ground and another's gone off with £300,000.'

'Hmm,' he nodded, thoughtfully, 'it's always the way, isn't it?'

The game finished 1-1. In the social club the fans fretted but it was warm there too, everybody had a drink and plenty of people were still smiling. Steve Beck clutched his pint, mused:

'When I started supporting, we were known as the friendly club – we have to get back to that.'

Michael Sinclair, said to be feeling terribly guilty, was considering a bid to rescue the club but the figures looked hopeless and he withdrew on 14 January. The administrator's deadline was up two days later. Nobody – not Batchelor, not Craig, not two other bidders looking into it – came forward with any money. At this point, Craig's plan for the club could have come to pass. It would have gone into liquidation because nobody wanted to save it. The sale of Bootham Crescent to Persimmon would have gone ahead, and the holding company which owned it was free of the FA's rule on distribution of assets, so the directors would have pocketed all the money. By this time the trust had raised £92,000, a tremendous effort. If they handed all their money over, it was going to be spent in four weeks keeping the club going, paying players. If they didn't, the club was gone forever. They gave it to the administrator.

Relying only on themselves now, the trust launched their own bid to raise £500,000 and take over the club. In February, sure enough, the administrator ran out of money. The trust put out an appeal on 20 February to raise £60,000. Two days later they had a home match – against Bury, a dream tie for bucket collections. The collectors rattled like fury, staggered back to count the money and found they had raised £20,000. Mike Brown put an appeal on the trust's website, and donations came in, from all over the world, raising another £20,000. They found £60,000 for the administrator, but this time they didn't just pour it into the black hole; they wanted it to be a down payment on a deal for them to take over the club.

York's total debts at the time were £1.8m. Financially, the trust just managed to cobble together enough for a CVA; Jason McGill, Sophie's brother, who has his own packaging business in York, contributed £50,000 and bought a club house which was used by young players for £300,000. That was crucial, and McGill became

Bootham Crescent: York City v Cheltenham, 17 April 2004

Hillsborough: Sheffield Wednesday v Brentford, 10 April 2004

Away fans: Wimbledon v Derby,
National Hockey Stadium, Milton Keynes, 9 May 2004

Surrey Street, Glossop, 2004

Sixfields Stadium:
Northampton Town v Manchester United,
FA Cup Fourth Round, 25 January 2004

Kingsmeadow Stadium:
AFC Wimbledon, Champions of the Combined Counties'
League Premier Division 2003–04, 8 May 2004

Wimbledon fans outside Selhurst Park, August 2002

Valley Parade, Bradford, 2004

Old Trafford, 2004

Arsenal victory parade, 16 May 2004

Ageing faces: Chelsea v Monaco,
Champions League Semi-final, Stamford Bridge, 5 May 2004

Gigg Lane, Bury, 2004

Highbury, 2004

Raymond Pinn in his workshop at Ashburton Grove, Islington, April 2004

The Football Association, 25 Soho Square, London, 2004

a minority shareholder in the club, but with an agreement that the trust still had control over its running. On 28 March 2003, at 1 p.m., they finally concluded a deal with the administrator, agreeing to pay the Inland Revenue 63p in the pound. Leicester, bought by a consortium of local businessmen, had got away with 10p in the pound, rising to 20p on promotion. Steve Beck, whose commitment had verged on the incomprehensible, was made York City's new chairman. The first thing they did was to take down the sign outside the ground and call York a football club again. The following day, before York's match against Southend, hundreds of fans marched from the Minster to the ground, behind a banner which read SAVED CITY.

The players came out on to the pitch at Bootham Crescent to heartfelt applause, and, in turn, they applauded the fans. When I talked to him later, Lee Nogan told me that as a senior player he was very happy the trust had taken over: 'We know they're fans of the club and they'll be here forever. You can't do much better than that.'

The *Evening Press* hailed the trust as 'a remarkable body of men and women. From the Trust's astonishingly successful launch to its takeover of the club, they have played a blinder. The magnitude of their achievement is plain. They have saved the club not once, not twice, but over and over again.'

At half-time, Steve Beck and some of the trust's stalwarts went onto the pitch to herald the new era. Paul Rawnsley's family was there; his wife Mhairi, pregnant with their third baby; Josh, three, and Jessica, eighteen months, both of them signed up Junior Reds, who hadn't seen too much of their daddy so far in their little lives. Rawnsley took the microphone and made a speech:

'Unfortunately,' he told the crowd, 'through the actions of the previous owners, over recent years our club had been driven to the brink of extinction. Don't ever forget how close we came to losing our club.

'Others have come and gone. Many people said the club was

beyond salvation. However, it was all of us here today – the supporters – that stood strong and would not let them kill York City.'

'This,' he said, 'is the start of a new journey. Working together, we will create a community club for the benefit of future generations.'

The crowd – apart from a bemused couple of hundred in the away end – were beside themselves. Rawnsley clenched his fist:

'Be proud to be York City,' he went on. 'And thank you to every one for the continuing support. They'll never kill York City.'

At that his son Josh came toddling onto the pitch. Paul scooped him up in his arms, turned to the Longhurst End, and shouted: 'Come Oooooonnnnnn!' And they all went crazy.

They also won 2-0. The trust proved, as at other clubs, that because their priority is survival they were the opposite of irresponsible dreamers. They immediately released four players as part of the cost-cutting plans. They also parted company with the manager, Terry Dolan. They weren't soft and they weren't hanging about. They appointed as player-manager Chris Brass, their former Burnley centre half who had been solid throughout. Nogan was his assistant. Done in the early flush of ownership, you have to wonder if that was a good decision. Dolan, of the old school in the notoriously insecure, sacking-bedevilled job of football management, had not taken immediately to their plans for a new, community-focused club, and the trust board hadn't liked him much. He was, though, an experienced lower division campaigner who had kept them up throughout the crisis. Brass, at just twenty-seven, was by a long way the youngest manager in the League. However, the new club board still say that they had no money at all to work with, and they could not afford the wages of a new manager. Alongside a few players who came through the youth system, the unruffled defender Leigh Wood, and busy midfielder Christian Fox, they picked up the odd player from more senior clubs, like Darren Dunning from Blackburn, and scoured the non-leagues, signing Aron Wilford from Whitby, Dave Merris from Harrogate Town. The wage bill was cut, down from its previous suicidal heights to 50 per cent of turnover. The club was doing well on the pitch, at first, and moving towards breaking even.

Steve Beck, who moved back to York with his wife, 'a dream come true', had, with Jason McGill and the other board members, to negotiate with the council for Huntington Stadium, but their hearts were never in it. They felt that, after all the work, a move out there could kill the club anyway.

Craig still wanted his money, and he had a deal with Persimmon. Jason McGill looked for a way round it, while Persimmon, loaded down with bad publicity, the Friends of Bootham Crescent picketing some of their new estate openings, began to want out. Craig had never improved Bootham Crescent much, so the club still had £2m available to claim in grants from the Football Foundation. McGill began to lobby them for a grant, to buy out Craig and the other directors and leave the club at Bootham Crescent. After months of hustling, cajoling, politicking, charming, in June 2004 he wrested from the Foundation an agreement to lend York City £2m at half a per cent over base, to be used to buy 76 per cent of Bootham Crescent Holdings. After ten years, the club is committed to moving to a new, purpose-built, 10,000-seat stadium – on their own terms. OK, they thought, Craig would be getting his money, as would Webb and Swallow, the old playing hero who had said nothing throughout the affair. The fourth major shareholder, John Quickfall, had already cheered the fans by announcing he would give any proceeds back to the club. York City, for now, were staying at home.

'It's been tough,' said Sophie McGill, 'but perhaps things happen for a reason. In the end we got the club and ground, owned by the fans, for a lot less than Douglas Craig was asking originally.'

They plan to move away from the fusty idea that the boardroom is some inner sanctum, separate from the people outside.

And they have a different vision of what the football club is for: they want to take it into the community, play a real part in the life of the city. They swept through the place like a smile.

Then, towards the end of the 2003–4 season, which had started so well, Chris Brass' team started to lose. I went to see them play Bristol Rovers in September and they played really convincingly: Dunning busy in midfield, Brass frighteningly committed at the back, Lee Bullock dangerous up front, and they won 2-1. Even in January, when they beat Rochdale then Carlisle, they were doing OK. Then they went into complete and utter freefall, drawing only four times, losing all fourteen of their other games, four points from fifty-four. As Carlisle rallied with some old heads – Andy Preece went there as a striker when Bury let him go as their manager – and Macclesfield signed the old managerial know-how of Brian Horton on a nice bonus to save them, York slid further and further down. On 24 April 2004, following two home defeats to Yeovil and Cheltenham, they lost 3-1 away at Doncaster, a result which effectively relegated them out of the Football League for the first time since they had entered it seventy-five years earlier.

There seemed no justice: 'Perhaps we were so concentrated on saving the club and the ground,' Jason McGill said, 'we forgot a little bit about the football, trusted the players to do their bit.' But they reflected that they had no choice, with no money to work with. Professional football is unforgiving. There will be no favours in the Conference either. But York will surely be back; this is a lower division club for which you can see a future. Unlike Bury, it does not have glamorous giants nearby, biting chunks out of its support; even Leeds is a fair drive away. York could draw support from miles around, with the right people in charge, committed to working with the fans and the community. You could see them carving out a healthy club here, with the catchment area they have, and the fight and talent the supporters have shown, their heartfelt commitment to the strange modern phenomenon of 'belonging' to a football club. On the final day of the season, York lost 2-1 at home to Orient, confirming they would finish bottom, and lost their League status after seventy-five years. The fans poured onto the pitch from the David Longhurst Stand. But they didn't swarm in front of the main stand to protest, shout abuse or slate the board. Instead the fans gathered in front of the directors' box, full of people who had given so much for their football club, and celebrated. They hailed the club's survival, the fact that there was a club there at all, and they showed support for Chris Brass, who was in tears. 'We'll support you everymore,' they sang, 'We'll support you evermore.'

After all the York fans went through it is bitter to reflect that Douglas Craig appears to have achieved one of his aims – York City were out of the Football League. He's been paid his money too, a strange, lonely revenge, although we don't know if it will make him happy. One thing, though, he didn't manage: he never killed York City.

CHAPTER 11

The People's Game

Wimbledon – one of English football's greatest and most important stories; the small club at the ragged ground playing its way from non-league, semi-professional football to scalping the game's biggest names. Proving that football is a shared passion, not an unchallengeable hierarchy, that given the right spirit and circumstances all clubs belong with and have a chance against each other. All true – but if only you could think a little more fondly about the way they went about it.

Throughout Wimbledon's rise from the Southern League to the Premier League, I was playing my football in local Sunday leagues around Manchester. Nearly everybody wanted to fight rather than play. You went round or tackled someone, they'd tell you they'd kill you next time, or break your neck. Most of it was talk, but out on the public parks there are no cameras, no crowd, no protection, just your team and some seriously fucked-up blokes, miles from anywhere after a bad Saturday night. Occasionally, something did happen. One Sunday, on the Littleton Road playing fields in Salford, miles of forsaken fields stretching into the murk, we were told some pub side player had stabbed another in the changing rooms. We believed it when the ambulance arrived. We were involved in one mass scrap over Christmas against a pub side mostly pissed from the night before, a hundred of their fans baying on the line.

In Moss Side we played thrilling, intense matches against FC

Astro, an all-black club and the indisputable champions of Manchester amateur football, many of their team playing on Saturdays for senior non-league or professional clubs, including their captain, Gus Wilson, who played 112 League games for Dario Gradi at Crewe. But we also played one side who turned out to be Man City's hard-core hooligans. That wasn't fun. We won a penalty and their skipper went around the forlorn, rutted pitch, saying, in a loud voice: 'Just break their fucking legs now', and we knew they did that sort of stuff for recreation. They intimidated much harder sides than us and won the League.

So when Wimbledon beat Liverpool in the FA Cup Final in 1988 I didn't read it as romance and I didn't find them a laugh. 'The Crazy Gang has beaten the Culture Club' was John Motson's Alan Partridge take on it, but for me it was a triumph for the crap we took every week, football as urban thuggery over a game of skill. When the story emerged that in the Wembley tunnel Vinnie Jones had threatened to rip Kenny Dalglish's ear off and spit in the hole, or whatever it was, I thought you had to be truly sad, or never have played the game, to find that anything but deeply depressing.

They had good players, many of whom moved on to long careers at other top clubs – Nigel Winterburn, Kevin Gage, Dennis Wise, Dave Beasant and many more – so their scouting, coaching and quality were clearly more expert than they let on. But to me Wimbledon's 'Crazy Gang' were spectacularly unfunny and they established the worst principle, that studs up, fists out and threats in the opposition's ear all work. It was never my idea of 'character' to put up with that to win a football match.

I can see it must have been great to be a Wimbledon fan, though. However horrible to the rest of us, these blokes were theirs and the fans lived a phenomenon of football history, watching their club rise, roughing up sides at small, gritty Plough Lane, respecting nobody, rising from semi-pro football to beating Liverpool, four times European Cup winners.

Sam Hammam was there throughout those years, the owner of the club, working his way into personifying the Crazy Gang spirit. His associate Ron Noades bought the club originally and took them into the League in 1977. Dario Gradi, a manager with a twinkly-eyed vision of what the beautiful game looks like, took them up in 1979 but they went down again and his former skipper, Dave Bassett, became the chest-out motivator who roused the rabble up and into the First Division by 1986. Noades took over Crystal Palace; he held on to Wimbledon initially and wanted to merge the two clubs, the first identity-destroying plan which Wimbledon fans organised to oppose. Hammam, who had become a director, bought the club from Noades in 1981, reportedly for around £100,000, and, a Lebanese businessman who describes himself as an engineer, took to the atmosphere like a natural. Telling me about his time at Wimbledon, which he loved, Dave Beasant said Sam was always there, in the thick, buying rounds of drinks for the players, egging them on. The club and its players were, Hammam said, his family, and his programme notes never stinted on hyperbole and a sticky mess of emotional guff.

Hammam was restlessly ambitious and knew Wimbledon could not stay at the top long term on the bulldog spirit, selling players and gates of a few thousand at Plough Lane. In 1987 he tried to revive the merger plan with Noades, create one south London 'super club' at Selhurst Park. The fans who campaigned against that discovered that Hammam owned acres of land around Plough Lane, and believed he stood to make millions if he moved Wimbledon and sold Plough Lane. Hammam, who thrived on being worshipped by supporters, was worn down by the hostility and he gave up on that one.

He then began a stop-start project to develop a new home for Wimbledon locally, in the London Borough of Merton, and in 1988 he applied for and was granted outline planning permission to build a stadium, with leisure and necessary moneymaking periphera, in the adjoining Wandle Valley. The planning permission required him to make improvements to the area but Hammam never proceeded with it. He always said the council failed him, that they never really did enough to help. The council say they always wanted Wimbledon to stay in the borough and did what they could, but Hammam never came through with the projects.

Plough Lane was protected by the common historic restriction imposed by councils, that it could not be used for any purpose other than sport or recreation. In 1990, saying he would need to develop Plough Lane to pay for another ground, Hammam bought out this covenant and had it cancelled; reports on the price he paid vary between £300,000 and £800,000.

Throughout that season there were rumours Hammam was going to move the club. Finally, the fans were told in Hammam's programme notes at the last match of the season against Crystal Palace on 4 May 1991: he was moving Wimbledon to Selhurst Park, where they would be Ron Noades' tenants. He said they had to move because the all-seater requirement of the Taylor Report would have reduced Plough Lane's capacity to 6,000. So the match turned out to be Wimbledon's last ever at Plough Lane, after ninety-two years. Palace beat them 3-0, Ian Wright scoring a hat-trick. For many Wimbledon fans, the *fait accompli* meant they never trusted Hammam again.

In Wimbledon supporter and journalist Niall Couper's wonderful labour of love, *The Spirit of Wimbledon*, participants tell Wimbledon's story from their perspective. Hammam is there, saying he tried everything to find a new home in Merton but the council blocked him. Supporters talk of a sense of profound betrayal at the sudden move. Tony Stenson, a *Daily Mirror* journalist who'd covered Wimbledon for the local paper back when the club was in the Isthmian League, writes of the move to Selhurst Park:

'There was never any need to leave Plough Lane. I looked into it at the time. The club had been given five years by the Football

League to get the ground up to scratch . . . Plough Lane could easily have become a 25,000-capacity stadium.

'Selhurst Park betrayed what Wimbledon was about. Suddenly it was all about money: the players were talking about it, Sam was talking about it, and no one was talking about Wimbledon.

'I'm not going to deny that football is about money, but it's also about heart, and somewhere along the line, Wimbledon lost that.'

The fans feared a merger again and organised to oppose it. Hammam told them there was no prospect of a move back to Merton, but the club's soul was freezing over at Selhurst. In 1997, at the highest point of football clubs' Stock Market standing, when the top clubs were gorging themselves on the second helping of Sky's banquet, Hammam made his move. Wimbledon fans discovered that he had sold 80 per cent of their little club to two seriously rich Norwegians, the powerboat-racing playboys Kjell Inge Rokke and Bjorn Gjelsten, for the outlandish figure of £25m. Hammam held the Wimbledon shares via a company registered in the British Virgin Islands, so he presumably paid no tax on his massive profit. His idea was to stay on to run the football side of the club, buying and selling players and negotiating their contracts, skills at which he had proved himself adept.

Then, in December 1997, came the next wallop for the Dons fans; the new regime had indeed decided to move the club, but not to Merton, not to Selhurst permanently, in fact, nowhere in London. To Dublin.

Wimbledon Football Club had been sold as the Premier League's Irish franchise for two foreign, multi-millionaire investors. Of the two, Rokke was the magnate, having built a fortune on fish processing and shipping via his own company, Aker. He and Gjelsten were old friends from school and Gjelsten worked for him, latterly as the company's chief executive.

The fans protested, pretty good at it by now. The Dublin move was approved by the Premier League clubs, which saw it as the opportunity to soak up the interest and money of the Irish, who have always supported English clubs, if not, perhaps, Wimbledon as their first choice. Hammam had told the Norwegians that the English authorities would not block the move, which was true, but they spent their £25m before the move was officially sanctioned. In May 1998, the Irish Football Association, a small body of part-time clubs but proud enough, blocked the franchise. The English FA simply stood by the decision of a fellow FA. The Norwegians were stuck with a club of 6,000 fed-up core supporters, with no ground, in a game whose wage bills in the Premier League were rising beyond the club's ability to keep up. The Norwegians soon fell out with Hammam and he left.

The supporters learned that in 1998 Hammam had sold Plough Lane to Safeway for a price reported to be £8m. As long ago as 1984, they learned, Hammam himself, through his holding company, Rudgwick Limited, had taken over ownership of Plough Lane from the club as payment for the loans he had made to bankroll its rise up the League. Since then, through fourteen Crazy Gang years, it had paid Hammam rent. Rudgwick's accounts for 1998 show a profit on the sale of a property of £5m.

Lawrence Llowne, who became a senior member and spokesman of the Wimbledon Independent Supporters Association (WISA), spoke for many fans:

'We feel Sam sold us down the river. He talked about the club being his family but he took over a community club which people had supported loyally for generations. OK we had great years on the field, but he sold the club, sold our ground, and walked off £30m richer. It was shattering.'

The Norwegians were left with having to do something with the club and a few thousand alienated and homesick Dons. In 2000, they appointed a new chairman to try to steer them a course; Charles Koppel knew Rokke and Gjelsten through powerboat racing; for a year he had promoted the sport and sold the media rights. In April 2000, Koppel and his partner Matthias

Hauger bought the remainder of Hammam's shares via their company, Farian, for a reported £1.5m.

Hammam didn't take long to find another club: Cardiff City, a genuine potential giant, and he lost no time trying to turn them into the 'franchise' for the whole of Wales. There, he struck the wrong note, invoking Celtic mythical legends and old battles with the English, saying it was about fighting for Wales and every away match should be like war. Many Cardiff fans needed little encouragement to behave that way, but the Swansea fans' reaction to the idea that Cardiff was the club for all Wales woke him up to the parochial facts on the ground. At Cardiff, already, he has the club in the First Division and on the threshold of a massive stadium development, with retail on the side and a group of fans who believe in him as the saviour. Their club, now a subsidiary of Cardiff City Football Club (Holdings) Limited, is registered, like Rudgwick, at the London offices of Kennedys, Hammam's solicitors.

In 2000, after fourteen years in the top flight, Wimbledon were finally relegated from the Premier League. That year they made a loss of £3.25m. The drop in income from the Premier League to the First Division meant the Norwegians were staring at massive losses to keep the club going, not what they had in mind when they invested in the Whole New Ball Game in 1997.

Koppel did not see a smorgasbord of options. Wimbledon needed a home, but the idea of building a new stadium from scratch in Merton cannot have been central to the Norwegians' original dream. The fans campaigned for a move back to Plough Lane – Safeway had been refused planning permission – or to another site in Merton, but Koppel said there were too many problems.

In August 2000, Peter Winkelman, a shaggy-haired music producer with a salesman's silver tongue, approached Koppel with the idea of moving Wimbledon to Milton Keynes. Winkelman, himself based in Milton Keynes, was part of a consortium, whose members he would never reveal but was known to include Asda, who wanted to build a superstore in this growing, prospering, consumerist new town. Planning was tricky; the Government had stemmed the spread of out-of-town shopping centres. However, the idea was to build a stadium, which the town didn't have, then the retail around it, including the superstore, would be granted planning permission because it would be 'enabling development', paying for the building of the stadium. So, Wimbledon, the old proud non-league club, became a pawn in another property deal involving a supermarket chain.

Milton Keynes has been a standing joke for concrete sterility since it was established in January 1967, but Winkelman talks a tremendous pitch about its dynamism, growth, the wealth of its inhabitants who, poor things, do not have a senior professional football club to support. The local clubs have had no success establishing themselves; it hasn't been the MK way to rally behind a club at the bottom of the football pyramid and work hard to create a professional club. Winkelman produced a finding that Milton Keynes was the largest town in Europe without a professional football club and he wanted to parachute one in there, ready-made.

Since 1998 he had been touting to troubled southern clubs the idea of landing in Milton Keynes; he'd approached Luton, Queens Park Rangers and even Barnet, and they'd all said no. Koppel, a South African, was captivated; here was a solution, a ready-made audience, a franchise for the club. If it landed in Milton Keynes as a Premier League or senior First Division club, it would make a major impact in a town which liked large-scale branded entertainment. The football followers, who currently left on the train to support London or Midlands clubs, possibly popped across to Northampton, would stay in MK. This was Dublin-lite and a way out for the Norwegians. In July 2001, Wimbledon had a board meeting in which a majority agreed to sign up with Winkelman for the move to Milton Keynes. The older directors who had been there since the Plough Lane days voted against. Wimbledon fans, needless to say, were bitterly opposed and utterly outraged at what was being done to their club.

Koppel wrote to the Football League on 2 August 2001, aware that the club needed permission to move. It was a revelation to many fans that the sense of belonging to a place, which football clubs inspire in fans, is actually incorporated in the League's rules. They say: 'The location of the ground, in its relation to the conurbation . . . from which the club takes its name or with which it is otherwise traditionally associated, must meet with the approval of the Board.'

The League's board met on 16 August 2001 and didn't take long unanimously to say no. Franchising was out. Clubs had to have some relation to the places whose names they bore. You couldn't up a club and its membership of the League and move it to the middle of a population you thought would give you a better financial return. The football pyramid is based on promotion and relegation by footballing success; in fact no club illustrated that principle better than Wimbledon. You can – or you could – rise by your efforts, wherever you were from.

'This is a victory for the football supporter,' said WISA of the decision, 'and we urge the board of Wimbledon Football Club to take heed.'

Koppel instead took legal advice and appealed. He argued that the League's board had not considered fully enough the club's punishing financial situation and how it would be improved by the move. The League agreed to decide the issue via arbitration, a service provided by the FA, and so Wimbledon fans were sent on a journey through football's leaky rulebooks. The FA set up a three-man panel which sat in January 2002; a barrister, Charles Hollander QC, was the chairman with two experts. They were David Dein, who had not long before bid to buy Wembley for Arsenal, and another pillar of the football establishment with clear views on clubs' relations with their homes, Douglas Craig.

York fans were incredulous; this was three weeks after Craig's announcement that he was kicking the club out and selling the ground for housing. When Wimbledon fans heard about it, they too were dismayed, but the panel's membership was unshiftable. Craig's presence on that panel always compromised the League's reaction to what he had done at York; he was one of their great and good, in fact they were relying on him to vote for tradition and against the move to MK. The League, taken up with the Wimbledon challenge, never seemed to grasp how far Craig had gone with his own club.

His panel, anyway, kicked the question back to the League, saying the board should consider it more fully, although they made some comments which suggested they were sympathetic to the move.

'Is it better for WFC to go into administration . . . than to permit a move to Milton Keynes?' They seemed to accept that the move could be Wimbledon's salvation.

The Football League was tiring of the issue, and its clubs reluctant to take on more legal costs, so in April 2002 the League asked the FA to set up an independent panel to decide the issue. This, again, was a curiosity of the rules; the FA itself was against the move, because it upholds the pyramid principle, but its rules allow two football parties to resolve their disputes by using an FA-appointed 'independent commission'. It is part of the game's insular culture of wanting issues to be decided 'within football', not let 'outsiders', like courts, get involved.

The three members this time were Raj Parker, a commercial solicitor from Freshfields, Nic Coward's old firm, Steve Stride, Aston Villa's £162,000 a year operations director, and Alan Turvey, the chairman of the Ryman League, down below the Conference in the pyramid. The FA has never said how or why they appointed those people, nor do the rules set out the process or qualifications for the appointed people. Turvey was assumed by fans to be sympathetic to them, Stride, maybe, as a commercial Premiership sort, perhaps erring towards Wimbledon's financial view of the issue, but they didn't know. Parker, they hadn't a clue. They didn't see how anybody could vote for an idea so obviously contrary to football's culture, but you never knew.

The commission sat for four days in May 2002. Lou Carton-Kelly, the chair of Wimbledon fans' supporters' trust, the Dons Trust, formed with the assistance of Supporters Direct, and Kris Stewart, WISA's chair, had to fight for the right to give evidence, then, when they had been accepted as witnesses, to see the case the club was putting forward. By now, at Selhurst, the atmosphere had curdled: black-card protests, fans turning their backs on the game, sit-ins, bitterness towards Koppel and the Norwegians, a torrent of indignation in the fanzines and on the web, with Koppel adamant all the while about the move. Stewart, a management accountant in his day job and a Wimbledon fan since 1989, told the commission that if the club moved to Milton Keynes he would regard it as dead; it wouldn't be Wimbledon any more. If that happened, he hoped to resurrect the club and start again at the bottom of the football pyramid.

The commission delivered its verdict on 28 May 2002, a date engraved in the folk memories of Wimbledon fans. Reading the judgement is a dispiriting pastime. The members were very much moved by the losses Wimbledon were making, £20,000 per day, although this ignored the fact that Wimbledon had always been a selling club and had sold players like Carl Cort (£7m), Ben Thatcher (£5m), Herman Hreidarrson (£4m) and John Hartson just recently. The commission were worried for the Norwegian shareholders, who, they said, put in £6.7m the previous year to keep the club going, and a further £3.8m in 2002.

'WFC shareholders have made it perfectly clear they will be forced to close the club down if they see no sound financial future for the club.'

The commission said there was no available site in Merton 'or anywhere else in south London'. Pete Winkelman, who had set out his stall about the joys of Milton Keynes, had, they found, 'infectious enthusiasm', was 'obviously genuine' and 'passionate and frank'. Steve Clark, on the other hand, from Merton Borough Council, who said the club could build a 20,000-seat stadium on Plough Lane, was dismissed as 'not a financial expert'.

To cut to the chase, the commission allowed the move.

The vote was 2-1. There is no doubt that Alan Turvey voted against, although he has always kept to the confidentiality agreed by all the panel members. His thinking was: this is Wimbledon Football Club, not two shareholders. If the club has got itself in a pickle, they have to get out of it. That might entail relegation, maybe more than one, no doubt some financial pain, but if the club is living way beyond its means that is the medicine. It happens in football; clubs rise, clubs fall. The other two believed, as it said in their judgement, that they were providing 'the WFC board and shareholders' with 'an opportunity to put the club on a more solid financial footing'.

They went on: 'Furthermore, resurrecting the club from its ashes as, say, "Wimbledon Town" is, with respect to those supporters who would rather that happened so that they could go back to the position the club started in 113 years ago, not in the wider interests of football.'

WISA issued a statement saying they would do whatever they could to overturn the decision. 'Franchise FC', Wimbledon were labelled; the move was contrary to the identity of Wimbledon Football Club, its history and where it belonged. It was purely based, they argued, on pulling two international investors out of a financial hole they had dug themselves when they gave Hammam £25m, intending to move the club to Dublin without all the permissions in place. The fans were furious at the Norwegians, contemptuous of Koppel for grasping on to Winkelman's Asda solution, and now outraged at the governance of football, the realisation that the League and the FA could both oppose the move yet somehow allow their rules to wave it through. But if the fans thought this kind of thing was unprecedented in football, that a core principle of the game was for the first time being trampled, that wasn't true. The League, professional clubs themselves, have always been compromises between sporting values and making money, and commercial imperatives kicked into football from the beginning. What of Bradford, invited into the League without kicking a ball, to become football's West Yorkshire franchise? What of Henry Norris, transporting Woolwich Arsenal to Highbury, then talking the club into the First Division? Dons fans here were the original old Arsenal fans, left in Plumstead, robbed of the local club they had always followed – except that piracy like this was supposed to have been outlawed by the League long ago, since footballing merit, not closed elections, became the route for clubs to advance.

There was, WISA said, a Plan B, which they had been preparing in case the decision went against them. Two days later they held a mass meeting at the Wimbledon Community Centre. The fans there were faced with two choices: continue to protest as their club was dragged up the M1; wave black flags, release black balloons, pound on and on – or treat that club as dead and launch their own. Kris Stewart had already committed himself to forming a new club, and researched the practicalities with Ivor Heller, another supporter, and Marc Jones, the fanzine editor and website whiz. Stewart said later that he hadn't even decided how he was going to phrase his rallying call that evening, until he picked his way through the hot crowd towards the microphone, then said, with weary understatement: 'I'm tired of fighting. I just want to watch football.'

He hit just the right note. When they put it to a vote, a forest of hands went up. It was unanimous. The fans of this small club, who over years had been propelled into a dismal world of land deals, overseas conglomerates, planning wrangles, and now, football's tortured and seriously flawed governance, threw themselves into the constructive business of creating a football club of their own. Somebody hung a banner on the gates of Selhurst Park: 'WFC RIP'. Then they considered a name for their own club. They decided it should not be reactive, or a protest slogan, but positive, an affirmation, something simple: AFC Wimbledon. When they filled in the form to apply to join the London FA, Stewart put, for the club's start date: '1899'.

'We thought of it as our club. Wimbledon had become Franchise FC and they were gone,' he told me. 'We were the ones continuing the tradition.'

They applied to join the Ryman League, but although Turvey was supportive and they gained 87 per cent of the clubs' votes, they were short of the 95 per cent necessary, so they trooped out, rejected. They joined instead, at still a reasonable level in the pyramid for a new club, the Combined Counties League, and quickly returned close to home, agreeing to groundshare, in the short term, with Kingstonian, at the Kingsmeadow Stadium in Kingston, south-west London.

For their manager they turned to Terry Eames, a former player who had joined the club in 1976 when Allen Batsford was the manager, and played in the side which won entry to the Football League. He'd come to Wimbledon for the Selhurst Park Fans United day, joining the protest against the move, as did many old boys.

AFC Wimbledon announced that Eames would be holding trials for players on Wimbledon Common on 29 June 2002 and hordes of hopefuls turned up. Eames ultimately gathered his side mostly from contacts and players he'd known during years managing in the non-leagues, but the Billy's Boots dream did come true for a few who'd come to the trials, including Joe Sheerin, a Chelsea player in his youth, who had turned up in the sunshine and shone.

Stewart and Heller arranged AFC Wimbledon's first friendly, away at Sutton United, for 10 July 2002. They didn't know how much support they would get, but the word was spreading, something exciting was happening, the media was interested; this was a supporters' football club forming out of the ashes of football as a failed financial investment. For the Wimbledon fans who had seen their little old club kicked about, abused, exploited by speculators looking for a return, this was truly a new beginning. On the night, the crowd was officially given as 4,500, but some Sutton people said they thought 6,000 people were there. It was a lovely summer evening, grown men cried and faith was restored in the sense of the club as a community of supporters, who belonged somewhere. They shouted, chanted, smiled, hugged each other and blinked in disbelief. Sutton won, 4-0, yet many Dons who were there talk about feeling more moved that day than they did after Wimbledon won the FA Cup. AFC Wimbledon was born.

A month later, Wimbledon FC began their season in the Football League First Division at home to Gillingham. Next to nobody came; the crowd at the 26,400-capacity Selhurst Park was 2,476. The next home games were Brighton, Wolves and Leicester, clubs with decent away followings, although, still, the highest attendance was 3,223, for the Wolves match. The players, haunted at first in the empty ground, rallied then, professionally, and began to win. The AFC Wimbledon fans scanned the list for a fixture which would strip out away fans and show the size of the home following left. That came with Rotherham at home, midweek, on 29 October. Wimbledon won, 2-1, Neil Shipperley and David Connolly, who would save the season for Wimbledon, scoring the goals. The crowd was 849, the lowest ever in the First Division. The astonishing feature of the Wimbledon fans' response was its unanimity; so often only an informed few supporters even know what is happening to their club, and are motivated to protest; here the club was being moved seventy miles north and the fans rejected it as one.

Their own scratch team lost nine pre-season friendlies before beating Enfield Town, another supporter-owned new club fleeing a loathed chairman. Then, on a hot summer's day, 17 August 2002, AFC Wimbledon played their first league match, away to Sandhurst

Town, who normally expect seventy fans to stand behind the railings round their pitch at Bottom Meadow in Berkshire. More than 2,500 turned up, to see AFC Wimbledon win their first ever competitive league match.

On the following Wednesday, Kingsmeadow completely sold out for the first home game, against Chipstead, Stewart being told by police he had to turn people away when the crowd reached 4,262. He went outside with a megaphone and thousands of people were still queuing. Some had come from miles away, and he had, sorrowfully, to tell them they couldn't get in. When the team trotted onto the pitch, the fans let it all out, because this was truly the rebirth.

Chipstead – and this is an impressive feature of the strength of English football, the depth of ability down the pyramid – stood up strong on the field in front of so huge a crowd, and, with a last-minute goal, won 2-1. Forming the club may have felt like a dream, but the game itself, as their own team had proved when clattering its way up the league, is not fairy-tale stuff. Kris Stewart was proud, a chairman with a lump in his throat:

'It's been very emotional. After all the campaigning and the death of the old club, this was restoring our club to its supporters. It was a wonderful night, we're so happy that the fans have come with us. We want to build a club here which stands for all the right things: community, and loyalty.'

Marc Jones posted a message on the website: 'This is something very special here. A cottage industry in the middle of a globalised trading estate. A corner shop perched between hypermarkets. A community football club in the midst of greed and desperation.'

Throughout the first season AFC Wimbledon's crowds at Kingsmeadow Stadium, in the Combined Counties League, were higher than those of Wimbledon FC at Selhurst Park in the Football League First Division. Wimbledon had 1,255 people shivering against Walsall in November; a new low, 664, against Rotherham in the League Cup; 1,336 against Grimsby. Unheard-of crowds. At

Kingsmeadow, they were on a high. Many Wimbledon fans could remember the club playing in the non-league anyway, and many who couldn't were steeped in the stories. They hadn't ever felt that their club, their experience of football, was all about staying in the Premier League. Back at a small ground in south London playing non-league football, they felt at home.

And all of this, according to two members of the FA Commission, which decided the issue, was 'not in the wider interests of football'. Where did they get those guys?

Alan Turvey, the third member of the panel, told me: 'I don't agree with that statement. How can it be wrong for a club to reform? What the fans are doing is marvellous, and I do wish them well.'

AFC's crowds tailed off a little as the euphoria solidified into a football season. In the summer, the Dons Trust organised a share issue for the club and raised £1.1m, while the democratic, supporter-owned structure was maintained by preserving for the Dons Trust itself 75 per cent of the voting rights. Kingstonian were in administration and the Trust bought the ground. They did a generous deal to make Kingstonian the tenant, although this could be seen as a jarring note, that in the end they bought another club's ground, but Kingstonian were in a mess and at least the tenancy kept them at home. Their fans, forming a trust and facing their own struggle, were full of admiration for what the Dons Trust were achieving, as were football supporters across the country.

Wimbledon FC, still with a strong team, finished tenth in the First Division. The Norwegians, however, had had enough anyway. Football had torn itself apart over a decision to salvage some of the magnates' money, and the decision was based on them continuing to fund the club until it moved to Milton Keynes, but in the end they didn't stick around. Rokke, one of Europe's richest men, had taken over half and become the chairman of the industrial and shipping conglomerate Kvaerner. In late 2001, Kvaerner had run into extreme difficulty, losing 4.96bn Norwegian krone (£428m), and they were rescued from going bust only by a late merger with Rokke's company, Aker. His need to marshall all his resources to turn Kvaerner round was thought to be behind his decision in November 2002 to cut his Wimbledon losses. He quit, passing his shares and loans to Gjelsten. Gjelsten said he would take the club to the end of the season and Milton Keynes, but in May he said he too could no longer continue and he pulled his funding out. Koppel, who had faced all the fury from Wimbledon fans, was forced into the humiliation of applying to put the club into administration.

With nobody to fund it, Wimbledon were days from liquidation then Winkelman came forward to say his MK Consortium would pick up the losses. He still didn't publicise who was in the consortium, but the administrator, Andy Hosking, and the Football League, were shown a letter from Asda Wal-Mart saying they were part of it. The debts were £25m, including £22m ploughed in by Rokke and Gjelsten which now had to be written off. The backers had lost their money anyway so they could have stayed where they were, or moved to Kingsmeadow themselves.

Hosking set about cutting costs, shipping players out: strikers Shipperley and Connolly, the goalkeeper Kelvin Davies, and midfielders Trond Andersen and Damien Francis. Some twenty non-playing staff were made redundant in what Hosking described as a process 'brutal at times'. Winkelman and his team worked hard to get Milton Keynes' National Hockey Stadium, a temporary home, fit for football, and on 13 September 2003, Wimbledon FC played their last ever home match in London. Wigan came down to Selhurst Park, 1,054 people turned up and Wimbledon lost 4-2. Two weeks later they played their first match in Milton Keynes. Koppel's idea had been to launch a top Premier League or First Division club on Milton Keynes' consumer society; instead, they got a battered husk of a club, a team of youngsters bottom of the League, the pariahs of football, their games boycotted even by many away fans. Winkelman said he had a sellout for the first game, against Burnley: 6,789 came to watch. Gradually, over the season, they garnered 3,000 regulars. Winkelman is adamant they want to build a club the right way, run an academy and a full community programme. He might build his stadium eventually and make his fortune, but it will be hard work, much harder than he thought originally.

'We're sorry for the pain it's caused,' he told me, always irrepressible, 'but it is all for the good in Milton Keynes.'

I had several exhaustive conversations with him over the years, and he would say why it was all worth it, roll out statistics, facts and slogans about Milton Keynes, why it should be allowed, an exception made, how great it would be for football to land in the town. He clearly won over the FA Commission, who found it all infectious. Once, at the end of the conversation, Winkelman paused, quite tired, and said a little more quietly: 'I think you'll agree I'm a pretty good salesman.' No doubt about that.

A fortnight later I went down to the Kingsmeadow Stadium. Because of the way the club was born, the intensity of the campaigning – and its brilliance, the WISA leaders, all professionals, calmly blowing holes in all the arguments – I'd thought AFC Wimbledon might have a self-righteous feel to it. I thought the people might be turning up as a gesture, to make a statement of principle, to Koppel, the Norwegians, Hammam, the FA, that they were mad as hell and weren't going to take it any more, that the talk would be thick with football politics rather than football.

It was a lovely day, T-shirt weather in October. I took the train to Norbiton and wandered around a bit lost in some semi-detached suburbia before latching onto the Kingston Road and heading upwards. London suburbia really does go on for ever; it must be hard to carve out an identity in the waves of sprawl. You can see why the club's roots, its location, meant a lot to the supporters.

A few Dons fans in blue and yellow eventually appeared, dotted in the cafés and shops. Finally I reached Kingsmeadow's long, sweeping drive. The first fans I saw outside the ground were a small group, drinking pints in the sunshine. Others were standing around, chatting, eating chips. A bloke was selling programmes; they were playing Sandhurst again, their first ever League opponents. The programme's centre spread had an unusual team shot, featuring everybody involved in running AFC Wimbledon – the stewards and turnstile attendants as well as the players. Kris Stewart, the chairman, was squashed in on the far right between Tim Pointer, from the police, and Gavin Ainslie, a programme seller.

In the bar some Dons fans were selling merchandise: shirts, DVDs of their resurrection, badges. I got chatting to one of them, Kevin Chatfield. He was born in Wimbledon and comes to all the matches – from his home in Wakefield, West Yorkshire.

'I feel proud to be part of it,' he said. 'Plough Lane had a family atmosphere, and here, it's back. It means something to be Wimbledon.'

There was a warm, laid-back feeling to the place. No anger, no protest, no righteous indignation, just people enjoying themselves, sipping a Guinness or two, looking forward to a football match. Inside the ground were some 3,000 spectators. This was an outrageous crowd, a full stadium, for a league like this. The terrace behind the goal was busy, ringing, within minutes, with blokes moaning at the referee. When Wimbledon attacked, the crowd gave a genuine rumble of expectation. Several people told me it was strange, but they hardly notice the drop in standard from the First Division. Here, it's decent anyway, most of the players have been around, on senior clubs' books; the fans are just caught up in supporting their club. This second season AFC started to win, to hammer sides. In the previous two games they'd beaten Chessington United 7-0, then Merstham away, 5-0, and Eames was in the programme complaining that they hadn't played well.

When Sandhurst threatened the fans panicked until Matt

Everard, huge at the Wimbledon back, mopped it calmly up. A Sandhurst sub warmed up; he had a mullet, so the fans on that side took the piss. It was, in other words, football. This was what the campaign, the bitter battle, had been fought for: the right to enjoy the simple pleasures and involvement of supporting your local football club.

At half-time you could change ends. The burgers are free-range, locally sourced, and there are chips and plenty of banter. In the second half, Sandhurst never lost it; they were tough and quite polished – English football runs deep and determined. Then Everard scored a booming header from a corner and Kevin Cooper, Wimbledon's promiscuous scorer, found himself in acres and Wimbledon drew away.

The only mention of the old Wimbledon FC all afternoon was a song by a few blokes on the terrace, once AFC were winning, to the tune of 'Yellow Submarine': 'We're going up and the Franchise are going down, the Franchise going down, the Franchise going down', sung with cheery contentment, not bitterness. At the end of the season it turned out to be true. AFC Wimbledon walked away with their championship and were going up to the Ryman League. Wimbledon FC were relegated, bottom of the First Division, bought out of administration at the last by Winkelman's consortium – using a company called MK Dons Ltd. He will need all his salesman's skills and a lot of money behind him to keep the club going, even in a new stadium built by the US hyper-might of Asda Wal-Mart, who want to keep the football club alive to facilitate a store in a honeypot new market. After football's new money came in and the game went corporate, the money was squeezed so unequally at the top that there was no room left for the small club punching through – even Wimbledon, the one which had shown it was possible. They took on too much expense to try to stay up there, rather than being allowed to reverse, with some honour, to a ground like Kingsmeadow and find their level. Instead, their status, hard and at times horribly fought for by the Crazy Gang, became a commodity, tradeable, moveable, disposable, the club a mere shell. On Monday 20 June 2004, Winkelman announced that the Football League had agreed to the club changing its name to Milton Keynes Dons FC. For all the talk about preserving the club's identity and heritage, Wimbledon FC disappeared that day.

What the fans did, deciding they had had enough, that they wanted their club back, how they left all together and organised themselves, has been a landmark response, its impact likely to spread a long way from south-west London and far into the future, a model for supporters looking for a more wholesome way for football and its clubs to be run.

'We're a true football club, owned by the fans, for the fans,' Kris Stewart told me. 'We've built something truly precious here, something I don't believe Wimbledon's former owners, or anybody else involved with the franchise in Milton Keynes, can ever really understand.'

CHAPTER 12

No Change at Crewe

They are proud, at Crewe Alexandra, of their main stand, unveiled in 1999 in place of the patched-up, ramshackle, 1932 stand and paddock, the fourth and final plank of the complete rebuilding of the Gresty Road ground into a 10,000-capacity stadium – all-seater, as required of First Division clubs. Just ten years earlier, when Crewe were in their twentieth consecutive season in the old Fourth Division, their fans would never have believed the club could come so far. Crewe's journey could be a lesson to all of football – if anybody was prepared to listen. Like the game itself played well, here they have simple principles, which they apply with hard work. They don't throw money at a short-term gamble but plan and invest for the future, a considered approach to their mission in life which the new stand's sponsor, in this famous railway town, could have done with considering. It was, when it was unveiled, the Railtrack Stand.

Dario Gradi, the longest serving manager at any club in English football, granted me an audience in the canteen of the Reaseheath training complex, a splendid new facility for Gradi's famous academy, a football factory with a gym, dressing rooms and nine full-size pitches yawning away into the Cheshire plain. We had oxtail soup, with white bread and marge for dipping, a strangely rudimentary menu for a state-of-the-art football club, but then again Gradi did run a couple of caffs in south London before he became football's most secure manager, granted ten-year contracts with a slice of the transfer fees he earns for the club.

These bonuses, in his time, have been huge, the number of well-schooled players trained by Gradi little short of awesome. He chewed on his bread, smiled, looked around him at the vast facilities and said: 'Seth Johnson paid for all this.'

Gradi spotted Johnson as a twelve-year-old, playing for a team in Devon where Crewe's kids were on tour, and he brought him gradually through a youth system Gradi has perfected more into science than art. Johnson was still only twenty and had played just ninety-three matches for Crewe when Derby County paid £3m to sign him in May 1999. Two years later, Leeds paid £7m to add him to their extravagant fistful of midfielders and Crewe earned nicely again from a sell-on clause. Johnson's £35,000 per week wages became one of the more notorious millstones from Peter Ridsdale and his board having lived the Leeds dream on borrowed money, while back in Crewe they were spending the real money steadily, on their infrastructure.

Gradi himself was originally a schoolteacher and a non-league defender – 'the poor man's Bobby Moore', as he modestly describes his efforts to play the game the elegant way. He had been bounced around the hire-'em-fire-'em coaching world – youth development at Chelsea, Wimbledon manager, Crystal Palace under Noades, youth team again at Orient – when he answered the advert to become the eighth manager in ten years at Crewe, the Football League's second bottom club. He harried hungrily for an interview, kept calling the chairman and his enthusiasm led to the club giving him a go.

He talked me through what he found when he arrived in June 1983. 'Gresty Road was covered on just two sides, it was really downtrodden, they had shale on the ground behind the two goals. We used to train on a school pitch we hired. The club had just had to seek re-election to the Football League after finishing second bottom. It was what you might call a challenge.'

He had, though, firm ideas about how a club could do well, about coaching individual players technique, teaching them painstakingly to play the game with skill and style. And he had a good eye for players, kicking off by picking up rejects from the bigger clubs within reach, most famously, in January 1985, nineteen-year-old David Platt, who'd been released by Manchester United.

Three years later, John Bowler, a regional marketing director of the pharmaceutical company Wellcome, who had been on Crewe's board since Gradi arrived, stepped up to become chairman. He has served time on the Football League's board, and he played the politics doggedly enough, but you feel he really ought to be listened to rather more. What he brings is not the braggadocio of the self-made wheeler-dealers but the calm experience of somebody who has actually been involved in running a large, successful organisation. He saw his local football club, the Railwaymen, the Alex, formed in 1877 and a founder member of the Second Division in 1892, as no different. They were a long-established football club, not doing too well; his job was to run the club long into the future. That meant they had to have a purpose, to understand what they were, where they ought realistically to be aiming to go, and how they would do it. So rather than promise the top flight in five years and hunt for the odd former star on his way down, Bowler implemented an idea not too often seen in the football boardroom: a plan.

'The club represents a small town, surrounded, not too far away, by major clubs, in Manchester and Liverpool,' he explained. 'We were never going to get huge crowds, and make the income like that to improve and grow. We looked at what we could do and realised we could pay our way and thrive by developing young players, then earn money by selling them on to bigger clubs. In Dario, we had the perfect manager to achieve that plan.'

Gradi himself grins when he hears about the chairman's considered youth strategy: 'I think the board only made a policy of it once I brought the money in. Really when we sold David Platt to Aston Villa.'

Geoff Thomas, the first prominent player to come through Gradi's system, had been signed from Rochdale and sold to Crystal Palace for £80,000 in June 1987. In February 1988, the same year Bowler took over, Graham Taylor, then Villa's manager, paid Crewe £200,000 for Platt, who played wonderfully when Villa came second in the First Division two years later, then volleyed himself into stardom in the World Cup in Italy. For Crewe, the money was manna. Whichever way round it was, or who thought of it first, the chairman, board and manager all agreed that Crewe would dedicate itself to youth development.

The following season they won promotion. Gradi had been there six years, laid foundations for scouting and coaching young players and managed the first team to take them out of the Fourth Division for the first time since 1969. That summer, they sold another player, Peter Billing, who Gradi had picked up from Everton reserves, to Coventry for £120,000. In March 1990, Coventry paid £300,000 for another of Gradi's graduates, Paul Edwards, signed originally from Altrincham. Crewe spent part of that on a minibus equipped with a video, to allow Gradi to give lessons to his players on the move. They were up to that, already.

It seems a wondrous journey, the fast track at Crewe, but Bowler has always said it was basic management:

'Look at the successful football clubs. They've all had settled sides with long-serving managers. It's crazy sacking the manager every time something goes wrong, as is continually signing players believing you can drop them in and immediately succeed. As in any business, you need the right people and they need time to develop, experience counts for a great deal. The only reason why football people don't see it is because there are so few examples for them to follow.'

It's true, when you think. The most successful manager now,

Alex Ferguson, joined Manchester United in November 1986, three years after Gradi joined Crewe. Charlton Athletic, another of the very few football clubs generally regarded to be run excellently, have stuck with Alan Curbishley since 1991, 1995 on his own. Arsène Wenger has now been at Arsenal since 1996, his system of introducing new players growing more formidable with the years. Think of the great clubs, their successful eras are characterised by a manager who had time to create a system, not just dish out half-time bollockings: Arsenal – Herbert Chapman; United – Matt Busby; Wolves – Stan Cullis; Liverpool – Bill Shankly and Bob Paisley; Forest – Brian Clough. Look at the struggling clubs; their lists of managers run on forever.

At the end of the 1989–90 season, Bowler made Gradi that first unheard-of offer, a ten-year contract. The very next season, despite the video-laden minibus, Crewe were relegated back to the Fourth Division. There was, though, no thought of sackings. In *The Gradi Years*, the account, by Jules Hornbrook, an Alex fan, ringing with awed disbelief at the club's transformation, Gradi is quoted accepting the relegation calmly, in the context of the club's developing philosophy and system: 'I didn't think it was a massive set-back. We'd got the infrastructure in place. I felt that we'd soon have a decent team at the club. Large amounts of money would never be available for players. We'd have to continue wholeheartedly with the youth policy. We would go where our players took us, not get the players to go where we want to go.'

Gradi's approach to coaching was professional; he had done all his badges through the much-maligned regimes of the FA technical heads Allen Wade and Charles Hughes, whom he cited as inspirations, and he knew the difference he could make to young players. Part of Crewe's attraction for him was geographical: close enough to the big clubs for senior cast-offs, far enough away, in his pocket of Cheshire, to have a large population area to himself. He seems to see the map, England itself, in terms of catchment areas for young footballers.

'A very good area, this,' he smiled, sipping his soup. He was like a fisherman discussing a stretch of sea.

The early successes paid for better coaching facilities. The first team moved off the hired school field and on to their own training ground. Gradi introduced a youth policy which soon had 120 children aged from eight to sixteen coming for coaching – proper coaching – in organised age groups on the club's new Astroturf. He'd seen the frenzied meat markets at clubs elsewhere and wanted it done with proper care. His is still a ruthless world, assessing children for their potential to become professional sportsmen, and to make money for the company and Gradi himself, but there is a decent way to do it, he insisted:

'At other clubs, kids would go training but they wouldn't even know the people coaching them, or have any real connection to the club. Here, the coaches stay with their age group, and the young kids know them, and they know what they are doing and why.'

He accepted that only a few come through, but believed the young people benefited from good quality coaching and the association with Crewe.

'People tell me our boys are well turned out and polite, and I say: "Good, so they should be."' There is paternalism here, very strong; Gradi has never married or had children of his own and there is a sense that the Crewe youngsters are surrogates for a man who loves kids. But it's strange, because he talks like a trader, too.

They sold a player every year, sometimes more than one. Rob Jones, the first celebrated graduate of Gradi's own youth system, one who came through from childhood rather than a buffed-up big club reject, was rolled off the production line to Liverpool for £300,000 in October 1991. Craig Hignett, picked up from Liverpool originally, played four full seasons as a dashing attacking midfielder for Crewe then was sold to Middlesbrough for £500,000 in November 1992. Just before he left, he scored four for Crewe in a 6-1 hammering of Wrexham in the FA Cup First Round. Crewe were still in the bottom division but they spent their money on Gresty Road, not short-term first team signings, building a new stand with a family area at the old Railway End.

They picked up Ashley Ward, a Manchester City reject, whom Gradi had watched for years, for £80,000 from Leicester, Crewe's most expensive ever signing at the time. He blossomed in the expressive and stylish play allowed by Gradi, who is a purist, his coaching about improving touch, control, passing: 'Football is a game of skill,' is one of his axioms. 'When I hear people talk about great battles and character, I think they should be watching *Gladiators* on television.'

Ward scored the goal at their local rivals Chester which finally took Crewe out of the Fourth Division in 1994. That December, Ward, duly polished, was sold to Norwich for £500,000. Robbie Savage, signed for free from Manchester United, joined in midfield Neil Lennon, the Manchester City cast-off, and they helped to work Crewe to heights which felt surreal to everybody in football: the First Division, in 1997. Lennon was sold with the side heading upwards, in February 1996, for £750,000 to Martin O'Neill at Leicester, where Gradi would watch him smoothly excel. Savage went in the 1997 close season, also joining Leicester for £400,000, going on to annoy people at the highest level for the rest of his career.

By then, Gradi's graduates, trained in his ways from an early age, were coming regularly through to the first team. The club was making more money to spend on the ground, the next stage of Bowler's five-year plan: training facilities first, the youth policy, now Gresty Road itself. In 1995 new stands were built at the Gresty Road End and on the old Popside, the end of standing there. They're named after their sponsors, the Advance Personnel and Blue Bell BMW Stands, but, hey, that's business.

It was mostly paid for by selling players, and Gradi himself was earning seriously, his salary up from £96,452 in 1995 to £184,115

in 1996. Crewe, a small-town club, forever ragged and bottom of
the League, had achieved all this with planning, professionalism
and expertise, playing their way smoothly up, achieving respect
as an institution, while all around them bigger clubs thrashed
around with lolloping wage bills, firing managers and alienating
fans. Crewe's response to promotion in 1997: they sold Danny
Murphy, one of Dario's original boys, to Liverpool for £1.5m. Dario
Gradi no longer ran his two cafés in south London as a safety
net. He himself was an institution, fourteen years at Crewe, who
made a profit that year, before tax, of nearly £2m.

Behind the march of progress was John Bowler, steady, a business brain and also a committed Christian. Along with the passion
and sense of belonging which a football club inspires, he believes
there is a social role to play:

'It can sound a bit Holy Joe,' he said, 'but we believe football
has a special place in society. It unites people around a common
cause, and we have a responsibility to use that to benefit the
community.'

The club's community programme, if not at the cutting edge
of social work like some of the most progressive, is wide ranging,
reaching a great many children – Gradi keeping a weather eye on
promising candidates – including the poor and disabled. The
supporters, generally, think what the club has done is wonderful,
have good relationships with it and love Dario Gradi.

So here is a football club which makes a profit, has had the
same manager since 1983, well over one thousand matches in
charge, develops its own young players, many of whom have gone
on to the highest levels, has good relations with its fans, a decent
community programme, a respected presence in the town, with
major companies sponsoring it. And with all that, they are arguably
competing way above their natural level, lasting five seasons in
the First Division before going down then bouncing straight back
again. Crisis in football: what crisis?

Bowler believes many clubs get it sadly wrong, punt and lurch for success rather than do even the first step of thinking through what they are about. But he is a diplomat, keeps his counsel unless provoked. The idea after ITV Digital collapsed, supported by Geoffrey Richmond, that all clubs should go into administration and sack their players drew the predictable outright rejection from Bowler. Crewe, like all the then First Division clubs, were set to lose £4m they had expected to receive over the next two years, but Bowler told me they would manage. They had some reserves, they would have to budget to make a loss, revise their forecasts and they'd get through it. To make it worse, they went down. Did they sack Gradi in response? Have a guess. This time, they held on to most of the players. They were on to the next phase, the Seth Johnson money having helped to complete the new main stand and Reaseheath, so they were up to spending a little more on the team. They had a little gamble on making a loss of over £1m to get back up with the squad intact and it worked. Then, in a game whose transfer market had collapsed, Crewe managed to sell their striker, Rob Hulse, to West Brom for £750,000.

Interestingly, Bowler does not go along with either of the solutions most often advanced to solve football's gap between the super-rich and the rest; in fact, he does not see it needs solving at all, accepts it as the system. He is not in favour of the so-called 'salary cap', the idea trialled in the Third Division in 2003–4 to stop the clubs spending too much of their money on wages simply by applying an upper limit, set at 60 per cent of their turnover. Bowler told me that this was removing the possibility of competition and strategy, of making the odd well-judged push to move on. He thought the example of badly run clubs, who had blown their money and gone bust, was being allowed to frame the rules for all of them: 'If we want to do things a different way, to spend more for a season or two, that should be up to us. Otherwise you will have a strict hierarchy where you really are what you earn, the clubs with most income can spend most on players and so usually do better.'

Nor does he even believe, perhaps surprisingly, that there should necessarily be more redistribution of money from the top clubs through the divisions. 'That would reward everybody for failure,' he said. He is adamant that football clubs can run themselves very well and decently, be a credit to themselves and an enriching part of their supporters' lives, as the system stands. He's not soft: 'Clubs have got to stand up on their own, not blow their money, succeed on their own merits. Everybody wants to watch the big clubs on television, they are competing in Europe and have global support, so they are entitled to the revenue from that. The other clubs can do well, if they understand their limitations as much as their strengths. You don't want to have a system which just shares it out regardless of what clubs have done to deserve it.'

At Charlton, they think differently; they believe football's money should be shared much more equally, even though theirs is also a story of extraordinary revival within the post-1992 divided structure, becoming solid performers in the Premier League. Their rebirth was inspired by the passion of supporters, after Charlton left their home, the Valley, because of financial problems in 1985. The weeds overgrowing the Valley's pitch and terraces became, along with the locked gates at Middlesbrough, a defining image of 1980s decline, but the fans at Charlton, as at all the other clubs, would not let their club wither. They even formed a political party, The Valley Party, gaining 10.9 per cent of the vote in local elections for Greenwich Borough Council on the single issue of winning planning permission to rebuild the Valley to enable the club to return. When the council granted it, the fans raised money and went tooled up with spades and shears, ready for work to start.

When Charlton made it triumphantly back to the Valley in December 1992, it was not to become a corporation ripping off that loyalty for directors to make a killing. They did float on the Alternative Investment Market, which raised them some money, and have since had further share issues. Some individuals have substantial shareholdings, like the chairman, Richard Murray, who owns nearly a third of the club, but along with Premiership status and making the money they can from commercial activities, they subscribe to a community approach, with a director elected to the board by the fans, the wonderfully named Wendy Perfect. Their wider work includes a longstanding anti-racism initiative in the area, which is close to Eltham, where in April 1993 the black teenager Stephen Lawrence was murdered, according to the inquest jury, in a racist stabbing by five white men.

Charlton too found the manager they wanted for long-term team building – Alan Curbishley – and supported him. They made it to the Premier League through the play-offs in 1998, didn't blow their windfall, went down again, then yo-yoed back up and have since steadied in the top flight, playing neat football, given a flourish lately by Paolo Di Canio, the full Valley glowing delightedly.

For all that success, Murray does continue to call for fairer distribution of money through the game and a more decent approach to life from the clubs. Charlton are bigger, in a different position from Crewe; they want to compete in the Premier League but cannot make the money to compete with United, Arsenal, Chelsea, Newcastle or Liverpool. He believes the present predictability of English football will ultimately turn off fans and TV viewers if the clubs do nothing about it. Charlton are also realistic enough to contemplate the possibility that one season they could be one of the three clubs to be relegated, which, given the huge income gap between the Football League and the break-away, would be a major problem. Murray has been unusually forthright in his criticism of the structure, saying in 2001:

'For the game to flourish and remain attractive . . . it must have a competitive structure with many teams able to challenge for honours. If it does not, the success of the few may well lead to the failure of the many . . . The additional money coming into the game is fuelling wage inflation and spiralling transfer fees and the destabilising activities of some players' agents only serve to increase both . . . Clubs are mortgaging their futures, yet the number who can be successful remains relatively small.

'The current spread of revenue distribution is too narrow, with the top clubs benefiting most from the current arrangements. This unequal distribution should be radically changed to provide greater competition within the leagues.'

Within the limits and hazards of this needlessly self-destructive structure, Charlton have striven to run themselves the right way, shot through with self-knowledge. 'We shall do our best to achieve whatever we can on and off the field,' Murray said in 2002. 'We want to continue with our growth and we want further success, but we also want a club that stands for good things in the game, with affordable pricing, strong family orientation and a firm community base.'

The Charlton directors, just three of whom are paid, take modest salaries compared to those lapping it up at other Premier League clubs: Murray was paid £54,000 in 2001, the year Peter Ridsdale's pay packet was £645,000, and he actually took a reduction to £50,000 the year after, close to unheard of. Charlton stayed in the Premier League, completed the £10m development of a new North Stand with all the trimmings, which was opened by a supporter, David Butlin, in April 2002, and played to crowds almost always full to the Valley's capacity of 26,875. Murray said:

'Ten years ago, everyone connected with the club shared a dream – to see Charlton Athletic back playing at the Valley among English football's elite with a team capable of competing with the very best in a modern family-oriented stadium packed to capacity – to be part of a football club which stood for something and one of which its supporters could be proud.

'Sometimes dreams do come true.'

The decency with which these clubs have been run can be seen throughout their operations, including the players they bring through. In February 1996, I spent a day with the England schoolboy under-15 team before their match, live on Sky, against Northern Ireland at Middlesbrough's Riverside Stadium. These were the very best young players in the country, heading, they all believed, for stardom and fortune. One of the teachers who ran the team told me the reality of professional football was that two of the squad might make it big; the others would fall away. I monitored them all carefully in the following years, as they became adults in a football world imploding financially. It wasn't pretty. Francis Jeffers, a spotty kid keeping pretty quiet in freezing Middlesbrough that day, burst through first, for Everton, and earned a dream move to Arsenal; but there his progress stuttered. Two were at Manchester United, Paul Wheatcroft and Ian Fitzpatrick. They were totally dedicated, Fitzpatrick gave the club most of his childhood, then, at nineteen, they were casually dumped, sent out to play a friendly where they found, without notice, scores of scouts lining the pitch, notebooks and licked pencils at the ready. Fitzpatrick stood up to the challenge of Third Division football with Halifax, played in the season they were relegated from the Football League in 2002, then in the Conference, but they released him. He went to Shrewsbury, but struggled there too, and was loaned out to Leigh RMI.

I met him in a TGI Fridays near his home, where he sipped a Coke and, still only twenty-one, reflected on his time in the game: 'When United want you,' he said, 'they're nice to you. Then, when they don't want you any more, they get rid of you like a piece of rubbish.'

Wheatcroft, a bright lad and a stinging striker, went to Bolton when United told him there was no place for him, but he was never given much of a chance after a mazy dribble on his debut. He then went to Rochdale, where he played very well but got injured; Scunthorpe, where he was frozen out; then drifted to training with Stalybridge Celtic, the UniBond Northern Premier

League club, where he was not even paid his expenses. At the time of writing, he is twenty-one and not playing football at all.

Just two of the players from that group came through smoothly; given their chance at nineteen at the club they'd been at since they were kids, learning quickly, then becoming fixtures in the side. One was at Charlton: Scott Parker. He earned rave notices in his third season, 2003–4, before Chelsea's unholy Russian chequebook was waved in his face and he left, Curbishley railing at the departure. Parker told me of the course of his career: 'I'm glad I was at Charlton rather than those big clubs, because the club believes in youth and I did get my chance.'

The other player to make it said the same: Stephen Foster, at Crewe. Groomed by Dario Gradi, promoted when he was ready, his performances now, at full back or centre back in the First Division, breathe authority. None of the rest of that under-15 team has made it steadily; so eager when they were taken on, they have suffered the twists of fate, injury, constant turnover of managers to win over, the financial convulsions of the clubs which then had to cut wage bills and shed players. At Crewe, almost the whole first team squad have been in Gradi's system since they were children.

Gradi, master of all he surveys at Crewe, part father figure, part proprietor, acknowledges there is a high failure rate but maintains that if you do it the right way everybody benefits, including the young people. A trip to Crewe is one of English football's pleasures, even if the trains don't run on time these days. Gradi's team plays delicious football, on the ground, the players comfortable in their technique. The stadium is proud of itself, the fans who have stuck with the Alex for years are passionate and totally disbelieving. All done with no scandals, no brutal managerial sackings, no lamentable waste, no rampant greed, no rip-off of the club's soul, no justifiable calls to sack the board. Bowler, for all his work over twenty years, full-time for many of them, has never been paid a penny, and the club, out of all the profits, has never issued a dividend.

'A number of chairmen today take a consultancy fee,' he told Jules Hornbrook, smiling. 'This is my charity work, I suppose.'

I called David Burns, the former chief executive of the League, to tell him I was writing this book. He lost the support of the bigger First Division clubs in the summer of 2002, when they tore into him after he signed the deal with Sky which replaced the bombed ITV Digital. Delia Smith, who with her husband Michael Wynn Jones has sunk £7m into Norwich City and tried to run her club the decent way, was at that League meeting, her first ever. She described it to me as a 'bloodbath', a 'kangaroo court', and told Burns afterwards she felt sorry for him. He resigned, however, with the familiar cry of the football-loving professional who has been quite shocked at what he found behind the game's closed doors: I don't need this.

He asked me which clubs I was concentrating on. I told him Bradford, Wimbledon – he'd been implacably opposed to the MK move – and the others which collapsed and he sort of grunted. Or growled; I'm not sure.

'OK,' he said, 'but don't forget the good clubs, the well-run ones, there are some.'

'Oh, yes,' I said, 'I'm very keen to show the good examples. Who would you point to?'

'Crewe,' he said immediately.

'Yes, I know Crewe very well,' I told him. 'I'm planning a chapter on Crewe. Who else would you point to?'

And he thought, hard, for a long time.

CHAPTER 13

Big Obsessions

Outside the Football League, just ten miles but a world away from football's richest plc, up on a hill past a twenty-four-hour Tesco, through a blue wooden door and an old waist-high turnstile, is a gloopy, bumpy football pitch, sandwiched between two rickety stands. It's pouring, and seventy or so souls are hunkered down under the corrugated iron roof of the stands. The home side, in blue, are playing fast, brightly, on the break; the greens, giving it everything, sliding into trouble. With a couple of minutes to go, one of the blues' strikers goes through on the keeper. He takes it wide, too wide, has to go all the way round to the byline, from where he dinks a cross back in for his partner, a little guy whose touch has been in all night. Diving to his right, he glances a header to his left, arching it into the far corner of the net, a touch of class. The fans are cheered: 'Brilliant, Billy! Well done, son!' Minutes later the referee blows. As they walk off, it's not the ref who takes the taunts for a change, but one of the opposition's players, Nigel Gleghorn. He used to be a pro, played well for Manchester City during one of their characteristic slumps at the end of the eighties, played for Birmingham and Stoke, and now he's forty-one and he's been turned over on this rutted field. He still had the skill, though, slaloming round players, even in this mud, but he looks weary. 'Go on, Foghorn!' some old blokes are shouting, 'Go home!' Everybody troops into the clubhouse, a prefab which runs along behind the goal. It's warm in there and there are pints of John

Smith's, crisps, fags, some hearty piss-take, the results on Sky.

This is Surrey Street, home of Glossop North End. They've just beaten Nantwich, in green, 3-0. Glossop, the small town hunched against the wind at the foot of the Pennines, will surely always remain the smallest town ever to have a football club in the top flight, having, on the cusp of the twentieth century, played Aston Villa, Manchester City, Liverpool, Everton, Newcastle and the rest in the First Division.

They are aware, and proud, of their history; a few salvaged mementoes are tacked onto the clubhouse walls: a programme from when Glossop played Chelsea; a team picture from the club's final League season, a glorious black and white affair with a fine gold frame, taken before Glossop played Birmingham City, which a local man found in a junk shop in Bombay. Apparently Birmingham hammered them, 11-1. Now, the club is maintained by a hardworking band of volunteers, battling to try to maintain Glossop as a town able to support a club in the First Division of the North West Counties League. Every season is a heart-stopper, clumping around at the bottom with the likes of Atherton Collieries, Ramsbottom United and St Helens Town, taking a few hammerings, rarely without a fight.

In the pyramid, the champions win promotion to the UniBond Northern Premier League, serious football, whose own champions go into the Conference. So even at this level there are some well-backed, well-stocked sides at the top, like Mossley, Glossop's local rivals, usually with a complement of ex-pros, managed now by the former Manchester City striker Jason Beckford, who expect to lord it over Glossop twice a season. The likes of Salford City have been bankrolled by a local steelman made good, who funded the signing of former pros and non-league dashers like Ryan Giggs' brother Rhodri, without, it has to be said, much return. Wages for big names can go up to £200 a week, says the rumour mill. At Glossop, they pay their players £10 per match, just to stay respectable, and even that's difficult to find.

There are a few perks for the directors: a half-time brew and flaky sausage roll in a separate area for entertaining the opposition's directors, a League requirement which they've complied with by dragging another Portakabin onto the site. They work hard, all hours, for no pay, to keep the club alive. Barry Jones, all grizzled warmth at the end of its tether, takes the nets down after the match. There are announcements on a tinny loudspeaker to make for Adrian Priestley, a salesman in and out of work these last years. Refs to pay, kit to gather up, dressing rooms to muck out.

In the clubhouse, a lottery goes round, a quid a go, to raise money. They're always skint. Barry complains that the floodlights cost £35 every time you turn them on. They did get a grant to build the stand on the far side, in front of the swampy slope where they're always losing balls at £30 a go. The rest of the ground could do with fixing up but there's never any money. They haven't had a sponsor for years: they've tried all the big names in what is a hard-working, prosperous town, but the factories are mostly owned by bigger companies now, some based overseas, and they're not interested. The league itself has no sponsor; clubs and leagues at this level struggle increasingly in the shadow of the glamour at the top of football. Firms earn rather more kudos from a box at one of the big clubs' expanded grounds than from sticking their name on the shirts of clubs like Glossop as a goodwill gesture. In Tesco, just across the road, the tills are forever ringing, the car park rammed with four-wheel drives filling up with dog food and Cava. They're said to make over £30m a year at this one store, but they don't sponsor locally.

In the clubhouse, a plaque sits above the bar in memory of a fan, John Catlow, who died in 1998: 'A big supporter and a big man' it says. 'Small clubs exist because of big obsessions.' In 2003, one of their long-serving players, Chris Ringland, was killed in a plane crash, and they devoted the whole clubhouse to him.

Priestley, stressed, tells me how he fell in love with the place. Like many here, he's a Manchester émigré, moved out for the gentler pace of life: 'I was a City fan always. We moved to Glossop on a Friday, then on the Saturday I came down to look for the football club. Since then, I've hardly been away.'

Many of the players are local, quite a few came through a committed complement of boys and youth teams. Other senior players have been around a bit at this level, hustled and hunted for by the manager, Chris Nicholson. The captain, centre half Louie Bovis, a salesman, turned up for training one day, said he'd moved to the area from the South East, where he'd played at a decent non-league standard, and fancied a game. He turned out to be a warrior, born to the job of keeping Glossop just one clearing header from relegation. There is pride here; they may have fallen a long way, but they draw the line at the North West Counties League First Division. They struggle, but they still serve a town, a catchment area; they all believe it is important that they keep senior football going here. Priestley needs little prompting to sail away on the tradition they are battling to safeguard. 'The club is very important to the town now, and it has a distinguished and unique history. It's a rich part of English football's story, and we feel very responsible for keeping it alive. But it's bloody hard at times, and thankless.'

It would be a mistake to think that people in Glossop in the twenty-first century spend much of their time, or any at all, worrying about the Hill Woods, the local mill-owning family which dominated the town in the nineteenth and early twentieth centuries until they left for London, and Arsenal. Glossop is a bustling place without too much unemployment; a working-class town with work still around; there's a skateboard park to fence off the teenagers' scallywag tendencies, a market, railway station, wagonloads of pubs, a curious epidemic of nail shops. They get on with it. If you want to know anything of the town's history, however, you come very centrally to the Hill Woods.

Local legend had it that the man who started it all, John Wood – great-great-grandfather of Peter Hill-Wood, the current Arsenal chairman, so not that long ago – arrived in Glossop with a shoe on one foot and a clog on the other. Endearing, but like most tales endowing men who make money with some kind of magical, mystical quality, not true. He was thirty by then, had money, or access to it, and, although a Yorkshireman, several years' experience in the Manchester cotton industry. Glossop sits in a valley of fast-running brooks, and from 1784 speculators had set up mills powered by the water, although cotton, like all boom industries, was more difficult and unpredictable than it looked and many failed before the shrewd or lucky few powered through to make fortunes.

John Wood took over two empty mills in 1815 and worked his way towards negotiating the ebb and flow of the business. He did well because he thoroughly understood his industry and his machinery and he was a workaholic with exacting standards. He beat on and expanded while others dropped, building within twenty years a huge mill along the river which, with the houses around it, effectively became the centre of Glossop itself. The Duke of Norfolk owned most of the land and, seeing the rents which could be made, built up the place, with a Town Hall, market square and, later, a railway station, which gave Glossop some civic integrity and connected it to the wider world.

I wanted to know what conditions had been like in the Hill Woods' mills. The town is still configured around them – huge stone buildings, some converted into factories, some derelict, and most people live in rows of what were previously millworkers' terraces. You can still feel the hard graft which went into making the millowners' fortunes. Joyce Powell, secretary of the Glossop & District Historical Society, told me that life in the Woods' mills was not well documented, but, 'From what we know, they were no better, and no worse, than all the mills generally in the area at the time,' she said. There was child labour, no security, workers were laid off when business was slow. The housing was basic, with no sanitation.

To give me a flavour of life at the time, she lent me a book, *A*

Memoir of Robert Blincoe, written by John Brown in 1832, which tells the story of a boy who spent his youth from the age of seven in two cotton mills. Robert Blincoe was an orphan in London, at the St Pancras workhouse, from where the governors sold him, with other children, as apprentices to the owners of Lowdham Mill, ten miles from Nottingham. There they were worked in the mill from 5 a.m. to 7 p.m., beaten and whipped, served watery porridge and splodges of bread; effectively imprisoned, owned by the proprietors of the mill. They all suffered nasty accidents; when Blincoe lost a finger in the machinery he was sent to the surgeon who stitched it back on, and the overseers put him straight back to work. Yet in Blincoe's hindsight, that mill became a civilised haven compared to the hell of the place he was sold to next when, after four years, Lowdham Mill went bust.

'It was his evil fortune,' the book recounts, 'with a multitude of fellow sufferers, to be turned over to Mr Ellice Needham, of Litton Mill, near Tideswell in Derbyshire.'

There, Blincoe met almost unimaginable abuse and cruelty. There was no food to speak of, the children were worked sixteen hours a day; they were filthy, half-starving – they stole food from the pigs – and dispensable. They died, diseased, without lament, in a routine procession to the paupers' corner of the local grave-yard. The children were beaten for the smallest misdemeanours, or just for fun, by the 6-foot, strapping overseers, with sticks, belts with buckles, even whips, till the blood ran. The overseers toyed with the children, making them balance above machinery which could kill or maim them if they fell into it, tying Blincoe's legs up to his hands behind his back, then punching him in the face or throwing heavy iron rollers at his head which would make deep wounds. The batterings left his head and body so bruised he had to sleep on his stomach. When his head was overrun with lice, the doctor used by the mill applied a pitch cap to Blincoe's head, left it on for a time until it stuck, then pulled it off so it actually scalped him. On and on like this, for ten years. How people survived it, we can hardly understand. Blincoe did, somehow, he grew up and left the mill, married and had children, and made sure his experiences were recorded. Giving evidence to a parliamentary inquiry into child labour in 1833, he was asked whether he sent his children to work in factories. He said he would rather have them transported to Australia.

I asked Ms Powell if she was suggesting the Hill Woods' mills had been as dreadful as this. No, she said, the local historians had found no notable abuse recorded from the Woods' mills, once the inspection system was in place. 'But they wouldn't have been a great deal better. That was mill life. The Woods' mills did have child labour.'

John Wood's own three sons, John, Daniel and Samuel – Peter's great-grandfather – were themselves 'put through the mill' from around fourteen, going through every department of the huge, rattling complex, learning the business from floor to office, before taking the company over in 1844. After he died in 1854, his sons loosened up a bit; Daniel and Samuel built Moorfield, a grand house in fields just above the town, with manicured gardens and an ornamental lake, where they started to enjoy their money. Samuel married Anne Kershaw Sidebottom, who busied herself in good works in the town, building, towards the end of the nineteenth century, churches and schools, Wood's Hospital, Wood's Baths and the ornamental Howards Park, laid out in 1887 and still appreciated by the locals today.

Samuel Hill Wood, 'Young Sam', Peter's grandfather, was born to Samuel and Anne in March 1872. He was that difficult third generation: born in the mill town to enormous wealth in a vast house with servants, then sent to Eton, where he discovered sport, hunting and lounging around. His father and his uncle Daniel both died in 1888, the year the Football League was established. As Young Sam was only sixteen, a public schoolboy without a clue about the mill – or, being honest, much interest in it – the business was run by a succession of managers. Whether he did what even we, let alone nineteenth century millworkers, would recognise as a real day's work in his life, isn't a sure thing. He came back to a town like so many others, whose people had come through the worst scourges of industrial revolution, and, although work was still hard and money scant, they had for the first time some leisure and the health to enable them to do something with it. Cricket was older established; football was brought to the North and Midlands by the middle classes or the likes of Hill Wood, who had spent their youths away from the poverty and graft, in public schools where 'games' had become central to the creation of gentlemen. Football was received in places like Glossop with rougher, urgent passion, its excitement and skill thrilling in a world of grey work, the men grasping hold of the local clubs as expressions of identity, as well as places to drink and let off steam. All that suited Young Sam, who appears to have spent as little time as possible fretting over trouble at t'mill, and as much as he could playing games.

Hill Wood didn't actually found Glossop North End; it was established by local men in 1886, named, somewhat hopefully, after the great Preston club which won the Double three years later, the Football League's first season. Samuel played for Glossop from the early 1890s, on the wing; in the summers, he captained Glossop Cricket Club and from the mid-1890s was captain of Derbyshire, where he found fame for once scoring ten runs off a single ball.

Quite why he decided to extend his enthusiasm for sport into sinking a large weft of the family fortune into Glossop North End is not certain. He was no doubt keener personally on football than any other aspect of life as a pillar of Glossop society, where his mother was still opening churches in a relentless swish of good works. Some theories have it that Samuel was using the football club to boost his profile and launch his political career; in the days before universal suffrage, he'd been elected to the local council, as a Conservative, in 1897. Glossop were then playing in the Midland

League, which was senior football, already hosting solid names, and Glossop, a small-town club, were not doing much. They should have been allowed nowhere near the League; they finished ninth out of twelve clubs in 1897–8. However, Samuel Hill Wood, well-connected and a social class above the brewers, butchers and pub landlords then taking a commercial interest in football, approached the League, which was looking for four more clubs. He apparently promised that he would bankroll Glossop, sign quality professionals and guarantee the club was financially stable. Who knows what deals were done; the upshot was that the League agreed.

Records from the time, compiled by local historian Dennis Winterbottom, show that Hill Wood took over the club completely, owning 194 of 200 shares, leaving a token one each for the six original backers, all with humbler local addresses. Hill Wood hired a secretary-manager, George Dale, and gave him a budget to scour the country for a side which could compete strongly in the Second Division. Dale released all but five of the players he inherited and signed four from Luton, two from Liverpool, three from Scotland – rich football terrain then – including the splendidly named striker Hunter McCosh. To supplement their football wages, several were given soft jobs in Hill Wood's weaving sheds, with time off in the afternoons to train. The town's stories have it that the closest local players got to the team was when men were dragged away from their looms to the fields opposite Moorfield, where the North End pros would use them as practice fodder.

On 3 September 1898, a crowd of 5,000 hummed into the North Road ground for Glossop's first ever game in the Football League, against Blackpool:

'They watched the game with great interest from beginning to finish,' said the *Glossop Dale Chronicle*, 'giving Glossop much encouragement with their cordial shouts, and refraining from the odious practice prevailing on so many football grounds of instructing individual players as to what they ought to do, in language impolite to say the least of it.'

Glossop won 2-1, the new team getting a good write-up: 'Not a duffer among them,' said the newspaper.

Two weeks later Glossop hosted Newton Heath, who would later become Manchester United. They lost 2-1 in a tough, close game, and Glossop were congratulated by the correspondent from *Athletic News*: 'Football professionalism has apparently been firmly established in the town, and with such a true sportsman at the head of affairs as Samuel Hill Wood, there is every reason to believe that the Glossop Club has a bright future.'

Glossop didn't storm the Second Division; Manchester City did, winning promotion six points clear. Glossop, scrapping, did well, losing only eight games, then on the final Saturday of the season they beat Loughborough 4-0, the result which saw them into the First Division. 'This history of the progress of the club is probably unique,' beamed the *Glossop Dale Chronicle*.

First Division football the following season was, however, beyond even Hill Wood's pockets. The Second Division had some quaint sounding names of yore – Gainsborough and Burton Swifts, along with others on their way to becoming giants – but the First was already manned by the great clubs, playing to major crowds. Glossop didn't get much out of trips to Aston Villa, Wolves, Derby, Nottingham Forest, Everton or Liverpool; in fact they won only four games and finished bottom.

Glossop stayed in the Second Division into the new century, finishing fifth in 1900–1901, but were sucked gradually into battling near the bottom. The rising cost of maintaining a team which could compete was highlighted when Glossop were fined £250 by the FA in 1903 for making illegal payments to players and 'wholesale dismanagement and deception'. Hill Wood had married in 1899, by all accounts a fearsome woman, Anne Selina Decima Bateman Hanbury, the Decima because she was the tenth child in her family. He became mayor of Glossop, supported the town's Conservative Club, and in 1910 was elected MP for the High Peak. He was in Parliament nineteen years but he never made a single speech.

The accounts vary of how much Hill Wood spent on the wages of players and upkeep of a club which was, in truth, way beyond what the town could sustain. Some say £10,000, a vast sum when millworkers were paid £1 a week for backbreaking work; the *Glossop Dale Chronicle* had it in his obituary, years later, as £33,000. As the First World War approached, the cotton business faced tougher competition from overseas and Samuel had to pull back. In 1915, the year the League played controversially on into the onset of war, Glossop finished bottom. When they half-heartedly applied for re-election to the League, in 1919, they were refused. While Henry Norris was tirelessly working the League's decision-makers to spirit Arsenal into the First Division, Glossop were out, dropping into the muscular local rivalries of the Lancashire Combination League.

In 1921, Samuel Hill Wood sold up. The cotton industry was heading for terminal decline in the face of cheaper imports, and the great old mills were shedding staff, closing down, stumbling into the 1930s. The Hill Wood family sold to a new company, which retained the name, Woods Bros (Glossop) Ltd, but had no connection. He sold Moorfield, ended the association with many of the good works and philanthropic legacies, dumped the football club, packed up and left for London. There he found a new club to support – Arsenal – being driven from luncheon at his club to the home matches. Henry Norris invited him on the board, then, six years later, when Norris was finally nailed by the Football Association for leaking a bit of money out of the club, Hill Wood became Arsenal's chairman. He bought shares and went on to furnish the club with their golden, art deco age under Herbert Chapman.

If Arsenal have never gone down since, Glossop mostly continued to fall, fighting for pride through the lower non-league levels of senior football: nineteen years in the Manchester League between the wars, another twelve from 1945 to 1957, the Lancashire Combination, then back in the Manchester League, the Cheshire League Divisions One and Two – strong competitions all these – then, in 1982, when non-league football was reorganised with the advent of the Alliance, later the Conference, the Lancashire Combination and Cheshire Leagues merged to form the North West Counties League. Glossop have stayed defiantly in its top division ever since.

It has not been easy. After the Second World War, the cricket club booted the football scruffs out of the North Road ground and they fetched up at their current, patchy Surrey Street home. As the Manchester clubs grew in stature and transport improved, Glossop's crowds fell away gradually to a kernel of die-hards. A benefactor kept them going through the 1950s, for which he had the honour of the haggard ground being named after him: the Arthur Goldthorpe Stadium. The club has always relied on volunteers and enthusiasts to keep it going. Peter Hammond, the club's current secretary, was taken to matches as a boy and has worked himself to exhaustion on every area of the club. Eric Monk has been helping for decades to reseed, mow and vainly try to level the pitch. Steve Baron, a bewhiskered pensioner, turns up in a shirt and tie, helps to collect the footballs after the game and cheers on the lads.

Even little Glossop suffered at the hands of a disastrous chairman, which nearly wiped them out. It had some familiar elements: a chairman arriving whom nobody knew, taking a fancy to the ground. Peter Smith, who was from the Midlands but renting a house nearby, arrived in 1989 making big promises, bought a majority of the shares and the club actually signed good players and made it to the last thirty-two of the FA Vase. The trouble started when Glossop were suspended from all competitions by the FA for failing to pay Lincoln City £3,000 for the goalkeeper Andy Gorton. That in turn led to the club being fined by the league for failing to fulfil their fixtures. The £3,000 was eventually paid and the bans lifted, but then, in late 1990, Smith left. Peter Hammond and other supporters discovered that without their knowledge he had agreed to sell the Surrey Street ground to the local council for £70,000, and been paid half of it as a deposit. The money, £36,000, came in on 6 December; it cleared a then £20,000 overdraft and some other creditors were paid, but £11,620 was withdrawn in cash. The supporters later discovered that the Andy Gorton money had been obtained by a short-term £5,000 mortgage, of which £1,200 was also withdrawn in cash.

Peter Heginbotham, a local solicitor and football supporter, was asked to help. He became chairman and spent five years and a lot of money shoring the club up. Like many before him, he was smitten by the place, a ragged little ground with an unshiftable air of history and commonplace magic. He managed to deal with the black hole by continuing with the sale of the ground, making the club a tenant of the council, had his law firm sponsor the club, worked hard to marry the club to the community and junior section, which is run separately, cut the wage bill, even put up floodlights. He failed early on in his appeal against the league fining the club for not playing fixtures when it was suspended by the FA – 'double jeopardy', as he called it. 'That was my first experience of the harshness in the way football is run,' he said. It was a game whose governors allowed men like Smith to walk into clubs without question or check, but were sticklers for unjust rules oppressing the supporters trying to mount a rescue. Heginbotham thoroughly enjoyed five years travelling to Barrow, Newcastle-under-Lyme, darkest Lancashire and furthest Merseyside, chasing the football dream, and Glossop had some success, winning the Manchester Premier Cup in 1997 at Old Trafford and in 1998 at Maine Road.

By 1996 he realised he couldn't carry on but he said he was careful not to be the sugar daddy who pulled out, which has got so many clubs into trouble.

'I told them straight: after this season, that's it. They were obviously worried, but it meant they were at least able to prepare for it. It cost me quite a lot of money but I thoroughly enjoyed it and hope I made a valuable contribution to the club and the community.'

The club has never found anybody similar to replace him, and hasn't had a sponsor since. Priestley says they need around £7–8,000 a year to be financially secure, pay the players, floodlights, running costs and fix things up. In football, swimming in billions now, you might think there would be a way to safeguard clubs like these, which have somehow survived a century, and provide a strong presence for the game, a route into playing for young kids, a football focus for the community, the base of the pyramid. However, there isn't. Clubs can apply for grants from the Football Foundation for facilities or particular community projects, but they cannot get help with the grinding, petty headaches of electricity bills, upkeep, which could be eased for a year with the amount a top player spends in a spot of recreational shopping. At Peter Hill-Wood's Arsenal, the wage bill in 2002 was £61.45m. That is vast, unthinkable money to the wider population of football. Just a speck of it could sustain so much. If Sol Campbell, along with several other players, is earning £100,000 a week, then one week of his wages would keep a whole club like Glossop going, with all the people it serves, for twelve years. At clubs like these you can see how a small part of the post-1992 bonanza could have been used fruitfully, not dished out to them to spend on players' wages – that would be a waste, fuelling wage inflation down the game – but on doing the grounds up, paying for the basics, so that the volunteers who maintain the clubs out of love and commitment can spend their time on more fulfilling and interesting areas of the game than how they will pay the gas bill.

One summer Adrian Priestley was giving the stand behind the goal a new coat of paint – and he ran out of paint. 'I realised, there was nothing in the kitty. We'd spent everything. All the money from the pie hut and lottery and bar and turnstiles, spent. We didn't have the money to buy a pot of paint.'

Twice, Priestley has written to Peter Hill-Wood at Arsenal. He's keen to stress they weren't begging letters: 'I just wanted him to know the state his grandfather's old club was in. That's all. If he wanted to do something for us, fine, but I didn't ask.' Proud, they still have Peter Hill-Wood named as their patron, although they've never heard from him. He didn't reply to Priestley's letters.

In Howard Park, near the little fountain on the rockery where Glossop's newlyweds pose for photographs, there is a statue dedicated to Samuel and Daniel Wood. The local kids haven't been too disrespectful: the classical figure has a hand missing, which once held a cotton shuttle, and a pair of specs has been scrawled in black marker onto each man's face. The pigeons have shat heartily all over them. Glossop people, let's be clear, aren't forever worshipping at the plinth of the Hill Woods. It's just that the family created the town, their legacy is still in its structures. The people here who know, remember the history and are gruffly grateful to the Hill Woods – the family may have grown rich then left, but they made a late nineteenth-century, pre-Welfare State contribution which still civilises the place today.

When Sir Samuel and his wife Decima died, they were buried back in Glossop, in what amounts to a family tomb at St James' Church, one of the ones Decima helped to build. A few years ago, some kids went in and smashed it about. The churchwarden wrote to Peter Hill-Wood at Arsenal, saying the church keeps the graveyard tidy but can't afford to pay for the upkeep of the graves; that is the families' responsibility. Hill-Wood sent a couple of hundred quid back with a stern letter saying he really hoped it'd be the last time the church asked him for help. Those who know about it don't think too much of his responses. They see him in the chair at Arsenal, the club making £56m in 2003–4 from television and prize money alone and paying £5m a year to a single player, building the new stadium for £357m, and they feel he might owe a little nod to the town where his family's fortune and involvement in football was built. When he agreed to see me for an interview for this book, I told him I wanted to talk about the Glossop history and link with Arsenal and was prepared to give him a grilling about the way he has left it so far behind.

I thought I'd get bluster from him, sincere blandishments, spin, you might call it. But he was disarmingly straightforward about all this, too. He did his best to give a nod to his roots; he'd fished out some old photos of his grandfather to show me, a little half-heartedly. 'This is up near a place called Moorfield, I think,' he said. The pictures were of Samuel and a few friends, up on the heather moors behind the house. They're the kind impossible to take seriously any more, the stuff of a thousand TV spoofs; upper-class fellows in plus fours with pipes and droopy moustaches, having jolly japes. In one or two, Samuel was shooting wildlife. Presumably, the mill was rattling with work, not a mile away.

'I must admit,' Peter Hill-Wood said, 'we were very bad at discussing family history; I know we came from Manchester and Derbyshire and my grandfather grew up in Glossop and ran Woods' mills, but we've never been very good at keeping family records.'

His version of the story was interestingly unromantic; the family reckoned Samuel had spent a decade too long in Glossop when the writing was on the wall for cotton and he'd lost a lot of money in that time.

'Nineteen seventeen, or was it the end of the First War, the textile industry got into terrible trouble. When the mills went wrong he kept them going which was probably financially not sensible. He should have closed them down ten years before he did.'

His grandfather had, Peter said, 'some other money around, which he lived on for the rest of his life.' He didn't, Peter added, leave much for them all to inherit. 'We don't really regret it, you know. It would have been nice but we didn't and so what.'

Regretting *rien* is clearly Peter's philosophy of life, but he doesn't quite carry it off; his eyes look fed up. Sir Samuel never worked again, paid for servants and a cook. Peter, after Eton and the army, went into Hambros merchant bank, and worked for a living. To Glossop people, he seems as if he must be fabulously rich, descended from millowners, chairman of Arsenal. From where he sits, he seems to feel it's all been a struggle, he's somehow kept missing out on fortunes. He has his mews house in Chelsea and a weekend place in Sandwich, Kent, where he likes to play golf, but it seems pretty modest to him: 'We've all had to make what we've made, really.'

He's a decent, pleasingly unaffected sort, but Peter Hill-Wood is not the man to reach back to support the town which made his family. Glossop is just not, he told me, part of his life; he's only ever been twice, for his grandparents' funerals. And he clearly has the southerner's fear of the north. 'When I went there it was sort of gloomy and dark and rainy and I can't remember whether I saw the Woods' mills or Wood Street or whatever it's called. I just don't recall. I do keep meaning to go back there and just sort of see what it looks like, but somehow other things always get in the way.'

Rather than me having to confront him with it, he volunteered the story about the church, grumbling that they'd asked him for money:

'I had the request to repair the vandalism on the family grave in Glossop and I told them I really hoped it was the last time. If they're going to keep vandalising it, I'm not going to keep repairing it.'

As for the club sending him letters, suggesting he might help out, or send an Arsenal side, he won't:

'A lot of people are hard up,' he said, looking at me sadly over his glasses.

'It's all a long time ago?' I asked.

'It's a long time ago,' he nodded.

And that was it. He had to walk the dog before the park shut. He was polite and personable as he said goodbye.

I told Joyce Powell what he'd said about his family; that he hadn't been to Glossop, was never immersed in their story. She, her house full floor to ceiling with books on local history, thought it was very sad: 'When I think of the pride people have discovering something about their family histories, something very ordinary, it seems a great shame.'

It's the same with football. The big clubs aren't interested any more in where they came from, in the thought that without the pyramid there would be no apex for them to sit on, raking it all in. Without the smaller clubs, they'd have had nobody to beat and clamber over and grow bigger than. Even now, Manchester United and Arsenal are still giants because there is a teeming world of football below them. There is certainly, from the big clubs, the plcs, the breakaway guys, the money men, not much sign of sentiment for the history. They haven't the time; there's little thought that they should maintain the game for its own sake and the sake of England's uniquely rich depth and range of football clubs. At Glossop North End it was hardly a revelation to hear that Peter Hill-Wood doesn't care. There was the odd mutter in the clubhouse, about Hill-Wood fortunes having been made off the backs of generations of local people, but they're proud, capable blokes here and they knew the score before. Behind the bar, Peter Hammond shrugged, said he might remove Hill-Wood from the title of patron. Glossop, for all their heritage and historic link with Arsenal, are no different from all the clubs in the wide tapestry of English football. The game began in this country and has always been powered with phenomenal force, fierce appetite, and from the beginning, while it turned into a commercial enterprise, the FA and leagues strove to maintain a collective culture. But, generations on, the enormous money which could make all the clubs strong, sustain a modern sport, is hoarded at the top, by the few big city clubs who made it through. The rest are on their own, living or dying by the unpaid efforts of volunteers. Small clubs, existing because of big obsessions.

CHAPTER 14

Taking It All

W hen I set out to explore what has happened to English football, the bust and inequality it has managed to fashion from its greatest ever boom, I wanted to track down and talk to the people most centrally involved in the Premier League break-away, which has so divided the game. Since the twenty-two Football League First Division clubs were backed by the Football Assocation to go into the vastly improved satellite TV rights deals with Sky, free from the arrangement to share 25 per cent of the money with the Second Division clubs and 25 per cent with the Third and Fourth Division clubs, they have reaped unprecedented windfalls. The £305m-five-year deal in 1992 was followed by £670m in 1997 for four years. The 2001–4 deal, done when the financial and media industries' optimism about the value of internet and tele-vision 'content' was at bursting point, was £1.6bn. From 2004 to 2007 the deal negotiated in a more temperate climate still adds up to £1.1bn. The total, for fifteen years of the Premiership: £3.675bn. You have to wonder how such a deluge of money into a sport, just three years after its most terrible disaster at the end of its bleakest decade, can have been allowed to leave any finan-cial problems at all, any club struggling for the basics, or facili-ties left desolate. Instead, the Premier League clubs shared next to none of it with the Football League or the wider game until the 2001 deal, when, because they were facing a challenge from the Office of Fair Trading to their right to bump up the money received by acting collectively as a cartel and selling their rights exclusively to Sky, they agreed to distribute a mere 5 per cent of the next one to grass-roots facilities via the Football Foundation. They now claim that their £20m a year, matched by the FA and Government, is transforming the landscape. Think how much could have been achieved with a little more trickle-down.

Yet even the bonanza at the top has been misspent, as it has been distributed to reward the already rich and therefore concentrated success in the hands of the winners, a duopoly by Manchester United and Arsenal – getting a bit boring, dare we say. 'There are now two leagues,' Richard Murray said in 2003. 'Arsenal, Chelsea and Man U in one and the rest of us in a league of seventeen teams.' The competition between the clubs, for whom success is ever more dependent on money, has led to agents and players being able to negotiate up their payments and wages to a level few who follow the game believe to be decent. The clubs have mostly done up their grounds – with grants, and at rising cost to supporters – and the money has certainly attracted some of the world's most accomplished stars to the top clubs, albeit at the expense of opportunities for young British players, despite the burgeoning trawls of kids from as young as eight into the big clubs' academies. Inflation of wages has soared right down the leagues, because they are still connected by promotion and relegation, without the distribution of income to balance it. Some, many, clubs in the lower divisions and in the Premier League have not been responsible in the way they have gambled for sporting success or survival, but the game's structure, with the rewards at the top and a financial battering for failure, does tempt them all to speculate, to 'live the dream', to varying degrees. The gap between the Premier League and Football League meant that in 2001–4 a club relegated from the Premiership immediately earned around £20m less from TV alone. In 2003–4, Arsenal's £56.6m from TV (including £19m for Champions League rights) was twice as much as all seventy-two Football League clubs made from TV together. Such a gap was always going to create a financial crack-up for the three clubs destined to go down every season. So, since 1992, the richest period the game has ever known and also a time of booming popularity and rising crowds at all levels of football, thirty-six of the Football League's seventy-two clubs, exactly half, have been in one form of insolvency or another, usually administration. Several of these have been large clubs, which have collapsed almost immediately on dropping out of the Premiership, owing many millions to creditors large and small. Yet still, nobody who can make a difference in football is addressing this inequality, or the spectacle of a sport, rich beyond imagining, leaving a trail of petty bad debt among the people and organisations which serve it. The FA, the governing body which backed the idea of the breakaway originally in 1990 for myopic, petty political ends, still says nothing about the chasm which the nation can see has opened up.

I wanted to know how the big clubs swung it originally, wondered what David Dein and Noel White can have possibly said to persuade the governing body that it was in its interests and the right thing to do, to back their breakaway. Can they have been as blatant as to say they wanted to do a whacking TV deal and not have to share it with the other clubs, in the way the League had always worked? I've always wondered how they justified it to each other, what they said, facing each other in the Lancaster Gate plotting rooms, to rationalise it all. Was there something we haven't understood, an underlying reason, which made the move by the FA genuinely coherent and well-advised? Dein and White have never, from what I have seen, explained the case they made to the FA. Dein has said many times that the big clubs wanted, needed, to escape the Football League's voting arrangements, by which they could be outvoted by the small clubs, although that was less true since the big clubs gained increased power via the 1985 'Heathrow Agreement'. Irving Scholar told me the big clubs' chairmen knew they were sitting on oceans of potential and, in the wreckage of the eighties, felt held back by the small:

'We said, "you lot can stay and destroy yourselves but we're not going down with you".'

That somewhat ignores the fact that the Hillsborough disaster happened at a First Division club's prestige ground; the 1980s decline and neglect was far from confined to smaller clubs. But that was the case most commonly made publicly, that the top clubs wanted to be in control of their own destiny. The chairmen, like Scholar and Dein, have always been somewhat reticent about saying that they did not want to share the big money about to pour in, or that they, personally, stood to get rich.

However they actually put it, they couldn't have found the FA more amenable. Millichip was fretting about the perceived threat to the FA of the joint board proposed by the League in *One Game, One Team, One Voice*, which, if he'd stopped to think, he'd have seen came from the big clubs anyway and was a sensible starting point for the new era. However, rather than negotiate, the FA was determined simply to crush the idea and smash the League once and for all. Arthur Sandford, who was the chief executive of the League at the time, moved on to become the chief executive of Manchester City Council. For a while I worked for a TV company opposite the Town Hall, so one day I made an appointment and popped across Albert Square to see him. His abiding feeling was that *One Game, One Team, One Voice* had been the correct way ahead and was rejected only because of the narrowest of vested interests: 'I'm still convinced,' he told me gloomily, 'that if we'd offered to give them seven seats on the top table and reserved only five for the League, rather than six-six, or whatever, it would have gone through. We wanted unity for football but the FA saw only their own petty positions.'

I never managed to talk to Sir Bert Millichip in detail about it; he died in December 2002. The tributes at West Bromwich Albion, the club where he was the chairman, were warm and genuinely affectionate; the supporters believed he was a wise old head who had done a lot for the club and held together a board of directors genetically programmed to infighting. Not long before he died, I interviewed him about a less salubrious story – that shortly after the Hillsborough disaster and the Taylor requirement that the grounds become all-seater, one of his fellow West Brom directors, Mike McGinnity, now Coventry's chairman, had formed a seating company, Pel, to take commercial advantage of the new work. McGinnity had taken on Ted Croker, the retired FA secretary for, we were told, his football contacts, and Pel had gone on to make a great deal of money winning the seating work at several major clubs. When Sir Bert retired from the FA in 1996, he worked for Pel as a consultant, to win overseas work for Pel by tapping the contacts he had made in European football while at the FA.

Sitting in the velour chairs in the chintzy lounge of his commodious pile in Barnt Green, the North Worcestershire suburb for Brummies-done-good, I asked him whether Pel had paid him. His answer opened a window onto his life:

'Not much,' he shrugged. 'Just enough to keep me in gin and tonic and Eccles cakes.'

He said some strange things about Hillsborough. Like so many football people he was oddly unemotional, even though he was there on the day, in the directors' box, seats reserved with his wife, and this was his, the FA's, match. His main memory was of how inconveniently long they were kept in the lounges before they were allowed to leave:

'The wives were getting very impatient,' he recalled. And that was about it. He was, to be fair, old by the time I talked to him.

My previous meeting with Graham Kelly was in 1997. He was still in position as the FA's chief executive, and he saw me in his office at grand, stolid, fetid Lancaster Gate. Used football kit was strewn on the floor; and defeat, even a waft of depression, was in the air. There was no sense that he or the FA was in control, or facing up to the game's problems, or had any plans to fix them. We went through the motions, he saw me out past the trophies and glories in the FA's silverware cabinets, and it was all pretty dispiriting.

Kelly was forced to resign in November 1998 following the revelation of the £3.2m in grants the FA had agreed to pay the Welsh FA while the FA chairman, Keith Wiseman, was looking for the Welsh FA's vote towards a seat for him on the council at football's world governing body Fifa. Kelly, sacked by the FA then later cleared by Fifa of any impropriety, has not worked full-time since, but has been busy with various football activities, popped up as the invited director at Luton, and has generally garnered more affection from and towards supporters, in whose battles he usually seems to find himself on the right side these days. He damned the Wimbledon franchise and the procedures which allowed it to get through.

This time we arranged to meet near his home between Preston and Blackpool, and fixed the place as the canteen – they'd like, I'm sure, to call it a restaurant – at Bolton West Services on the M61, southbound. I parked on the northbound side and walked across the windy overpass, past the shop and empty, flashing, games arcade and found Graham loitering outside the café. Always surprisingly tall, his ginger hair was greying; he looked gaunt, quite a lot older, in his black slacks and polo neck, than he had a few years before, stuffed in his suit, behind the top man's desk at Lancaster Gate.

Like many people spat out of organisations, his years on the outside have allowed him a freedom to speak, and also a cleaner perspective on events. He's still consumed by football, loves the game: watching it, being involved with it, reading, talking, writing about it. He'd been reading the spate of autobiographies of 1960s heroes: Nobby Stiles, George Cohen. He's a bit of a Man United fan. In the hot summer of 2003, he told me, he had taken a course to gain his coaching badge, lining up with all the dads for two days at Lancashire County FA. He had also reregistered as a referee; his weekends are now taken up with refereeing under-10s football on Saturday mornings, where he isn't too impressed with the attitude of some of the watching parents. Saturday afternoons he watches a League match, Preston, Blackpool, occasionally Liverpool. Sunday afternoons he coaches a team of under-11s, which he loves.

We sat on the green plastic chairs attached to the square tables, nobody else in the place, and sipped muddy coffee from a cloudy cafetiere. It was freezing in there, and we didn't take our coats off. Graham looked down at the table:

'Yes,' he said finally. 'The game still runs very strongly in me. I don't know why.'

Tentatively, with some long pauses, he felt his way into discussing his time at the FA, and the breakaway. He told me what actually happened.

'The Football League were going round the FA counties at the time with their plan, and it was seen by the FA as a problem, as a proposal for powersharing. White and Dein went to see Millichip first, and he then sent for me. He told me: "They're seeking to get out of the Football League, the TV contract is up for renewal." He wanted me to arrange to see them and explore the feasibility of the FA supporting it.'

I asked him what they said when he met them.

'They said they were fed up with the structure, they had to break out then, not wait three years, because the TV deal was up before then.'

He didn't remember if they explicitly mentioned that they wanted to break away from sharing money with the rest of the Football League. It is difficult to believe that the FA didn't see the plot in precisely those terms but apparently they didn't: 'That wasn't the tenor of the conversation. I don't remember thinking they just wanted to keep all the money,' Kelly said. 'I'm not sure either if they said it was all in the best interests of football.' He looked up, his eyes knowing: 'Would I have believed them if they had? I hope not.'

But if it seems that the FA was turned over, thinking bureaucratically about its committees and supposed footballing administrative pre-eminence while the men at the clubs could smell the money, Kelly is adamant still that *The Blueprint* could have been good for the game. Its better intentions, he said, were genuine, the ideas for a streamlined top division, a national plan for well-designed new stadia including ground-sharing, youth development and other initiatives which were never followed through. The FA, he said, thought it would run the Premier League from Lancaster Gate like another of their competitions, like the FA Cup, that he would be the chief executive and the FA would have a real partnership with the big clubs.

He began to realise that this was not going to happen, that the big clubs had other ideas for where they were going, when Charles Hughes told some chairmen in a meeting that they already had their chief executive, referring to Kelly. There was, Kelly said, a very long silence. Then Millichip sold the pass, telling the clubs they did not have to stick at eighteen, that it was up to them how many clubs they wanted in the Premier League.

'I looked outside,' Kelly remembered, 'and the FA flag was flying on the balcony. I didn't see the three lions, just the white background. I thought that's it, it's the surrender. From then, there was no possibility of the FA controlling the Premier League, or even restraining it.'

The FA gave the clubs a breakaway, of which the clubs could previously only dream, which they must never have thought they would actually achieve with the governing body's backing, yet the FA negotiated and insisted on nothing in return.

'We wrote a blueprint,' he said after some deep thought, 'but we were too weak to deliver on any of it.'

Yes, he told me, he knew very well that many of the Premier League boardroom men, including Dein, have since made fortunes for themselves. 'I hope they're enjoying their money,' he said.

'What do you mean?'

'Just that,' he said, and he looked up and smiled. 'I hope they're enjoying it.' Then he laughed. And I laughed too, although I still can't quite explain why it was funny. Dry, I think you could call his sense of humour.

We had another cafetiere. There isn't much else to do at Bolton West Services. Not on the southbound side, anyway. Graham thought again, for a long time. Staring down into the far corner of the table, he said:

'We at the FA missed a golden opportunity. The clubs were desperate for their freedom, and they would have given virtually anything to be granted that. We could have done so much more to get it right, by saying that the FA is here for the good of the whole game, and developed a structure which worked. So many things have come back to haunt us, which could have been dealt with by establishing principles then: on the financial integrity of the game, on agents, good management of clubs, putting country before club. I still do not believe that big clubs should subsidise small clubs which are badly run, but we should have ensured a more equal distribution of the money, not allowed them to break away and keep it all.'

He thought for ages again, looking intently down. He'd bought a Cellophane-wrapped, stale-looking piece of fruitcake and he had a munch on it. He paused, put his cup down: 'We were guilty of a tremendous, collective lack of vision.'

I bumped into Graham Taylor in the press room at Highbury, where he was summarising for Radio 5. I told him I was writing a book about how football had changed, and that I had always been struck by his boldness, to rubbish the breakaway publicly at its launch, even though he was the England manager at the time. He was immediately open to talking about it. Was it really true, I asked him, that they produced their glossy *Blueprint*, purporting to be all about improving the England team, but never discussed it with him, the England manager?

'Absolutely true,' he smiled, 'they never mentioned it openly. I just knew what was going on because you heard the talk.'

His main memory of the time was the day he saw Graham Kelly and Charles Hughes across the corridor, in Kelly's office, after the meeting at which Millichip had caved in to the clubs: 'They were absolutely fuming.' Taylor smiled. 'They were furious. My God, they were spitting feathers.'

He believed at the time it was the wrong move for the FA to be backing, that it was indeed based on the greed of the big clubs, and that was why he said what he said: 'The idea that it was for the benefit of the England team is nonsense. As I saw it, the big clubs wanted all the money, and the object of the FA was to cave in, to meet those demands. The FA have to hold their hands up and be responsible for the demise of the Football League, for having broken it up.

'The FA believed that it would have the authority and run the Premier League for the clubs, but it has happened the other way around; the big club chairmen have steadily worked their way into committees and boards and positions of importance at the FA and undermined its authority.'

The resulting change to football's culture and structure has not been to his taste: 'Look, you have to accept change. But I try to listen to my heart, my guts. Although I can see the improvements since the Premiership was formed, I worry about the heart and soul of the game. I believe football is about much more than the big clubs. It belongs to the nation, to everybody. Now, though, it is obsessed with money, and run, totally dominated, by the big clubs.'

As a football man, Taylor is long overdue a reassessment. OK, he allowed Channel Four in where he shouldn't have, and they captured him, fly on the wall, floundering as the England manager, clearly, to put it kindly, not in his element. But it is too superficial to base a view of Taylor on the do-I-not-like-that piss-take which flowed from the programme.

He spent most of his career with underdogs, and wonders if that formed his view of the game. He joined Grimsby Town after school, played 189 league games and became their captain, before they sold him to Lincoln in 1968 for £4,500. He played 169 times for them, then, when he retired through injury in 1972 aged only twenty-eight, Lincoln made the bright young man their manager. Four years of team-building later, Taylor got the Imps promoted. He was impressing people, had an offer from Millichip to join West Brom but in 1977 chose the security of a five-year contract and the ambition of Elton John at Watford. Elton John's style was not Jack Walker or Abramovich vulgarity, waving blank cheques for the manager to buy a winning team, and Taylor signed mostly solid, experienced professionals to mesh with the young players, like John Barnes and Luther Blissett, who were coming through.

'My strength was really building for the long term, putting structures in place, and motivating players. Watford had finished seventh in the Fourth Division in 1977. Six years later, we were runners-up in the First Division and qualified for the Uefa Cup.'

Along with Wimbledon's rise, it is one of football's great small-club achievements, and, although Taylor's Watford did launch the long ball, they had John Barnes weaving on the left, Nigel Callaghan jinking on the right and were all round more appealing than the 'Crazy Gang'. At Aston Villa, for whom he left Vicarage Road ten years later, Taylor is very well respected by the fans for constructing a team, again with no glamour signings, who passed their way, David Platt excelling, to runners-up in the First Division in 1990. He left there for England, never the right appointment, then managed at Wolves and his second stint at Aston Villa, which he left in 2003, fuming about Doug Ellis' chairmanship of the club. He is no fan of the Premier League revolution:

'The players are on enormous wages and I can tell you that many of the foreign players, particularly, don't care about the clubs and the local pride at stake – why would they? I can tell you as a manager, they are difficult to motivate.'

The club itself, Taylor said, was wholly different when he returned to it:

'When I left in 1990, Aston Villa was a football club, an FC. All the staff knew each other, from the players to the secretaries, and they felt part of it. When I went back in 2002, it was a plc. There were three times the staff, people didn't know each other, and the heart had been stripped out of the place.

'Football was never a means to make money by owning shares but people have come into it from other businesses and made easy money. I can understand it; it must be very tempting. I can see too that it is a lot easier to make money in football as an executive, a director, than outside in the real world. It's a lot more pleasant too, and the hours are better, if you're running a football club rather than, say, an engineering company. But many of these people who have come into football as a business know nothing about the game itself, they are ignorant of its history and they don't care about the smaller clubs.'

Of the breakaway's prime movers, David Dein, who is now the vice-chairman of the FA as well as Arsenal, refused me an interview. The e-mail from his secretary said: 'Unfortunately, Mr Dein will not be able to assist.'

I did, though, get hold of Noel White.

CHAPTER 15

The Football Man (1)

L et's be clear about it: I caught him on the hop. I'd written to Noel White at Liverpool asking for an interview and he'd sent back a nice, polite, typewritten letter, saying he was too busy. 'My commitments for the next 5/6 weeks,' he wrote, 'are extensive.'

He stapled his card to the letter, which gave his address as a house called 'Rustlings', in Hale. It's a leafy Cheshire suburb for Manchester people who've made decent money. It used to be footballer belt before the players earned more than the directors and moved into the truly minted fringe of the Cheshire set. The card gave White's status as a director of Liverpool FC, a life vice-president of the Football Association and the current chairman of the FA's International Committee. His phone numbers were on it, so I thought: what the hell, give him a ring.

I had found out a bit about him previously; one of the old Manchester City directors, Chris Muir, told me one time when I'd been trying to make sense of City's endemic chaos that Peter Swales – who Muir, an ally, maintained was sadly underrated by the fans – had been in business with White. White & Swales: they had done pretty well out of it. Muir said 'Swalesy' had been a sharp operator since taking over at City in the early seventies and pointed out that for all the antipathy of the fans Swales had never mired City into the depths Franny Lee achieved within just a couple of years of his 1993 takeover, which City fans had welcomed as the Second Coming at the time. While Swales was City's chairman, he had worked himself onto the FA council and was made the chairman of the International Committee, the FA's most coveted position, which made him responsible for appointing the England manager, including Graham Taylor. He had previously been at non-league Altrincham alongside Noel White, which always seemed a saving grace, proof of his roots in the game, that it wasn't all about ego, self-promotion and free trips.

When I phoned Noel White he was evidently enjoying a brief interlude in his extensive commitments. It was about four in the afternoon on a weekday and I found him at home, minding his granddaughter. She answered the phone first and he had to shuffle her off it. I told him I was following up his letter and knew he was busy but wondered if we could just have a chat. He said OK. His accent and voice I recognised instantly: the sandpaper Mancunian spoken by the men who ran the football teams I played in as a kid; market traders, dealers in some strand of the textile industry, dads who smoked loads of B & H, or Hamlets if they fancied themselves more the urban philosopher, sheepskin coats for a touch of the Don Revies. Men who lived for the football at the weekends. He filled me in on his background.

He's seventy-four now, and he and Swales had begun working together back in 1955, when he was twenty-five: 'We started off selling gramophone records, the old 78s, then we moved into TV rentals, which was the backbone of the business. We moved from one shop to several others, doing the TVs and white goods, before they were known as white goods.'

They did well enough and sold out in 1968. White bought the Bowden Hotel, local to Altrincham, and ran that for eighteen years. He's pretty much retired now, apart from his football commitments at Liverpool and the FA. He and Swales, local businessmen who'd made a bit, had taken over Altrincham, their local semi-professional club, in 1961. After a while, seeing themselves as a senior non-league club, they pushed and lobbied the FA to accept the formation of a Northern Premier League. You might think of that as grass-roots stuff, but it was about the creation of an elite, controversial, because it skimmed off the cream of clubs in the major, semi-professional leagues of Cheshire, Merseyside, South Yorkshire, Lincolnshire and the North East. They pulled it off though, and the Northern Premier began in 1968, stocked with famous old names like Northwich Victoria, Gainsborough Trinity, Worksop Town – one of Herbert Chapman's clubs as a player and latterly a post-retirement canter for Chris Waddle – Boston United, who are now in the Third Division of the Football League, South Shields, Ashington, Altrincham and others.

By 1967, Swales was itching to clamber up the football pyramid and he made it onto City's board, from where he mounted his coup to become the chairman shortly after City's trophy-winning years. Chris Muir told me all the details; they clearly saw themselves as daring Young Turks employing devilish tactics, but it was all before my time and, given City's subsequent decline under Swales, the story of his rise just left me feeling vaguely miserable.

After Swales left Altrincham, White stayed on for nearly twenty years. He took the club from the Northern Premier into becoming founder members of yet another elite he was involved in forming: the Alliance Premier League, the forerunner of the Conference, which started in 1979 as a national league for the most senior semi-pro clubs. Alty won it in its first season, and stayed in this top section of non-league football for eighteen years. In his time, the club became famous for its FA Cup runs, regularly making it through the qualifying rounds and standing up to League clubs. In 1979 they drew 1-1 with Tottenham at White Hart Lane, although they lost at home in the replay. In 1986 their finest hour was beating Birmingham at St Andrews, 2-1, in the Third Round. That was White's final season there.

He had joined the FA in 1976, as a council member, representative of the senior clubs in Merseyside and Cheshire. Gradually, he made his way up the monkey puzzle tree of council and committees. That led him to get to know the Liverpool directors quite well, and eventually in 1986 one of them, John Smith, asked him to join the board at Anfield. 'I felt I'd taken Altrincham as far as I could. We'd had a lot of success. The Liverpool people were impressed with what I'd done and wanted me to help increase the club's earning power, so I joined.'

In early 1990, he was even made Liverpool's chairman for eighteen months: 'Then David Moores [part of the Moores family which owned Littlewoods] bought a large stake in the club, and he fancied being the chairman so I stepped down. That was about the time I got interested in the Premier League formation.'

Yes, I told him, I've always been interested in that: what was behind it all?

'It's a long, long story, with many twists and turns,' he said, which sounded promising. 'We felt a top tier was needed to help us to compete in Europe, have a stronger division and a better voting structure. We carried the message to Sir Bert Millichip and took it as far as we could. Graham Kelly was very helpful and we gathered support for the idea. It was like the Northern Premier League, the clubs wanted it, and we had to gain support from within the FA.'

I asked him what reasons he and David Dein gave the FA when they asked the governing body to back the breakaway.

'Well, we were going through rebuilding after Hillsborough. It was essential that big money became available. That was one of the reasons.'

But most of the money hasn't gone on ground rebuilding, has it? Wasn't it more generally about the top clubs keeping all the money?

'Yes, the Premier League takes all the money; they provide the entertainment, take the risk in signing players and creating big stadia. We were losing top players to Europe at the time and this would allow the top clubs to be able to keep more of the money and pay players more. We thought we'd get a collection of clubs together which could compete with clubs in Italy and Spain to pay the wages of the top foreign players. It's been very successful and attendances have increased.'

It's created a huge gap financially between the Premier League clubs and the Football League, though, hasn't it?

'Clubs do struggle when they go out of the Premier League. Clubs run into trouble because they gamble to try to keep up with the Joneses. You have to live within your means. But none of them have ever turned down the chance to join. People are forever optimists.'

I tried to probe his reading of the broader context. Did he not think at the time the League's proposal for unity was a good one, and in fact what he had done damaged the League?

'The League's suggestion had a lot of merit. This wasn't meant with any bitterness. The direct object wasn't to belittle any other club. There was nothing vile, nothing vicious. The Premier League idea appealed to me more.'

Was he surprised the FA backed the breakaway?

'No, I wasn't surprised. This was a response to the League's proposals.'

The FA said in their *Blueprint* that the main advantage was going to be helping the England team by reducing the Premier League to eighteen clubs. Was that discussed much?

'That,' he said, 'was one of the fringe benefits.'

I asked him the question I had always wondered about his involvement, once I'd been told about his background. David Dein was a man who bought into Arsenal in 1983 and was in a hurry to do the best for his big club and himself. But White had spent a full twenty-five years at Moss Lane in Altrincham, working away making a local suburban club a proud non-league force. It seemed very odd that within so short a time he should have put his energies into a breakaway of the very richest city clubs in the country, to keep all the money about to flood into football, rather than share it with the football population at large.

'Well, yes,' he said, 'but I thought there was merit in it, it was something which made sense.'

Yes, but it has split football and concentrated all the money at the top, so many smaller clubs have been in financial crisis.

'Well,' he said finally, 'there was a bit more to the background. Another reason for it.'

At last, I thought. The breakaway seems to have been so nakedly a move for money and power by the big clubs, so blatantly wrong for the FA to have backed, I'd always thought perhaps we were missing something which made sense of it, beyond greed and short-sightedness. And now, here it was: the real detail, the behind-the-scenes grit, the true picture of why the men who ran football backed the breakaway.

What was it then, I asked, this other, deeper reason?

'I can't say,' he said.

'You can't say?'

'No, I can't.'

'Is it confidential?'

'No. I can't remember.'

'You can't remember?'

'No, I can't remember. I'll have to look up my notes.'

CHAPTER 16

Not Forgotten

'It wouldn't happen now,' Hilda Hammond is saying, sitting on the sofa in the family's living room in January 2004. 'If there was a disaster, in which ninety-six people died, and it turned out the safety certificate was ten years out of date, the place was unsafe, and the police made a huge mess of the operation, the authorities would all be absolutely hammered. Heads would roll. There would be no question about it.'

Phil, her husband, now the chairman of the Hillsborough Family Support Group, is sitting in the armchair, the wide-screen telly showing Sky Sport; looks like England being bamboozled at cricket by Sri Lanka, again. Since I was last here nearly six years ago, when they were still deep in the legal struggle, wrestling with tons of files and documents, their semi-detached home in Aigburth, a comfortable Liverpool suburb, seems airier. They've had the floor done, and the fresh white walls make the room brightly cosy. When I first met some of the families who lost their children at Hillsborough, along with being struck by how much they loved their children, how devastated they were when they died, how hard they were prepared to fight to seek the truth, I always noted how ordinary they are. The idea put about that they were some sub-human species of Scouse hooligan could not have been more wrong, which was why it was so damaging.

Phil Hammond was a post office manager until he retired on the grounds of ill health after flogging himself through over a decade of battles against the legal system which he had trusted before he lost his son, Philip, who was fourteen. Hilda is a nurse manager in the Intensive Care Unit at The Walton Centre, a Liverpool hospital for neurosciences. People went to that football match from all walks of life; working class, middle class. We aren't surprised about that now, but then, just fifteen years ago, football supporters were caged in like animals, one of Margaret Thatcher's 'enemy within'. The Hillsborough victims weren't all from Liverpool either. The Hewitts, who lost their two sons, Nicholas and Carl, were from Coventry. The Murrays, who lost Paul, were from Stoke. Inger Shah, a mother who died, lived in London. Driving around to see some of the families is a trip through middle England. These people were brought together by the worst imaginable circumstance, the death of their loved ones, and many had nothing else in common. Over the years there has been friction between some families, which led to them eventually giving their support to another group, the Hillsborough Justice Campaign, which included survivors.

While the football authorities and clubs mostly forgot what little they ever learned about the disaster, rolled on with their political machinations, took the money, built the grounds, raised the prices and held a minute's silence every year on 15 April, for the families there has been no forgetting. In the Hammonds' home, Philip's room upstairs is still much as it was, full of papers but bereft of him.

Football, reborn, ballooned into media fodder, front page and back in the years after the disaster, but the families' long, lonely battle to establish exactly what happened that day, and to see that the people responsible were sanctioned, was mostly not touched by the press. It was too much of a reminder of dark days the country and its national game were feverishly putting behind them. Hilda told me that at first, when Philip was killed, they had thought there had been a tragic accident. It was only after Taylor, in his first report, identified the causes, the unsafe ground and police negligence, that they realised how pernicious and avoidable it all was. After that, the families were outraged that the Director of Public Prosecutions, after an investigation by the West Midlands Police, decided not to charge anybody. Then the families suffered the inquest, where they felt the evidence was weighted against them, producing the verdict of accidental death in March 1991. The families undertook long-drawn-out appeals against both these decisions, and lost. The country mostly forgot about them until Jimmy McGovern's drama-documentary in 1997 blasted back with the truth of what happened on the day and the lingering whiff that there was a cover-up, that the evidence presented to the inquest and the DPP was skewed against the fans and in favour of the police, to ensure there would be no prosecutions.

In February 1998, the new Labour Home Secretary Jack Straw offered some hope, announcing a limited reopening of the case, the appointment of a judge, Lord Justice Stuart-Smith, to conduct a 'scrutiny' – an odd format which had no formal legal basis – of the new areas of doubt. The judge dropped a clanger the first day. Phil, hobbling with a walking stick because of his artifical leg, arrived first, and Stuart-Smith said to him: 'Where are the others? Are they going to arrive late, like the Liverpool fans did?' Phil shakes his head, remembering it: 'I wish we'd walked out on him. Apart from the fact he was so crass, it made it clear he had made his mind up and we'd be getting nothing from him.'

So it turned out. The serious new doubts about the police story that a crucial video camera, Camera 5, had not been working on the day – dismissed. Medical evidence which challenged the coroner's decision to limit the inquest only to what happened before 3.15 – thrown out. Another serious issue had come to light: South Yorkshire Police officers had been asked by the police solic-itors, Hammond Suddards, after discussions with senior officers, to change their statements about what happened. The statement of PC David Frost, who first came forward with this revelation, was included in Stuart-Smith's report. It showed that criticism of senior officers was deleted. In all, 147 statements out of 400 made by South Yorkshire policemen were changed; Stuart-Smith said sixty involved a 'minor ambiguity or error', which left eighty-seven, more than a fifth, which had been substantially changed. Stuart-Smith, however, rejected the argument that this process amounted to a cover-up.

'There was an understandable desire,' he said of the South Yorkshire Police after the disaster, 'not to give anything away.'

That was it. They got nothing. Public opinion was on their side for the first time but the legal establishment was still impenetrable. The families decided to go it alone. They held a concert to raise a fighting fund, and went for a private prosecution themselves.

Phil sits back in his chair. 'The most important day in the history of the Hillsborough Family Support Group was the day in Leeds when Chief Superintendent Duckenfield and Superintendent Murray, his second-in-command, were committed by the magistrate to trial for manslaughter. They'd put every obstacle in our way, but we had them in the dock. There was a case to answer, which they had to face.'

Phil himself toiled through the legal work, self-taught, doing what he could to help the group's solicitor, Ann Adlington, and their barrister, Alun Jones QC. At the trial, they argued that the police had been so negligent in the care and safety of the supporters that it amounted to manslaughter. Duckenfield and Murray pleaded not guilty. In July 2000, Murray was acquitted by the jury. They could reach no verdict on Duckenfield; they were hung. The judge refused the families' request for a retrial, ruling it would be 'oppressive' to expect Duckenfield to face trial again.

They couldn't see why – the Leeds players Lee Bowyer and Jonathan Woodgate and the other defendants in the Sarfraz Najeib GBH case were all retried after the first case was abandoned following an article in the *Sunday Mirror* deemed by the judge to be prejudicial. The families also took issue with the judge's summing up, in which he had told the jury they needed to consider more than just the particular facts of the case, and worry about the general impact a guilty verdict could have on the police and other services: 'You are entitled to ask yourselves whether it would send out the wrong message to those who have to act in an emergency of this kind.'

They believe that was a misdirection, but they discovered yet another detail in the legal system which has so completely let them down: there is no right of appeal in a private prosecution. With the issues still unresolved, nobody having taken responsibility, I'd thought I would find Phil and Hilda still in torment. But they seem, I tell them, more at peace, lighter in spirit, than when I saw them last. Hilda says that is because they can now say, whatever the result, that they themselves have done right by their children, by fighting as hard and as far as they possibly could:

'We could so easily have been where we were in 1993,' Hilda says, 'stitched up by the police, waved away by the legal system, the whole case closed as accidental death, but at least now we can face our children in heaven and say truthfully that we did everything we could.'

They are convinced there is a lot they still don't know. Even now, Phil says: 'Every time the phone rings, every single time, my first thought is Hillsborough. I have this feeling that someone, sometime, one of the police officers, will finally tell us everything.

'Perhaps somebody will lose a son or daughter, then have to go through what we've been through. Then they might think of us, come clean about what went on. Before I die, I am convinced that will happen, that we will find out.'

Of all the outstanding questions, one huge area has been largely overlooked. Most of the attention has always focused on the South Yorkshire Police, which mismanaged the match, failed to close off the tunnel, failed even to recognise the crushing which was happening right in front of their control box, and said later that the relevant camera, Camera 5, had not been working. Roger Houldsworth, who ran the CCTV system at Hillsborough, said it was working, yet he was never called to give evidence at the inquest. He emerged as a result of the Jimmy McGovern programme, only to be dismissed by Stuart-Smith. However, the force which conducted all the investigations, for Taylor, the coroner and the DPP, was the West Midlands Police, and their role and the personnel involved are overdue some scrutiny.

Headed by Chief Constable Geoffrey Dear, West Midlands were appointed immediately after the disaster to gather evidence for Taylor. They handled the huge volume of evidence which Taylor marshalled to produce his clear conclusions that the police were to blame and the ground unsafe, and that the South Yorkshire Police should be criticised for presenting the tale that the fans had been drunk and misbehaving.

At the time Geoffrey Dear had a very major problem of his own in the West Midlands. Shortly after Taylor reported, on 14 August 1989, Dear had to take the momentous decision completely to disband his force's elite group of detectives, the West Midlands Serious Crime Squad. They had been responsible for obtaining convictions in the region's most violent offences for decades, including the six Irish men jailed for the bombing of a Birmingham pub in 1974, and the four convicted of the 1978 murder of the newspaper delivery boy Carl Bridgewater, all of whom had always protested their innocence.

In the late 1980s, a rash of Serious Crime Squad cases had been collapsing following allegations that the squad's police officers had fabricated evidence, forged confessions or used violence to 'fit up' people for crimes they had not committed. Clare Short, the MP for Birmingham Ladywood, had in January 1989 called for a Home Office inquiry to clean up the squad. Dear tried to deal with it internally, but as he mused later to the *Birmingham Post*, it didn't work: 'I now know that there were people who apparently decided to stick two fingers up at the boss.'

Clare Short was unhappy enough with the lack of progress to help to set up an independent inquiry funded by the Civil Liberties Trust, led by the Birmingham University law lecturer Tim Kaye. They looked into twenty three cases brought by the Serious Crime Squad in the previous ten years in which charges had been dropped, or the defendants acquitted, after the defence argued that police officers had fabricated confessions, planted evidence, put undue pressure on witnesses or committed other serious malpractices to convict innocent men.

Kaye's report, *Unsafe and Unsatisfactory*, was published in May 1991. 'The reasons for the failure of many of these prosecutions are nothing short of alarming,' he wrote.

Two months earlier, the 'Birmingham Six' had been freed after spending sixteen and a half years in prison, when the Court of Appeal quashed their convictions following evidence that West Midlands Police officers had forged notes of an interview. In 1997, the three surviving members of the 'Bridgewater Four' were released having spent nineteen years in prison, when a confession was proved to have been forged. There was a spate of quashed convictions throughout the 1990s of men who had spent many years in prison, following evidence brought to their appeals of violence by Serious Crime Squad officers, fabrication of confessions, 'plastic bagging' and torture.

The Hillsborough families, consumed by their own grief, never greatly registered any of this. They had no reason to think that they were going to be dragged in any way into this dirty, savage world. They had sent their children to a football match, from which they had never come back, and now, following Taylor's identification of what happened, they expected those responsible to take the blame. Just two days after Dear disbanded the Serious Crime Squad, on 16 August 1989, the DPP announced a criminal investigation into Hillsborough, and the West Midlands Police was confirmed as the investigating force. In some newspapers, this was portrayed as a valuable face-saver for Dear and his force.

The families expected justice to be done. They have for ever after believed it wasn't. Because the DPP inquiry was taking a long time, the coroner decided to hold very limited 'mini-inquests' into the deaths of all the victims, from April 1990, which provided no opportunity really to test the evidence or cross-examine witnesses because of the ongoing criminal investigation. The DPP then came out on 30 August 1990 and said there would be no prosecutions.

Peter Wright, South Yorkshire Police's Chief Constable, had told the *Sheffield Star* immediately after Taylor reported that: 'The criticisms have to be accepted.' However, he later told the same paper that alcohol had played a much greater part than Taylor had accepted: 'There will be a lot of additional evidence presented to the coroner's inquiry which was not presented at Lord Justice Taylor's inquiry, which may put a different complexion on the end product.'

At the main inquest, the police, far from withdrawing the allegations dismissed by Taylor, repeated them with renewed vehemence. The families always believed that the South Yorkshire Police were allowed to do this, that their case to the coroner's inquest was presented in the best possible light to obtain the verdict of accidental death. They protested that the West Midlands Police – two junior officers were named – had put pressure on some witnesses to change their evidence, particularly to support the 3.15 cut-off. That was another allegation later dismissed by Stuart-Smith. The families did notice at the time, during the main inquests, that the coroner was constantly deferring to and taking advice from a West Midlands Police officer, seemingly acting as his right-hand man. Phil Hammond told me the families never took to the officer much, and he never really talked to them. He was Detective Superintendent Stanley Beechey.

He was clearly playing a central role in the evidence gathering. When the mini-inquests concluded on 4 May 1990, the coroner thanked several West Midlands Police officers for all their hard work. He said that Beechey, together with another officer, Chief Inspector Tope, 'had an awful lot to do' with preparing the evidence summaries of how each victim had died.

'I sent them back with dozens of comments,' Dr Stefan Popper, the coroner, said, 'and everybody had to go back and recheck. That was in the preparation, but throughout these two and a half weeks they [Beechey and Tope] have been making sure that things were going smoothly, doing the back-up, watching, undertaking anything that needed checking. Thank you very much indeed. We could not have managed without you and I do appreciate it.'

At the main inquest, Beechey himself had given evidence. He confirmed to the coroner a part of his role in the investigation; he had been present in a monitoring room in Sheffield when the West Midland Police interviewed some of the central people, including Duckenfield, Murray and Graham Mackrell. The interviews had taken place in June 1990, except for Duckenfield's, which was done on 3 July. Beechey's job, he said, was to be handed sealed audio-tapes of the interviews. Beechey said that he was responsible for the tapes and would produce them for the inquest 'as and when we need them'.

Phil Hammond remembers that at the full inquest the coroner constantly referred to Beechey, asking him what evidence was coming next. 'They used to go out for little chats, then come back in.' There is a reference to Beechey in the inquest transcripts in March 1991: asked by one of the barristers what was in store on the following Monday the coroner said: 'I will ask Mr Beechey if he can think of anything else.'

Under the weight of the failed appeals and the campaign which followed the DPP decision and inquest verdicts, they never concentrated much on Beechey. Then, in mid-1995, Anne Williams, one of the Hillsborough mothers, was contacted by a man called George Tomkins, who had seen a *Cook Report* television programme about her case. Anne lost her fifteen-year-old son Kevin at Hillsborough, and has campaigned ever since that the circumstances of his death were misrepresented after witnesses were leant on by West Midlands Police. Those arguments were also dismissed by Stuart-Smith. Tomkins told Williams that in November 1984 he had been tried and acquitted on a charge of robbery following an investigation led by Beechey. Tomkins went on to claim to Williams that when Geoffrey Dear disbanded the Serious Crime Squad, Beechey had been suspended from duties, and so should never have been on the Hillsborough inquiry at all.

I went to see Dr Tim Kaye to see how much there was to Tomkins' claim that Beechey had been connected to the Serious Crime Squad and was 'suspended' at the time of the Hillsborough investigation. It turned out to be uncomfortably close to correct. When Dear disbanded the squad, he asked the Police Complaints Authority to investigate. They appointed West Yorkshire Police to look into the miscarriages of justice and alleged malpractices – another case of police force investigating police force, a system which Kaye believes to be seriously unsatisfactory. While that investigation was being carried out, Dear did not formally suspend the Serious Crime Squad officers, because there has to be strong evidence of specific disciplinary offences for that to happen. Instead, Dear transferred them to 'non-jobs', well away from criminal investigations, pending the outcome of the inquiry. He termed the officers' new areas of work, in a public announcement, 'non-operational duties'. The force listed the most senior Serious Crime Squad officers who were being transferred. Beechey was on the list.

He was described as a former head of the Serious Crime Squad. At the time, in August 1989, he was the deputy head of West Midlands CID. His transfer, as stated on Dear's list, looked innocuous enough perhaps, although even then it might have been thought a touch inappropriate: 'Studying technical aspects of Hillsborough'. To give a flavour of the tameness of the officers' new postings, other examples were Superintendent Roger Corbett, one of Birmingham's former heads of CID, who was transferred to the personnel department, and Detective Inspector Bob Goodchild, the head of Chelmsley Wood CID, who was put in charge of 'road safety and talks in schools'.

Ultimately, West Yorkshire's PCA investigation into the Serious Crime Squad said that ten officers ought to have faced charges – Beechey was not one of those ten – but they had all already retired. Four of the squad's officers were punished for minor disciplinary breaches. Following an announcement by Geoffrey Dear's successor, Ronald Hadfield, Beechey was returned to operational duties on 30 November 1990.

Although he was never charged with any disciplinary offence arising out of the investigation into the Serious Crime Squad, the fact remains that from 14 August 1989, to 30 November 1990, Beechey had been formally placed by his force on 'non-operational duties'. In the Hillsborough investigation, that period took in the preparation and conduct of the mini-inquests, the whole course of the DPP inquiry, and even the early sessions of the main inquest, which began in Sheffield on 19 November 1990. Yet there Beechey was, clearly working on more than 'studying technical aspects' of the disaster. He was centrally involved, as the coroner had said, with preparing the evidence summaries for the mini-inquests, supervising the police interviews of the disaster's central figures and, by the time of the main inquest, seeming to the families to be the most senior officer involved.

Tim Kaye was initially not too struck with this news of Beechey's involvement in the Hillsborough investigation. The effect of it depended, he said, on what Beechey had been doing. I wrote to the coroner's office in Sheffield to find out what, officially, Beechey's role had been at the inquest. Dr Popper, the coroner at the time, has retired. The present coroner, Christopher Dorries, wrote back promptly to say Dr Popper would not do an interview because he never does. However, Mr Dorries had talked to him and 'Dr Popper was able to confirm for me that Superintendent Beechey was one of a large number of West Midlands officers dealing with the

Hillsborough Inquiry and Inquests. He was not the most senior of these officers, that being Assistant Chief Constable Mervyn Jones. Like the other officers, Mr Beechey was engaged on various duties at various times. Dr Popper suspects that he would have been the second most senior officer (i.e. directly under Mervyn Jones) at the time of the main inquest.'

This, when he was still officially on non-operational duties, under investigation for his part in one of the most notoriously corrupt police squads in modern history. When I told Tim Kaye about the seniority of Beechey's role, his attitude changed. He was silent for some time, then he said: 'That seems very serious.'

When preparing for the Stuart-Smith 'scrutiny', Ann Adlington, the Hillsborough Family Support Group's solicitor, asked to see any statement made by Beechey relating to Hillsborough. In November 1997 she was told by the South Yorkshire Police, which has all the documents, that his statement was covered by Public Interest Immunity (PII), meaning it can never be disclosed. No reason was given.

I wrote to Beechey himself, who is now retired, via the West Midland Police press office, asking him to talk about his role in the Hillsborough investigation and his view of the outcome, including the inquest jury's verdict of accidental death. The police confirmed the letter had been sent on. Beechey never replied.

I made contact with Geoffrey Dear. He had a distinguished record in the police force; commended for bravery in 1979, an assistant commissioner in the Metropolitan Police from 1980 to 1985, and when he had arrived in the West Midlands he had genuinely confronted the Serious Crime Squad. When he moved shortly afterwards, in April 1990, he became HM Inspector of Constabulary. He is now retired from the police and has a number of directorships and senior posts with public bodies.

He was happy to talk and did so at length. He was very impressive and straightforward; it was a relief to find somebody involved who could immediately recall the detail of the disaster and the precise Taylor findings, especially compared to most football people, who never bothered to find out much in the first place, cling to the old lies and seem to have a lingering notion that it was all somehow unfair on them. Bert Millichip, when I talked to him, couldn't even remember the year Hillsborough happened.

Dear's view of the Hillsborough inquiry was that Taylor had done a superb job, cutting through the false arguments, producing a report following the largest investigation ever undertaken, at 'breakneck speed'. Dear clearly relished working with Taylor and agreed, on the evidence, with all the findings: 'Duckenfield was a very nice man as an administrator, but he hadn't commanded a match before, and, as Taylor said, he froze. He opened the gates and he hadn't sealed the tunnel. The ground was substantially in breach of the Home Office safety guide, but really everything else was peripheral to that decision, and the consequences were horrific. As Taylor found, the crowd weren't ugly, in fact they were quite jolly before it all happened.'

Dear said he understood the families feeling outraged that nobody was held legally responsible, but his view was that, although Duckenfield's inadequacy and the police operation amounted to a breach of civil duties of care, they were not criminal. As far as he was concerned, there had been no cover-up.

I asked him about the Serious Crime Squad. He explained that he had moved the senior officers to 'non-jobs' pending the West Yorkshire PCA investigation because he could not actually suspend them. I asked him if that was what 'non-operational duties' meant, and he chuckled: 'I had to call it something. The principal idea was to keep them away from any ongoing investigation.'

I mentioned the Hillsborough investigation and he said he would not have put any of those officers on to it. I asked him if he remembered Beechey and he said: 'Yes, he was a former head of the squad. Are you telling me he was on the Hillsborough inquiry?'

I told him that the description of Beechey's transfer was that he was 'studying technical aspects'. Dear recognised the term; he said it was likely to have been trying to enhance video footage, some of which was blurred, using computer equipment which would seem archaic now.

'We never deployed those officers to do the serious bits of Hillsborough,' he said. I told him about Beechey having been involved in handling the audio-tapes of the interviews. He was quiet.

'That surprises me,' he said. He hadn't, as the Chief Constable of a huge force, known where every officer was. 'It does surprise me if Beechey was involved in active policing on the Hillsborough investigation. But still, I don't think you could possibly worry about the inquests being derailed because of doubts, at the time, over one man. You could if he was at the top, but the investigation was being run by more senior officers.'

I told him that the coroner had said Beechey had been second-in-command by the time of the main inquest. And that he was certainly involved at a very senior level before that. Dear thought for a while.

'It definitely was not what I had in mind when I transferred him. If I had been told, I would have taken him off the investigation. I wouldn't have had Beechey working on that or any other inquiry. Not because he might be doing anything wrong, but because it was not appropriate.'

There is nothing to suggest that Beechey did not play everything by the book on the Hillsborough investigation, but everything to suggest he should simply not have played the role he did. Back in Liverpool, Phil Hammond finds all this another outrage, another layer of nightmare into which the Hillsborough families have been drawn, dragged into contemplating the murk of the West Midlands Serious Crime Squad, while football rebuilt, launched itself into money and moved on. He wants an inquiry: 'What was this officer doing in such a senior position in a major criminal investigation into a disaster as huge as Hillsborough, while he himself was under investigation? The West Midlands Serious Crime Squad was probably the most notoriously bent police squad in modern times, and it turns out we had a former head of the squad investigating the deaths of our children. To know that he had been transferred to non-operational duties, but contrary to that, had a senior role in the investigation, it stinks. They can't have thought much of Hillsborough if that was non-operational duties.

'We are entitled to an official inquiry into this part of it: how Beechey got on to the inquiry and why he was allowed to flout the transfer to non-operational duties. We didn't even know who he was, or anything about the Serious Crime Squad at the time; why would we? We were devastated by grief and we trusted the legal system. We want to be told what on earth was happening inside that investigation and the inquest. And we have a right to know.'

CHAPTER 17

The Football Man (2)

E ver since Graham Mackrell resigned because West Ham played
Emmanuel Omoyimni for eight minutes of a Worthington
Cup quarter-final, I'd wanted to talk to him. It was quite a big
story in the football press; quirky, but a serious enough error to
be worth bashing a club with. Described variously as a 'fiasco',
even as 'the Emmanuel Omoyimni affair', with the internet insom-
niac and ravenous for English football news, it went worldwide.
Mackrell's comments were widely carried:

'It patently wasn't correct [that Omoyimni was eligible to play]
and as a result I'm responsible, and I felt the only honourable
thing to do was to resign. It was a little error but unfortunately
it has had large consequences for the club.'

The West Ham chairman, Terry Brown, was quoted thanking
Mackrell for his hard work in the just six months he'd been there,
saying: 'Graham has made an honourable decision.'

Not a single newspaper recalled that Mackrell had been Sheffield
Wednesday's secretary and safety officer, responsible for the
ground on which ninety-six people were killed, but hadn't resigned
then. He had, in fact, stayed on at Hillsborough for ten years after
that. The football media's short-term memory and obsession with
the game itself, rather than its human consequences, should
surprise no one, but I was always curious to know how Mackrell
squared it with himself, staunchly defending his corner at
Hillsborough in the face of so much anguish, saying life – meaning

football – must go on, then clearing his desk with a gentleman's sigh over an inconsequential footballing cock-up at West Ham.

He had, I'd heard, worked with an internet company, InterClubNet, after he left West Ham, run by Nick Roach, the son of Dennis Roach, the players' agent who has dallied in recent years with several shades of controversy. There was, in fact, potential for embarrassment; the Football Association began an inquiry in 2000 into Roach's activities after Manchester City and Everton reported him for, the clubs alleged, demanding enormous commissions from them for working on the transfers of Paolo Wanchope and Duncan Ferguson, while at the same time acting for the players. Acting for a club and a player in a transfer is a clear conflict of interest and so, for obvious reasons, against the rules, and the FA made solemn noises about taking the 'Roach affair' seriously and launching an investigation. Roach, however, took legal proceedings, claiming that as a Fifa-registered agent, he could not be sanctioned by the national FA, only by Fifa. That was the last we heard of any investigation and the affair has stalled since. Throughout all this, however, the FA was working very closely with InterClubNet on developing computer software for County Football Associations which would bring them surfing online out of the nineteenth century. Mackrell was the managing director.

Phil Hammond always told me that he had not found Mackrell overhelpful to the Hillsborough families. People in football describe Mackrell as chirpy, matey company, a good bloke for a drink and a game of golf. I gave him a call and he was very happy to talk; we arranged to see each other at Berners Hotel, which he said he uses for meetings when he's in London on business.

The hotel was off the midday bustle of Tottenham Court Road and Oxford Street; old-fashioned London posh, men in coats and caps smiling scrapingly outside, a creamy ceiling in the lobby so ornate it made you queasy. There were flowery couches and armchairs arranged for that intimate business talk, the inevitable piano in the corner, thankfully unattended. I had a skim round the clumps of suits and odd middle-aged tourists, then a bloke in slacks and a green blouson, hair brushed back, fifty-ish with a briefcase, flashed me a grin: Graham Mackrell. Handshakes all round and one cafetiere please.

Small talk was no problem; football chat, a few quips, the problems of lower division clubs – they all live beyond their means, he said. He'd looked into a couple of smaller clubs for 'friends' who might invest in them and found them a real mess, impossible to touch if you wanted to make money. All the fault of clubs paying players more than they could afford, the gap between the Premier League and the rest is now unbridgeable. What can you do?

He told me he had worked at InterClubNet until mid-2002, doing 'stuff for the FA and stuff like that'. The company floated but the dotcoms were crashing. 'My share options weren't exactly worth a lot,' he said, arching his eyebrows knowingly. He left and now has his own consultancy, works from home, a bit of this, a bit of that on the commercial side of football. He specialises in 'event management'. He works as a 'venue director' for Uefa on the Champions League. He'd been responsible for Rosenborg in Norway in 2002–3, in 2003–4 he was doing Ajax's matches at the Amsterdam Arena: 'It's really coordinating the football with the sponsors' rights and the television to make sure that everything goes off OK. Particularly, obviously, with my background, making sure the football side gets sorted out.'

He's also a match delegate, an official observer, for the Premier League. He makes a living, he shrugged, and we chatted about the perils of working from home, how you have to give yourself a structure, make sure you shave, or you don't get enough done.

We got down to talking about his background. I said obviously I knew what had happened at West Ham because it had been so well publicised. This being football, there turned out to be more to his resignation than the clean falling on his sword which he and the club had announced, but West Ham paid him off so he can't talk about it much. Speaking rapidly in a high-pitched voice with an accent piped out of southern suburbia, he was clearly well practised in the football art of making a suggestion or two while not revealing much at all.

'There are terms of a confidentiality agreement which both parties have always honoured, you know what I mean, so I won't break that. It was a disappointing situation, but that's life.'

It turned out that he hadn't really got on well at West Ham and hadn't liked it, and it all came to a head when the mistake was made with Omoyimni, not by him but somebody working in his department:

'Technically you're responsible for the actions of your staff and officially I resigned because of that. But it was really down to personalities. To be fair to West Ham we agreed it wasn't going to work, you know what I mean, so we parted company and that's it really.'

Originally, he told me, he wasn't football mad, as most people tend to be who've managed to work their jobs into the game. AFC Bournemouth was his home town club; he qualified as an accountant and his firm were the club's auditors. He didn't want to stay with an accountancy firm and the club was looking to take somebody on, so he joined, in 1974. Later, he moved on to become the club's secretary, staying at Dean Court seven years before he got an offer to move to Luton, the year they won the Second Division with David Pleat's wonderful, flair-packed side. The chairman was David Evans – the Tory MP forever infamous among football fans for trail-blazing Margaret Thatcher's identity card scheme, which made going to matches at Kenilworth Road a marginally less welcoming experience than seeking entry to Greenham Common.

'I learned a lot working for him,' Mackrell smiled. 'He was an incredibly shrewd, interesting operator, a really nice guy. If you did well for him, he did well for you, you know what I mean.

Some of the things he did he utilised for his political career, but at the end of the day, I've seen a lot worse things in football than that.' I was beginning to feel that I might not get a great deal solid out of a conversation with Graham Mackrell.

He had been doing well at Luton when, in 1986, Bert McGee asked him to go to Sheffield Wednesday, a good promotion. Wednesday already had an accountant and Mackrell went there as club secretary, although he emphasised he was, in effect, the chief executive. He found it a nice club; McGee, 'obviously of the old school', had hauled the club out of its financial mess and onto a sounder footing. Mackrell's job was to handle contract negotiations with players and also to improve the commercial side.

'I was there to bring things forward, modernise a little bit, make things a little bit more outgoing in marketing terms, to look particularly at raising the profile of the club.' The way he talks, you can imagine stolid old Sheffield toolmaker McGee feeling he had just the sort of go-ahead man to bring a touch of the modern to Wednesday. Talking about his time at Hillsborough, Mackrell said he had: 'Some really good times there; I had some obviously difficult times, you know what I mean, but who doesn't in any job?'

I hadn't been prepared for quite so huge a degree of glibness about the 'difficult times' Mackrell encountered at Hillsborough. I asked him about the disaster. He said it had been a stress for everybody at the club, but this, it seemed, was mainly because of what came out in the media afterwards: 'Football is high profile and television cameras were there; it was one of those situations where lots of things were said and written and people I'm sure were misquoted.'

He didn't elaborate much on what he meant by that. It seemed that there was not too much soul-searching at Sheffield Wednesday after the disaster. He said that his job was to defend the club through the legal processes. 'Like in any incident', the insurers took over and they appointed lawyers to take the club through the Taylor and police inquiries and the inquest. 'It was agreed that I would handle all the legal side because I was deemed to be the one who was full-time at the club and best suited to do so.'

I asked him how they felt when the Taylor Report was published and pointed out that the safety certificate was out of date and all the ways in which the Green Guide had not been complied with: 'The thing is,' he said, 'it's very easy to do things like that afterwards. If you'd gone to every ground in the country you'd have found exactly the same, you know what I mean? And also, the Green Guide is a guide, it wasn't mandatory; it was an interpretation.'

He said that at the time he hadn't believed there was any safety risk at the ground: 'You know, in retrospect and hindsight it's very easy to sit there and say the reason was X. Life's not like that.'

He didn't seem exactly traumatised by what happened; he was talking about a stressful and difficult time in his work, a part he clearly didn't want to dwell on. They'd got through it but the whole business had been wrapped up with legal settlements and confidentiality agreements not worth opening up again. I asked him if he had gone through a period of agonising, of thinking that if only some specific aspects of the ground had been differ-ent, the barrier not removed, the capacities of the pens worked out properly . . .

'No,' he said instantly. 'I realistically don't think you do. From that point of view, you're going to sit there and say a lot of those things you're talking about happened before I joined the club.'

He elaborated a little on this, suggesting that Eastwoods, the engineers, were the experts on whose advice the club had relied: 'You employ people to do certain things that you assume are done'. But he stopped short of concrete thoughts; which parties had been liable for what had been a legal swamp. 'Culpabilities', he said, were 'a very moot point.'

It was a while before he mentioned the families at all, or that people had actually died as a result of the 'unfortunate set of circumstances' we were discussing. When he did, it wasn't about the human catastrophe, but about 'media stuff', in which 'both parties were making accusations and so as a result people become defensive'.

I asked him about the lingering resentment I'd found at Sheffield Wednesday, where so many fans still seem to think the Liverpool fans pushed from the back and it had all been their fault. He said:

'I think you would talk to people in Sheffield who say: would it have been in the interests of everybody to have a different result at the inquiry, you know, they could even question whether all the right witnesses were called and things like that. But you know, I think you just have to try and put a line under it and you go forward in life.'

He didn't seem to acknowledge willingly that the ground was unsafe, or the club at fault: 'Well, obviously, legally the club was criticised and you take that criticism on board.'

I asked him about his own responsibility, as the officially designated safety officer:

'Did you ever feel that you had to consider your position?'

'No, never,' he said.

'Why?'

'I think it was a totally different set of circumstances.'

I asked him what he meant. The main cause of the disaster, as identified by Taylor, was the opening of the gates, which was a police decision. 'No way would I have any involvement in that whatsoever.'

The changes to the Leppings Lane had, he said, happened before his time, and 'other people' were involved with that. So none of it was his responsibility.

He said they'd needed to get back playing football matches again: 'I think people, particularly from Liverpool, found that very difficult, but you know, whilst it was an awful tragedy, the majority of the people who were there weren't from Sheffield, so the Sheffield people, it was their ground still, you know what I mean? So they expected to – unfortunately trains still go through King's Cross don't they, you know what I mean?'

He said Wednesday had not put a memorial up for so long because they were worried it would be vandalised, and he dismissed any of the other explanations which do the rounds, some darker than others, about why for ten years under Richards and him they never did so, despite the constant requests of the families, football supporter groups and Sheffield City Council.

'What do people want?' he said of the families' campaign. 'The legal process went through, people tried to get prosecutions which failed. It's easy to say they want a head on a stick but they weren't ever going to get it so where does it go? It couldn't have had more publicity, it's been well aired and obviously on a number of occasions it's been felt that it was not in anybody's interest to proceed.'

I'd thought maybe he didn't have kids himself – not that you have to to empathise with the Hillsborough families' loss, just that it would be harder not to if you did have children yourself. Actually, he told me, he had two, grown-up boys, and he did acknowledge then it was a parent's worst nightmare:

'Of course it is. Burying your own child must be the most ghastly thing that could ever happen.'

We slipped back into chatting about football, the way the game changed after the disaster, the Premier League breakaway, the financial gap between the two leagues. He had a quip in there: 'If you were talking to Manchester United fans – you know, probably in Exeter or somewhere,' he said, grinning.

We kicked all that around. He said when you are at a club you don't think about the good of football at large, just about your own club and stealing a march on your immediate rivals. That was what lay behind all the clubs taking eager part in the breakaway; they only thought about how good it would be for them, how much money they would make, not what it was doing to the other three divisions or the wider game, or even that they might get relegated. He said the game's problems will never be addressed because of self-interest. He mentioned Abramovich, said Chelsea fans were never going to worry about who he was or how he made his money if he was going to spend it bringing good players to the club. 'Fans would have Barabas playing for them if they could get a result, you know what I mean?' he smiled. 'It's totally bread and circuses to them.'

I returned him to his own story, the glaring contrast in his career. OK, I said, he'd explained that there was more to his leaving West Ham than the story of honourable resignation which they'd given to the media, but still, I said, the public facts were that he resigned for that clerical oversight, but not after the horrors laid bare at Hillsborough: 'There was the disaster at the ground when you were the chief executive and, officially speaking, the safety officer, and you never felt that you had to resign for that, but then there was the player who played eight minutes in the Worthington Cup and you had to resign for that . . .'

'No,' he replied. 'I think they're two totally different sets of circumstances on two different occasions. I think to put any analogy between them would be inappropriate. They were totally different things. One was a totally different set of circumstances.'

And he didn't want to talk about it any more. He didn't come across as heartless, nothing as dramatic as that. Defensive, perhaps evasive, when it came to the disaster, but in his work he was a matey sort, bit sharp, ready with a joke, clearly ambitious. On day-to-day patter he was helpful, cheery, indiscreet enough to be a tease. I could see why he's got on so well in football, how he'd negotiated all the politics and the chairmen, done the commercial stuff they wanted, smoothed his way personally to win work with the governing bodies too.

After the disaster at his ground, he did his job, which, as he and his bosses saw it, was to defend the club and get some football matches back on again as quickly as possible. They did the work on the Leppings Lane end, didn't stop to think too much about their own failures and faults the disaster had exposed, and a couple of years later joined the Premier League. Mackrell stayed on to see Wednesday through the Charterhouse deal and into signing some of the expensive players' contracts they went down with in 2000. It had been stressful at work at the time of the disaster, but he'd got through it. If there seems to be something missing where human sympathy for ninety-six people dying might be, he shares that with football generally, whose men decided the show must go on, and, if called upon for an emotional reaction, content themselves with a platitude or two. Mackrell came out with one of the standards; the new Premier League stadia, he said, were 'monuments to those people who died'.

Rising to his feet, he said, 'I'll let you look after that, David', and pushed the bill across the table. I thought it was a bit steep for coffee: you clearly pay for the ambience at Berners; the pianist had even started up. We shook hands; he's always at the end of a mobile, he said, if there's anything else I need, I shouldn't hesitate to call. Then he was off, through the revolving doors, chasing up some football business in the West End.

CHAPTER 18

A Positive Future

The search for football's soul takes me one windy Tuesday lunchtime to a strip of Astroturf pitches, marooned behind Office World and Pets Corner on the outskirts of Stockport. Beyond the leafless trees, the M60 whistles frantically by, a ring road full of work. On the only occupied pitch, ten lads, fourteen and fifteen in assorted training gear, are listening sullenly to a couple of tracksuited coaches. They gob a bit – well, a lot, let's be honest – then shuffle over to do their drills. Passing, man in the middle, possession. The coaches, a man and a woman in their mid-twenties, hand out the well-dones, much-betters, and briskly set up another exercise. The lads slouch off to do it. Soon, when they forget themselves, they put the effort in and seem to enjoy it; they're really itching to have a game, but the coaches hold this cunningly out of reach until the end, a reward for good behaviour.

It's a weekday and these lads should be in school, but that's the whole point. They've all been excluded, or referred here because their schools can't cope with them. This is the optimistically named Positive Futures, a Government-funded scheme run by a charity, Fairbridge, which is trying to reach out to fifty of Salford's most 'at risk' teenagers through the one structured activity they might respond to: football. The beautiful game. 'At risk' here means they are falling out of school and edging into crime, drug abuse, or being a nuisance where they live, in Seedley

Langworthy, one of the most notoriously shattered corners of the whole country. If you are one of the fifty most at risk young lads in Salford, an always tough city now cracked by industrial decline, you are not in a good situation.

The Fairbridge office is a two-storey, modern, redbrick affair, next door to one of Salford's cemeteries, fortified as if its few computers inside are Brinks Mat bullion. Maggie Heavey, the administrator of the Positive Futures programme, a nice, friendly woman with years experience working with young people, gave me some details about the boys' backgrounds. I said I wouldn't use their names because there was no need, and anyway she didn't give me surnames. On the Astroturf they were just pale lads with bumfluff and trainers, a bit monosyllabic perhaps, but ordinary seeming enough. Their lives, though, are chaotic; one, already into offending, is estranged from his parents and lives with his grandparents. There don't seem to be many dads in any of their families. They are mostly persistent truants, behave badly in their neighbourhoods, are messing with drugs and crime, some have psychiatric problems. One, whom Maggie describes as a 'prolific offender', is on the child protection register. When the welfare authorities assess a top fifty who are 'at risk' the indicators are quite precise; one of the waif-like lads is number one: excluded from schools which say he is uncontrollable, a persistent offender, possibly a victim of child abuse. There is a fleck of knowing humour in Maggie's descriptions; of one, fifteen, already a regular drug user, with attention deficit and hyperactivity disorder, who regularly flits from home overnight, she says: 'Football is his only legal interest.'

Perhaps it's here, on the outer fringes of society, that you get the truest picture of the reach of football's appeal and popularity. These boys, so young, are dropping out of education and onto the wrong side of the law; their grip on normality is fingernail thin, yet the one activity which can get them out of bed, into trainers and kit, taking instructions obediently from their elders, is football. Asked what their long-term goal is when they join Fairbridge, many of the boys say they want to be professional footballers. Positive Futures is premised on the idea that the game might give the boys at least a foothold to clamber out from their dead ends, even if their chances of ever earning like Beckham are zero. Fairbridge tries to work the enthusiasm for football into some solid steps for the young people to be able to develop 'life skills', and here we're talking basics: calming down, organising themselves, gradually, hopefully, coming to believe they could have a constructive future, then wobbling tentatively towards it. The staff's major aim is modest enough: to get the kids back into school.

The football clubs, the glamour clubs, could have a great part to play in this kind of work. United, the world's richest and most overblown club, is in the air round here; you can just about see Old Trafford from the second floor of Fairbridge's building. Alex Ferguson went to the launch of Positive Futures, along with the Chancellor, Gordon Brown, and Andy Cole, the ex-United striker. There's a poster of it downstairs, with that unlikely threesome grinning their endorsement. Fergie, Maggie says, was 'invited by London'. They've had nothing from United here: 'It would be a huge reward we could use for our young people just to have a ticket or two to Old Trafford to give away. Salford is United's community; I hope they haven't got so big they don't think that any more, but because it's so expensive most of our young people have never been to a match there. It would be a massive help to have some support from United. We've asked many times but not had anything.'

Out on the draughty Astroturf, the coaches, Ian Worthington and Wendy Priscott, are organising possession; two groups in a circle, two-touch, one lad in the middle trying to intercept. It's standard training ground stuff, as is the next instruction from Ian:

'Let's talk to each other!' he calls. 'We all want the ball, but nobody's calling for it. Call each other's names!'

Anybody who has played football recognises the basics: talking. Let your team-mates know what's on. Yet here it has more significance; communication is an essential faculty the boys are lacking in their lives.

'They live in very difficult situations and all their lives they've been told they're no good,' Maggie tells me. 'Even the ones who act like hard nuts very often have no self-esteem and confidence underneath. Acting big is a way of coping; push people away so nobody will come near them.

'In football, you have to communicate with other people to be effective, and they can understand that. You have to work as a team, work with other people as part of a common objective, and trust other people, all things our young people find very difficult.'

And you realise: football, the game itself, has some life-affirming qualities. They're reaching out to these kids with the essentials of the great team sport, and it can help them with some of the building blocks of life. The kids don't know that, they just want to do it because it's football; everything else is boring or too hard. For all its commercialisation, their exclusion from Old Trafford as well as everywhere else, football still has massive appeal and credibility, even to these lads.

Haltingly, a bit embarrassed and under their breath at first, they begin to call out to each other: 'Dwayne!' 'Yes, Carl.' 'Pass it, Daryl.'

Ian and Wendy are trained in youth work as well as football coaching. They look for sparks of response and commitment in the boys, then they and other Fairbridge staff try to build on them with other work. There are sessions on healthy living and drug awareness, and the opportunity to do more: art, mechanics, lots of outward bound courses – climbing, kayaking, horse riding – in which Fairbridge has always specialised.

They've had some grief since the funding came in for the football course, grumblings in the local press that they're rewarding the bad kids. Yet they say it's an attempt to show the wrecked children of the inner city a way into a more wholesome and satisfying world. Wendy says it is hard at times, but:

'You do see some progress, and even if we don't, we'd like to think there is some good being stored in there for the long term.'

Both she and Ian have taught rich kids, at summer schools in America and in the perma-tan Cheshire suburb of Wilmslow. They prefer this.

'To be honest, there isn't that much difference in the young people,' Wendy says. 'The middle-class kids could be very bolshy. And often they didn't particularly want to be there. Here, they do, and they don't necessarily have much else. When we see some progress, if one of the young people thanks us, tells us it was a good session, they enjoyed it, we can feel we've made a difference.'

There have been some good results. Three or four lads have joined local football clubs, a couple went on to sports courses at Salford College. They tell you glowingly at Fairbridge about a boy from Seedley Langworthy who came to them after he'd been beaten up in the local park. Three lads just set on him for nothing, broke his ribs, fractured his nose and dislocated his jaw. He was emotionally wrecked afterwards, suffered from severe agoraphobia and wouldn't go anywhere without his mum. When he arrived on the Fairbridge induction course, he wouldn't look any of the staff in the eye, or talk to them. They persisted, gradually he felt safer, and slowly he unfurled. He went on to do some work experience as a lab technician, found it interested him and now he's doing a science degree at university. The Fairbridge workers, he said, 'Deserve a Purple Heart for bravery.'

Maggie talks me proudly through his story, but the fact that this one boy stands out highlights how rare the real successes are: 'There aren't very many places to fall from here,' she says, 'it is a bit of a last chance for many of them.'

'Come on, we don't need all the fancy flicks,' Ian's shouting, the perennial complaint of the football coach. 'Play it simple, and we find our men, don't we?'

They're getting into it now, calling each other's names, enjoying themselves. They want a game but Ian gives them another exercise first, a drill where they have to keep moving for a solid minute. If they stop, the minute starts again.

'I've seen this done in just two minutes before now,' he says. 'The longest it's taken is forty-eight. It's all about you; your attitudes and working together as a team.'

They're doing pretty well now; they want the ball and like it when they have it, pass and move, pass and move, call a name, keep it going. Before too long, Ian puts them out of their agony and tells them they can have a game. They have a quick drink, gob prodigiously, then they're in teams, Ian and Wendy joining in. The lads show a bit of skill, express themselves, a couple of them are nice little players who clearly spent a long time kicking a football around before sport lost out to teenage temptations. Towards the end, Ian lets loose a bit, starts indulging himself with some of the flicks he was telling the lads off for a minute earlier.

The session is over; they wander back, a little out of breath, red about the cheeks, and sit down by one of the goals with bottles of water. One of them, a stocky little guy, has a bandage on his arm. Maggie leans down sympathetically.

'What happened to you?'

He doesn't turn to her, looks down at the pitch: 'Stabbed,' he scowls. There's not much you can say, really. He's sixteen.

Afterwards I talk to a couple of them. They're shy with me and twitchy. They tell me they like playing football because they enjoy it and it keeps them off the streets.

'There's just nothing to do anywhere so it keeps us out of bother and that.'

One of them is at school, one isn't; school's boring, you get a better life doing stuff at Fairbridge. No, they haven't got any idea what they might want to do when they're a bit older. They don't really look at me; they've done really well just volunteering to talk to the journalist with the microphone. One of them, Maggie tells me afterwards, mostly sleeps rough in a disused shop. He's fifteen.

Twenty years ago, even ten, these kids would have been going to Old Trafford every fortnight for a couple of quid. The average ticket price at United in 1989–90 was £4.71, so it must have been less than £3 to stand. The price rises at the major clubs post-Taylor have been the national game's contribution to 'social exclusion', yet, back to basics, football can do so much good. In our divided country, for all the greed, self-interest and financial messes at the professional clubs, the outrageous fortunes of the players, the game's out-of-control and distorted priorities, it still holds, in its essence, the greatness of sport. Even as the Premiership plcs interpret football's appeal in terms purely of commercial power, others are rediscovering the game's founding principles and inherent benefits, social, physical and – let's come out with it – moral.

One of the pioneers of this football outreach work is Neil Watson. He was a PE teacher originally, and in April 1989, the same month as Hillsborough, he got a job running the community scheme at Leyton Orient FC. It was different from most such schemes attached to clubs, which tended to see their community programmes as marketing devices, a way to take the club's name to young kids in their areas with coaching sessions run by ex-pros. Such schemes, attached to the professional clubs, were organised nationally on the initiative of the PFA in 1986, under the umbrella of Football in the Community. It was the low point of football's image and fortunes, and the aim was to try to improve football's standing while providing work for the PFA's members, players retiring without many prospects. It was hard to persuade the professional clubs that this was something they should be doing at all, to get them to see beyond the business of signing players, sacking managers, chasing League position. The clubs were implacably opposed to spending a penny on it, so from the beginning the PFA had to persuade them that the schemes would be 'self-financing', which meant earn their own money, some in sponsorship, some by charging the schoolchildren for the coaching courses. Most clubs, not all, signed up eventually, and as it cost them absolutely nothing but did provide decent PR, they saw the benefit to themselves and allowed the schemes to grow. More recently, some progressive thinking has penetrated to some of the larger clubs, actively promoted by the Premier League who see community work as their best avenue for good PR, a way of showing the Government how much good they do. Yet even today, however much they crow about their schemes, the clubs themselves mostly put no money into the Football in the Community departments which bear their name. There is a small contribution to each club's scheme from the PFA centrally, and as the PFA gets its money from a small slice of the Premiership's TV deal, the money does come out of that, but it's peanuts.

Roger Reade has been the national administrator from the beginning; he got the job having previously built up Manchester City's Junior Blues club – he's the man guilty of hooking a generation of kids into the lifelong angst of being City fans. I was a member myself; I used to go to matches with the Junior Blues silk scarf tied round my wrist, although I never went to any of the jamborees which still today reduce beery fortysomething City fans to tears of nostalgia.

'Clubs are a lot more positive now about their community schemes and they do see the advantages of it,' Reade, an enthusiast, told me, 'but it's still a principle that the schemes have to be self-financing.'

The Premier League has made enormous publicity play of literacy and numeracy schemes which run at Premiership clubs' grounds, and which boast some sparkling results with kids the schools can't get motivated in the normal run of the timetable. Yet even those schemes are not funded by the multi-million-pound clubs themselves but the Government. The clubs' contribution is usually to provide a room or two in a stand, perhaps some of the equipment. OK, it's something, but it hardly makes them the Red Cross. The community schemes have grown hugely, reached a great many children and widened participation in football through coaching courses, but still clubs mostly see them as a cross between marketing, PR and a trawl for promising youngsters who might be drawn from one of the sessions into a centre of excellence or academy.

Orient's scheme was different because it was managed by the Sports Council and the local authority, Waltham Forest, not the club itself. They wanted the programme to reach out to neglected communities, young people, people with disabilities, the over-fifties, girls and women. Neil Watson was on his own journey of discovery about the power of football. He was not, it would be fair to say, central to Orient's sense of itself.

'I had a desk in the sponsors' room, and on a match day I had to clear all my stuff away. Later we moved to a crappy office upstairs. Then Barry Hearn, Orient's chairman, was building a bigger sponsors' lounge, so we went in a Portakabin outside.'

In 1995, the community programme commissioned a theatre company to produce a play dealing with the exclusion of the Asian community from football, both professional and grass roots. It ran for 650 performances around the country. The response of the children and teachers to the realisation that some communities were living mostly outside organised sport led to the idea of building a dedicated 'social inclusion' programme, which would reach out to 'difficult' groups of people through the medium of sport. This was harder, more purposeful, work than other clubs' standard Football in the Community programmes and eventually Watson and Orient's trustees decided theirs would operate more effectively if it were independent of the expectations and small amount of central funding which came with the PFA's programme, so they opted out of it.

'In 1996, we decided to do the work which nobody else wanted to do. We organised football on housing estates, with adults in the drug treatment services, travellers, young adults on community service orders. We still did the run-of-the-mill stuff which all the big London clubs were doing; you couldn't move without tripping over a coaching course then. But the challenge was to work with those who were excluded, marginalised, suspicious of authority, leading chaotic lives.'

Out often late at night on the tough estates, Watson discovered a simple truth about football: most people, boys at least, really do love it. 'So many kids are cynical and alienated because of the situations they've found themselves in, but football is a catalyst for reaching them. Being attached to a professional club gives it some glamour, too – they were always aware of Orient's moderate place in the football pecking order, but they were still fascinated to be part of something run under the name of a Football League club.'

The scheme even separated itself entirely from the club itself, after Barry Hearn made some infamous remarks about asylum seekers on Radio 5 – 'I think it's disgraceful we let all those people into this country' being one of them. The Leyton Orient Community Sports Programme's trustees issued a statement 'deploring the views' of the club's chairman. They were working with refugees, asylum seekers and ethnic minorities at the time, and said Hearn's views 'contradict completely the principles of the Community Programme', which were to work for 'social inclusion through the medium of sport'.

Watson is reassuringly realistic, not evangelical, about the difference such programmes can make: 'Of course schemes like these can't put right endemic social problems on their own, but, working properly and professionally with other agencies, they can help people, and I have seen hundreds of people whose lives have been turned around.'

Watson discovered an army of public bodies and charities eager to fund and weave football projects into wider programmes to help reduce crime, drug use, build social cohesion, healthy living and other benefits. I went down to see some of the Orient work in progress. You might think there would be some magic formula, but there isn't. The twenty or so men I saw at the Lowhall Sports Centre in Walthamstow, on a hot Monday afternoon in July, had been referred from drug rehabilitation agencies and the Probation Service. The basis of what I saw was simple: give a bunch of guys a football and a decent pitch and they usually want to play. Senior development worker Ose Albhangee was overseeing the session, a fierce, fast, possession-based game which the participants were tearing into:

'We're trying to get them into playing sport and feeling a bit more about themselves,' he said. 'Trying to raise their self-esteem and improve their fitness. It's easy for us to attract people with football into doing some meaningful activity which isn't anti-social, and which they'll get something out of.'

Simple stuff. I talked to a few of the guys. One was a young refugee from Sierra Leone who had had a terrible time since arriving in this country, drifting from place to place; another had, he told me, turned his life round after serving four years in jail for robbery.

'I started playing football, getting fit, and it changed my outlook. I think the project is very good; so many kids get stuck in the crime life, but they don't really want to be in that life, and this is a very good way of coming out of it. If you have a love of football, it's never too late to play.'

That's also true. I saw it for myself in my thirties. I played in a game of five-a-side with an extended group of mates of mates on a Thursday night, which went on for years. I'd always played in teams, but most of them hadn't, had been turned off it at school by the cold shower, it-hurts-so-it's-good-for-you PE teacher approach to sport. Here, with nobody growling at anybody, only encouraging, all abilities welcome, everybody loved it and turned up religiously every week. I was struck by the speed of progress of the guys with no real playing experience. Quite soon, the ones with some speed and natural athleticism were catching up those of us who'd wasted our childhoods and adolescences trying to bring a football to heel. We even formed a team, Dynamo Thursday we called it, and went into a league, which was rather less forgiving but tremendous when we did get a result or two. Grown-up blokes, all working, paying our tax and £1,000 council tax, we used to go out on the local parks in Manchester, have to change outside in the rain because there were no dressing rooms, then play on mudbaths which came close to degrading. I used to try hard not to think about United and City, raking in football's new millions just a mile or so away, and concentrate on trying to get close to some nippy teenager on the opposition's side, just once.

Ose Albhangee told me that he would get men on his courses who had done no exercise for as long as they could remember, were trying to come off habitual heroin use and lives of crime, and if they stuck at it and came regularly, they would be physically fit within six weeks. Having seen the transformation of some of our lads, that didn't surprise me.

The fruits of the Leyton Orient work came to much wider attention and Neil Watson was headhunted by the Home Office to head Positive Futures when it launched as a national project in March 2000. It is specifically part of the Home Office's strategy to reduce drug abuse, to use sport to reach the fifty most 'at risk' young people in the country's 20 per cent most deprived neighbourhoods. Fairbridge, in Salford, are delivering just one of 104 projects nationally, from Teesside to Devon, Newport to Cumbria.

Watson acknowledges that sport is not everybody's cup of tea: 'We asked young people to write down their experience of sport and there were more negative responses than positive. Sport, particularly football, can be harsh, and where it's very competitive it can reinforce people feeling negatively about themselves. This project is about using the interest in sport to bring people together in positive ways, to build confidence, and then, to use the jargon, provide a gateway to a different, more positive way to live.'

In 2002, Positive Futures was given £3.9m from the Home Office, Football Foundation and Sport England. In 2003, the funding was increased to £15m and the scheme expanded further nationwide. The scheme itself commissioned an independent evaluation of its impact, and the conclusions, published in February 2004, were admirably cautious, saying they need to do more work to assess how far the sports projects have really benefited the young people and their communities long term. Of the immediate results, however, they found that of 35,000 young people who took part, only 15 per cent performed poorly or dropped out, and 14,000 gained employment or training, improved their educational performance, joined a local sports club, improved their social relations or had some other positive impact in their lives.

The programmes are run mostly through organisations like Fairbridge, charities established and experienced in working with young people. Mostly absent is the one group whose participation could make a huge difference – the professional football clubs. There are a few exceptions: Charlton, according to Watson, are 'very good and capable of leading these projects'. Colchester, a club which generally punches above its weight, are also good and leading a similar scheme. Chelsea are beginning to work in Wandsworth with Cranstoun Drug Services, while Arsenal too have started a more difficult project, working with the Peabody Housing Trust. Other than that, Watson said, a few other clubs are dipping their toes into the work, but most are keeping clear. So they will mostly miss out on the £15m funding available.

'It's a huge shame because I would ideally like to run every course through a professional club. They've got the credibility and the appeal with the young people, and we could achieve so much with real commitment from the glamour clubs. But they're not interested. Something I hear from them is: why should we work with the bad kids?

'But that's a wholly wrong approach. The point is that football clubs are part of their communities. The communities are rich in variety, and full of difficult challenges too. As a football club, you should want to be part of that, working in and with the community, not shutting yourself away from it.'

When the Football Foundation was set up in 2001 with the first crumbs of the Premier League and FA's new TV money, it was predominantly to put some money into repairing local public sports facilities, the sodden playing fields and absent changing facilities. There is a small fund set aside, £1m, for the professional football clubs to bid for to run social inclusion projects. Watson was on the panel to consider applications. Throughout the period since the fund's inception, not a single club's Football in the Community scheme has applied.

'They don't want to do the work,' Watson sighed. 'They think it's too difficult, which is a desperate shame. This is true community work, but they don't think through what their community is.'

You could take this further. Do the clubs, football people, ever stop to think through what the business is in which they are involved; what sport is, what it could do, what its place, its true heart, its purpose is or could be, in society, in the country, in modern life? I interviewed Jez Moxey, Wolverhampton Wanderers' chief executive, in his office at Molineux, about Wolves' well-regarded community scheme, the Twilight and Midnight Leagues. These are late-night football sessions aimed at giving kids something constructive to do in the evenings and reduce crime and teenage pregnancies in rundown parts of the Black Country. The results have been impressive: the staff introduce advice sessions on health and safe sex as part of the kids' participation in the leagues, and local statistics record that it works. Wolves get the kudos but put no money in at all; the leagues were running on £200,000 public money from Wolverhampton Health Action Zone, £30,000 from the Government's Sportsmatch programme and

£30,000 from a local sponsor, the Birmingham Midshires Building Society. Moxey, no doubt getting through that sort of money in a single week's wages to a handful of his players, told me he saw the Football in the Community programme as 'a PR department for the football club'.

I suggested to him that if the clubs really devoted themselves to their community work, they would not be doing something radically new or precious; in fact they would be true to their original heart when they were formed – Wolves were St Luke's Church team when they started back in 1877. The club I grew up supporting, Manchester City, grew out of a team formed in 1880 by the vicar's daughter at St Mark's Church, Gorton, a tough area in industrial east Manchester, to give local youths something decent to do, rather than 'scuttling', beating each other up. Many of the now great clubs, including Everton, Aston Villa, Southampton, Bolton and Barnsley, were formed by churches; others were started for similar reasons by schools and more enlightened companies to provide some recreation for their workers. That was sport; something good, something decent, not just another avenue for making money.

The clubs have grown phenomenally since then, and the competition among the ninety-two clubs has become the consuming soap opera which we now think of as football, but the glamorous status they have evolved only makes the clubs more appealing to their communities, more able to make a huge contribution. Moxey, standing in his overheated little executive's office, with its pot plant, insipid watercolours and in-tray full of numbers, looked at me a little at a loss. His job is to try to give Sir Jack Hayward – 'Mr Wolverhampton', who is based, naturally, in the Bahamas – some return for the £50m tax-free fortune he has applied to building up the Wolves. The club is a business, the community scheme a small part of its PR. He didn't really get what I was saying; in fact he looked as if he felt rather sorry for me.

It shouldn't be so outlandish an idea for football clubs to rethink themselves as social institutions, as charities in the broadest sense of the word. They are, after all, *sports clubs*. That ought to mean more than reaching for the money, paying enormous salaries out to a few players, pounding on for points. If they spent their huge money wisely – all of them, so one doesn't lose out by doing it more than another – they could run vast community programmes, organise many teams, see their grounds used as the hub of general public participation in sport, while still running their first teams as intensely and ruthlessly as ever. Indeed, the two complement each other naturally. The clubs, if they thought through what they are, could see this as a central part of their purpose, rather than a useful commercial add-on they were talked into a few years back, assured it would cost them nothing. Maggie Heavey, running the scheme in Salford for some of the furthest flung young people we have, says the glamour clubs could make a huge difference if they wanted to:

'I do think they have forgotten about their communities. Perhaps they've forgotten an important part of what sport is. Certainly they've lost sight of providing access. There is so much good they could do; football is still the most attractive activity for our young people, a great way in to addressing some of society's problems'.

'I don't know why,' she smiles, admitting it finally. 'Football has left me cold since George Best retired.'

CHAPTER 19

Room at the Top

I f you feel that football is a great game, booming but out of control, its priorities as a sport distorted by money, greed, self-interest, short-term gratification and a host of human failings which are natural but have come to dominate it rather too much, it isn't too difficult to come up with an alternative, more positive vision for the game. Since the elation at football's rebirth began to curdle in the late 1990s, official reports into what ails it have come along like buses – the Government's Football Task Force, the Independent Football Commission, the All-Party Parliamentary Football Group – all having long inquiries, a deep think, then coming up with near-identical analyses. Football is at a peak of glamour, popularity and riches but is spoiling its great gift with poor management of the cash by clubs wasting it on enormous wages and payments to players and agents. An overwhelming majority of people involved in football believe that the Premier League has far too much of the game's money – a key finding of research commissioned by the FA itself, which we'll come to in a moment. This has concentrated success in the hands of a couple of clubs, while creating the conditions in which nearly half of the Football League's clubs have gone bust since 1992. Ticket prices are punishingly high, wholly contrary to the Taylor Report; professional football is pricing out the poor and the young – although the absence of the next generation has not been adequately recognised by the clubs,

348

the worthy inquiries or even the fortysomething season ticket holders themselves.

The clubs have been allowed to see themselves as commercial companies, plcs, rather than community sporting institutions, which could be a force for so much good if they only wanted to be. No less a figure than Florentino Perez, the elected – yes elected – president of Real Madrid, arguably the world's most glamorous club with its firmament of star players, the *galacticos*, told the *Observer* in June 2003 that while he is a workaholic businessman who has made a great deal of money in the construction industry, Real Madrid is different, more than a business:

'No one believes in plcs more than I do. I've got one that is very big in the Stock Market. But football, when you really come down to it, belongs in the sphere of human emotions. Real Madrid is a kind of religion for millions all over the world. You can't have that in the hands of one individual. It's as if the Catholic Church belonged to one person. It wouldn't be right.'

Yet in England, where the game began, we have to put up with it. Our clubs – we still call them clubs, for sentimental old time's sake, or to kid ourselves – are bought and sold like fertiliser companies, picked up for plaything or profit, by one man, consortia, merchant banks. Roman Abramovich told the BBC he sniffed over the top clubs in Spain – Real Madrid and Barcelona – but couldn't buy them because they are still membership clubs. Here, all were available. Many people in football now agree the plc model is not only wrong in principle for football clubs, contrary to the longstanding rules of the Football Association, but their experience since they were allowed to rush to float on the Stock Market shows that they do not work. A football club is not a commercial enterprise properly devoted to distributing its profits to shareholders looking for a buck, but a sporting endeavour.

What to do? As Bill Shankly is supposed to have said, it's a simple game. That did not mean it is easy to play well – that takes hard work, dedication, teamwork, a sense of determined purpose – but that its essence is simple. At the heart of football's enduring appeal is that you do not need cumbersome technical equipment, just a ball, and with only that, if you master it, you can paint lilting patterns. As with the game on the field, so off it, the fundamentals are not difficult. The huge money needs to be shared much more evenly and widely to benefit the game throughout, for all involved with it. That does not mean it should be thrown away to lower division clubs to blow on players' wages – but nor should the Premier League clubs be allowed to do the same. Management at the clubs needs to be improved to ensure the money is looked after and to protect them against corruption. Their huge TV and commercial bonanza should be subsidising ticket prices to allow all sections of society access to the national game. The professional clubs, including the great names, should be woven into a sporting structure with a sense of purpose as a force for good, which connects the top glamour clubs to the Football League clubs below, strengthens the pyramid of stalwart non-league clubs and gives as many people as possible the opportunity to play the sport to their preferred level in decent conditions. It is not rocket science. To achieve this considered approach, the sport surely needs unity, not division, between its elite and the rest, and for that it needs a governing body with the strength and confidence to run the game in the balanced interests of all. There, however, we have a major problem. Faced with a financial meltdown whose existence it could no longer simply deny, the FA has belatedly faltered towards some semblance of governance, but at its heart the governing body looks even weaker, less capable of doing what is necessary, than it was when it made the fateful, fatal howler of backing the Premier League breakaway back in 1991.

In January 2000 the FA announced a bright dawn for a new future with the appointment of a chief executive, Adam Crozier, who was presented as the man to take the old body from its hidebound past, embodied by the likes of Graham Kelly, into a dynamic world of bright shininess. Football would shed its outer skin of buffers and, under this new man from the advertisers Saatchi & Saatchi, grasp today's challenge. What this actually was, what job Crozier was free to do as the FA saw it, was never made very clear. Certainly true, however, was that a few months before he started, the scope of what he could do had been narrowed and the major Premier League clubs had further cemented their power over the FA.

In the vacuum after Graham Kelly left, the FA had been restructured. It established for the first time a means of bypassing the FA Council, the old, unwieldy decision-making forum in whose ninety-two members the development of the game can be traced: the public schools, Oxford and Cambridge, the army, air force and navy, a representative from each County Football Association and, following sundry power struggles, increased places for the professional football clubs. Still no representative for the Football Supporters Federation, or any women, or any non-whites – the game's evolution appears to have stopped a decade or three ago, except when it came to ceding to the major clubs. The pressure to sideline the FA Council came predominantly from them, and their prime concern was, of course, money; the desire to gain control of the FA's commercial decisions, without having to refer to the Council members the big clubs see as amateurs in blazers.

For anybody with a memory of football's previous political upheavals, the Premier League's grumbles and demands in the late 1990s rang many bells. TV deals were a major area of confrontation: the FA still did its own deal with broadcasters for the FA Cup and England matches, which were only lucrative because the big clubs and their players took part in them, yet the Premier League had no say over the deals or how the money was distributed. England matches: the FA still paid no compensation to clubs or real wages to players for their participation, a point David Dein was keen to push. Sound familiar? Yes, indeed, these were the very points of natural conflict between the major clubs and the FA which led to the League's proposals in *One Game, One Team, One Voice*, which the FA believed it had defeated by backing the breakaway of the biggest clubs. Far from achieving that, while the governing body had vindictively hammered the seventy smaller clubs which had had little to do with the suggestion of a joint board in the first place, the FA had only made the rich clubs much stronger and richer. Their campaign for more power at the FA, over the same commercial issues, pressed on, but now they were more difficult to resist.

The peace deal this time, in 1999, was brokered by Frank Pattison, a Council member on the grass-roots amateur side, a retired solicitor representing Durham FA. The arrangement was smoothed by the Premier League's pledge to the Football Task Force, made to buy off the challenge to the broadcasting arrangements from the Office of Fair Trading, that the Premiership would distribute 5 per cent of its next TV deal to help to rebuild public playing facilities. So grateful were the amateur members for these unprecedented droppings from the top table that they agreed to concede their own power in the FA Council on commercial matters completely, and create instead a senior, main board made up of equal members from the professional clubs and the game nationwide. There would be four representatives from the Premier League, two from the Football League, balanced by six representatives from the wider, amateur population of football, known as the National Game. The FA's chairman, Geoff Thompson, would sit on this board together with the new chief executive. 'The suits sweep out the blazers!' went the superficial headlines in the press as the change was welcomed for its 'modernisation', the creation of a dynamic, streamlined, more nimble, 'new' FA.

The laughable, depressing aspect of this for anybody with a little knowledge was that it was almost exactly what the Football League had proposed nine years earlier in *One Game, One Team, One Voice* in order to resolve conflicts with the FA: a joint board of League and FA representatives. It was deemed so anathema then that the FA backed the breakaway of the First Division clubs to smash it. Now, the FA was solemnly giving those clubs, which were behind the original proposal, exactly what they had wanted, but instead of having to operate within the old League structure in which money was shared 50:25:25 it was costing them only 5 per cent of their next deal. The FA split professional football in 1992 and created punishing financial inequality, in the interests, back then, of stamping its feet as football's top governing body. Now came the logical consequence of its short-sightedness: it was handing its own top table to the breakaway cartel of rich clubs. In theory, the FA said that its main board was balanced because the National Game had equal seats with the major clubs. In practice, the Premiership clubs now hold football's purse strings, which invests them with rather more clout than the well-meaning men of the National Game, who rely completely on the few drops of trickle-down. With the establishment of this main board, the top clubs were finally gaining a grip on the ultimate power over football to which they had been seeking access for decades. The four Premier League representatives? David Dein, Ken Bates, Peter Ridsdale, and, of course, Dave Richards. With his record, at Sheffield Wednesday and in business, what top table would allow itself to be without him?

Crozier, the new broom, swept into this environment with the wide eyes you can see in all the young professional men handed their dream of getting out of boring business and into working in the game they love. At Saatchi & Saatchi he had moved in to steady the company when the Saatchi brothers, the advertising architects of Margaret Thatcher's Tories' years in power, left to set up on their own again, and Crozier had risen to be the joint chief executive. The selection panel at the FA, which, dominated by the big clubs, was saying it wanted a culture change to become more 'commercial', bestowed on him the job of giving the old organisation a makeover. Crozier said that the opportunity to shape the game nationally was 'irresistible'.

I went to interview him shortly after he took over, when the FA was still hunkered down at Lancaster Gate. He was in Graham Kelly's old office, from what I could remember, but it looked stripped down and there was no mucky football kit on the floor. Crozier, small, smiling, bright as a tack, was bristling with ideas, big on eye contact and enthusiastic about the job in hand. I wondered if he knew quite what he had got into, as he shone with the glee and privilege of being involved in football. I asked him what he thought he would need to do about the FA's relationship with the Premier League, and the clubs' growing dominance, and he waved such concerns away: 'We have to get away from all these divisions,' he said.

He set about his new responsibilities in the way chief executives are no doubt trained to do and it seemed eminently sensible. He looked carefully at every aspect of the FA, what it was there for, what it was doing in different areas and then considered what it ought to be doing and how it might do it better. He then produced a considered plan for the organisation, setting targets to be achieved within 100 days, a year and three years. The FA, in the document he produced, was given a stated, unifying purpose: 'To lead the successful development of football at every level.' And a vision: 'To use the power of football to build a better future.'

Nobody ever refers to his plan any more, and, like all the documents which have come and gone identifying a better way ahead for football, it has no doubt found its resting place in some far, neglected corner of the FA's library. At the time, I didn't like his vision slogan; I thought it was too Saatchi & Saatchi, too vague, warm, waffly. Now, reading again what he said, I'm sorry I didn't recognise it more charitably as a good start. Within the FA, and outside, there were people who fell on his document with almost pathetic gratitude. They were cheered simply because here at last was a plan, a basic for any organisation but a revolutionary innovation for the FA. And Crozier, coming from outside as a football lover, had seen immediately that participation, playing the game at the grass roots, the game striving to be a force for good, should be central to the FA's purpose. That was instructive and refreshing.

There were some nuggets in the detail; there was to be a Financial Compliance Unit, as part of a department, headed by Nic Coward, which would make the FA on financial matters 'more powerful and investigative', and have 'a clear regulatory structure with teeth'. Crozier acknowledged there were problems of financial governance which had to be addressed. The grass roots, the National Game, was a central part of his vision, and he promised it would have a national strategy for developing facilities and participation, another huge step. The two concrete aspects which made some headlines were his plans for managers to have mandatory coaching qualifications, and for there to be a professional women's football league within three years. The FA, he said, was going to be 'accountable, responsive, passionate and inclusive'.

There was one page, headed simply 'NB':

'Football, led by the FA, needs to understand the role it plays as part of the fabric of life in England.

'It provides a sense of belonging and purpose for millions of people, reaching and touching people in a way that no other organisation can match.

'Our vision must, therefore, reflect what football can put back into society.'

The fascinating portent for the future was how the Premier League reacted to this broad-hearted, generous statement of purpose for the game. They turned up at Crozier's door with sour faces. There wasn't much cooperation or welcoming of the new future. Instead they were indignant, complaining they hadn't been consulted on several of the issues, like the proposal that all managers should be licensed. Dein, Richards, Ridsdale and Bates said they had been bounced into it all, because they thought Crozier's document was going to require their approval at a main board meeting, but instead they arrived to find it was already launched.

'Many of the proposals require the consent of the clubs,' said the Premier League's spokesman Mike Lee, a former New Labour official who introduced the black arts of spin to protecting the interests of football's richest clubs and their chairmen. 'We were not consulted on it as thoroughly as we would have liked.'

It was an immediate slap on the wrist and a lesson for Crozier. The Premier League representatives were installed in the heart of the FA and they expected to have control. Whatever else people would subsequently say about him, he proved himself a fast learner of football's *realpolitik*. The Premier League representatives had a clear conflict of interest: they were main board directors of the FA but their paid, day jobs were to run Premier League clubs. Often, particularly over money, the two positions were in opposition. To take an example, when David Dein, as the vice-chairman of Arsenal, argued that the clubs should be paid for the use of the players for England internationals, that was the kind of decision he, as a director of the FA, would have to consider. Presumably by arguing with himself in the mirror. Yet nobody in football appears to recognise there is a problem with conflict of interest right at the top of its governing body.

Crozier implemented notable change and progress in several areas, although not always as set out in his initial vision. The National Game division was staffed and set out a strategy to develop grass-roots football for the first time ever. Steve Parkin, appointed the National Game's director, made the strange corporate leap from the European marketing division of the confectionary company Mars, but he established a structure for his department as a company would, logically. He commissioned research which showed that the state of neglect of playing facilities nationally was so longstanding and deep it would take £2bn to put right. This is a problem for the nation, because most of the facilities which have been left so desolate are in parks owned by local authorities which have been starved of the cash to create decent public spaces comparable to those in much of Europe. The FA and Football Foundation's money could only ever patch things up, but nevertheless they were going to do their bit. There were, predictably, turf wars between the two bodies, but they slowly grappled into a resolution and the Foundation began to distribute money; between 2001 and 2004 they provided £92m in grants towards 685 projects worth £180m, a start on repair of the municipal wastelands. The County FAs were getting computer systems and development officers, and slowly the more progressive of them were able to evolve from dusty HQs processing fines for disruptive pub players to sports bodies trying to make a difference to their communities. In Manchester, the County FA worked with the local councils and other public bodies in a dedicated effort to provide football as something positive in the deprived and difficult communities, producing, in June 2003, a local football facilities strategy for the whole region. Littleton Road in Salford, site of my desolate experiences as a teenager, is to be overhauled by a £4.5m development into a modern 'sports village', with £1m from the Football Foundation and public money going in to promote 'social inclusion' and sport for all.

Crozier was never exactly a tiger of follow-through in this area. The joke grew in the National Game department that the lift from Crozier's seventh floor did not stop on their second floor. Yet while he may not have taken a personally active role in this less glamorous core of the FA's work, the new staff were encouraged to get on with it, and began to make a difference.

Other strong intentions similarly led to progress but not quite to the degree envisaged. The Financial Compliance Unit began life symbolically diluted into the 'Financial Advisory Unit'. It was a team of three accountants who went to clubs to look at their finances, but only in leagues from the Football League down, the Premier League clubs being immune from the process. They found some appalling examples of management, including the fact that

42 per cent of clubs in all leagues kept 'poor records' of gate receipts, but, rather than operating, as promised, as a regulatory body with teeth, instead they agreed a system with clubs whereby they issued reports, in confidence, to the clubs' chairmen, who were then free to ignore them. The detail of regulation was not one of Crozier's strong points; he genuinely wanted the FA to play its governing role strongly to clean up the game, but under Coward progress was painfully slow and Crozier seemed to find it difficult to pick his way through the grittier, more tedious parts of what was necessary.

Some have suggested his new era was more style than substance, in line with the times in England. Certainly the simple business of an office move was invested with some kind of epoch-changing transformation, as the FA moved out of Lancaster Gate and into new premises at Soho Square in 2001. Lancaster Gate had been a grouchy old warren, its backstairs and hideaways seemingly built for intrigue, and moving was sensible enough. Crozier was, it's true, very taken with changing the FA's image and the move to a hipper part of London was part of that. It had its unpleasant side too. Crozier consciously set about lowering the average age of the FA's employees, which saw some long-serving staff, including the receptionists, sacked to make way for younger women. Many argued there was too much of an influx of marketing people and press officers; Crozier argued always that he was trying to do his best for the FA and football.

The National Game, regulatory matters and other elements he saw as central in the first flush of fresh-faced optimism may have rather fallen away simply because Crozier, very bright, was drawn into the battles of the FA's real business. He had slipped into his initial plan that 'within 100 days' the funding for the new Wembley Stadium would be 'finalised'. He was to spend well over a year wrestling with the project after it failed to attract funding first time round, and in that time he organised the removal of Ken Bates as Wembley's controversial chairman. Crozier always believed that, having crossed Bates, he was thereafter on borrowed time.

The England management was another unexpected issue which started to suck up his time. Crozier had no notice that Kevin Keegan would quit in the toilets after the drizzly 1-0 home defeat to Germany in October 2000, the last ever game at the old Wembley. Crozier leapt into the need to find a replacement, and here, as was never the case when he had been concentrating on improving mucky playing fields and changing rooms, he found vast media attention, which must have been magnetic. Crozier played a large part in drawing Sven-Göran Eriksson away from Lazio, ever after cited as his greatest coup.

In all these ways, events and the pressures of the job drew Crozier away from the simplicity of his original vision, but it stayed broadly intact throughout his honeymoon period which lasted long into Eriksson's time in charge. On the top floor of Soho Square, however, where the main board meets in padded armchairs around the large table, the air was getting thicker. The FA had, like the Premier League, enjoyed a boomtime TV deal – £405m for 2001–4 – but now both were up for renewal. As the time for doing the next deals approached in 2003, everybody around that table knew that the media rights and dotcom bubbles had burst and the money was going to be saner.

It is said that the Premier League regard the TV landscape as connected. There is, in other words, one pot. There is Sky, and there are the terrestrial channels. They have a certain budget to spend on football, and they will spend some of it on the Premier League, some on the FA. In their day jobs, the Premier League representatives on the FA's main board have as their main interest getting as much as they can for their own clubs. Crozier began to believe that they saw the FA as a competitor, not as another organisation for whom they were going to strive to get the biggest deal possible. While actively talking up their own deal, some Premier League people began to talk down the FA's, muttering that Crozier had radically underestimated the likely drop by budgeting for a reduction of only 25 per cent. Nor did they mostly act like directors of the FA; people who worked there told me they never even met these men from the big clubs, who would arrive at reception and be whisked up to the eighth floor to make all the decisions. One quite senior person told me he had the most respect for Dein, because Dein, unlike the others, at least knew people's names and would say hello in the corridor. This in an organisation with only around 200 staff.

The longer he was there, Crozier became increasingly convinced that the Premier League representatives were there to serve their own power and make money for themselves, not to act in the best interests of the FA. After the spat over his initial vision and the crisis over Wembley, he had several skirmishes which made him cautious and defensive, and he believed the Premier League was briefing against him. So, soon after he arrived with bright-eyed plans for the game, saying, like so many before him, that he was interested in football, not the dismal politics of its administration, Crozier found himself in a constant scrap, grappling with lurking dangers and vested interests. Before three years were up, in the autumn of 2002, he was flung headlong into crisis. The catalyst was a demand from the Premier League clubs for yet more influence in the FA, calling for the establishment of a new body just below the main board, a Professional Game Board. It could seem reasonable enough; there was a National Game Board, which mediated policy, allowed the National Game directors to get their thoughts together before their proposals went up to the main board. Crozier, though, dug his heels in. He was having nothing to do with it; he would not sanction it. From nowhere, this obscure, seemingly clerical issue developed into a row so serious that the bright young man in whom the game had invested its hopes suddenly became a target, forced-resignation material. Stories, deeply hostile to Crozier, began to tumble out of the FA's main board itself, usually into the *Daily Mail*, always a ready mouthpiece.

At the root of the issue was, surprise surprise, money. Not just money, but the same old battles: England matches and the FA Cup. The big clubs, now with their joint board in more favourable circumstances than they could ever have imagined, were still pushing. They fell out with Crozier over some alleged misdemeanours so arcane they were difficult to understand. One concerned the sale by the FA of perimeter advertising at Premier League clubs' FA Cup matches. This was deemed by the Premiership as 'excessive commercial demands'. There was a problem over the England players' pool, then one row and unfavourable rumour after another about the new England and FA Cup sponsorship deals, the Premier League complaining the FA was treading on its clubs' toes. The Premier League representatives were repeating the complaint they made at the very beginning of Crozier's time: they were not being consulted, being bounced into decisions. Very soon, the knives were out, unsheathed.

One public spat with his opposite number, Richard Scudamore, the chief executive of the Premier League, encapsulates the Crozier era at the FA. Crozier had commissioned research from Mori to find out what people involved at all levels of football considered to be the game's most urgent issues. The survey was impressively wide and deep ranging: participants included 40 professional and semi-professional players, 153 chairmen, chief executives, managers and coaches from 106 professional and semi-pro clubs, 1,569 amateur players, 4,535 regular match-going supporters, plus referees, journalists, police officers, sponsors, schoolteachers, MPs and football administrators.

Yet when it was finally published, the survey produced more headlines out of the argument it provoked with the Premier League than what was actually in it. Scudamore had asked for advance sight of the research before it was published. Crozier had agreed; however, the Premier League has a history of leaking reports to spin them favourably to themselves, which Crozier was keen to avoid. Scudamore was furious that Sunday journalists were briefed before the Premier League had a chance to see the report and tore into Crozier, publicly. Crozier never responded but he clearly had not wanted to suffer any leaks.

The research itself illuminated why he was so keen to avoid this, and also illustrated how destructive all this politicking, self-interest and commercial avarice is to the central purpose of trying to do what is right for football. Mori had found that 'the most pressing concerns', at all levels, were about the game's financial structure. Everybody interviewed cared desperately about the morass the game was in: 'Spiralling wage demands at all levels of the professional game, combined with uncertainty about future broadcasting revenues, are seen to threaten the survival of many football clubs.'

It went on: 'Most club officials are in favour of major change to combat this issue, with widespread support for a more even distribution of TV money and a player salary cap.'

Here was the most resounding conclusion: 'The vast majority of groups believe that FA Premier League clubs take a dispro-portionate amount of the money available within the game – a view shared by many club officials within the Premier League.'

On average, 95 per cent of all people involved with the profes-sional game, including supporters, agreed with the statement that: 'Premiership clubs take too much of the money available in the game.'

The Mori research, entitled *State of the Nation: A Survey of English Football*, became yet another instructive document which was never heard of again. It isn't clear what Crozier planned to do with the findings, but he always said he wanted them so that he could base his policy arguments on solid research. Perhaps he was going to mount an argument for more even distribution of the money, and take on the Premier League. If so, he was never given the chance. The final week of October 2002 was vicious, a negative story about Crozier appearing in the *Daily Mail* every day, some clearly emanating from within the main board. The FA was now suddenly said to be in commercial turmoil, Crozier culpable of one management failure after another. The ballooning of staff at Soho Square and their high wages was made a major issue, this from the Premier League whose representatives, like Dein, paid £250,000 that year, Ridsdale, £383,000, and Scudamore, paid £717,468, had, as we used to say in the playground, no room to talk.

Crozier would not budge on the professional game board. All six professional representatives now agreed they wanted him out, including the two from the Football League, one of whom, John Elsom, had recently run Leicester when it went into administration, and had then decamped to Grimsby Town as a director, which maintained his place on both the League and FA boards. The casting decision fell to Geoff Thompson, the chairman of the FA and quiet man of football politics. He apparently failed to fight for Crozier, who emerged onto the Soho Square pavement late on Thursday 31 October 2002 to tell the bright lights of the TV cameras, before which he had always felt so much at home, that he had resigned. Thompson made a show of thanking him for his efforts, although the FA's official statement acknowledged Crozier had 'a difference of opinion on how the game should be run and regulated'.

In fact, Crozier had become convinced that the Premier League clubs' demands for more money and control of the FA were insatiable. The Professional Game Board would be just the next stepping stone; he believed the original breakaway by the big clubs in 1992 had been only the start and the end was complete control of the FA. Certainly, he was ousted in a row over the very same commercial demands which had, if the FA had only seen it, lain behind *One Game, One Team, One Voice*. The FA back then had been myopic and misguided, but Crozier, whatever his faults, and he wasn't perfect, was a fighter. To his great credit, he was not like so many before him, who arrive in the game with the ideals of the football lover but sell out to the cynicism that infests the professional game. He was adamant he was going to cede no more, and he was basing his decision not on paranoia about the motives of the men on his main board, who ultimately employed him, but on solid evidence.

Friends of Crozier at the time let it be known that he believed he was fighting for the independence of the FA, and that the Premier League clubs were on a crusade for more money and power. The truth, which never emerged then, was that, on 4 October 2002, Crozier had received a letter from Dave Richards, on Premier League headed notepaper, enclosing a draft contract which Crozier was asked to sign on behalf of the FA. It was seeking to wipe out the arguments between the FA and Premier League with a proposal for their future relationship. The letter, which I have seen, and went round and was agreed by all Premier League clubs, wanted ultimate control over all commercial decisions affecting the FA Cup and England matches. The Premier League wanted to approve all the friendly fixtures which England played and have commercial control over the FA Cup. They wanted the new Professional Game Board to be independent of the FA Council and therefore effectively free of control, not that the council was ever likely to raise much of a row anyway.

Richards' letter said that in return the Premier League clubs would commit to play in the FA Cup and Community Shield for five years. Crozier is understood to have regarded that as a clear threat of withdrawal from the FA Cup. That was nothing new anyway; I have it from three members of the FA's main board that Dave Richards was constantly threatening to withdraw the Premiership clubs from the FA Cup, or saying the clubs would withdraw, if he didn't get his way on an issue, usually over money. The sources complained that they could not debate with Richards in any detail; he would fly off, be dismissive, or issue a threat. I put this question, whether he threatened that the Premiership clubs would withdraw from the FA Cup, to Richards through the Premier League press office because he never talks publicly. He was walking past and they asked him, and he said: 'Bollocks.'

At the bottom of his letter, Richards said that several representatives of the Premier League – Dein, Ridsdale, Richards himself, Robert Coar of Blackburn, all members of the FA's main board, and Maurice Watkins, a lawyer and Manchester United director – would be coming to a meeting on 21 October and they expected the contract to be agreed. They, Richards' letter said, 'have a mandate to go further should we not reach our objectives'.

So there it was. Dave Richards, the club he chaired heading for the Second Division, his business in ruins, rather than staying at Sheffield Wednesday and grappling with the problems caused in football by the gap between the breakaway Premier League and the rest, was instead being paid handsomely to throw his weight around and seek to strengthen the Premier League's stranglehold on the game and its governing body.

Crozier thought he had to draw a line, and he drew it at the Professional Game Board. So, he was out. Paid off – £750,000, sanctioned by the board, as revealed in the FA's accounts – and an undertaking not to discuss what went on round the top table of English football. The bright young man was gone and the FA itself was in shock. I was told subsequently that there was a backlash from the staff, who had found it chilling that the organisation was so blatantly run by the Premier League, whose representatives, men whom most of the staff had never been even introduced to, were the directors of the governing body and in their own interests could remove its chief executive. Frank Pattison, who had brokered the original settlement which set up the main board, resigned. He has not spoken publicly since, but he was said to have felt betrayed by the Premier League's continuing demands.

In the vacuum, there was plenty of activity again. The cry went up from Soho Square that the FA was in financial crisis. Crozier, the commercial genius signed up for a dynamic future with a new main board of commercial men, hadn't, we were suddenly told, had a clue about money. The FA reached for its time-honoured solution: a new committee. Its job was to hack away at costs and it was staffed, among others, by those denizens of financial restraint, Peter Ridsdale and Dave Richards. Sixty staff were sacked, at all levels. Richards, we were told, took the lead, this pat on the head coming from his close associate, Ken Bates.

The truth was rather more fuddled. Crozier's FA does seem to have been expensive; staffing increased from 218 in 2001 to 273 in 2002, and wages had increased 21 per cent, to £22m. Yet this was on the back of the FA's huge TV deal, and the wage bill did not account for a large part of the FA's costs; they turned over a whopping £184m, and made a profit before tax of £12m. Their overall costs did seem high and were not broken down, but the FA's job is to distribute money around football, not to make and keep a profit. It is difficult to assess the state they were in without more detail but it certainly didn't look like a crisis compared to . . . ooh, let's think, Sheffield Wednesday, Leeds United or Chelsea.

Rather undermining the Premier League's case against Crozier was the fact that he was the highest paid person of all: his salary package was £567,000 in 2001 and £408,000 for his ten months in 2002, awarded, approved, by the main board. As, come to think of it, was the way he was running their organisation, so it was strange for them to find themselves in so much crisis yet be able to blame it all on Crozier. Privately, I was told by one or two people working on floors at the FA, actually trying to get on with running football, that they felt Crozier's FA had been quite profligate, that a great deal of money was washing around and costs never greatly questioned, but for that they wanted to know why the board never exerted any control.

The cost-cutting itself revealed the greed at the heart of the power struggle. Of the FA's costs, which the Premier League clubs professed themselves to be so pained about, a large slug, some £30m, was paid to the Premiership clubs themselves in FA Cup money, for winning matches in the later rounds and receiving

£265,000 for each game televised live. For winning the Cup, David Dein's Arsenal were paid £4m in prize money, much more in TV payments. Now, although financial problems were supposedly pressing because the new TV deal was going to be lower, and, overseen by Richards, staff were being sacked, the big clubs would not accept any reduction in their own FA Cup payments. The following season, 2003–4, the prize money paid to clubs winning the Cup's later rounds remained the same, but payments in the earlier rounds, which had produced good money for non-league and lower division clubs, were cut. Around £2m is said to have been cut from the wage bill by sacking people; that figure could have been more than taken care of with a shaving of the FA Cup payments to the already rich clubs. They, however, would not entertain it, and the threat of their withdrawal from the FA Cup was always in the air when it was suggested.

The cry went up: look at the trouble a bright young man with vision got us into, we need a safe pair of hands now. We were told the finances were so awful the FA needed an insolvency practitioner actually to run the organisation. They reached for the hard-faced figure of Mark Palios, from the corporate restructuring department of the accountants PriceWaterhouseCoopers, who had once been a professional footballer with Tranmere Rovers and Crewe. Quite a few of Crozier's people were soon out of the door: Paul Barber, the head of marketing; Steve Parkin, the National Game's director. Palios was not one for 100-day strategies or three-year plans, and he didn't talk to the press much at all. That, after Crozier, was held to be a good thing. We'd gone from one extreme to the other.

Palios had a look at these supposedly desperate finances. He put the planned National Football Centre, about to be built at Burton-on-Trent, on hold. He also cancelled a loan which Dave Richards had been energetically negotiating, £130m from the American bank Bear Sterns, which Palios now deemed unnecessary. A few more people were sacked and, what do you know, the FA was sound again. Crozier had been criticised for having only budgeted for a

25 per cent drop in the FA's TV deal, yet when the FA renewed, that turned out to be right. The black hole did not appear to have been so deep after all.

Quite what Palios planned for the FA was never quite clear. From the start he knew very well who he had to keep happy: the twelve people on the top floor of Soho Square, most centrally the men from the billion-pound Premier League who will brook no restraint on their power and not a penny off their takings. Palios' view, I was told, was old-fashioned: mind the pennies, run the organisation efficiently, save money. In his talks to business schools and chambers of commerce, arenas in which he felt comfortable, he stressed the money he had saved the FA. Internally, I was told, he was not a big vision man, saying that grand ideas are all very well, but an organisation must prove itself capable and competent.

Palios quickly found himself battered by events; he had no apparent experience in doping issues, yet within weeks he was forced to confront the massive media interest in the failure by Manchester United's Rio Ferdinand to turn up for a random drug test at the club's training ground. Palios faced United, and a threatened England players' strike, over that, and Ferdinand was given an eight-month ban, but one can only guess how that went down with the power brokers. Then Eriksson was found to have been talking to Chelsea's new chief executive Peter Kenyon, whom Abramovich had tempted away from United, and Palios was forced to lump another £1m on Eriksson's contract. Months later, Palios himself resigned, in a mess of office affairs and corporate intrigue. There isn't much time, for anybody, calmly to set about trying to steer football on to the right course, whether they see their job that way or not. After such an upheaval, it is not easy to see how FA staff can get excited on the tube to work in Soho Square every morning.

The FA did belatedly respond to the financial crisis in the game at large, setting up in the summer of 2003 yet another committee. Called the Financial Advisory Committee, it produced a report to the FA's main board which contained a picture of desperately poor management within clubs, which they said they wanted to improve with a code of good practice to which directors would have to report. They were also going to finally establish a 'fit and proper person test', which would weed out criminals, bankrupts or serial directors of bust companies from taking over a football club, by the end of 2004. That had first been urged on the FA in a report it commissioned itself seven years earlier, by the former deputy commissioner of the Metropolitan Police, Sir John Smith. Then in December 1999 the need for such a test, as a minimal protection for the game's historic clubs, was reiterated by the majority report of the Football Task Force. Coward always rejected it then, and the game's authorities replied to the majority Task Force report by arguing they could solve the game's problems with 'a more inclusionary approach to key stakeholders', a lump of jargon which can shorten your life if you even begin to think about it. They recommended only that there should be an 'Independent Football Commission', to produce an annual report on the authorities' running of the game. The Government, not at all interested in legislating for football and deciding, in the end, it preferred to cuddle up to the game for good publicity, granted them that. A barrage of clubs tumbled into administration almost immediately afterwards: Swindon Town, Hull City, Lincoln City, Queens Park Rangers, Chesterfield, Port Vale, Bradford, Leicester, Ipswich, Wimbledon, Barnsley, Bury, York, Notts County, Carlisle, Oldham, Huddersfield and dozens more at all levels were in financial difficulties. The FA had to acknowledge there was, after all, a problem of some sort, and so it limped towards setting up the committee, in the summer of 2003.

Reform has been painfully slow, a point emphasised by the Independent Football Commission itself, once it was established and reporting. In 2003, the IFC turned round and bit the FA, calling for reform of the FA Council to include representatives from the ethnic minorities and for greatly improved governance and financial regulation, drawing specific attention to the way in which the FA had allowed its own rules on companies, in Rule 34, to be bypassed by clubs forming holding companies. The other reports came to similar conclusions; the All Party Parliamentary Football Group of 150 MPs and peers produced its report in February 2004, calling for more redistribution of money, better management and more attention to the grass roots. Aware that football's magnates hate any criticism, they, like the others, were keen to stress they came as friends, that as football lovers they wanted what was best for the game. It is, after all, the national game, and all who play, watch or are involved in it feel they in some way belong to it, and that it belongs to them. The Football Task Force majority, noting the scale and gift of the 1990s boom, pointed out the need for unity and a strong governing body, to mend a beautiful game disfigured by financial inequality and petty politics. The Government did flirt with becoming involved, with the idea of installing a 'regulator' to compel football to run itself properly, but they saw in the Task Force how brutally the big clubs fight for their power and decided that wrestling with them was more trouble than it was worth.

Yet the FA has shown itself unable to govern independently because it has become inexorably controlled by the Premier League and is bedevilled by the conflicts of interest around its top table. Whatever progress it falters towards, it will never be allowed to grasp the nettle of the breakaway itself, the disunity it created and the consequent imbalance of cash. Although it is so blatant, the rest of football is now so dependent on the Premier League that the subject of greater distribution of money has become unmentionable. Because of this, there has never been serious consideration of the issue, just, as with the 'fit and proper person test' before it, a series of limp objections.

The main one is that if the money were shared with the lower division clubs they would simply spend it on paying higher wages for players, to 'live the dream' of competing above their station.

That is fair; it would be a waste of money if they did, but that objection should form part of a considered approach to steering clubs away from paying more than they can afford to players. As the FA's Mori poll revealed, most people in football are in favour of a salary cap. This bears no relation to the hated maximum wage in which players' wages were for years oppressively and, as it turned out, illegally held down to a level which left them to struggle when they retired. We have come a long way from that. The conclusion most people have come to, including the PFA, is that clubs should limit the amount they spend on their wages to a healthy proportion of turnover. The Football League, faced with the implosion of so many of its clubs, did finally introduce, for the 2003–4 season, a trial in the Third Division, whose clubs were asked to limit their expenditure on players' wages to 60 per cent of their turnover. The experiment was extended to the Second Division in 2004–5 and the League wants eventually to have that as standard practice throughout. The Premier League has introduced no such reform, and, for all its talk of irresponsible lower division clubs, has done nothing to address the likes of Leeds, Chelsea or other Premiership clubs which have overspent, or those which have been wholly unprepared for relegation and collapsed when they went down. So the question of better management of finances is one for all clubs, not an argument against redistribution. The stories of Leeds under Ridsdale, Bradford under Richmond, Bury under Hugh Eaves, show that clubs at all levels have a propensity to gamble. Those within the Football League who argue – quietly – for more equality agree it should be combined with measures to ensure clubs do not blow their good fortunes.

The Premier League clubs argue they need the bulk of the money to compete with the top European clubs, pointing out that at least the Premier League does a collective deal, while in Spain and Italy the clubs do deals individually, which leaves the major clubs very much richer than the rest. However, that argument is flawed too, and one would want a lot more detail before having to agree it provides a rationale for so much inequality here. It has, for a start, less power since the Italian clubs suffered their own financial meltdown at the end of the 1990s. That leaves the giants of Real Madrid, but their financial position is unique, sorted out with a deal to sell the training ground to their local authority which, at the time of writing, is being investigated by the European Commission. One unfeasibly rich or lucky club in Europe, operating in a different system, ought not to determine the distribution of football's money in this country. That is an argument to fuel inflation, the idea that all clubs must reach to pay as much as the Continent's single richest club, in order to attract players to compete. Ultimately, a line has to be drawn. Investigate the argument with any rigour, as so seldom happens in football, and it would surely fall apart; it cannot be true, for example, that if our clubs had just slightly less to lavish on players' wages they would get none of the top stars. English clubs might have to be a little more careful or have slightly smaller squads or pay some players rather less, but the players will continue to come. And anyway, a massive wage bill does not guarantee success; Liverpool won four European Cups in the 1980s with players who came from Northampton, Scunthorpe and Chester, when all the world's glamour players were going for the money to Italy. In 2004, the European Champions League finalists were Porto and Monaco, clubs shrewdly managed whose players combined formidably in a team. Manchester United and Real Madrid dropped expensively to earth.

Few people have ever argued that the major clubs, whose matches the TV companies are paying to broadcast, should not earn more of the money to allow them to grow and compete – although even that is a discussion worth picking over. If the money were shared out more, so would be success, and so the TV companies would be interested in more clubs. Here, the rewards for success take the already rich away from the others.

A more even spread of money will help to iron out the two fundamental problems in the professional leagues: the very un-English monopoly just a couple of clubs have on success and the catastrophic financial consequences of relegation. The Premier League clubs have a duty to ease the financial impact of relegation, so that their clubs are no longer going down and going bust, leaving a trail of miserable creditors unpaid in this richest-ever era.

Still, the idea of spreading football's huge wealth only within the Football League, awarding clubs, many of which have been very badly run, is not tremendously attractive. It has to be done to ensure proper competition, but it is difficult to be persuaded that millions should reach down to some clubs in the lower reaches, which serve local populations and have gates of below 5,000. There, rather than considering large amounts of money to bring them into unrealistic competition with the bigger clubs, the money could be tailored simply to help them survive and thrive. The experiences of clubs through their crises in the 1980s and then in recent years makes redundant the argument, long rehearsed and even Football League policy for a while, that English football has too many clubs. They have proved themselves resilient; bust in the 1980s because of mismanagement in a series of crises, bust in the 2000s because of mismanagement and financial inequality in a time of boom, the clubs have been pulled through by the efforts and commitment of their supporters. They have survived over a century and are very profound rallying points in their towns and communities.

Rather than provide a slice of the game's money to fuel a drive by first teams for promotion, the money could be spread, lower in the Football League and in the pyramid, on easing the perennial struggle simply to stay alive. Perhaps some of the basics could be taken care of, and money could be tailored for use in such areas as youth development, community programmes, even marketing efforts, so that clubs can attract more people from their areas to be part of football. There is, put simply, no reason why football clubs should be struggling in this time of boom. Leave the money at the top, and the big clubs themselves only spend it on players' wages which most people find repellent; a small drop in their swollen levels will be good for everybody's health. And if it reaches down to make the pyramid strong, that will itself help the top clubs, which sit at its apex. The Football Foundation bursts to proclaim its good works with just 5 per cent of the bonanza: think what the sport could achieve with much more, 50 per cent coming down through the pyramid, as it used to do through the League before the breakaway. The precise proportions – how much to which divisions of the Football League, how much to the pyramid, how much to facilities and the National Game development, together with the reforms required to ensure the money is not blown – all of that is detail which a concerted inquiry could work out. It is a simple game, if only there were a will to run it well.

It will not happen, however, because the Premier League clubs broke away from sharing and have no intention of being drawn back into it. They see themselves very differently, as individual corporate beasts hungry for money, competing in the jungle against each other, increasingly looking to Europe for their competition and the world for their commercial markets. The idea of an actual European breakaway from domestic competition has gone away somewhat; Manchester United have always been keen to stress that the Premier League is their bread and butter, providing many millions of pounds and massive TV deals from thirty-eight matches a year. They want some more control over the sale of some of their TV rights, lobbying, for instance, for the right to sell overseas rights themselves, but they are not angling for a breakaway. They are, however, members of the G14 group of top European clubs, which continues to push for more influence and money, a process of pressure on Uefa which is similar to the campaign the big clubs have waged domestically to wear down the FA. A breakaway is not likely in the foreseeable future, but the continuing participation of the top clubs in the expanded European Champions League, which swings them another £10–£20m in TV money alone, further concentrates cash and power in the hands of the big clubs. We are heading for a 'consolidated' sport, in which a few clubs are global brands, the rest struggling in varying states of inferiority.

Richard Scudamore walked into the All Party Parliamentary Group's inquiry at the end of 2003 and said, on the question of redistribution of money, that the Premier League believed the 'balance is about right'. He was paid £628,000 that year, which included a bonus for delivering the Premier League clubs their massive TV deals. Scudamore and others from the Premier League talk of their largesse, of the 5 per cent they give to the Football Foundation, the 'parachute payments' they give to the relegated clubs, and money they provide to the PFA, extracted last time round only after the players threatened to strike, and say they are a generously distributive league. It is important to remember, when such talk is rolling, that the breakaway process began back in 1985 with the comment by Martin Edwards of Manchester United, that 'The smaller clubs are bleeding the game dry ... they should be put to sleep.' The experiences of those clubs, still alive and fighting nearly twenty years later, kept alive by the defiant loyalty of their supporters, suggest they are the backbone of a tremendously rich game, which should be nurtured, not destroyed.

Spectating is, for all the problems of clubs, booming. In 2003–4, more people went along to Football League matches than in any season since 1963–4, a forty-year high. The total attendance in Divisions One, Two and Three was 15,889,750. The First Division had crowds of 8.9m, the highest for forty-eight years, the Second Division crowds increased 6.5 per cent from 2002–3, which itself had been a record season. The most startling increase was in the Third Division, that basement of strugglers, where crowds increased by 21 per cent, a lot of it due to the renaissance of Hull

City in their new stadium, but testament too to the continued appeal of live football and supporting a club. Although televised weekday glamour and European matches take a bite out of local clubs' gates on cold nights, attendances even at non-league level are generally phenomenal. Whatever it is people crave from football – a sense of belonging, community, colour in a dull world, entertainment, getting out – they are finding they get it and coming back for more.

The Football League, this upsurge salted with the crisis of insolvent clubs and a restive First Division, quietly set about introducing some reforms while the FA and Premier League did nothing. Their strange choice of chairman, the ex-Tory Party chairman Dr Brian Mawhinney, began to stress the need for 'improved governance'. Along with the 60 per cent salary cap, in the summer of 2004, the League at last became the first body to introduce its own 'fit and proper person test' for directors and major shareholders of clubs. All payments to agents by clubs as part of transfer deals are to be published – which should finally show us where the bulk of football's money has been going. The League has been showing the way to the other bodies, that reforms are necessary to help the game prosper. The most powerful example of that was the Taylor Report, which led to Government legislation to make grounds safe. Without it, who knows if clubs would even now be bothering to make their stadia decent. Yet instead of welcoming reform, the big clubs fight any hint of action by the Government which could help the game.

Quietly, almost completely unnoticed by the thumping sports sections of newspapers, underneath the screwed-up governing body, the infighting, the out-of-control greed for money in the top professional clubs, good work has nevertheless continued, trying to build football at local levels. The appetite for playing football has not been higher for a very long time, although the traditional eleven-a-side game on Saturdays and Sunday mornings declined by 20 per cent in the three years from 2000 to 2003, largely because of the awful facilities. The FA's National Game division, recognising this, is looking to work more with five-a-side and other forms of football, which better suit modern lifestyles. Effort is being made to improve facilities and to take football into a more fulfilling role for itself, a means of bringing people together and helping to enrich their lives. To be a sport fit for the modern world, with a sense of what that ought to involve, not a mere vehicle for commercial exploitation, local or global.

It is deeply frustrating, seeing the national game revel in a boom, which could take it so far, yet drive itself so needlessly into dysfunction and failure. The prescription for change is simple, but it is difficult to see from where the strength will come to bring it about. The men running football need somehow to be shoulder-charged into abiding by some of the basics of the great, simple game, of which they are still only trustees – custodians, to cite the word they once used of themselves, before it fell out of fashion. I never liked the phrase Crozier coined, and it still has too much puff about it for my personal taste, but on reflection there are worse starting points than the vision unveiled by that bright young man they hired from advertising because it seemed a good idea at the time. To use the power of football to build a better future. No wonder he didn't last long, coming out with crazy talk like that.

April 2005

The end of a football season is habitually written up in the back pages as 'the run-in', borrowing from a breathless finish on the turf, the jockeys out of their saddles cracking the whip, crowds of punters in the stands roaring them on to the last. The image has just about held up in the Premiership years: at least the run-ins have been two- (and occasionally even three-) horse races. But in 2004–5, the description dignified the Premier League with a competitive excitement it no longer has. There was no run-in, because Chelsea raced away with it. Even Alex Ferguson, English football's most unforgiving fighter, still dangerously obsessed by winning at the age of sixty-three, admitted weeks before the season's end that the title was Chelsea's. The commentators still scream at the style and panache of the hammerings that Chelsea dish out, desperate to justify the 'product' the TV channels pay millions for; the newspapers cover Chelsea as though they are a proper football club. But it is difficult to find a fan, away from the white middle-aged men occupying the hideously expensive seats of Stamford Bridge, who doesn't find the spectacle at least off-putting, if not a touch shaming, or – let's be honest – obscene.

Since the first edition of this book, a little more information has seeped out about how Roman Abramovich emerged from the Boris Yeltsin years as one of the handful of men who own the vast bulk of what were Russia's state-owned resources. His own spokesman, John Mann, told me straight that, yes, Sibneft – the oil company Abramovich bought – was 'undervalued' at the time, and the auction in which he carried it off was 'not perfect'. With football providing an insight into the post-Communist carve-up of Russia, we watched as Mikhail Khodorkovsky – owner of the country's largest oil company, Yukos, and the richest of the oligarchs – was suddenly arrested by the authorities, charged with massive tax evasion and fraud, then, in May 2005, convicted and sentenced to nine years in prison. Khodorkovsky's company was stripped, picked, beaten up then sold off in a strange auction. The world took that as a sign that Vladimir Putin's government, along with 95 per cent of the Russian population, was no longer happy to see thirty or so individuals sitting on so much of the nation's wealth. Does this give us a clue as to why Abramovich bought Chelsea: that owning a Western football club would make him world famous and so more difficult for the Russian authorities to humble? John Mann told me no, Roman is a responsible businessman who adds value to his companies, has broken no laws and has stayed out of Russian politics; he had no need to use English football as a twenty-first-century escape vehicle. It was as simple as this, Mann assured me: Roman had just fallen in love with the beautiful game, as we all have on some floodlit, rain-soaked night.

Whatever, Abramovich has sent one very clear message to the game he now loves, and 2004–5 made that very clear: it's all about money. We knew that before, but now we can have no romantic doubts. It is true that Chelsea's manager José Mourinho is, for all his self-obsession, an expert coach, and that his players are, by definition, not at all bad, but Mourinho's reported £10m-a-year package, and the players' £100,000-a-week wages, are beyond the pockets of any other club. In January 2005 the first Chelsea accounts of the Abramovich era were published. They told us that Chelsea spent £175m on players in 2003–4, the year I wrote this book, and watched Crespo wallop his 25-yarder at Highbury. And the wages, for Crespo, Cudicini, Duff, Lampard, Mutu and one or two others who didn't last; £115m. The club itself, clearly, could not sustain spending like that, so it made a loss of £88m. Abramovich picked up the shortfall, bankrolling the whole spectacle with loans of £115m – small change from his extraordinary wealth, so long as it lasts.

All of that managed to make Manchester United plc look like some earnest northern sporting cooperative, the lads valiantly doing their best in the face of overwhelming and vulgar riches. In 2004–5, United plodded in third; their wage bill the previous year was £77m, almost exactly half Chelsea's, a frightening statistic for anybody who believes a league should involve some degree of meaningful competition. Arsenal, puffing in second, but yards off the pace, are still pinning their hopes on oceans of cash to be wrung out of 60,000 people in their new stadium, whose name they sold to an airline. Early in 2005, Raymond Pinn and the other Ashburton Grove businesses lost their fight against Deputy Prime Minister John Prescott's decision to allow the compulsory purchase of their premises to make way for the development, despite the negative report he had received from his own planning inspector. All in the London Borough of Islington will make way in 2006 for the Emirates Stadium.

English football's lack of competitiveness at the top and its proclamation that sport is all about money, are subjects the media is uncomfortable talking about; the Premiership is complacent; and the FA, the governing body for the whole of football, is silent. The FA staff come over all nervy and uneasy when you bring it up; the Premier League's representatives still weigh heavily on the FA's board, so the FA mumbles about clubs being independent companies, the leagues running their own show. Since it sold out its principles by backing the breakaway in 1992 the FA has been neutered; over the last thirteen years the big clubs have only cemented their power.

There was a little episode in February 2005 which laid bare, for all to see, the attitudes of those running the game in England.

Uefa, European football's governing body, having consulted around Europe for a year and researched the sporting, legal and financial implications, decided it had to do something about the severity with which success was being concentrated, all over the continent, in the hands of just a few mega-wealthy clubs. The proposal they arrived at was modest enough: by 2008–9, 8 players in a 25-man squad should, to some extent, be 'homegrown', having come either through that club's youth system, or that of another domestic club.

The proposal was uncontroversial across the rest of Europe; the vast majority of clubs in Spain, Germany and France either already field a smattering of their own kids, or believe it is right they should try to. Immediately, however, David Dein came out furiously to say that this idea threatened to undermine 'the product' – Premiership football – which was fine as it was. He told the BBC that the Premier League would oppose such a proposal absolutely and be prepared to go to the European Court to fight it. That raised the faintly hilarious prospect of England's grandest clubs mounting an expensive legal action against European football's governing body, for the right not to play their own young players.

Uefa's language was stronger than its proposed measure, raising the cheering possibility that this is only a start.

'Should we accept that a very rich club can buy an unlimited number of players, pay them massive salaries and ensure that their smaller rivals never have a chance to win a competition?' Uefa asked. 'That is not what sport is about. There needs to be some degree of balance, some means to keep the playing field at least reasonably level.'

Common sense, but you would never hear sentiments like that expressed by our own governing body in Soho Square. Elsewhere, Uefa's proposals were accepted as a decent first step in trying to reintroduce some measure of equality to the game, restoring clubs' links with their local areas, and giving 'native' young players a chance. For that last reason in particular, Europe's football associations, which run the national sides, supported the idea – more opportunities in first teams for their own players has to mean more good, experienced players from whom to pick a national team. In fact, every national football association in Europe went to Zurich to speak in favour of the proposal – except one: our FA. Its chairman, Geoff Thompson, went along to put the Premier League's view, which was that the idea was bad for the game, unnecessary, a restraint of trade and all the other miserable free-market arguments which have trampled on a decent way to run a sport. It was a glaring example of the way the big clubs have taken over the FA; Italy's Serie A was the only other European league besides the Premiership to oppose the measure, but, unlike in England, the Italian FA stood firm, even saying it wanted the proposal introduced into domestic football. Our governing body, however, has no such independence, and David Dein found his own conflict of interest, as both a director of Arsenal and a director of the FA, again nakedly exposed.

For a brief few weeks in the autumn of 2004, all the Football League's clubs were suddenly out of administration. Bradford City had finally agreed a settlement enabling the club to come out of its second period in administration. Julian Rhodes, inevitably, sank yet another slice of the family fortune into the stricken football club it has been his misfortune to support. The talk was that the post-ITV Digital medicine was working, that there was a 'new realism' to the financial management of clubs in the lower divisions, which was true, to an extent.

But it took no time for the next crisis club to yelp in pain: Wrexham. This was a saga of – wait for it – property developers buying the club, seeing money to be made out of the ground. The protagonists were Mark Guterman, the owner of Chester City when they went into administration in 2000 and now Wrexham's chairman, and Alex Hamilton, a former solicitor and season-ticket holder at Liverpool. Their first, smart move was to buy the free-hold of the historic Racecourse Ground from the owners, the Wolverhampton and Dudley Brewery, for £300,000. Wrexham's previous owner, Pryce Griffiths – a local man cast from the usual lower division club chairman's mould – had as recently as 1998 negotiated the club a 125-year lease to secure its tenure at the ground, for which he had paid £750,000 up front. As the brewery was receiving no rent, it thought £300,000 was a nice year-end boost to the balance sheet; Hamilton and Guterman knew they had a bargain: the Racecourse stands at the 'gateway' to the North Wales town and is eminently developable.

Hamilton himself stayed entirely in the background, while Guterman went on with being the chairman, running the club and talking about various possibilities for the ground. Then the club ran out of money paying an outsized wage bill, and Guterman went back to Hamilton, who had bankrolled their venture. Hamilton, furious, agreed to put £300,000 into the club to stave off a winding-up petition from the Inland Revenue, but insisted on tearing up the old 125-year lease and replacing it with one which allowed him to give just twelve months' notice to quit. Despite the fact that Hamilton owned both the club and the ground, he behaved like a landlord arguing with a hard-up tenant.

Hamilton then fell out with Guterman, emerged from anonymity to reveal himself as the owner of both club and ground, then banged on the local council's door insisting he be allowed to flog the whole Racecourse Ground site for £20m, and turn it into a B&Q DIY superstore. He would, he said, be prepared to build the club a new ground outside town, and wipe out their debts. By the time he'd finished, he'd drive back up the M53 some £6–8m richer. Everyone would be a winner. The fans, however, who had not been consulted at all, and indeed had found out only with difficulty about the lease and freehold, decided Hamilton was seriously bad news. They marched, formed a trust and protested about what they saw as a threat to 133 years of football history in the town. The council wanted the Racecourse to stay where it was, a more inspiring first impression of the town than an immense B&Q. Hamilton, furious again, played his joker in July 2004: he issued the club, which he still owned, with a Notice to Quit, giving Wrexham a mere twelve months to find a new home.

I talked to Hamilton about all this in a long session at his Cheshire home. He insisted that Wrexham was just a bust, failing company like any other, and the answer, to sell its ground, build a new one and pay off the debt, made perfect sense. Which perhaps it did. What didn't was that he had failed to explain it to the fans. If he was going to be thwarted, he told me, and somebody else wanted the club and the ground, they would have to give him 'a fat cheque'. Wrexham then blotted the Football League's newly sound look, becoming the thirty-seventh club since the 1992 Premier League breakaway to fall into formal insolvency, going into administration after Hamilton refused to put any more money in to cover losses.

Other clubs began to report difficulties. Most spectacular was Cardiff City. It seemed Sam Hammam had stayed true to his promise to put only £3.14m into the new club he had fallen in love with, so the Bluebirds' flight up two divisions had, it turned out, been achieved with loans and debts of £30m. At the end of February 2005, the money ran out, and the club were late paying the players and staff their wages. In the crisis that followed, despite receiving loans from the PFA, Cardiff were forced to sell their captain, Graham Kavanagh, to Wigan, before settling the wage bill. Then it emerged that the club had paid Hammam's company, Rudgwick, £300,000 in 2003 for what were described as management services, and £583,000 in 2004. Sam's halo began to slip, even among the most besotted of Cardiff's fans.

At Easter, Bury cried for help, saying they had staved off two winding-up petitions in early 2005. They called on crowds to come to Gigg Lane in their thousands for a special game on Good Friday, or the club might not survive. Football people around the country had to shake off disorienting attacks of déjà vu before lending their support. Cambridge United, rock bottom of the League and shipping money, agreed to sell the club's ground, the Abbey Stadium, to a company run by one of the club's directors, John Howard, for £2m to pay off debts; the cash was gone in weeks, Cambridge still went into administration – the thirty-eighth club insolvent since 1992 – and were relegated out of the league. Grimsby moaned loud and long about a tax bill. Ken Booth, the scrap metal man who had steel-plated Rotherham's overachievement in the First Division, finally bailed out from supporting the club financially, and took the Millmoor Ground as payment for his £3m loans.

Even Rushden and Diamonds, that synthetic creation, in-house entertainment of the Dr Marten's boot empire, provided a moral lesson on oligarchs and benefactors, had the English media lifted its eyes from Mourinho's every drama to give it a look-in. Rushden and Diamonds was moulded originally from the merger of two minor local clubs, Rushden Town and Irthlingborough Diamonds, and built into a Football League outfit, complete with gleaming new stadium, with millions of pounds from Max Griggs, a born-again Christian and the owner of Dr Marten's. Then, in 2002, Dr Marten's stomped into financial trouble, and Griggs shipped out the trademark English boot to be assembled by less-well-paid workers in China. Some 1,000 skilled Northamptonshire cobblers were put out of work by the relocation. Griggs decided that the football club was no longer an expense he could financially justify, and announced he was to pull the funding. By early 2005, in a turnaround which brought tears to the eyes of the hard-working people of Supporters Direct, Griggs was asking the fans to form a trust so that he could hand the club over to them.

There are signs of enlightenment, hope, everywhere: more fans who understand the fabric and culture of the game and believe it does not have to be this way. Trusts have formed at nearly every club – admittedly some in better shape than others – and there are more supporters asking plain questions and not being satisfied when the answers don't come. Recognition does seem to be slowly evolving that football clubs must do more than cash in on the loyalty of their fans, and even the Premiership clubs do seem to want to do more in their communities, if only to claim they have 'corporate social responsibility'. There is increasing alarm about the junk we eat, and how little we exercise, so it can surely not be too long before that discussion gets round to wondering whether our national sport and its clubs could be doing more to get people playing football, rather than hooking them into consuming it on television or in the £50 seats.

Manchester United spent the whole year after I first wrote this book fighting off the very odd takeover bid from the American Malcolm Glazer, which managed to unite a very large number of United fans in the principle that their club was 'not for sale'. The strength of the opposition was remarkable: it wasn't restricted to a small core of keen or interested fans but extended to many thousands, standing up strongly for the club to have an identity of its own. United fans even talked about walking away if Glazer did actually buy it, and forming their own club, an acknowledgement from the fans of the biggest club in the world to those of AFC Wimbledon, who won another promotion up the football pyramid, this time to the Ryman League Premier Division. In a startling development, the Manchester United plc board announced it agreed with the principle of a supporters' trust, and said it would work with the supporters' group Shareholders United to form a trust which would enable fans to hold shares mutually and, the board hoped, provide some stability for the company. So here was the game's formerly most brutal and clinical plc discovering that being permanently for sale on the Stock Market wasn't, after all, the best way to run a football club, and rediscovering the principle that a football club is, in fact, a club. The emotional call by the early campaigners of the Independent Manchester United Supporters Association, to 'roll back the plc', which had seemed utterly fanciful just a few years earlier, now seemed to form part of the policy of the plc itself. Then, on 12 May 2005, Glazer shocked the fans, the board which had rejected his business plan as 'aggressive', and the whole of football, by paying £227m to the two Irish investors, John Magnier and JP McManus, and taking over United. His deal was financed with huge mounds of debt which, it seemed, he was ready to load onto United. His motives, and his plans, were a mystery to most, the fans were outraged, and the future of United, of all clubs, was suddenly fundamentally uncertain.

Looking at the game in 2005, you can be an optimist or a pessimist. You can be appalled at Chelsea's buying of success, and believe English football is setting the the world the worst possible example. Glazer's takeover could make you feel that a part of English football had died, yet in the fans' campaign, there was enlightenment, a glimpse of possible change over the horizon. There is the potential, with pressure, with argument, that the game will find its soul again, make itself whole. But the best chance of that happening will be if a previously too timid Government finally decides to intervene in the game's administration. That change is far from imminent, however, so for some time yet we will continue to come back to Hillsborough, not just to remember the victims and the grief of the families who lost them, but for the lessons the game never learned from its most terrible disaster. There was some suggestion in 2004 that the Government might look into the questions raised by the presence of Detective Superintendent Stanley Beechey on the Hillsborough investigation, until the Home Secretary, David Blunkett, got into a terrible pickle over an affair he had had with an American millionaire socialite and was forced to resign. The

Hillsborough families, still, call for justice. And, sixteen years on, football lovers must wait a while longer yet for Lord Justice Taylor's 'fullest reassessment of policy' for the game, and a 'new ethos' for football.

Bibliography

Football: General

Rothmans Football Yearbook, various years

Sky Sports Football Yearbook 2003–04, edited by Glenda Rollin and Jack Rollin (Headline)

Encyclopedia of British Football, by Phil Soar and Martin Tyler (William Collins 1977)

100 Seasons of League Football, by Bryon Butler (The Football League 1998)

The Official PFA Footballers' Factfile, edited by Barry J. Hugman (Stanley Paul)

The Sunday Times Illustrated History of Football, by Chris Nawrat and Steve Hutchings (Octopus Publishing 1998)

League Football and the Men Who Made It, by Simon Inglis (Willow Books 1988)

Football Grounds of Great Britain, by Simon Inglis (Collins Willow 1996)

England, their England, by Nick Harris (Pitch Publishing, 2003)

The Cassell Soccer Companion, by David Pickering (Cassell 1995)

The Official History of the Football Association, by Bryon Butler (Queen Anne Press 1993)

Broken Dreams, by Tom Bower (Simon & Schuster 2003)

Sweet FA, by Graham Kelly (Collins Willow 1999)

The Father of Modern Sport, by Keith Booth (Parrs Wood Press 2002)

Clubs

Arsenal

The Official Illustrated History of Arsenal, by Phil Soar and Martin Tyler (Hamlyn 2003)

Herbert Chapman, Football Emperor, by Stephen Studd (Souvenir Press 1998)

Wenger, by Jasper Rees (Short Books 2003)

The Glorious Game, by Alex Fynn and Kevin Whitcher (Orion 2003)

Hillsborough and Sheffield Wednesday

Hillsborough: The Truth, by Phil Scraton (Mainstream 1999)

No Last Rights, by Phil Scraton, Anne Jemphrey and Sheila Coleman (Liverpool City Council 1995)

A Quarter of Wednesday, by Daniel Gordon (Wednesday Publishing 1995)

Football in Sheffield, by Percy M. Young (Dark Peak 1981)

Sheffield Football: A History, Volume I, 1857–1961, by Keith Farnsworth (The Hallamshire Press 1995)

The Romance of the Wednesday 1867–1926, by Richard Sparling (Desert Island Books 1997)

Manchester City

Manchester, the Greatest City, by Gary James (Polar Print 1997)

Bradford City

A Game That Would Pay, by A. J. Arnold (Gerald Duckworth 1988)

The Real McCall, by Stuart McCall with Alan Nixon (Mainstream 1998)

Notts County

Steak . . . Diana Ross, by David McVay (Parrs Wood Press 2003)

York City
They'll Never Kill York City: How the Supporters Saved City (York City Supporters Trust 2003)

Wimbledon
The Spirit of Wimbledon, by Niall Couper (Cherry Red Books 2003)

Crewe Alexandra
The Gradi Years, by Jules Hornbrook (Jules Hornbrook, 2000)

Glossop North End
The Lawlines Minibus, by Peter Heginbotham (Parrs Wood Press 2002)
The Book of Glossop, by Jack Hanmer and Dennis Winterbottom (Baron Birch 1993)
Glossop North End Football Club, Season 1898–99, compiled by Dennis Winterbottom (Glossop and District Historical Society 1971)
Glossop Dale, Manor and Borough, by Scott J. H. Smith and Dennis Winterbottom (Glossop and District Historical Society 1986)
A Memoir of Robert Blincoe, by John Brown (Caliban Books 1977)

West Midlands Serious Crime Squad
'*Unsafe and Unsatisfactory?*', by Tim Kaye (Civil Liberties Trust 1991)
Forever Lost, Forever Gone, by Paddy Joe Hill (Bloomsbury 1995)
Murder at the Farm, by Paul Foot (Review 1997)
Error of Judgement: The Truth about the Birmingham Bombings, by Chris Mullin (Poolbeg 1990)

Reports
The Hillsborough Stadium Disaster: Inquiry by Lord Justice Taylor: Interim Report (HMSO 1989)

The Hillsborough Stadium Disaster: Inquiry by Lord Justice Taylor: Final Report (HMSO 1990)

Scrutiny of Evidence relating to the Hillsborough Football Stadium Disaster, by Lord Justice Stuart-Smith (The Stationery Office 1998)

Committee of Inquiry into Crowd Safety and Control at Sports Grounds: Interim Report, by Mr Justice Popplewell (HMSO 1985)

The Blueprint for the Future of Football (The Football Association 1991)

One Game, One Team, One Voice: Managing Football's Future (The Football League 1990)

The FA Premier League National Fan Survey, 2000, 2001, 2002–3

Deloitte & Touche Annual Review of Football Finance, 1993–2003

Ticket Pricing, Football Business and 'Excluded' Football Fans, by John Williams and Sean Perkins (Sir Norman Chester Centre for Football Research 1998)

Investing in the Community: Report by the Football Task Force (January 1999)

Football: Commercial Issues: A Submission by the Football Task Force to the Minister for Sport (December 1999)

English Football and its Finances: All Party Parliamentary Football Group, First Inquiry Report (2004)

The Independent Football Commission: Annual Report 2003

Manchester Local Football Partnership Facility Strategy (Manchester County FA 2003)

Financial Advisory Committee: Report to the FA Board and IFC (2004)

State of the Nation: A Survey of English Football (Mori 2002)

Annual Reports and Company details from Companies House

www.soccerbase.com was particularly helpful for player and manager details.

Index